D1174972

305.4
W63

S.U.

"WICKED" WOMEN AND THE RECONFIGURATION OF GENDER IN AFRICA

Edited by
Dorothy L. Hodgson
and Sheryl A. McCurdy

HEINEMANN
Portsmouth, NH

JAMES CURREY
Oxford

DAVID PHILIP
Cape Town

Nyack College Library

Heinemann
A division of Reed Elsevier Inc.
361 Hanover Street
Portsmouth, NH 03801-3912
USA
www.heinemann.com

James Currey Ltd.
73 Botley Road
Oxford OX2 0BS
United Kingdom

David Philip Publishers (Pty) Ltd.
208 Werdmuller Centre
Claremont 7708
Cape Town, South Africa

Offices and agents throughout the world

© 2001 by Dorothy L. Hodgson and Sheryl A. McCurdy. All rights reserved. No part of this book may be reproduced in any form or by any electronic or mechanical means, including information storage and retrieval systems, without permission in writing from the publisher, except by a reviewer, who may quote brief passages in a review.

ISBN 0–325–07005–9 (Heinemann cloth)
ISBN 0–325–07004–0 (Heinemann paper)
ISBN 0–85255–695–0 (James Currey cloth)
ISBN 0–85255–645–4 (James Currey paper)

British Library Cataloguing in Publication Data

"Wicked" women and the reconfiguration of gender in Africa.
—(Social History of Africa)
1. Women—Africa—Social conditions 2. Sex role—Africa
I. Hodgson, Dorothy L. II McCurdy, Sheryl A.
305.4'096
ISBN 0–85255–645–4 (James Currey paper)
ISBN 0–85255–695–0 (James Currey cloth)

Library of Congress Cataloging-in-Publication Data

"Wicked" women and the reconfiguration of gender in Africa / edited by Dorothy L. Hodgson and Sheryl A. McCurdy.
   p. cm.—(Social history of Africa, ISSN 1099–8098)
   Includes bibliographical references and index.
   ISBN 0–325–07005–9 (alk. paper)—ISBN 0–325–07004–0 (pbk. : alk. paper)
   1. Women—Africa—Social conditions. 2. Sex role—Africa. I. Hodgson, Dorothy Louise. II. McCurdy, Sheryl, 1956– III. Series.
HQ1787.W53 2001
305.4'096—dc21   00–040882

Paperback cover art: Detail from work by artist George Lilanga printed on cloth purchased at Nyumba ya Sanaa in Dar es Salaam in the mid-1980s.

Printed in the United States of America on acid-free paper.

05 04 03 02 01 BB 1 2 3 4 5 6 7 8 9

Copyright Acknowledgments

The editors and publisher gratefully acknowledge permission to reprint revised versions of the following articles:

Thanks to the *Canadian Journal of African Studies/Revue Canadienne des Etudes Africaines*, for permission to print revised chapters based on four articles published in the 30:1 (1996) issue: Judith Byfield, "Women, Marriage, Divorce and the Emerging Colonial State in Abeokuta (Nigeria) 1892–1904," 32–51; Dorothy L. Hodgson, "'My Daughter . . . Belongs to the Government Now': Marriage, Maasai and the Tanzanian State," 106–123; Margot Lovett, "'She Thinks She's Like a Man'": Marriage and (De)Constructing Gender Identity in Colonial Buha, Western Tanzania, 1943–60," 52–68; and Richard Schroeder, "'Gone to Their Second Husbands': Marital Metaphors and Conjugal Contracts in The Gambia's Female Garden Sector," 69–87.

We thank Cambridge University Press for permission to print a revised version of Jean Allman's article, "Rounding Up Spinsters: Gender Chaos and Unmarried Women in Colonial Asante," *Journal of African History* 37 (1996), 195–214. Reprinted with the permission of Cambridge University Press.

Thanks also to the University of Chicago Press for permission to publish a revised version of Barbara Cooper's article: "The Politics of Difference & Women's Associations of Niger," *Signs: The Journal of Women in Culture and Society* 20:4 (1995), 851–882.

CONTENTS

Illustrations ix

Preface xi

1 Introduction: "Wicked" Women and the
Reconfiguration of Gender in Africa
Dorothy L. Hodgson and Sheryl A. McCurdy 1

PART I: CONTESTING CONJUGALITY

2 Women, Marriage, Divorce and the Emerging
Colonial State in Abeokuta (Nigeria) 1892–1904
Judith Byfield 27

3 "She Thinks She's Like a Man": Marriage and (De)constructing
Gender Identity in Colonial Buha, Western Tanzania, 1943–1960
Margot Lovett 47

4 Wayward Women and Useless Men: Contest and Change in
Gender Relations in Ado-Odo, S.W. Nigeria
Andrea Cornwall 67

5 "Gone to Their Second Husbands": Marital Metaphors and
Conjugal Contracts in The Gambia's Female Garden Sector
Richard A. Schroeder 85

PART II: CONFRONTING AUTHORITY

6 Dancing Women and Colonial Men: The *Nwaobiala* of 1925
Misty L. Bastian 109

7   Rounding Up Spinsters: Gender Chaos and
Unmarried Women in Colonial Asante
Jean Allman   130

8   "My Daughter . . . Belongs to the Government Now":
Marriage, Maasai, and the Tanzanian State
Dorothy L. Hodgson   149

PART III: TAKING SPACES/MAKING SPACES

9   Gender and the Cultural Construction of "Bad Women" in
the Development of Kampala-Kibuga, 1900–1962
Nakanyike B. Musisi   171

10   You Have Left Me Wandering About: Basotho Women and
the Culture of Mobility
David B. Coplan   188

11   Urban Threats: Manyema Women, Low Fertility, and Venereal
Diseases in Tanganyika, 1926–1936
Sheryl A. McCurdy   212

12   Negotiating Social Independence: The Challenges of Career
Pursuits for Igbo Women in Postcolonial Nigeria
Philomena E. Okeke   234

PART IV: NEGOTIATING DIFFERENCE

13   The Politics of Difference and Women's Associations in Niger:
Of "Prostitutes," the Public, and Politics
Barbara M. Cooper   255

14   "Wicked Women" and "Respectable Ladies": Reconfiguring
Gender on the Zambian Copperbelt, 1936–1964
Jane L. Parpart   274

15   Gender and Profiteering: Ghana's Market Women as Devoted
Mothers and "Human Vampire Bats"
Gracia Clark   293

Index   313

About the Contributors   323

ILLUSTRATIONS

MAPS

1   Colonial Africa Map   xiv
2   Contemporary Africa Map   xv

PHOTOGRAPHS

5.1 Second husbands: Gardens in many parts of The Gambia
     now generate such substantial incomes for women that
     they have become largely self-sufficient in meeting their
     own financial needs.   89

5.2 Reversal of fortunes: For the first time, Mandinka women's
     cash crop incomes outstrip those of their husbands.   92

5.3 Discretionary income: Many men resent the fact that
     women gardeners can now afford to purchase personal
     items such as radios, jewelry, clothing, etc.   99

6.1 A well-to-do young Igbo woman of the 1910s.   115

6.2 Early twentieth-century Igbo market scene, showing
     informal spatial arrangements and women's dominance.   121

10.1 Nthabiseng Nthako, dancing at a tavern in Lower Thamae,
     Maseru, Lesotho, 1988.   198

10.2 Unidentified informal tavern singer, Mohale's Hoek,
     Lesotho, 1989.   201

15.1 Yam travelers rest and count money in a shed beside the wholesale yard.   296

15.2 A yam traveler bargains with farmers.   308

FIGURE

11.1 A *waungwana* Manyema woman of the early 1890s.   217

PREFACE

The topic of this book first emerged in a conversation between the editors in the corridors of the 1993 annual meeting of the African Studies Association (ASA) in Boston. Fresh from the field (where we had met in the archives and hostels of Dar es Salaam) and intellectually invigorated by the rich range of research and ideas presented at the conference, we discussed the innovative work being done by junior scholars on gender in Africa. The papers we liked best were attentive to the intersections of culture, power, agency, and structure in the constitution and transformation of gender, and grounded in interdisciplinary training in the methods and theories of history, anthropology, and other fields.

Initially, we organized a double set of panels for the 1994 ASA meeting in Toronto to showcase this work. Susan Geiger and Marjorie Mbilinyi served as our discussants, and both sessions were extremely well-attended and sparked intense debate and discussion. Subsequently, six of the panel papers (Hodgson, McCurdy, Schroeder, Scully, Lovett, and Byfield) were published together in 1995 as a special issue of the *Canadian Journal of African Studies,* which we edited. In response to interest in the special issue, and our own desire to widen the scope of the topic by incorporating additional themes and perspectives, we decided to expand the issue into an edited collection. After distributing a call for papers over the Internet and through the mail to potential contributors, we then faced the difficult task of winnowing the many worthwhile proposals to a manageable book length. We had to cut even more chapters at a later date when the series editors and readers felt the volume was still too unwieldy. Each round of rejections was painful, and we are grateful to the many scholars who wished to contribute for their graciousness in accepting our limits. In addition to new contributions, authors of already published chapters have in most cases substantially revised their chapters to incorporate new insights and strengthen the clarity of their arguments.

From the beginning, our interest in the topic has been more thematic than geographic. No single collection could (or should) ever hope to fully cover all of the regions of Africa in both historical and contemporary perspective. As a result, the volume is unbalanced from a regional perspective, with the majority of chapters from former British colonies and a clustering of articles from Tanzania and Nigeria. While some readers may view this as a weakness, we see it as a strength for comparative analysis and teaching. The chapters from Nigeria, for example, can be read closely against one another for the subtle and not so subtle similarities and differences in gender relations and female agency according to different historical moments and cultural locations. More importantly, each illuminates a different theme or perspective on "wicked" women and gender. We would have liked to include more francophone and lusophone material, but we received very few proposals from those areas, despite our international call for papers. We believe this is more a reflection of the continuing divide between scholars who research and write in English and those who work in French than of the absence of "wicked" women in the former French, Belgian, and Portuguese colonies.

A project of such long duration incurs numerous debts. Dorothy would like to thank the Research Council, Faculty of Arts and Sciences, and the Department of Anthropology at Rutgers University for financial and administrative support. Sheryl thanks the Population Research Center at the Pennsylvania State University and the School of Public Health at the University of Texas-Houston for crucial administrative and financial support. Together, we would like to thank Robyn Stone, Belinda Blinkoff, and Nia Parson of Rutgers University for research assistance. We are grateful to the contributors as well as to Sara Berry, Susan Geiger, Jean Hay, Gregory Maddox, Jamie Monson, Marjorie Mbilinyi, Barry Riddell, Hanan Sabea, Elizabeth Schmidt, Pamela Scully, and Luise White for their encouragement, guidance, and advice at various stages of the project.

As the series editors, Allen Isaacman and Jean Allman have been tremendously helpful in assisting us to conceptualize, structure, and contain the book. Jim Lance has provided support and encouragement throughout the process. But of course it is our friendship and families that have borne the brunt of our efforts, and fortunately we have all survived relatively unscathed. Ironically, we both gave birth to and nurtured sons in the course of this project on wicked women. Hopefully, one day when they are old enough to read this book, they will appreciate our efforts and learn from the stories within. In the meantime, we hope that they learn from their feminist fathers to appreciate, support, and encourage female initiative, autonomy, and accomplishment. To Rick and Luke, and Pier and Anthony, thanks.

D.H.

S.M.

22 June 2000

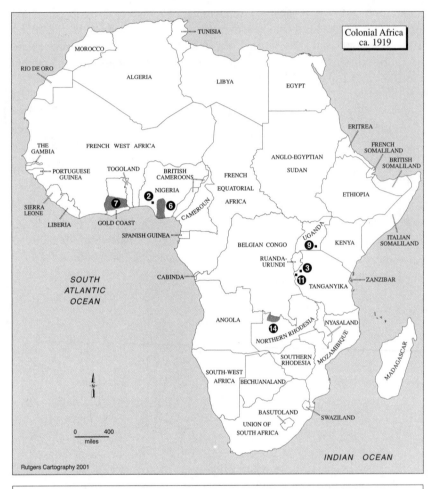

Colonial Africa
ca. 1919

Places Discussed, Colonial Period, by Chapter Number

❷ Abeokuta, Nigeria (Byfield)
❸ Buha, Tanganyika (Lovett)
❻ Owerri & Onitsha Provinces, Nigeria (Bastian)
❼ Asante Region, Gold Coast (Allman)

❾ Kampala-Kibuga, Buganda (Musisi)
⓫ Ujiji, Tanganyika (McCurdy)
⓮ Copperbelt Region,
   Northern Rhodesia (Parpart)

Map 1   Colonial Africa.

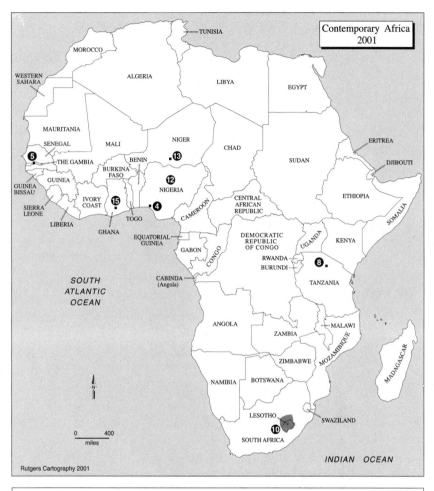

Contemporary Africa 2001

TUNISIA
MOROCCO
WESTERN SAHARA
ALGERIA
LIBYA
EGYPT
MAURITANIA
SENEGAL
MALI
NIGER
CHAD
ERITREA
❺
THE GAMBIA
BENIN
⓭
SUDAN
DJIBOUTI
GUINEA BISSAU
GUINEA
BURKINA FASO
⓬
NIGERIA
ETHIOPIA
SIERRA LEONE
IVORY COAST
⓯
❹
CENTRAL AFRICAN REPUBLIC
SOMALIA
LIBERIA
TOGO
CAMEROON
GHANA
EQUATORIAL GUINEA
GABON
CONGO
DEMOCRATIC REPUBLIC OF CONGO
UGANDA
KENYA
RWANDA
BURUNDI
❽
SOUTH ATLANTIC OCEAN
CABINDA (Angola)
TANZANIA
ANGOLA
ZAMBIA
MALAWI
MOZAMBIQUE
ZIMBABWE
MADAGASCAR
NAMIBIA
BOTSWANA
LESOTHO
❿
SWAZILAND
SOUTH AFRICA
INDIAN OCEAN

-N-

0   400
miles

Rutgers Cartography 2001

Places Discussed, Contemporary Period, by Chapter Number

❹ Ado-Odo, Nigeria (Cornwall)
❺ Kerewan, The Gambia (Schroeder)
❽ Monduli, Tanzania (Hodgson)
❿ Free State, South Africa & Lesotho (Coplan)

⓬ Nigeria (Okeke)
⓭ Maradi, Niger (Cooper)
⓯ Kumasi, Ghana (Clark)

Map 2   Contemporary Africa.

1

Introduction: "Wicked" Women and the Reconfiguration of Gender in Africa

Dorothy L. Hodgson and Sheryl A. McCurdy

They call me a vagabond,
But I am not a vagabond; I am taking care of business.
Should I mind when they wink at me?
They spread evil of me in secret whispers,
Yet they fear to speak out.
　　　　　—female Basotho shebeen singer (Coplan, this volume)

"Vagabond," "prostitute," "wayward," "unruly," "indecent," and "immoral" are just a few of the terms used to label and stigmatize women whose behavior in some way threatens other people's expectations of "the way things ought to be." Yet, like the shebeen singer, many of these "wicked" women are struggling to do whatever is needed to "take care of business" and support themselves and their children. In the process, they are chastized and criticized as "vagabonds" or worse by others, who "spread evil of [them] in secret whispers." *"Wicked" Women and the Reconfiguration of Gender in Africa* analyzes how the ideas and actions of such "wicked" women are pivotal in transforming gender relations and other domains of social life. Whether accused of adultery, abandonment, or insubordination, their lives and actions often reflect and produce contradictions and contestations of power within the intersecting and shifting landscapes of the individual, family, community, nation-state, and global arena. By analyzing the processes through which some women become stigmatized as "wicked," the nature of their alleged transgressions, and the effects of their actions, the chapters in this volume document how "wicked" women and the paradoxes they generate become sites for debate over, and occasionally transformations in, gender relations, social practices, cultural norms, and political-economic institutions.

Together, the chapters examine the myriad ways in which certain African women, individually and collectively, push the boundaries of "acceptable" behavior, demonstrating the permeability of these boundaries, and sometimes producing changes in gendered relations of power. As individuals, women have struggled to wrest control of their marriages from their fathers and unwanted husbands, exploited new economic opportunities to increase their financial autonomy, assumed and maintained political power in the face of active opposition, and mediated contradictory notions of moral authority and responsibility. In groups, women have challenged injustices perpetrated by colonial and postcolonial states, created new economic and social spaces for themselves in urban areas and migrant towns, circumvented sexist barriers to employment, established formal political associations, and pursued financial autonomy in the face of mounting hostility. As a result of their individual and collective challenges, the "wicked" women described in the collection have succeeded, however slightly, in reconfiguring the gendered orders in which they live. Of course, "wicked" women are not the only actors to produce gender, but the historical depth and geographical breadth of the chapters in this book demonstrate that they are and have always been key to processes of gender production and transformation.

A LEGACY OF RESEARCH ON GENDER IN AFRICA

This collection builds on a long legacy of research by Africans and Africanists on women and gender. While space and time constrain our ability to write a thorough historiography of the accomplishments and contributions of our (primarily) foremothers in this introductory chapter, we do want to briefly outline the key theoretical trajectories that inform the themes of this volume. In numerous collections and monographs in the 1970s and 1980s, scholars built on several earlier works (such as Kaberry 1952; Paulme [1960] 1963) to examine aspects of women's lives and social, economic, political, and spiritual roles in countries throughout the African continent.[1] Influential historical research demonstrated women's strategies (Wright 1975) and the ways they influenced community politics through their associations (Strobel 1979;

Berger 1981). Some feminist researchers used life histories to illuminate the complex negotiations and contradictory structures that shaped women's lives as they juggled their roles as daughters, sisters, lovers, wives, mothers, farmers, healers, initiates, and political organizers.[2] Together, these writings retrieved women's lives from their invisibility in previous studies of African history and society and demonstrated the diversity and significance of their experiences.

Drawing on this work, other scholars argued that in order to understand the meanings of being a "woman," one must understand the meanings of being a "man." They therefore studied "gender," that is the cultural and social relations of power between and among men and women. They argued that the meanings and practices of being a man and a woman were historical and cultural products that sometimes had little or nothing to do with biological differences between the sexes. In fact, accounts of "female husbands" and "male daughters" challenged common Western assumptions about binary gender codes (cf. Amadiume 1987). While these studies demonstrated the variability and flexibility of gender roles and relations across time and space, they often masked the agency of these same men and women in producing, reproducing, and transforming gender. How and why do the ideas and actions of some people result in temporary or enduring cultural and social changes? Are certain people more pivotal than others in initiating such transformations?

To address these questions, recent feminist work in African studies has foregrounded issues of gender, power, and social change.[3] These interests have produced several influential, overlapping lines of inquiry. One set of studies has examined the complex collaborations between colonial administrators and male elders as they attempted to assert and maintain patriarchal authority over women and younger men through the construction and reinforcement of "customary law" and "traditional authority."[4] Related work has explored the women who, as runaway wives, prostitutes, or insubordinates, contested assertions of patriarchal power (e.g., Pittin 1983; White 1990a; Mbilinyi 1988, Parpart 1994). Some researchers have challenged assumptions about the unitary, cohesive nature of the "household" to explore the dynamic interactions between men and women over issues of production, consumption, and resource distribution and control.[5] A few have specifically explored how certain technological and environmental changes prompted women and men to renegotiate their marital and household obligations.[6] Others have exploded previous distinctions between "political" and "domestic," and "public" and "private" by showing the penetration of the state into people's most intimate domains, including those of female circumcision, childcare, and personal hygiene.[7] Recent studies have also explored the production of African masculinities.[8]

The work of African and African diaspora scholars has been central to these debates. Some have used ethnographic and historical data to challenge Western assumptions about the homogeneity of the category "African women" (Sudarkasa 1987), the universality of binary gender models (Amadiume 1987), and the relative significance of domains of female power (Amadiume 1987, 1997). Others have debated the relevance of Western feminist political agendas for African women (Steady, 1987; Gaidzanwa 1992; Okeke 1996; Nnaemeka 1998), and denounced the ongoing structures of political and economic inequality in academia that restrict research and publication by all African scholars, especially African women and feminists (Okeke 1997). Some African women have questioned the relevance and utility of the category of "gender" for analyzing relations between African men and women. (Amadiume 1987; Oyĕwùmí 1997; but cf. Imam, Mama, and Sow 1997). In addition, important applied and theoretical work has been produced by the numerous research institutions, networks, and collaborative projects designed and implemented by African women scholars and activists. They include, to name but a few, the Tanzania Gender Networking Programme (TGNP) (1993), the SAPES Gender Project (Meena 1992), the Association of African Women for Research and Development (AAWORD; see their Occasional Paper Series), and several projects sponsored by CODESRIA (e.g., Imam, Mama, and Sow 1997). Through these projects and others, African women define their own problems and promote their own economic, political, and social demands (Hodgson 1999b).

This volume also draws on the methodological innovations of these diverse approaches. In response to the lack of primary written sources for most regions of Africa, scholars have turned to life histories, oral histories, legal cases, material culture, artifacts, rituals, performance, myths, songs, stories, spatial analysis, and other sources. Some use the early ethnographic accounts of travelers, missionaries, and colonial officials, as well as their diaries, letters, and pictures. Many researchers achieve proficiency in at least one if not several African languages, and combine extended ethnographic fieldwork with historical research. The chapters in this volume illustrate the tremendous explanatory power of these interdisciplinary methodologies to produce nuanced studies of local communities that intertwine culture and history, set within the broader political economies of region, state, and globe. Through an in-depth grasp of the different ways that individuals and communities operate, the authors present fresh interpretations of everyday lived experiences, illustrate the ways the past informs the present, and demonstrate how local and translocal processes intersect on the African continent.

The study of gender in Africa has made significant contributions to our understanding of gender roles and relationships as culturally diverse, historically dynamic, and inflected by differences of age, class, race, ethnicity, and nation. It has also demonstrated the centrality of gender as an organizing principle of society in Africa and elsewhere. Accounts of African women as the primary economic providers for their households in their roles as farmers and traders[9] and descriptions of the complicated gender and generational rights and responsibilities for household production, consumption, and distribution[10] have challenged prevailing Euro-American understandings of marriage and households as partnerships in which men are the main providers and household resources are pooled for consumption and distribution. The myriad ways in which African women express their demands and exercise power have also provoked a rethinking of theories of gender and power. Studies include those on organized movements and protests (e.g., Ifeka-Moller 1975; Van Allen 1976; Presley 1992; Ekechi 1996), the production and use of performance, costume, and material culture,[11] and involvement in spirit possession cults and other forms of spiritual expression.[12] All have helped further our understanding of how gender relations are produced, reproduced, and occasionally transformed through the everyday lives and practices of men and women.

GENDERED TRANSGRESSIONS: OF "WICKEDNESS" AND "WOMEN"

So why "wicked" women? How does the concept of "wickedness" advance our theoretical and empirical understandings of gender in Africa and elsewhere? Although for some the term may seem offensive or impertinent, we believe that it encapsulates the interplay of the multiple dimensions—agency and structure, discourse and practice, culture and political economy—that constitute both continuity and change.[13] "Wickedness" is produced at the intersection of and by the interaction of these domains as men and women operate within certain structures of power that constrain or enable their actions, either reproducing or transforming the very structures themselves. In some of the chapters, "wickedness" is a discourse of primarily masculine power that seeks to control or oppress women by stigmatizing certain actions, whether normative or unconventional. Culturally and historically variable concepts of stigma and prestige at once reflect and uphold dominant cultural norms (themselves historical products) and political-economic relationships such as relations of production, consumption, and distribution. But for others, "wickedness" refers to a manifestation of feminine power whereby women purposefully and effectively challenge political, social, or cultural constraints on their behavior. The seemingly stark differences between these two concepts of wickedness reflect some of the central theoretical tensions of the book: How does "wicked" as an analytic category correspond to local interpretations of women's actions? If "agency" is such an ambiguous, slippery term, is it even possible to compare and analyze different accounts of female transgressions? Rather than put forward some dogmatic definition of wickedness, we find it more instructive to read the chapters against one another, seeking to understand whether the similarities, differences, and contradictions between cases are a matter of culture, history, or interpretation.

Many women are labeled "wicked" because they disrupt the web of social relationships that define and depend on them as daughters, sisters, wives, mothers, and lovers. Often these women directly or indirectly challenge normative expectations of "respectability"; they are no longer the "good" wives or daughters they are supposed to be. Although the criteria for what determines "respectability" vary, "respectability" is a potent force in delimiting and regulating the dominant configuration of gender, that is, the "norms" of "appropriate" gender roles, relations, responsibilities, and behavior. Transmitted by socialization and internalization, buttressed by appeals to "custom" and "tradition," and reinforced by mechanisms of social surveillance and control, gendered norms of "respectability" often become the basis for local and even national moral and social orders. Thus, when women (or men) overstep these boundaries, whether intentionally or unintentionally, they not only challenge dominant norms of gendered behavior, but threaten the moral foundation of society. Furthermore, social norms of "respectability" are mutable and sometimes contradictory, and often transformed under outside influence, as missionaries, state administrators, Euro-American feminists, and others insinuate and impose their ideas in direct and indirect ways. Although such transgressions, like the roles and expectations they challenge, are culturally and historically particular, their trans-historical and cross-cultural prevalence attests to the need to distill common patterns.

Each section of the book examines a distinct domain or strategy of "wickedness." The chapters in the first section, "Contesting Conjugality," explore how marriage and household relations, as the primary locus of production, reproduction, consumption, distribution, and social control in societies, become key sites of struggle in the context of broader economic and social transformations. In particular, women who earn independent incomes must often struggle with their husbands to retain control over their earnings, negotiating and renegotiating their household financial obligations. Related debates can occur over how women allocate their labor and time or their control of and access to economic resources such as land, livestock, agricultural inputs, water, and fuel. Some women directly challenge and disobey male directives; others quietly defy their families and persistently circumvent restrictions on their sexual autonomy and social mobility as they seek companionship and work of their own choosing. Although often articulated in terms of moral crisis, contests over conjugality are really about shifting power relations. Marriage rights, roles, and obligations between family members are dynamic; ideas of what it means to be a "wife" and a "husband" are challenged not just at the level of the household, but by larger socioeconomic, religious, and political processes such as labor migration, urbanization, and missionization. Furthermore, these multiple meanings and forms of marriage reveal that what we gloss as marriage embraces a diverse array of relationships: from the serial domestic unions of migrant Basotho, Baganda, and Zambian women in urban areas to long-term partnerships in other places.

Given the centrality of marriages to male-female relationships, debates about marriage, women as wives, and men as husbands appear in almost all of the chapters. But the four chapters included in the first section illuminate distinct aspects of the subject that resonate throughout the collection. Judith Byfield examines how Egba women in the early 1900s took advantage of the new economic opportunities and the alternative judicial arena presented by the opening of the railway to pursue financial autonomy, dissolve unwanted marriages, and legitimate desired relationships. In a similar context of economic change and social dislocation, Margot Lovett interprets the ways in which marriage and what constituted "proper" gender relations within that institution were altered after young Ha men became increasingly involved in labor migration during the colonial period in Tanganyika. Andrea Cornwall traces shifts in ideas about female waywardness and male prerogative over the course of the twentieth century in Ado-Odo, Nigeria, in response to socioeconomic changes. She analyzes what turns a "good wife" into a "bad woman," and "husbands" into "useless men." Finally, in his analysis of the dramatic increase in women's cash crop gardening in The Gambia, Richard A. Schroeder shows how discursive politics and economic practices interacted as Mandinka wives and husbands reconfigured their marital relationships and responsibilities to take account of the fact that women were now the primary household cash earners.

The chapters in the second section, "Confronting Authority," examine cases whereby women, either individually or collectively, directly challenged dominant authorities, whether male elders or state administrators. Some challenged established structures of political power within their own community; others responded to the imposition of new structures of power. As political leaders, legal combatants, or fierce critics, these women confronted and undermined state representations of and interventions in their lives, tailoring their methods to the prevailing structures of power. In the process, they upset the consolidation and privileging of public, political space as male and private, and domestic space as female, and created new sites for female action and expression.

Misty L. Bastian explores how women in colonial Nigeria formed dance groups to confront powerful Igbo men in order to express their anger over recent changes in the newly colonized and missionized southeast, threaten men with fines and divine retribution, and demand reforms. In her exploration of the "gender chaos" provoked by the transformations in women's roles in the cash economy in colonial Asante, Jean Allman investigates how "spinster" women confronted and undermined attempts by Asante chiefs to force them to marry. Finally, through an in-depth analysis of a 1992 court case, Dorothy L. Hodgson explores how a young Maasai woman's direct challenge to her father's authority and, by implication, the authority of local elders, lineages, and clans, forced her father and elder Maasai men to scramble, both inside and outside of the courtroom, to defend their "legitimate" authority, an authority premised on a certain configuration of naturalized and "proper" gender roles and relations.

The chapters in "Taking Spaces/Making Spaces" foreground issues of space, both metaphorical and material, to explore important questions about gender and power: the negotiation of boundaries of behavior; the relationship between autonomy and mobility; women's struggles to retain female-controlled spaces as well as to enter predominantly male spaces; the creation of new or alternative sites for female expression and activity; and the shifting and sometimes contradictory gendered meanings of certain spaces. Women are labeled "wicked" when they transgress ideological boundaries such as cultural norms of "respectability" or material boundaries such as legal restrictions on employment, residence, marriage, and divorce. By trespassing these boundaries, "wicked" women literally create new spaces in which other women can act and think.

"Wicked" women have long been attracted to liminal or so-called "hybrid" spaces such as border zones and urban areas where people from diverse ethnic, regional, religious, and class backgrounds live and interact. The dense interconnections of people provide a plethora of economic, social, and sexual opportunities and expose men and women to alternative social practices and gender orders. Thus, these heterogeneous, partly anonymous spaces are conducive to individual and collective attempts to escape or transform oppressive gender relations. Nakanyike B. Musisi analyzes such processes in her study of how women moved to urban

Buganda in order to reclaim their space, voice, bodies, and actions. Despite being stigmatized as "bad," these women used the liminal space of the city to assert their own visions of female sexuality, economic autonomy, and political expression. David B. Coplan examines a similar situation among Basotho women, who fled their hopeless rural situations for the new economic and social opportunities available in South African townships and mining communities. Women willing and able to service the needs of male migrants became food preparers and sellers, beer brewers, bar owners, prostitutes, entertainers, and providers of "all the comforts of home" (cf. White 1990a). Along the way, they developed new practices and companionships that helped them cope with the constancy of poverty, transience, and oppression. In an exploration of struggles over bodily spaces, Sheryl McCurdy explores how Manyema women in colonial Tanganyika retained control of their sexuality and fertility despite successive attempts by the British to legislate, cajole, and coerce them to change their practices. Finally, Philomena E. Okeke analyzes the strategies university-educated Igbo women in southeastern Nigeria use to access the professional economic spaces long controlled by men. Their tactics, especially the use of sexual favors, have sparked debates over what kind of behavior is "respectable" for elite, educated, professional women.

Chapters in the final section, "Negotiating Difference," explore how women use differences among themselves of class, ethnicity, identity, age, marital status, and kinship to transform economic, political, and sexual aspects of gender relations. Ideas about the "proper" behavior of women can vary significantly within the same society, depending on a woman's class, age, marital status, religious affiliation, ethnic identity, and lineage. Even as they may stigmatize one another, women in one category take advantage of the sexual, economic, and political freedoms of another group to claim new possibilities for themselves of political action, economic survival, and social and sexual relations.

Barbara M. Cooper analyzes how both married and unmarried women in the Maradi region of Niger use the politics of naming to expand notions of what public and political spaces are legitimately open to women. Rather than emphasizing some illusory female solidarity, women take advantage of their differences in age, marital status, education, occupation, and class to ally with different political parties, and thereby create distinct spaces for political action. Similarly, Jane L. Parpart examines how gender and class interacted in the ways that urban African women transgressed "respectable" behavior in colonial Zambia. The "wicked" behavior of lower-class women shocked and dismayed those Africans struggling to gain acceptance as "respectable" townsfolk, yet it also forged new possibilities for women and men of all classes. Finally, Gracia Clark explores how market women in Ghana at once embody and exploit the contradictory expectations, responsibilities, and opportunities of simultaneously being sisters, daughters, wives, and mothers in order to legitimate their economic activity and counter hostility directed toward them during times of economic crisis.

Collectively, the chapters reveal the broad range of women and transgressions that, in specific places and contexts, were deemed "wicked." These women differed by age, marital status, fertility, occupation, class, economic success/misfortune, and sexual history, among other characteristics. Their misbehavior varied from the mundane (trading) to the outrageous (sexually explicit dancing). It included direct or indirect assertions of power, individual or collective action, quiet persistence or flagrant defiance. Sometimes formal and informal associations provided the platform for challenging unwanted conditions. Often women took advantage of new economic, political, and social opportunities to alter their circumstances. Their detractors included men and other women: family, friends, strangers, missionaries, state officials, and others. The diversity of women and forms of perceived transgressions suggest that definitions of "wickedness" depend on the gender constructions of "women" in specific times and places; and that the "naming" of a particular woman, group of women, or their acts as wicked both reflects and constitutes social practice.

African men had diverse reactions to and encounters with "wicked" women; they could restrict or encourage female "misbehavior." In colonial Ghana, while some male chiefs tried to force unmarried women to marry, other men helped the women subvert the chiefs' edicts by posing as their husbands or husbands-to-be (Allman, this volume). Many wayward women had men who supported them. Shebeen singers, for example, found lovers, friends, and companions among male migrants and local gangs (Coplan, this volume). Prostitution, in particular, created complicated alliances and antagonisms between husbands, fathers, brothers, lovers, and state officials who were concerned about controlling women's sexuality and fertility (Coplan, this volume; Musisi, this volume; Parpart, this volume; cf. White 1990a).

OF CRISIS AND CHAOS:
A CHRONOLOGY OF UNCONTROLLABILITY

Assessing the varieties of "wicked" women through a temporal frame raises different questions: What kinds of "wickedness" are most salient at particular historical moments and why? Why do certain issues/acts become sites of gendered resistance and thus foster debate over "wickedness" in the precolonial, colonial, and postcolonial periods? Is there a relationship, as some authors have suggested (Allman, this volume), between moments of widespread political, economic, and social crisis and efforts to intensify control over women? How does the changing role of the colonial and then the postcolonial state shape such encounters?

Although none of the chapters analyze "wicked" women in the precolonial period, this does not imply that women in that period were passive, that gender relations were static, or that transgressions and struggles similar to those documented for the colonial and postcolonial periods did not occur. Thanks to the efforts of historians (e.g., Berger 1981; Musisi 1991; Wright 1993; Greene 1996; Schoenbrun 1998; Larson 2000), art historians (Drewal and Drewal 1983; Perani and Smith 1998), and now archaeologists (e.g., Kent 1998) to reconstruct normative gender relations for particular periods and places from the fragmentary oral, written, and material evidence that is available, we know that gender relations were dynamic and diverse, and that women were central to state-building, trade, technological change, migration, and slavery. Yet the sources for the precolonial period still have limitations in terms of documenting the gendered dimensions of specific events or individual experiences. The emphasis on the later historical period in this volume is thus partly a consequence of the much richer archival and oral sources available (cf. Allman 1991).

But it is also the product of the immense social dislocations provoked by the implementation of colonial rule. Despite the many social, political, and economic changes in the precolonial period, the onset of colonial rule intensified struggles over normative gender relations. The imposition of boundaries—spatial, political, economic, symbolic—on people's movement and identities through the demarcation of colonial borders, the stereotyping and rigidification of ethnic identities, the creation of native reserves and districts, the restrictions on forms of economic endeavors and political participation, and the codification of customary law all had consequences for relationships between and among men and women. These dramatic shifts in economic, political, and environmental relations, informed by nineteenth-century Victorian ideas about normative gender relations, prompted fierce negotiations over what constituted "proper" female and male behavior.

During the early colonial period, the emergence of state institutions and structures that attempted to monitor and regulate local practices provided some men and women with new opportunities for and constraints to action. For example, colonial officials often wrote explicitly gendered legislation restricting the movement of people into or out of rural and urban areas (e.g., Barnes 1992). In Buganda, an 1899 law prohibited married women and men from visiting the foreign sections of town (Musisi, this volume). But other newly created areas were magnets for disgruntled women. In 1899, the Egba and Lagos governments of Nigeria signed an agreement that ceded jurisdiction over a strip of land on either side of a new railway to the British government. Unhappy Egba women took advantage of the newly created colonial railway space and used the jurisdiction of British authorities to divorce their husbands (Byfield, this volume). Both situations reveal that at the onset of the colonial period women were unhappy with the control their husbands exerted over them and they responded in varying ways, according to their opportunities, to that domination.

With the intensification of the colonial project in the 1920s and 1930s, African women again became significant sources of attention, debate, and concern. As part of rebuilding and fortifying the economic position of the colonies, colonial officials tried to bring order to the perceived chaos of African social, economic, and political relations by reshaping African ideas and practices. "Stabilizing" marriage and reinforcing patriarchal control became a key concern of missionaries and colonial officers (in collaboration with some African men and women) (e.g., Hunt 1990; Allman 1994), as did teaching Africans to be more "efficient" and "productive" farmers and herders (Chauncey 1981; Hodgson 1999c) and charging women to be "better" mothers responsible for protecting and improving society's morals (Hunt 1990; Summers 1991; Vaughan 1991; Allman 1994). Women responded to the shifting patterns of political authority, economy, and colonially sponsored propaganda by challenging each other, African men, and colonial authorities. Across the continent, women used local institutions like song and dance groups to express their anger and frustration over the rapid and sometimes violent changes in local practices and relationships. Some, like the *Nwaobiala* dancers in Nigeria, used their songs to demand a return to precolonial social ideals and practices of betrothal, marriage, chiefly authority, and gendered division of production and consumption (Bastian, this volume). Others responded to the changing political and economic system by collective attacks on colonial and native authorities (e.g., Ifeka-Moller 1975; Van Allen 1976) or defiantly refusing to obey orders (Allman, this volume).

Before World War II, female presence in cities was actively discouraged, but tolerated as a necessary evil. During and after World War II, however, African women's migration to cities increased dramatically (cf. Little 1973). As men's earnings increased, more people were living in urban centers, pursuing new forms of leisure (Martin 1995). Unable to stem the flow of women into cities, officials in Northern Rhodesia and South Africa elected to pass legislation and develop social welfare programs that might, at the very least, mold the sort of desirable urban dweller they preferred (Parpart, this volume; Coplan, this volume). Neither legislation nor social welfare programs succeeded in reforming the poorer, fringe elements of urban centers, but they did provide elites with standards of "sophisticated" respectability to aspire to, acquire, and use to distinguish themselves from other Africans (Parpart, this volume). In contrast, colonial officials in Uganda never quite gave up the hope that they could control Bagandan women. They used legislation and brute force throughout World War II and again during the mid-1950s to label unattached women as "prostitutes," round them up, and repatriate them to rural areas (Musisi, this volume). Identifying women as the source of moral "decay" in African societies allowed officials to deny the ways in which economic projects of economic restructuring, such as migrant labor schemes, transformed families and created a demand for new forms of sexual and domestic services.

As nationalism emerged during the 1950s, aspiring leaders lamented the evils of both elite and lower-class practices. Many nationalist leaders condemned elite women who pursued Western ways and chastised poor women for their disrespectful behavior, urging them to behave in "African" ways, central to which was respect for patriarchal authority (e.g., Urdang 1979). Mobutu's early doctrine of "authenticité" in Zaire, for example, demanded that women, especially the notorious "femmes libres" (see La Fontaine 1974; MacGaffey 1988), return to their "traditional" roles as obedient wives and good mothers as proof of their "patriotism" and "revolutionary consciousness" (Wilson 1982).[14] In Zaire, Tanzania, and other newly independent countries during this period, political leaders disregarded women's economic contribution, ignored their historical political roles, and launched cultural campaigns to ban "immodest" clothing such as miniskirts and tight pants, and "indecent" Western cosmetic products such as makeup, hair straighteners, and skin lighteners.[15] African women, however, had their own agendas during the 1950s; some left their husbands to move into houses of their own (Cornwall, this volume), others refused to stay out of urban areas or behave in a "respectable manner."

Despite gains in certain political and economic rights since the colonial period, women in contemporary Africa continue to struggle over many of the same issues: economic security, political power, and social control. As in the colonial period, the implementation of national and international development programs has had ambivalent consequences for women: some find their long-standing livelihoods under attack (Clark, this volume), others eagerly take advantage of new income-earning opportunities (Schroeder, this volume). Education has empowered some women to challenge assertions of patriarchal privilege and power (cf. Okeke, this volume), but uneducated women have long fought similar battles. Fortunately, some educated African women are in the vanguard of challenging the pernicious, persistent misrepresentations, policies, and practices that perpetuate gender oppression and inequality, through their scholarship and political activism (e.g., Okeke 1997; Meena 1992, describing the rich work of TGNP). Thus while women in Africa, as elsewhere, continue to challenge gender representations and relations, the parameters and content of those efforts have changed as a result of previous struggles and present contexts.

The chronology of uncontrollability is therefore a historical record of shifting power relations in local communities that reveals how women and men attempted, both individually and collectively, to negotiate social and economic transformations in the face of dynamic local and translocal processes. As many of the chapters illustrate, when communities faced particularly difficult social or economic circumstances, wicked women became the locus of moral panic. Anxious to preserve existing social orders, local and state officials blamed unconventional women for community problems, rather than acknowledge that their own programs and policies created difficulties. These women and their actions were construed as the cause rather than the symptom, thereby enabling others to lay the responsibility for all the scourges of society on their laps.

STRUCTURE, AGENCY, AND POWER

Any consideration of gender and social transformation must consider issues of power, agency, and structure. Women's agency is, of course, exerted within particular structures of power. Certain institutions and opportunities enable women (sometimes inadvertently) to challenge and transform repressive gender norms, while others constrain what women can do. National courts in both colonial and contemporary Africa provided an important venue for demanding change in betrothal, marriage, divorce, child custody, inheritance, and property rights. Women who brought such cases risked censure ranging from verbal abuse to physical banishment by their families and kin, but, if successful, created legal precedents for other unhappy women to follow. Yet the courts also created and codified new crimes and offenses such as "adultery" and "infanticide" in collaboration with community elders (Chanock 1982, 1985; Scully 1996).

The relationship between structural changes and female agency varies. Sometimes broader social crisis, such as the imposition and/or intensification of new religious, political, and economic regimes, caused the redefining of formerly normative actions as transgressive. For example, in response to the substantial economic and social dislocations produced by the imposition of structural adjustment policies in Ghana, Ghanaians vilified the long-accepted group of female traders, "attacking traders as women and women as traders" (Clark, this volume). At other times, female transgressions provoked broader social crisis. As increasing numbers of unhappily married Nigerian women fled to the railway zones under the jurisdiction of Europeans to divorce and begin new lives, their fathers and former husbands fought hard to restrict and control them (Byfield, this volume). More commonly, the interactions of structural change and female agency were tangled and complex. In Ujiji, for example, British colonial officials intensified animosities between rival ethnic groups by restructuring the court system. In response, women from these groups threatened each other through dance performances, causing anxious colonial officials to worry about political and economic unrest (McCurdy 1996).

The chapters also highlight some preferred forms of female agency and expression. Song and dance are common modes of individual and collective communication for women, whether in formal dance groups in Tanganyika (McCurdy 1996), organized protests in Nigeria (Bastian, this volume), or shebeens in South Africa (Coplan, this volume). The style, form, and content of these performances provide a means for women to report, comment on, and critique practices and policies with which they disagree, as well as propose their own alternatives. For example, Igbo-speaking women in Nigeria had a long-established practice of "making" *egwu* (songs/dances) in order to embarrass local male authorities and communicate women's collective grievances and demands. In 1925, women produced a new form of *egwu*, *Nwaobiala*, in response to the intensification of colonial and missionary interventions. These women incorporated sweeping, a quintessentially female task, into their performance, with groups of women doing a lengthy and ritualized sweeping of public places and big men's private spaces (Bastian, this volume).

These examples point to a central feature of many female performances, and of female critique in general, which is the use of metaphor as an indirect yet potent means to voice grievances. For the shebeen singer quoted in the epigraph, "taking care of business" alluded to the economic motivations shaping her choice of careers and companions. For Igbo women, sweeping signified the need to clean out the pollution of moral and social disorders brought by colonizers, missionaries, and collaborating male elders. In The Gambia, female gardeners spoke of going to "their second husbands" (*a taata a ke ya*) to describe working on their gardens, which fed and nurtured them, as their "first" husbands should have been doing (Schroeder, this volume).

Agency, as discussed above, is a difficult term to define and interpret, as it entails culturally and historically specific modes of action and interpretation. Furthermore, there is a tendency to either ignore or romanticize female agency, portraying women as victims or heroines (cf. Abu-Lughod 1990). By grounding their analyses in empirical data, however, the chapter authors depict the complexities and subtleties of gender, power, and social transformation. Through their use of language, performance, and new spaces and opportunities, and the assistance of men, women produce, reproduce, and transform gender representations and relations. As women embark on new lives and new ways of being they earn the scorn of some and the support of others, and at some point, inevitably, they will be labeled "wicked." Yet the cumulative effect of their actions, large and small, is to shift relations of power, and thereby reconfigure gender relations and representations.

CONCLUSION

By combining the theoretical and methodological insights of recent scholarship in both feminist studies and African studies, the contributions to this book establish the centrality of gender to the culture, history, and social transformation of African societies. Gender relations are no isolated concern, but shape and are shaped by people's involvement with processes and institutions such as labor migration, development projects, economic and political interventions by the nation-state, and religious change. Both women and men take advantage of the opportunities produced by the social and material changes in their lives to maneuver with their friends, rivals, family, community, and state for leverage, changes, and continuities. However derided and despised, "wicked" women are central actors in ongoing and multilayered negotiations of gender, power, and social change. With their rich attention to the interaction of agency, power, and structure, these complex, multilevel analyses challenge common stereotypes of African women as either passive victims or unrestrained resisters, and demonstrate once and for all that there is no "normative" African woman nor static gendered relation of power.

NOTES

We are grateful to Jean Allman, Sara Berry, Allen Isaacman, Jane Parpart, Claire Robertson, Luise White, and two anonymous readers for the press for their extremely helpful comments on earlier drafts of the introduction.

1. Some key readings include Wipper (1972b), Hafkin and Bay (1976), Strobel (1979), Okeyo (1980), Afonja (1981), Bay (1982), Hay and Wright (1982), Oppong

(1983), Robertson and Klein (1983), Hay and Stichter (1984), Oboler (1985), Robertson and Berger (1986), Stichter and Parpart (1988), Parpart and Staudt (1989).

2. Examples include Romero (1988), Mirza and Strobel (1989), Ngaiza and Koda (1991), Bozzoli with Nkotsoe (1991), Geiger (1997).

3. See, for example, Moore [1986] 1996, Hansen (1989), House-Midamba (1996), Abwunza (1997), Grosz-Ngate and Kokole (1997), Mikell (1997).

4. Chanock (1982), Mann (1982), Mann and Roberts (1991), Mbilinyi (1988), and Schmidt (1990).

5. Guyer (1984), Guyer and Peters (1987), Carney and Watts (1991), Dwyer and Bruce (1988).

6. Jackson (1976), Wright (1983), Vaughan (1987), Moore and Vaughan (1994), Maddox (1996), Sunseri (1997).

7. Examples include Allman (1994), Hansen (1992), Hunt (1988, 1990), Jeannerat (1997), Stambach (1999), Thomas (1996, 1998).

8. Hodgson (1999a), Landau (1995), Lindsay (1998, 1999), Shire (1994), White (1990b).

9. Boserup (1970) brought the dominance of African women in agriculture to international attention. For analyses of African women as traders, see Clark (1994), Robertson (1984, 1997).

10. The work of Jane Guyer (1981, 1984, 1988; Guyer and Peters 1987) and Sara Berry (1985, 1993) has been central to this topic.

11. Askew (forthcoming), Bastian (1996), Comaroff and Comaroff (1997), Fair (1996, 1998, forthcoming), Martin (1995), McCurdy (1996, 2000), Schloss (1996), Stambach (1999).

12. Alpers (1984), Hodgson (1997), Hoehler-Fatton (1996), Kratz (1994), Boddy (1989), McCurdy (2000).

13. Other authors have found the concept of wicked women similarly productive, including Brown (1996) for colonial Virginia, Davis (1995) for seventeenth-century France, Littlewood and Mahood (1991) for Victorian Scotland, and Rublack (1997) for early modern Germany.

14. History, as we already know, repeats itself. When Laurent Kabila took power in Zaire (now renamed the Democratic Republic of Congo), in 1997, one of his first acts was to use soldiers to enforce a ban on miniskirts and tight pants by attacking and humiliating women. James C. McKinley, Jr. "In Congo's Restive Capital, New Government Sows Resentment," *New York Times*, 25 May 1997, p. 7.

15. Letters to the editor of the *Daily News* in Tanzania at this time included, "Lets Have a Law on Obscene Dresses," 1 August 1972, p. 9; and "Miniskirt Addicts Deserve Very Hard Handling," 5 September 1972, p. 9.

REFERENCES

Abu-Lughod, Lila. 1990. "The Romance of Resistance: Tracing Transformations of Power through Bedouin Women." *American Ethnologist* 17(1):41–55.

Abwunza, Judith M. 1997. *Women's Voices, Women's Power: Dialogues of Resistance from East Africa*. Peterborough, Ontario, Canada: Broadview Press.

Afonja, Simi. 1981. "Changing Modes of Production and the Sexual Division of Labor Among the Yoruba." *Signs: Journal of Women in Culture and Society* 7(2):299–313.

Allman, Jean. 1991. "Of 'Spinsters,' 'Concubines,' and 'Wicked Women': Reflections on Gender and Social Change in Colonial Asante." *Gender and History* 3(2):176–189.

———. 1994. "Making Mothers: Missionaries, Medical Officers, and Women's Work in Colonial Asante, 1924–45." *History Workshop Journal* 38:23–47.

Alpers, Edward A. 1984. "'Ordinary Household Chores': Ritual Power in a Nineteenth Century Swahili Women's Spirit Possession Cult." *International Journal of African Historical Studies* 17(4):677–702.

Amadiume, Ifi. 1987. *Male Daughters, Female Husbands: Gender and Sex in an African Society*. London: Zed Books.

———. 1997. *Re-Inventing Africa: Matriarchy, Religion, and Culture*. London: Zed Books.

Askew, Kelly. Forthcoming. *Performing the Nation: Swahili Musical Performance and the Production of Tanzanian National Culture*. Chicago: University of Chicago Press.

Barnes, Teresa. 1992. "The Fight for Control of African Women's Mobility in Colonial Zimbabwe, 1900–1939." *Signs: Journal of Women in Culture and Society* 17(3):586–608.

Bastian, Misty. 1996. "Female '*Alhajis*' and Entrepreneurial Fashions: Flexible Identities in Southeastern Nigerian Clothing Practice." In Hilde Hendrickson, ed., *Clothing and Difference: Embodied Identities in Colonial and Post-Colonial Africa*. Durham, NC: Duke University Press.

Bay, Edna, ed. 1982. *Women and Work in Africa*. Boulder, CO: Westview Press.

Berger, Iris. 1981. *Religion and Resistance: East African Kingdoms in the Precolonial Period*. Tervuren, Belgium: Musee Royal de l' Afrique Centrale, Annales, Série In-8, Sciences Humaines No. 105.

Berry, Sara. 1985. *Fathers Work for Their Sons*. Berkeley: University of California Press.

———. 1993. *No Condition is Permanent: The Social Dynamics of Agrarian Change in Sub-Saharan Africa*. Madison: University of Wisconsin Press.

Boddy, Janice. 1989. *Wombs and Alien Spirits: Women, Men and the Zar Cult in Northern Sudan*. Madison: University of Wisconsin Press.

Boserup, Esther. 1970. *Women's Role in Economic Development*. London: George Allen & Unwin.

Bozzoli, Belinda with Mmantho Nkotsoe. 1991. *Women of Phokeng: Consciousness, Life Strategy, and Migrancy in South Africa, 1900–1983*. Portsmouth, NH: Heinemann.

Brown, Kathleen M. 1996. *Good Wives, Nasty Wenches and Anxious Patriarchs: Gender, Race and Power in Colonial Virginia*. Chapel Hill: University of North Carolina Press.

Carney, Judith and Michael Watts. 1991. "Disciplining Women? Rice, Mechanization and the Evolution of Gender Relations on Senegambia." *Signs: Journal of Women in Culture and Society* 16(4): 651–681.

Chanock, Martin. 1982. "Making Customary Law: Men, Women, and Courts in Colonial Northern Rhodesia." In Margaret Jean Hay and Marcia Wright, eds., *African Women and the Law: Historical Perspectives*. Boston: Boston University Papers on Africa, VII.

————. 1985. *Law, Custom and Social Order: The Colonial Experience in Malawi and Zambia*. Cambridge: Cambridge University Press.

Chauncey, George, Jr. 1981. "The Locus of Reproduction: Women's Labour in the Zambian Copperbelt, 1927–1953." *Journal of Southern African Studies* 7(2): 135–164.

Clark, Gracia. 1994. *Onions Are My Husband: Survival and Accumulation by West African Market Women*. Chicago: University of Chicago Press.

Comaroff, John L. and Jean Comaroff. 1997. "Fashioning the Colonial Subject: The Empire's Old Clothes." In John L. and Jean Comaroff, eds., *Revelation and Revolution: The Dialetics of Modernity on a South African Frontier*, Volume Two. Chicago: University of Chicago Press.

Cooper, Barbara. 1997. *Marriage in Maradi: Gender and Culture in a Hausa Society in Niger, 1900–1989*. Portsmouth, NH: Heinemann.

Davis, Natalie. 1995. *Women on the Margins. Three Seventeenth Century Lives*. Cambridge: Harvard University Press.

Davison, Jean. 1996. *Voices from Mutira: Change in the Lives of Rural Gikuyu Women, 1910–1995*. Second edition. Boulder, CO: Lynne Rienner.

Drewal, Henry John and Margaret Thompson Drewal. 1983. *Gẹlẹdẹ: Art and Female Power among the Yoruba*. Bloomington: Indiana University Press.

Dwyer, Daisy and Judith Bruce, eds. 1988. *A Home Divided: Women and Income in the Third World*. Stanford, CA: Stanford University Press.

Ekechi, Felix K. 1996. "Perceiving Women as Catalysts." *Africa Today* 43(3):235–249.

Fair, Laura. 1996. "Identity, Difference, and Dance: Female Initiation in Zanzibar, 1890–1930." *Frontiers: A Journal of Women's Studies* 17(3):146–172.

————. 1998. "Dressing Up: Clothing, Class and Gender in Post-Abolition Zanzibar." *Journal of African History* 39:63–94.

————. 2001. *Pastimes and Politics: Culture, Community and Identity in Post-Abolition Urban Zanzibar, 1890–1945*. Athens, OH: University of Ohio Press.

Gaidzanwa, Rudo. 1992. "Bourgeois Theories of Gender and Feminism and their Shortcomings with Reference to Southern African Countries." In Ruth Meena, ed., *Gender in Southern Africa: Conceptual and Theoretical Issues*. Harare: SAPES Books.

Geiger, Susan. 1997. *TANU Women: Gender and Culture in the Making of Tanganyikan Nationalism, 1955–1965*. Portsmouth, NH: Heinemann.

Greene, Sandra E. 1996. *Gender, Ethnicity, and Social Change on the Upper Slave Coast: A History of the Anlo-Ewe*. Portsmouth, NH: Heinemann.

Grosz-Ngate, Maria and Omari Kokole, eds. 1997. *Gendered Encounters: Challenging Cultural Boundaries and Social Hierarchies in Africa*. New York and London: Routledge.

Guyer, Jane. 1981. "Household and Community in African Studies." *African Studies Review* 24(2/3): 87–137.

————. 1984. *Family and Farm in Southern Cameroon*. Boston: Boston University African Studies Center.

————. 1988. "The Multiplication of Labor: Historical Methods in the Study of Gender and Agricultural Changes in Modern Africa." *Current Anthropology* 29(2):247–272.

Guyer, Jane and Pauline Peters, eds. 1987. "Conceptualizing the Household: Theory and Policy in Africa." Special Issue of *Development and Change* 18(2).

Hafkin, Nancy and Edna Bay, eds. 1976. *Women in Africa: Studies in Social and Economic Change.* Stanford, CA: Stanford University Press.

Hansen, Karen. 1989. *Distant Companions: Servants and Employers in Zambia, 1900–1985.* Ithaca, NY: Cornell University Press.

————. ed. 1992. *African Encounters with Domesticity.* New Brunswick, NJ: Rutgers University Press.

Hay, Margaret Jean and Sharon Stichter, eds. 1984. *African Women South of the Sahara.* London: Longman.

Hay, Margaret Jean and Marcia Wright, eds. 1982. *African Women and the Law: Historical Perspectives.* Boston: Boston University Papers on Africa, VII.

Hodgson, Dorothy L. 1997. "Embodying the Contradictions of Modernity: Gender and Spirit Possession among Maasai in Tanzania." In Maria Grosz-Ngate and Omari Kokole, eds., *Gendered Encounters: Challenging Cultural Boundaries and Social Hierarchies in Africa.* New York and London: Routledge.

————. 1999a. "'Once Intrepid Warriors': Modernity and the Production of Maasai Masculinities." *Ethnology* 38(2):121–150.

————. 1999b. "Organizing for Change: Forms of Collective Action among African Women." Paper presented to the Symposium on "African Development in the 21st Century," Smith College, Northampton, MA.

————. 1999c. "Pastoralism, Patriarchy and History: Changing Gender Relations among Maasai in Tanganyika, 1890–1940." *Journal of African History* 40(1): 41–65.

Hoehler-Fatton, Cynthia. 1996. *Women of Fire and Spirit: History, Faith and Gender in Roho Religion in Western Kenya.* New York: Oxford University Press.

House-Midamba, Bessie, ed. 1996. *Reconceptualizing African Women: Toward the Year 2000.* Special Issue of *Africa Today* 43(3).

Hunt, Nancy Rose. 1988. "'*Le bébé en brousse*': European Women, African Birth Spacing and Colonial Intervention in Breastfeeding in the Belgian Congo." *International Journal of African Historical Studies* 21:401–432.

————. 1990. "Domesticity and Colonialism in Belgian Africa: Usumbura's Foyer Social, 1946–1960." *Signs: Journal of Women in Culture and Society* 15(3):447–474.

Ifeka-Moller, Caroline. 1975. "Female Militancy and Colonial Revolt: The Women's War of 1929, Eastern Nigeria." In Shirley Ardener, ed., *Perceiving Women.* London: J. M. Dent and Sons.

Imam, Ayesha, Amina Mama, and Fatou Sow, eds. 1997. *Engendering African Social Sciences.* Dakar: CODESRIA.

Jackson, Kennell A., Jr. 1976. "The Family Entity and Famine among the Nineteenth Century Akamba of Kenya: Social Responses to Environmental Stress." *Journal of Family History* 1(2):193–216.

Jeannerat, Caroline F. 1997. "Invoking the Female *Vhusha* Ceremony and the Struggle for Identity and Security in Tshiendeulu, Venda." *Journal of Contemporary African Studies* 15(1):87–106.

Kaberry, Phyllis. 1952. *Women of the Grassfields. A Study of the Economic Position of Women in Bamenda, British Cameroons.* London: Her Majesty's Stationery Office.

Kent, Susan. 1998. *Gender in African Prehistory*. Walnut Creek, CA: Altamira Press.

Kratz, Corinne A. 1994. *Affecting Performance: Meaning, Movement and Experience in Okiek Women's Initiation*. Washington, DC: Smithsonian Institution Press.

Landau, Paul. 1995. *The Realm of the Word: Language, Gender and Christianity in a Southern African Kingdom*. Portsmouth, NH: Heinemann.

Larson, Pier M. 2000. *History and Memory in the Age of Enslavement: Becoming Merina in Highland Madagascar, 1770–1822*. Portsmouth, NH: Heinemann.

La Fontaine, Jean. 1974. "The Free Women of Kinshasha." In John Davis, ed., *Choice and Change*. New York: Humanities Press.

Lindsay, Lisa A. 1998. "'No Need to Think of Home'? Masculinity and Domestic Life on the Nigerian Railway, c.1940–61." *Journal of African History* 39(3):439–466.

———. 1999. "Domesticity and Difference: Male Breadwinners, Working Women, and Colonial Citizenship in the 1945 Nigerian General Strike." *American Historical Review* 104(3):783–812.

Little, Kenneth. 1973. *African Women in Towns: An Aspect of Africa's Social Revolution*. Cambridge: Cambridge University Press.

Littlewood, Barbara and Linda Mahood. 1991. "Prostitutes, Magdalenes and Wayward Girls: Dangerous Sexualities of Working Class Women in Victorian Scotland." *Gender and History* 3(2):160–175.

MacGaffey, Janet. 1988. "Evading Male Control: Women in the Second Economy in Zaire." In Sharon B. Stichter and Jane Parpart, eds., *Patriarchy and Class*. Boulder, CO: Westview Press.

Maddox, Gregory H. 1996. "Gender and Famine in Central Tanzania, 1916–1961." *African Studies Review* 39(1): 83–101.

Mann, Kristin. 1982. "Women's Rights in Law and Practice: Marriage and Dispute Settlement in Colonial Lagos." In Margaret Jean Hay and Marcia Wright, eds., *Women and the Law in Africa: Historical Perspectives*. Boston: Boston University Papers on Africa, VII.

———. 1985. *Marrying Well: Marriage, Status and Social Change among the Educated Elite in Colonial Lagos*. Cambridge: Cambridge University Press.

Mann, Kristin and Richard Roberts, eds. 1991. *Law in Colonial Africa*. Portsmouth, NH: Heinemann.

Martin, Phyllis. 1995. *Leisure and Society in Colonial Brazzaville*. Cambridge: Cambridge University Press.

Mbilinyi, Marjorie. 1988. "Runaway Wives in Colonial Tanganyika: Forced Labour and Forced Marriage in Colonial Rungwe District 1919–1961." *International Journal of Sociology of Law* 16(1): 1–29.

McCurdy, Sheryl. 1996. "The 1932 'War' between Rival Ujiji (Tanganyika) Associations: Understanding Women's Motivations for Inciting Political Unrest." *Canadian Journal of African Studies* 30(1): 10–31.

———. 2000. "Transforming Associations: Fertility, Therapy, and the Manyema Diaspora in Urban Kigoma, Tanzania c. 1850 to 1993." Ph.D. thesis, Columbia University.

Meena, Ruth, ed. 1992. *Gender in Southern Africa: Conceptual and Theoretical Issues*. Harare: SAPES Press.

Mikell, Gwendolyn, ed. 1997. *African Feminism. The Politics of Survival in Sub-Saharan Africa*. Philadelphia: University of Pennsylvania Press.

Mirza, Sarah and Margaret Strobel, eds. 1989. *Three Swahili Women: Life Histories from Mombasa, Kenya*. Bloomington: Indiana University Press.

Moore, Henrietta. [1986] 1996. *Space, Text and Gender: An Anthropological Study of the Marakwet of Kenya*. New York: Guilford.

Moore, Henrietta and Megan Vaughan. *Cutting Down Trees: Gender, Nutrition, and Agricultural Change in the Northern Provinces of Zambia 1890–1990*. Portsmouth, NH: Heinemann.

Musisi, Nakanyike. 1991. "Women, 'Elite Polygyny,' and Buganda State Formation." *Signs: Journal of Women in Culture and Society* 16(4):757–786.

Ngaiza, Magdalene K. and Bertha Koda, eds. 1991. *The Unsung Heroines: Women's Life Histories from Tanzania*. Dar es Salaam: WRDP Publications.

Nnaemeka, Obioma, ed. 1998. *Sisterhood: Feminisms and Power from Africa to the Diaspora*. Trenton, NJ: Africa World Press.

Oboler, Regina. 1985. *Women, Power and Economic Change: The Nandi of Kenya*. Stanford, CA: Stanford University Press.

Ogden, Jessica. 1996. "'Producing' Respect: The 'Proper Woman' in Postcolonial Kampala." In Richard Werbner and Terence Ranger, eds., *Postcolonial Identities in Africa*. London: Zed Books.

Okeke, Philomena E. 1996. "Postmodern Feminism and Knowledge Production: The African Context." *Africa Today* 43(3):223–234.

————, ed. 1997. *African Women in the Age of Transformation: Women's Voices from the Continent*. Special issue of *Issue: A Journal of Opinion* (African Studies Association) 25(2).

Okeyo, Achola Pala. 1980. "Daughters of the Lakes and Rivers: Colonization and the Land Rights of Luo Women." In Mona Etienne and Eleanor Leacock, eds., *Women and Colonization: Anthropological Perspectives*. New York: Praeger.

Oppong, Christine, ed. 1983. *Female and Male in West Africa*. London: George Allen & Unwin.

Oyěwùmí, Oyèrónké. 1997. *The Invention of Women: Making African Sense of Western Gender Discourses*. Minneapolis: University of Minnesota Press.

Parpart, Jane. 1994. "'Where Is Your Mother?': Gender, Urban Marriage, and Colonial Discourse on the Zambian Copperbelt, 1924–1945." *International Journal of African Historical Studies* 27(2):241–271.

Parpart, Jane and Kathleen Staudt, eds. 1989. *Women and the State in Africa*. Boulder, CO: Lynne Rienner.

Paulme, Denise, ed. [1960] 1963. *Women of Tropical Africa*. Berkeley: University of California Press.

Perani, Judith and Fred T. Smith, eds. 1998. *The Visual Arts of Africa: Gender, Power and Life Cycle Ritual*. Upper Saddle River, NJ: Prentice Hall.

Pittin, Renée. 1983. "Houses of Women: A Focus on Alternative Life-Styles in Katsina City." In Christine Oppong, ed., *Female and Male in West Africa*. London: George Allen & Unwin.

Presley, Cora Ann. 1992. *Kikuyu Women, the Mau Mau Rebellion and Social Change in Kenya*. Boulder, CO: Westview Press.

Robertson, Claire. 1983. "The Death of Makola and Other Tragedies: Male Strategies against a Female-Dominated System." *Canadian Journal of African Studies* 17(3):674–695.

———. 1984. *Sharing the Same Bowl: A Socioeconomic History of Women and Class in Accra, Ghana.* Bloomington, IN: Indiana University Press.

———. 1997. *Trouble Showed the Way: Women, Men and Trade in the Nairobi Area, 1890–1990.* Bloomington, IN: Indiana University Press.

Robertson, Claire and Iris Berger, eds. 1986. *Women and Class in Africa.* New York: Africana Publishing Company.

Robertson, Claire and Martin Klein, eds. 1983. *Women and Slavery in Africa.* Madison: University of Wisconsin Press.

Romero, Patricia, ed. 1988. *Life Histories of African Women.* London: Ashfield Press.

Rublack, Ulinka. 1997. "Wench and Maiden: Women, War and the Pictorial Function of the Feminine in German Cities in the Early Modern Period." *History Workshop Journal* 44(1):1–21.

Schmidt, Elizabeth. 1990. "Negotiated Spaces and Contested Terrain: Men, Women, and the Law in Colonial Zimbabwe, 1890–1939." *Journal of Southern African Studies* 16(4):622–648.

Schoenbrun, David Lee. 1998. *A Green Place, A Good Place: Agrarian Change, Gender, and Social Identity in the Great Lakes Region to the 15th Century.* Portsmouth, NH: Heinemann.

Schoss, Johanna. 1996. "Dressed to 'Shine': Work, Leisure, and Style in Malindi, Kenya." In Hilde Hendrickson, ed., *Clothing and Difference: Embodied Identities in Colonial and Post-Colonial Africa.* Durham, NC: Duke University Press.

Schroeder, Richard. 1999. *Shady Practices: Agroforestry and Gender Politics in The Gambia.* Berkeley: University of California Press.

Scully, Pamela. 1996. "Narratives of Infanticide in the Aftermath of Slave Emancipation in the Nineteenth-Century Cape Colony, South Africa." *Canadian Journal of African Studies* 30(1):88–105.

———. 1997. *Liberating the Family? Gender and British Slave Emancipation in the Rural Western Cape, South Africa, 1823–1853.* Portsmouth, NH: Heinemann.

Shire, Chenjerai. 1994. "Men Don't Go to the Moon: Language, Space and Masculinities in Zimbabwe." In Andrea Cornwall and Nancy Lindisfarne, eds., *Dislocating Masculinity: Comparative Ethnographies.* New York: Routledge.

Stambach, Amy. 1999. "Curl Up and Dye." In John L. Comaroff and Jean Comaroff, eds., *Civil Society and the Political Imagination in Africa: Critical Perspectives.* Chicago: University of Chicago Press.

Steady, Filomena. 1987. "African Feminism: A Worldwide Perspective." In Rosalyn Terborg-Penn, Sharon Harley, and Andrea Benton Rushing, eds., *Women in Africa and the African Diaspora.* Washington, DC: Howard University Press.

Stichter, Sharon and Jane Parpart, eds. 1988. *Patriarchy and Class: African Women in the Home and the Workforce.* Boulder, CO: Westview.

Strobel, Margaret. 1979. *Muslim Women in Mombasa: 1890–1975.* New Haven, CT: Yale University Press.

Sudarkasa, Niara. 1987. "The Status of Women in Indigenous African Socities." In Rosalyn Terborg-Penn, Sharon Harley, and Andrea Benton Rushing, eds.,

Women in Africa and the African Diaspora. Washington, DC: Howard University Press.

Summers, Carol. 1991. "Intimate Colonialism: The Imperial Production of Reproduction in Uganda, 1907–1925." *Signs: Journal of Women in Culture and Society* 16(4): 787–807.

Sunseri, Thaddeus. 1997. "Famine and Wild Pigs: Gender Struggles and the Outbreak of the Maji-Maji War in Uzaramo (Tanzania)." *Journal of African History* 38(2):235–259.

Tanzania Gender Networking Programme. 1993. *Gender Profile of Tanzania.* Dar es Salaam: TGNP.

Thomas, Lynn M. 1996. "'Ngaitana' (I will circumcise myself): The Gender and Generational Politics of the 1956 Ban on Clitoridectomy in Meru, Kenya." *Gender and History* 8(3): 338–363.

———. 1998. "Imperial Concerns and 'Women's Affairs': State Efforts to Regulate Clitoridectomy and Eradicate Abortion in Meru, Kenya." *Journal of African History* 39(1):121–145.

Urdang, Stephanie. 1979. *Fighting Two Colonialisms: Women in Guinea Bissau.* New York: Monthly Review Books.

Van Allen, Judith. 1976. "'Aba Riots' or Igbo 'Women's War'? Ideology, Stratification, and the Invisibility of Women." In Nancy Hafkin and Edna Bay, eds., *Women in Africa.* Stanford, CA: Stanford University Press.

Vaughan, Megan. 1987. *The Story of an African Famine: Gender and Famine in Twentieth-Century Malawi.* New York: Cambridge University Press.

———. 1991. *Curing Their Ills: Colonial Power and African Illness.* Stanford, CA: Stanford University Press.

White, Luise. 1990a. *The Comforts of Home: Prostitution in Colonial Nairobi.* Chicago: University of Chicago Press.

———. 1990b. "Separating the Men from the Boys: Constructions of Gender, Sexuality and Terrorism in Central Kenya, 1939–1959." *International Journal of African Historical Studies* 23(1):1–25.

Wilson, Francine. 1982. "Reinventing the Past and Circumscribing the Future: Authenticité and the Negative Image of Women's Work in Zaire." In Edna G. Bay, ed., *Women and Work in Africa.* Boulder, CO: Westview.

Wipper, Audrey. 1972a. "African Women, Fashion and Scapegoating." *Canadian Journal of African Studies* 6(2):339–349.

———. ed. 1972b. *The Roles of African Women: Past, Present and Future.* Special Issue of *Canadian Journal of African Studies* 6(2).

Wright, Marcia. 1975. "Women in Peril: A Commentary on the Life Stories of Captives in Nineteenth Century East-Central Africa." *African Social Research* 20:800–819.

———. 1983. "Technology, Marriage and Women's Work in the History of Maize Growers in Mazabuka, Zambia: A Reconnaissance." *Journal of Southern African Studies* 10(1):71–85.

———. 1993. *Strategies of Slaves and Women: Life-Stories from East/Central Africa.* New York: L. Barber Press.

PART I:

CONTESTING CONJUGALITY

2

WOMEN, MARRIAGE, DIVORCE AND THE EMERGING COLONIAL STATE IN ABEOKUTA (NIGERIA) 1892–1904

Judith Byfield

INTRODUCTION

The nineteenth century was a period of great turmoil across Yorubaland. The demise of the Oyo empire resulted in decades of intermittent warfare as potential successor states competed for dominance in the region. By the century's end, the political geography was transformed once more as Britain established control over the Yoruba city-states. Significant social and economic changes also marked the latter half of the century. In Abeokuta,[1] these changes entailed the emergence of an increasingly important Christian community, the rise of a new class of wealthy warrior traders, and the town's increasing incorporation into the international economy.

These larger developments created opportunities for dependent men and women to challenge their status and position in Egba society. During the 1890s, slaves increasingly deserted Abeokuta farms in their bid for freedom, while significant numbers of women left unsatisfactory marriages. Chroniclers of the town's affairs noted a substantial increase in divorce and adultery by the first decade of the twentieth century (Punch 1906, 17; Fadipe 1970, 92).

This chapter examines a number of marital disputes and divorce cases brought before the British Railway Commissioners in Abeokuta. Women's efforts to engage the Railway Commissioners in marital disputes during this early and fluid period of colonial rule illuminate the subtle but complex ways in which gender conflicts were woven into the fabric of state formation. In this chapter, I argue that as women entered the socioeconomic, political, and judicial spaces created by the extension of the railway, they helped to shape the evolving relationship between the Egba and colonial states. When women defected from "traditional" authority, their marital disputes and a variety of other cases that were brought to the Railway Commissioners became integrated into the colonial state's effort to maximize its authority over Egba affairs. This aim was made explicit in a 1913 discussion within the Colonial Office about the Lagos Supreme Court's jurisdiction in divorce cases among Christians in the protectorate and in Egbaland specifically. The proposed marriage ordinance from which this debate ensued was seen as an excellent opportunity for advancing the policy of indirect rule.[2]

Even though the colonial state benefited from the Railway Commissioners' intervention in marital disputes, the women represented in these cases were not mere pawns in the play of domination. Rather, they demonstrated initiative and agency as they tried to assert their interests and desires. In order to fully appreciate the historical context from which these women emerged, I begin with a discussion of women's roles and positions in Egba society prior to the expansion of British colonial power at the end of the nineteenth century. An examination of these roles and the nature of the gender struggles that accompanied British colonial expansion capture the contradictory impact of colonialism on women.

WOMEN, MARRIAGE, AND THE EGBA STATE, 1830–1899

Marriage was a critical feature of Yoruba social and economic life. All men and women were expected to marry, and all women were expected to procreate. Full Yoruba marriage, which was the preferred form of marriage prior to the end of the nineteenth century, was a protracted process. Over its course, lineages gave up their productive and reproductive rights over female members in exchange for the bridewealth, goods, and services that were transferred from the husbands' kin (Mann 1985, 36; Johnson [1921] 1973, 113–15). Marriage guaranteed the society's social, economic, and cultural reproduction and was an important avenue for individual accumulation of social and economic capital. Through marriage, men and women expanded the pool of people from whom they could acquire economic resources. Families raised money for social and economic ventures or settled existing debts by manipulating bridewealth. For example, young female *iwofas* (pawns) often lived with the lender from whom their family borrowed money until they were old enough to marry. A prospective husband had to pay the loan and the bridewealth in order to claim his wife (Fadipe 1970, 193).[3]

Marriage was also an important avenue to political power. This was especially evident at the height of the Oyo empire, but after its decline, marital symbolism was marginalized and new female roles emerged (Matory 1994, 14–15). The decline of the empire and of those who exercised power as "wives"[4] of the king can be contrasted to the increasing number of entrepreneurial warriors and traders who came to dominate the political landscape and the unprecedented rise of powerful and independent women such as the Iyalodes of Ibadan and Abeokuta.[5] Female power brokers emerged in these towns, in part, because there was no kingship in Ibadan, and Egba kings were historically weak (Johnson [1921] 1973, 777–78).[6] The kingship in Abeokuta was circumscribed by the powerful Ogboni society and the Ologun, the federal military structure (Biobaku 1957, 9).[7]

Men were disproportionately represented in Abeokuta's political structure; nonetheless, wealth and age were the primary determinants of status. The paucity of inherited titles and the weakness of Egba kings suggest that an aristocratic elite was relatively circumscribed. The Ogboni structure, on the other hand, allowed substantial mobility to men and women of wealth. The Ogboni, "a society of wealthy and influential men and a few old women," constituted the civic court, town council, and electoral college for the selection of the Oba (king) (Biobaku 1957, 5).[8] Furthermore, as individuals accumulated wealth, they were incorporated into the title structure. Thus, royal marriage was not the primary route to political power for the Egba women who rose to prominence during the nineteenth century.

Women's access to state power increased after the 1860s, and important titles were specifically created for wealthy women. The title of Iyalode of the Egba was given to Madame Tinubu in 1864 as a reward for her support during the Dahomey invasion (Biobaku 1960, 38–39; Yemitan 1987). Betsy Desola, named Iyalode of the Parakoyi (trade chiefs) in 1878, was a large-scale entrepreneur and a member of a small, but influential, group of Christian slave-holding women.[9] Important titles were also created for other members of the town's Christian community, which had become quite influential.[10] The title Balogun of the Christians was given to John Okenla, who had led his Christian army, comprised primarily of slaves, to battle in the Ijaye war (1860–82) and, later, in the 1864 Dahomey war (Oroge 1979, 233–39). All three met the criteria that came to define power in the nineteenth century: private armies, large households, and extensive trading and agricultural operations.

Although the nineteenth century ushered in new opportunities, new positions, and a new level of independence for some women, it did not marginalize the importance of marriage in women's lives. Great pressure was put on women to marry and remain married. In his *History of the Yorubas,* Samuel Johnson argues that divorce was very rare, "so rare as to be practically considered as non-existing" ([1921] 1973, 116). In addition, it was said that divorced women could not remarry (Johnson [1921] 1973, 116; Fadipe 1970, 90–91). Johnson and N. A. Fadipe suggest that women in the nineteenth century were more or less locked into their marriages.[11] Nonetheless, biographical anecdotes and other sources indicate a more complex picture.

The author of a biography of Canon Josiah Jesse Ransome-Kuti,[12] noted that the Canon's mother, Anne, a Christian, ran away from her husband after hearing rumors that her son, Josiah, would be killed because of her conversion. Anne, one of the earliest Christians in Abeokuta, was baptized in 1848. She subsequently returned to her husband, but she continued to assert her religious independence. She had Josiah baptized in the Wesleyan Church in 1859, but later, mother and son switched to the Anglican Church Missionary Society (CMS). Josiah's father was against his son's baptism, and often, after Sunday services, he carried Josiah "to the fetish groves to give him meat offered to idols" (Delano c. 1944, 8). A negotiated truce between the old and new religions appears to have saved the marriage.

Wives did not always return to their husbands, as the case of Madam Jojolola demonstrates. Jojolola succeeded Tinubu as Iyalode of Abeokuta. Like Tinubu, Jojolola was wealthy. She had many acres of farmland, slaves, and *iwofas* (pawns). She was also a cloth trader and *adire* (tie-dye cloth) producer. At one point in her marriage, Madam Jojolola left her husband's compound and returned to her natal home. Descendants claim that she returned because the other wives were envious of her wealth. Family members did not speak of her divorcing her husband, but if attempts were made to reunite Jojolola with her husband, they were unsuccessful. Jojolola eventually obtained land from her family and established her own compound, which became a major *adire* compound.[13] Her case suggests that although public opinion weighed heavily against divorce, separation was tolerated.

Customary law did allow divorce under specific circumstances such as adultery with a husband's blood relation, kleptomania, repeated insolvency, impotence, a husband's habitual laziness or drunkenness, infectious disease, and cruelty.[14] In 1855, T. B. Macaulay, a CMS missionary, witnessed a case in which a woman was granted a divorce because of her husband's public stealing and the disgrace it brought to her.[15] The mothers of Alake Gbadebo and Alake Ademola II divorced their first husbands and subsequently married men who became Alake.[16] Women also secured divorces by seeking refuge in the palace, a practice known as *dipomu*. In cases of ill-treatment, women went to the palace and took hold of one of the pillars. Their husbands could not touch them there because it was considered an insult to the king to touch a woman in "the land of refuge" (Delano 1937, 142).[17]

Divorce was not restricted to women in customary marriages. Within the Christian community, a Bishop's Court was created in either 1886 or 1887 to handle marital disputes, the majority involving allegations of adultery. The cases were heard by a European missionary, the chair of the court, and eight assessors chosen by local congregations.[18] Under J. B. Wood, the first chair, the Bishop's Court only considered cases in which it was clear that the petitioner had been wronged and had not committed any wrongs.[19] Wood noted that they would have heard many cases had they not so narrowly defined the court's scope. The court's existence did not appear to contribute to the rate of divorce in a significant manner. The dramatic rise in divorce was more specifically associated with the extension of British rule after 1892.

EGBA-BRITISH AFFAIRS AFTER 1892

The British bombardment of Ijebu in 1892 to force that kingdom to open its roads for trade between Lagos and the interior of Yorubaland marked a critical new phase in British-Yoruba relations. For many, it reflected the formal ascendance of British political power beyond the Lagos colony, and its readiness to use force to achieve that objective. In order to prevent a similar use of violence against Abeokuta, the Egba chiefs signed a treaty of peace and commerce with Governor Carter of Lagos. The Egba treaty differed slightly from treaties signed by other Yoruba city-states because it fully recognized Egba independence and promised that there would be no aggressive actions against any part of Egba country (Pallinder-Law 1973, 59).

Nevertheless, British officials assumed substantial influence in Egba politics. Governor H. McCallum, for example, was instrumental in reorganizing the Egba political apparatus into the Egba United Government (EUG), which centralized political authority around the Alake. Under the EUG, the Alake ruled in consultation with an advisory council, made up of the other three Obas, the Oba Imale (the head of the Muslim community), the Balogun of the Christians, the Olori Parakoyi (head of the trade chiefs), as well as several Ogboni members (Pallinder-Law 1973, 64). The new Council included representatives from interest groups that had not participated in the former political structure, but it excluded women completely.

In February 1899, the Egba and Lagos governments signed an agreement that allowed the British to build the railway through Egba territory, thus significantly increasing British influence. The agreement also ceded jurisdiction over a hundred-yard strip of land on either side of the tracks to the British government. Many Egba chiefs realized that this area would become a magnet for those who sought to avoid their authority, and some of the strongest objections came from wealthy slave-owners who feared that the railway area would become a sanctuary for runaway slaves (Pallinder-Law 1973, 72–74).[20] Despite this opposition, the Egba authorities acquiesced to the Lagos government. The colonial government was granted the right to build and maintain a railway on Egba territory, comprehensive judicial rights over the railway area, and the right to pursue fugitive offenders from the railway area into Egba territory. The Egba government also agreed to seek and follow the Railway Commissioner's advice on matters affecting Egba/British relations. The Railway Commissioner, in turn, was given wide discretionary power by the colonial Governor. He was to act as liaison officer between the Egba and Lagos governments, and interfere in cases of cruelty, extortion, and oppression. Initially, the Commissioner resided at Aro, an important trade terminus approximately eight miles outside of Abeokuta town, but by 1900, he had taken up residence within the town walls (Pallinder-Law 1973, 74–75).

THE ARRIVAL OF THE RAILWAY

The railway between Aro and Lagos opened for traffic in 1900 (Ajisafe 1948, 91). Colonial officials, who had long sought to open the Lagos hinterland to the steady and increasing trade with European merchants, greeted its opening with relief and anticipation. Many Egba citizens also welcomed the railway because of the increased ease and speed of transportation (Ajisafe 1948, 91). Yet the railway did much more than introduce mechanical transport beyond the Lagos coast. Its procedures and personnel, both staff and administrators, introduced new dynamics into the social and political affairs of Abeokuta. The colonial government vested in the office of the Railway Commission judicial authority that went far beyond matters pertinent to the maintenance of the railway and the railway area. In addition, the Railway Commissioners pushed the limits of their power as far as they could. For example, the second Railway Commissioner, Captain Ambrose, who was especially concerned about the difficulties European traders sometimes had collecting debts, initiated discussions with the Alake and Council to reform the methods of debt recovery (Pallinder-Law 1973, 85). The Egba government resisted his suggestion to establish a special court for debt recovery. Nonetheless, ongoing discussions eventually led to the creation of a new judicial structure in 1904.[21]

The Lagos government, in theory, respected Abeokuta's independence; nevertheless, it wanted to bring the town's political and judicial structures in line with the bureaucratic structures that were being created in other parts of the colony. Therefore, the Lagos government applied continuous pressure on the Alake and Council to make the requisite changes. The Commissioners' enthusiasm for intervening in local issues and reshaping the Egba polity was not always welcome. In a confidential letter to the Acting Colonial Secretary in Lagos, Cyril Punch, who became Railway Commissioner in February 1901,[22] admitted that there was dissatisfaction among certain groups because of the Commissioners' influence on the Alake and Council.[23] The Commissioners succeeded by using a combination of negotiation, pressure, and coercion. During the discussions on the railway, for example, while the Egba chiefs considered the proposals, a contingent of Lagos government soldiers was based at the Aro terminus (Pallinder-Law 1973, 73). However, coercion was not always necessary. British proposals were sometimes accepted because they enhanced the power of certain groups or individuals in Egba society. The 1904 judicial agreement, for example, greatly strengthened the Alake's authority.

The Railway Commissioners played at least two distinctive and competing roles in Abeokuta. First, they reinforced the power of the "traditional" rulers now realigned in the Egba United Government. They exiled chiefs who did not show proper deference to the Alake and summoned troops from Lagos when segments of the community rebelled against the Alake. Second, the Commissioners held a distinct base of power as the direct representatives of the imperial government. From the latter position, the Commissioners influenced the actions and policies of the EUG and recruited those who sought to redress wrongs or renegotiate their social positions in Egba society. For instance, in 1903, the people of Kemta township revolted when the Alake set aside a judgment made by a Kemta Ogboni chief and then attempted to arrest him (Pallinder-Law 1973, 104). Railway Commissioner Punch called in troops, who were accompanied by Governor MacGregor, to Abeokuta. Local historian A. K. Ajisafe reported that the Governor

> only blamed the Kemta people for taking such aggressive steps without complaining to the Commissioner in Abeokuta. "If in the future," he said, "you have a grievance against your authorities you should either write to the Alake and Council or send a deputation to them and state your grievance; *if you receive no satisfaction from them, you should appeal to the Foreign Government. It is for this cause the British Representative is stationed here.*" (Ajisafe 1948, 98, emphasis added)

It is not surprising then that even marital cases found their way to the Railway Commissioner.

MARRIAGE AND DIVORCE AT THE TURN OF THE CENTURY

In his classic volume, *The Sociology of the Yoruba,* Yoruba sociologist N. A. Fadipe argues that marriage in Yoruba society was in a great state of flux as a result of the diffusion of foreign ideas and the process of rapid economic growth. Fadipe explicitly connects changes in marriage with the advance of the railway:

> Divorce was considered to be closely connected with the question of bridewealth. In connection with both, as well as the custom of betrothing daughters mostly in childhood and without their consent, revolutionary changes had occurred during the last decade of the nineteenth century and since the end of the First World War. The opening up of the interior to trade, which began in 1896 by the building of a railway line from Lagos, accelerated these changes. (1970, 91)

He attributed many of these revolutionary changes to the presence of the railway construction camps. Women and girls frequented the camps, largely in pursuit of trade. Their contact with male clerks and artisans led already married women and betrothed girls to "defy both their parents and public opinion and become attached to some clerks or artisans as mistresses" (Fadipe 1970, 91). The connection between economic pursuits and the development of relationships with railway workers cannot be overlooked. From 1899 to 1904, a number of women ran away to the camps, prompting the Alake to write to the Railway Commissioners on behalf of the deserted husbands, fathers, and slave-owners. The letters requested the Commissioners' assistance in returning these women. To aid in identifying them, the Alake mentioned the occupations of the women's new partners: laborers, head laborers, carpenters, and stewards.[24]

Railway workers possessed certain economic advantages that made them attractive marriage prospects. Fadipe (1970, 92) estimates that the young men who took wage employment on railway construction and other public works projects earned in one year what many farmers needed three years to accumulate. From the end of the nineteenth century to 1914, opportunities for cash earnings shifted the center of economic gravity from chiefs and kings to the common people (Fadipe 1970, 214–15). A woman who aligned herself with a railway worker could potentially receive a tidy sum of money to establish her trade. She also cemented social and economic ties in a segment of the community with a relatively high percentage of disposable income. The presence of railway workers also stimulated trade in the surrounding areas. Markets grew at stations, particularly since traders could expect payment on the workers' payday for goods taken on credit (Oyemakinde 1974, 303). The railway thus provided a sanctuary from masters and lineage authority, new relationships and economic opportunities, and an alternative judicial arena.

CASES BROUGHT TO THE RAILWAY COMMISSIONERS

Egba citizens brought a wide variety of cases to the Railway Commissioners, including disputes over repayment of debt,[25] slave redemption,[26] illegal detention,[27] and marriage. Of the forty-five cases I located, twenty-three were initiated by women and twenty-two by men.[28] This section examines a number of the cases related to marriage gleaned from administrative letter books that recorded outgoing correspondence from the Railway Commissioners in Abeokuta from 1900 to 1904. These records present very little biographical data, and do not indicate how the cases were resolved. Although the letters present only one piece of what were undoubtedly multiple communications, they do provide insight into the way in which Egba citizens viewed and utilized the powers of the Railway Commissioners' office. The cases also reveal women's agency in establishing caring relationships, as well as relationships of their own choice.

Sir, In reply to the letter of the Alake of this date with references to a woman named Solape I am sending her to you with the request that you take her to the Alake and have her case inquired into. She left her first husband 13 months ago [and] says that he treated her cruelly. This should be enquired into. Please do so and report to me. She further states that Majolagbe with whom she is now living is willing to pay the dowry if time is granted. This would be the best arrangement.[29]

Sir, I have the honour to inform you that the woman Oni has brought her case to me, and I am referring her to the Alake. It appears she is a free woman, and having paid the amount of her dowry to her husband has a right to live with any man she pleases. Her brother is trying to force her to go to one of his friends and because she refuses has ill-treated her. If her statement is true he should be punished, and informed that he has no control over the woman.[30]

In each of these two cases, cruel treatment precipitated the women's decision to seek the Commissioner's assistance. The second letter offers important commentary on women's expectations once a marriage had ended. Oni had repaid her bridewealth and assumed that she would control her own future. Divorce, in her estimation, did not return her to the dependent status that gave her male lineage members the right to choose her next spouse. The Commissioner apparently concurred.

The desire to choose one's own spouse was shared by unmarried women:

Sir, A girl named Animatu daughter of the Olowu has come to me to complain that the Olowu wished to force her into marriage with one Jinadu, when she wishes to marry a young man called Peidu son of Agura. Also that he put her in irons for six days, and that she succeeded in escaping this morning.

I hope you will help her in the matter if her story is true. She should not be forced to marry anyone. I believe you have a law prohibiting people being put in irons; if so, I suppose you will deal with the Olowu.[31]

According to Captain Blackwell, the Railway Commissioner, this young woman was willing to go to great lengths to marry someone she chose, rather than to marry her father's choice. This case was very sensitive for a number of reasons. First, her father, the Olowu, was one of Abeokuta's sectional kings and a member of the EUG's governing Council. Second, she involved a British official in her dispute with her father. Third, her complaints raised the specter that this prominent member of the Council could be charged with a criminal act. In addition, it was likely that the Olowu had already accepted some gift or payment in return for promising his daughter to Jinadu.[32] When Animatu refused to marry Jinadu, she challenged the social contract between the two families and the rules of betrothal. Given her father's position, there was virtually no chance that the Alake and Council would have looked favorably on her decision to refuse Jinadu or even heard her case. Her appeal to the Railway Commissioner thus offered her recourse that she would not have had otherwise.

Men sought the Railway Commissioners' help to reclaim their wives or, on occasion, to facilitate a divorce as the following letter demonstrates:

Sir, The bearer, Mr. Young of Ago Owe township and a woman named Sholakunmi complain that they cannot obtain justice from the Alake. The woman was formerly wife to one Bankole but refuses to live with him. She wishes to live with Mr. Young and application was made to the Alake so that [the] matter of dowry being settled the woman should be free to do as she pleased. . . . The statement now is that the money has been paid to the Alake but not handed over to the husband Bankole and that the woman is still detained from going where she pleases. Possibly the matter has altogether another complexion if one heard the whole story but I shall be obliged if you will ask the Alake to give it his best consideration.[33]

Mr. Young clearly wanted to formalize his relationship with Sholakunmi, and the Commissioner's intervention promised to nullify the Alake's obstruction. Bridewealth disputes occurred quite frequently during divorce proceedings and often complicated a woman's effort to leave her husband:

> Sir, I have had the parties concerned in the case of Akiyemi Johnson before me . . . Johnson is willing to pay dowry but the question of fixing the amount presents difficulties. Edun (the husband) at once claimed £21 but . . . could only account for £12.16.6 and of this amount I should say many items were made up on the spot. The girl declares that £5 was the total amount given to her family and that he ill-treated her, tying her and flogging her. I found when I was in Jebu and had a great number of dowry cases to assess that £7 really was a very fair amount. I would bring pressure on Johnson to induce him to pay this amount. Edun refuses it. Will you consult with the Alake and let me know if the case can be settled for this amount.[34]

It is quite possible that Edun inflated the amount of the bridewealth and was using his wife's effort to divorce him as an opportunity to enrich himself or was trying to prevent her departure. In this instance, Punch's "standard fee" would have facilitated the divorce because it could be more easily accumulated by the woman or her new partner. While Punch's fee made bridewealth refunds easier for women, it also probably meant that some husbands did not fully recoup their expenses. Bridewealth usually included a certain sum of money in addition to items such as cloths, kola nuts, pepper, and sometimes alcoholic beverages. The amount of money required increased steadily over the nineteenth century. Johnson reported that "well-to-do families rarely required more than ten heads of cowries, though in earlier times one head was considered ample" ([1921] 1973, 113–15).[35] For much of the nineteenth century cowries were the medium of exchange in bridewealth payments, but the letters and Punch's comments suggest that British currency supplanted cowries in Ijebu and Abeokuta. Stipulating bridewealth refunds in British currency further encouraged Yoruba men and women to participate in the wage-earning or export-producing sectors of the colonial economy. Furthermore, the amount demanded in bridewealth sharply increased as young men took wage employment because it provided parents with the opportunity to enjoy a share of the enhanced standard of living (Fadipe 1970, 92–93).[36]

Many men put themselves in debt, often becoming *iwofas* (pawns), to raise the necessary capital for marriage. The strong connection between indebtedness and marriage hardened many men against divorce. Some of the men who approached the Railway Commissioners were husbands who wanted their wives to return. It was economically easier to take back an errant wife than to become entangled in an effort to reclaim the original bridewealth or to become further indebted by acquiring a new wife. If the wife could not be convinced to return, the husband was strongly inclined to demand a high bridewealth refund, as the following letter demonstrates:[37]

> Sir, I have the honour to invite your attention to my letter No. 226 of the 23rd . . . covering a statement of Swumi who complains that a man called Olaogun eloped with a woman Taiwo who was engaged to his brother, and that they are now in Lagos. He asks that the girl may be restored or that the amount of the dowry £25.2.6, may be repaid. I shall be glad to be informed whether anything can be done in this matter.[38]

The records document critical social changes occurring among the Egba. Divorce became even more common after Abeokuta was integrated into the colonial state. By the 1920s, Native Courts across Yorubaland were hearing thousands of divorce cases annually (Atanda 1969; Mann 1985; Renne 1990b; Matory 1994).[39] Other critical changes occurred in Yoruba marriage. Marriage by mutual consent, which previously had been largely confined to slaves and people without kin, became increasingly popular. Many families also abandoned the practice of betrothing girls in infancy (Fadipe 1970, 92). It is also evident from the letters that divorced women could and did remarry.

Moreover, these letters demonstrate how the colonial state accumulated authority in Abeokuta. Abeokuta residents initiated these communications between the Railway Commissioners and the Egba authorities. Even though none of the divorce cases involved railway personnel or had anything to do with the railway, petitioning the Railway Commissioners enabled the Commissioners, and thus the colonial state, to expand their judicial domain. Except for the cases involving charges of ill-treatment and the wife who had fled to Lagos, it is clear that the Railway Commissioners relied on a broad interpretation of their position to justify their involvement.

CONCLUSION

The extension of British power at the turn of the century was not a negative development for all women. It encouraged young women in particular to challenge the authority of senior members of their lineage to regulate their marriages. It gave younger women the option to factor mutual attraction, concern over physical well-being, and their own economic interests into their marriage deliberations. The ramifications of this development were profound because it weakened the social control that senior men and women exercised over younger women.

In this early period, colonial officials did not hinder these women's efforts to renegotiate marriage. The Railway Commissioners and other colonial officials advocated divorce for a number of different reasons. Some believed that African women were oppressed in polygamous households (Callaway 1987, 52). In some instances, divorce was introduced in order to eliminate female husbands. Many officials also viewed marriage without consent and without the option of divorce as *de facto* slavery (Renne 1990a, 37).[40] Slavery was of great concern to colonial officials because conquest was clothed "in the legitimating garb of an abolitionist crusade" (Young 1994, 124). Yet British officials did not abolish slavery, because they feared undermining the economy. Instead, they circumvented the institution by abolishing its legal status and expunging practices from other institutions, such as the *iwofa* system, which resembled slavery (Byfield 1994). In addition, officials often insisted that slave women's bids for freedom were divorce cases rather than redemption cases (Lovejoy and Hogendorn 1993, 84; Lovejoy 1988).

In Abeokuta, the Railway Commissioners' advocacy on behalf of women cannot be separated from larger political concerns. Colonial officials often inserted themselves into local dispute resolution in their drive to "make hegemony operational" (Young 1994, 115). The Railway Commissioners practiced this strategy by establishing themselves as a court of appeal for women seeking divorces and others who did not expect favorable hearings before the Alake or other Egba chiefs. In the process, their intervention further undermined the autonomy of the EUG.

Regardless of their motivation, British officials' apparent readiness to grant divorces intensified gender struggles in Abeokuta and other Yoruba towns. Since marriage, accumulation, and indebtedness were so intertwined, men had a vested interest in limiting their wives' ability to leave them. The rapid economic changes of this period, which placed a premium on access to labor and credit, accentuated the need to control wives and daughters. Nevertheless, women were not simply passive objects being transferred between men. Egba women were independent economic actors, who, as the letters clearly demonstrate, also took advantage of new commercial opportunities at the turn of the century. They expanded their long-held roles as traders into areas that depended on, or intersected with, the region's incorporation into the international economy. Many women became involved in the emerging trades in kola nuts and cocoa.

The dramatic rise in divorce as British rule extended to Abeokuta and other parts of Yorubaland reflected the convergence of competing hegemonic concerns and local gender conflicts. The fact that women's independence did not threaten the colony's economic base during this period also contributed to colonial accommodation of divorce. Yoruba women were crucial to the expansion of trade in British industrial products and to the processing of local goods for export. Whether women were married or divorced, their economic activities continued. The colonial state accommodated divorce until the 1920s, when the interwar economic crisis galvanized some men to argue that women's access to easy divorce added to men's overwhelming debt burden (Byfield 1994).

Even though British officials were willing to grant women divorces, they were not committed to treating Egba women and men equally. Instead, they protected men's disproportionate access to power and resources. This was clearly evident in the political arena. Women were among the important title-holders in Abeokuta under the old Egba state, yet no women chiefs were selected when the EUG was created in 1898. Even when the Council was enlarged several times between 1898 and 1914, women chiefs were never invited to join it. Women obviously were not invisible to colonial officials; nonetheless, these officials ignored them politically during the protracted process of colonial imposition in Abeokuta. This political neglect reflected British gender ideology. It also fashioned a new political template in Egba society. Women could no longer translate age or wealth into political power. Masculinity became another essential criterion for power. The absence of women from the political institutions that evolved after the expansion of British power requires further consideration; nonetheless, this case study demonstrates that gender was very much a part of the fabric of colonial state formation.

NOTES

This chapter is based on a paper originally presented at the African Studies Association Annual Meeting in 1994. I would like to thank Dorothy Hodgson, Sheryl McCurdy, Margot Lovett, Deborah King, and the participants in Dartmouth College Feminist Inquiry for comments on earlier drafts. Additional research for this paper was supported by a Rockefeller Humanities Fellowship from the Center for Afroamerican and African Studies (CAAS), University of Michigan. I would like to thank the members of CAAS for their insights and encouragement during my stay in Ann Arbor.

1. Abeokuta, one of the new Yoruba city-states established in the wake of the fall of Oyo, was settled around 1830. It was home to Egba refugees from the Egba provinces—Egba Alake, Oke Ona, and Gbagura—as well as refugees from Owu.

2. In this debate that unfolded a year before Abeokuta was incorporated into the protectorate, Lewis Harcourt, the Secretary of State for the Colonies, argued that the Lagos Supreme Court should acquire jurisdiction over divorce in Egbaland. The court's jurisdiction over divorce in Egbaland would fall in line with Lugard's proposal to "eliminat[e]

friction between the government and the native authorities by subordinating them in all essentials to the government and at the same time strengthening the position of the native authority vis-a-vis the natives under their jurisdiction." Letter from Lewis Harcourt, 15 August, 1913, CO 520/127 #27064 (Public Record Office, London).

3. Under the *iwofa* system in Yorubaland, the borrower worked for the lender, instead of paying interest on the loan. Borrowers also had the option of substituting a lineage member to work in their place. If the substitute was a child, he or she lived with the lender until the loan was repaid. For comparative analyses of pawning systems in Africa, see Falola and Lovejoy (1994).

4. The wives of the reigning Alafin (king of Oyo) often performed administrative functions. They served as heads of empire-wide priesthoods, as royal advisers, and as provincial representatives of the palace. Male and female *ilari,* a corps of palace delegates, who served as toll collectors, messengers, priests, and royal guards were also considered wives of the king (Matory 1994, 9; Biobaku 1952, 40).

5. The Iyalode settled disputes among women and had direct access to the king. Politically, this title was important because it institutionally acknowledged women as an important interest group. In addition, as Afonja argues, it indicated a power shift from royal to commoner women. The strength of the office varied among city-states. It was strongest in city-states like Abeokuta and Ibadan, which were less politically centralized and more fully integrated into the international economy (Afonja 1986, 147). See also Awe (1977) and Fadipe (1970).

6. S. Johnson also noted there was a common saying that maintained, "*Egba ko l'Olu, gbogbo won ni nse bi Oba*" ("Egbas have no king, all of them act like a king"), ([1921] 1973:77).

7. The original Egba provinces did not have an organized military apparatus. The Ode (society of hunters) was responsible for security. However, in 1780, the farmers' association formed a federal militia that launched the Egba revolt against Oyo. This militia was the antecedent to the Ologun (Ajisafe 1948, 3rd edition, 8–9).

8. Usually, there were six women in the Ogboni (Morton–Williams 1960, 368; Morton–Williams 1964), and the senior woman member, the Olori Erelu, sat on the Iwarefa, the six-member committee that conducted the affairs of the council (Biobaku 1956, 258).

9. James Johnson, letter to Wright, 2 August 1879, Church Missionary Society (CMS) Archives, Cooperative Africana Microfilm Project, Chicago Center for Research Libraries, CA2/056. Oroge argues that this group of Christian slave-holding women—Mary Coker, Betsy Desola, Lydia Yemowi, Fanny Fisher, and Susannah Lawolu—came to prominence in the 1870s and reports that Mary Coker was given the title of Iyalode of the Parakoyi. The discrepancy warrants future investigation; Coker certainly was an important personality during this period, and two of her three sons went on to hold important titles as well. Isaac became a Parakoyi chief in 1904 and Samuel became an assistant Christian Balogun, while Robert became a catechist for the CMS in Abeokuta (Oroge 1979, 257).

10. The first Christians in Abeokuta were Egba Saro recaptives who had been introduced to Christianity in Sierra Leone. They began returning to Abeokuta by the end of the 1830s, and missionaries soon followed in their wake. By the 1860s, a number of Christian Saros had become wealthy from trade. Other Saros were influential in politics and tried to restructure the Egba state in 1865. Their short-lived attempt to centralize the Egba state under the Egba United Management Board created a civil service of edu-

cated Africans as officials and advisers and established a Customs Department to support the central authority (Ayandele [1966]1981; Kopytoff 1965).

11. Fadipe does note that some spouses became estranged, but claims that reconciliation nearly always followed (1970, 89).

12. Canon J. J. Ransome-Kuti taught at the Ake School in Abeokuta and the CMS Girls' School in Lagos and held a number of church positions, such as Superintendent of the Abeokuta Church Mission, Soren-Ifo District, before he was named Canon of the Cathedral Church of Christ in Lagos in 1905. His son, Reverend I. O. Ransome-Kuti, was a noted educator and nationalist, and his daughter-in-law, Funmilayo Ransome-Kuti, was one of Nigeria's most important nationalists and feminists from the 1940s until her death in 1978.

13. In the 1980s, it was still known as Jojo's compound, even though she died in 1932. Interviews with Alhaji Oladunwo Soetan and Alhaja Ajoke Soetan, 11 November 1988.

14. Matory (1994, 113). He also suggests that Yoruba divorce applies to various degrees of estrangement, the most extreme of which occurs only when a woman has found a new partner and decides to legalize her union with him.

15. T. B. Macaulay, Journal Extract for the Quarter Ending December 25, 1855. CMS, CA 2/065.

16. In his *History of Abeokuta*, A. K. Ajisafe states that Gbadebo's mother was taken from her first husband by his father, Alake Okukenu, and subsequently gave birth to Gbadebo in 1854 (Ajisafe 1948, 90). However, in Alake Ademola's account of this story he stated, "She divorced Kuti and Alake Okukenu took her to wife . . . Just in the same way my mother Adebola Okodabi was . . . wife of one Onitade. She divorced him and became the wife of Oba Ademola I in 1871 several years after the divorce. She was wealthy and was of good position, she had her own house at Wasimi Ake." Minutes of Egba Council, 30 April 1936, ECR 1/1/74 Vol. 1, National Archives, Abeokuta (NAA). It is interesting to note the agency Ademola attributes to these women.

17. Before the twentieth century, *diploma* was not reserved to women; both men and women in crisis could seek refuge in the palace. By the 1920s, however, *dipomu* was transformed and became a mechanism through which women who divorced their husbands but were unable to refund the bride price were temporarily detained in the palace. They could leave during the day to conduct their trade, but had to return to the palace at the end of the day. They paid a small fee for their living expenses and remained in detention until someone was able to pay the amount that had been levied against them. Between 1927 and 1931, 605 women were held as *dipomu*. See Record Book for Dipomu from Courts, ECR 1/7/1, NAA.

18. Letter from J. B. Wood to Rev. F. Baylis, 1 August 1893, CMS, Yoruba Mission 1/7/2. The missionaries were expelled from Abeokuta in 1867 and did not return until 1875. They were brought back with the support of Ogundipe, the "unofficial Alake" of Abeokuta (Ayandele [1966] 1981, 46–47).

19. Wood, for example, criticized his successor for not dismissing a petition from Thomas Cole who wanted a formal separation from his wife, Linda, who had left him for another man. Wood argued that since Thomas had been unfaithful to Linda first, he had forfeited any claim for relief. Letter from J. B. Wood to Rev. F. Baylis, 1 August 1893, CMS G. 3.A.2/0–1/7/2; Yoruba Mission 1/7/2.

20. Desertion had reached crisis proportions prior to the construction of the railway. It was reported that in 1897 palm trees were left unharvested due to slave desertion and a subsequent labor shortage (Agiri 1972, 45–46). Many slaves fled to Lagos, but some stayed within Egba territory and established slave villages. Letter from H. Kopke, Acting Railway Commissioner, to the Acting Inspector General, 5 December 1900, Abe Prof 9/3, Administrative Minute Book Relating to Egba Affairs, 1900–1904, 2–4, NAA.

21. The 1904 judicial agreement effectively abolished the courts of the sectional Obas, and the private courts conducted by Ogboni chiefs. It retained the Alake's court as "the sole court of original jurisdiction for the use of all Egba litigants" (Pallinder-Law 1973, 110–11), and created a mixed court presided over by the British Commissioner and two Egba magistrates, appointed by the EUG (Pallinder-Law 1973, 98, 108).

22. Letter from Hermann Kopke, Acting Railway Commissioner, to the Superintendent of Native Affairs, Abeokuta, 18 February 1901, Letter Book, 1900–1903, 26, Abe Prof 9/2, NAA.

23. Their dissatisfaction revolved around the establishment of a court for the recovery of debt. Cyril Punch, Railway Commissioner, to the Acting Colonial Secretary, Lagos, 10 May 1901, NAA; Letter Book 1900–1903, 55–56.

24. See Copies of Correspondence, April 1899–March 1900, ECR 3/ 1/1, NAA, and Copies of Correspondence, 1900–1904, ECR 3/1/2, NAA.

25. For example, see the case of Motekun, who appealed to the Commissioner to help her recover money owed to her by the son of one of the town's military chiefs. Letter from Cyril Punch, Acting Railway Commissioner, to the Government Secretary, Abeokuta, 23 July 1902, NAA; Letter Book, 1900–1903, 235–36.

26. See the case of the slave woman Moriamo who appealed to the Commissioner because her owner would not allow her to redeem herself. Letter from Cyril Punch, Acting Railway Commissioner, to the Government Secretary, Egba Government, 6 August 1902, NAA; Letter Book, 1900–1903, 239–40.

27. See the case of Funlayo, whose child was held by a native doctor after the mother was unable to pay him for healing the child. Letter from Capt. L. Norton Blackwell to the Superintendent, Native Affairs, Abeokuta, 2 September 1901, Abe Prof 9/2, Letter Book, 1900–1903, 99–100.

28. The majority of cases were disputes revolving around slavery and marriage, twenty-one and eleven respectively. Six of the marriage disputes were submitted by men and five by women. All the women wanted to end a marriage or engagement, while four of the six men wanted their wives returned. Letters from the Alake to the Railway Commissioners confirm that a larger group of women were contesting their marriages or engagements and opting to leave. Of twenty-seven letters written by the Egba government on behalf of male complainants, twenty-six referred to wives, daughters, sisters, and aunts who had run away from their husbands. See Copies of Correspondence 1900–1904, ECR, 3/1/2, NAA.

29. Letter from Hermann Kopke, Acting Railway Commissioner, to the Superintendent Native Affairs, Abeokuta, 18 December 1900, Letter Book, 1900–1903, 7–8.

30. Letter from Capt. L. Norton Blackwell, Railway Commissioner, to the Superintendent, Native Affairs, Abeokuta, 5 November 1901, Letter Book, 1900–1903, 129.

31. Letter from Capt. L. Norton Blackwell, Acting Railway Commissioner, to the Alake, Abeokuta, 29 April 1902, Letter Book, 1900–1903, 196.

32. Betrothal was cemented when the parents of the boy sent the first installment of the bridewealth to the parents of the girl. The payment was often more symbolic than substantial, but the ceremony served to publicly announce that the young woman was promised to someone (Fadipe 1970, 73). Johnson states that girls were betrothed in childhood; Fadipe essentially concurs, claiming that the age of betrothal was about ten years, but Folarin argues that in the distant past girls were betrothed as infants (Johnson [1921] 1973, 113; Fadipe 1970, 70; Folarin 1928).

33. Letter from Cyril Punch, Acting Railway Commissioner, to the Government Secretary, Ijemo, 10 September 1902, Letter Book, 1900–1903, 250, NAA.

34. Letter for Cyril Punch, Acting Railway Commissioner, to the Government Secretary, Abeokuta, 1 July 1902, Letter Book 1900–1903, 228, NAA.

35. Ajisafe estimated that one head of cowries was equivalent to about 6d. (Ajisafe 1948, 37).

36. The demand for European currency declined the farther one moved away from the coast. At the turn of the century, European currency was still a curiosity in northern parts of Yorubaland (Matory 1994, 45).

37. The relationship between indebtedness and divorce became a particularly important subject of debate during the years of the depression (Byfield 1994).

38. Letter from Hermann Kopke, Acting Railway Commissioner, to the Superintendent Native Affairs, Abeokuta, 19 December 1900, Letter Book, 1900–1903, 9.

39. See Minutes of Council Meeting, 15 July 1935, ECR 1/1/67, Vol. II, National Archive, Ibadan (NAI). The number of divorce cases heard in Native Courts for 1927, 1928, and the first half of 1929 totaled 8,267. The number of adultery cases for the same period totaled 2,031. Copies of Correspondence, 2 July 1929, ECR 3/1/26, NAA.

40. The custom of becoming female husbands, which existed in many communities, allowed wealthy older women to marry younger women and gain custody of children. Also see Amadiume (1987).

REFERENCES

Afonja, Simi. 1986. "Women, Power and Authority in Traditional Yoruba Society." In Shirley Ardener et al., eds., *Visibility and Power—Essays on Women in Society and Development*, 137–57. Oxford: Oxford University Press.

Agiri, B. A. 1972. "Kola in Western Nigeria, 1850–1950. A History of the Cultivation of Cola Nitida in Egba-Owode, Ijebu-Remo, Iwo and Ota Areas." Ph.D. thesis, University of Wisconsin.

Ajisafe, A. K. 1948. *History of Abeokuta*. Lagos: Kash and Klare Bookshop. (3rd Edition).

Amadiume, Ifi. 1987. *Male Daughters, Female Husbands*. London: Zed Books.

Atanda, J. A. 1969. "The Iseyin-Okeiho Rising of 1916: An Example of Socio-Political Conflict in Colonial Nigeria." *Journal of the Historical Society of Nigeria*, 4(2):497–514.

Awe, Bolanle. 1977. "The Iyalode in the Traditional Yoruba Political System." In Alice Schlegel, ed., *Sexual Stratification: A Cross-Cultural View*, 144–59. New York: Columbia University Press.

Ayandele, E. A. (1966) 1981. *The Missionary Impact on Modern Nigeria, 1842–1914: A Political and Social Analysis*. London: Longman Group Ltd.

Biobaku, S. O. 1952. "An Historical Sketch of Egba Traditional Authorities." *Africa*, 22:35–49.

———. 1956. "Ogboni: The Egba Senate." In *The International West African Conference*, 257–63. Lagos, Nigeria: Nigerian Museum.

———. 1957. *The Egba and Their Neighbours, 1842–1972*. Oxford: Clarendon Press.

———. 1960. "Madam Tinubu." In National Broadcasting Company of Nigeria, *Eminent Nigerians of the Nineteenth Century*, 33–41. Cambridge: Cambridge University Press.

Byfield, Judith A. 1994. "Pawns and Politics: The Pawnship Debate in Western Nigeria." In Toyin Falola and Paul Lovejoy, eds., *Pawnship in Africa: Debt Bondage in Historical Perspective*. Boulder, CO: Westview.

Callaway, Helen. 1987. *Gender, Culture and Empire: European Women in Colonial Nigeria*. Urbana: University of Illinois Press.

Delano, I. O. 1937. *The Soul of Nigeria*. London.

———. c. 1944. *The Singing Minister of Nigeria—Canon J. J. Ransome-Kuti*. London: United Society of Christian Literature.

Fadipe, N. A. 1970. *The Sociology of the Yoruba*. Ibadan, Nigeria: Ibadan University Press.

Falola, Toyin and Paul Lovejoy, eds. 1994. *Pawnship in Africa: Debt Bondage in Historical Perspective*. Boulder, CO: Westview.

Folarin, Adebesin. 1928. *The Laws and Customs of Egbaland*. Abeokuta: Balogun Printers. (Reprint).

Johnson, Samuel. [1921] 1973. *The History of the Yorubas: From the Earliest Times to the Beginning of the British Protectorate*. London: Routledge & Kegan Paul Ltd.

Kopytoff, Jean H. 1965. *A Preface to Modern Nigeria: The "Sierra Leonians" in Yoruba, 1830–1890*. Madison: University of Wisconsin Press.

Lovejoy, Paul. 1988. "Concubinage and the Status of Women Slaves in Early Colonial Northern Nigeria." *Journal of African History*, 29:245–266.

Lovejoy, Paul and Jan Hogendorn. 1993. *Slow Death for Slavery: The Course of Abolition in Northern Nigeria, 1897–1936*. Cambridge: Cambridge University Press.

Mann, Kristin. 1985. *Marrying Well: Marriage, Status and Social Change among the Educated Elite in Colonial Lagos*. Cambridge: Cambridge University Press.

Matory, J. Lorand. 1994. *Sex and the Empire That Is No More: Gender and the Politics of Metaphor in Oyo Yoruba Religion*. Minneapolis: University of Minnesota Press.

Morton-Williams, Peter. 1960. "The Yoruba Ogboni Cult in Oyo." *Africa*, 30(4):362–74.

———. 1964. "An Outline of the Cosmology and Cult Organization of the Oyo Yoruba." *Africa*, 34:243–60.

Oroge, E. A. 1979. "The Institution of Slavery in Yorubaland with Particular Reference to the Nineteenth Century." Ph.D. thesis, University of Birmingham.

Oyemakinde, Wale. 1974. "Railway Construction and Operation in Nigeria, 1895–1911: Labour Problems and Socio-Economic Impact." *Journal of the Historical Society of Nigeria*, 7(2):303–24.

Pallinder-Law, Agneta. 1973. "Government in Abeokuta 1830–1914, with Special Reference to the Egba United Government 1898–1914." Ph.D. thesis, Goteborg, Sweden.

Phillips, Earl. 1969. "The Egba at Abeokuta: Acculturation and Political Change, 1830–1870." *Journal of African History*, 10(1):117–31.

Punch, Cyril. 1906. *A Report on the Native Law of Egbaland*. MSS Afr. s. 1913. Oxford: Rhodes House Library.

Renne, Elisha. 1990a. "'If Men Are Talking, They Blame It on Women': A Nigerian Woman's Comments on Divorce and Child Custody." *Feminist Issues*, 10(1):37–49.

————. 1990b. "Wives, Chiefs and Weavers: Gender Relations in Bunu Society." Ph.D. thesis, New York University.

Yemitan, Oladipo. 1987. *Madame Tinubu, Merchant and King-Maker*. Ibadan, Nigeria: Fastprint Ltd.

Young, Crawford. 1994. *The African Colonial State in Comparative Perspective*. New Haven, CT: Yale University Press.

3

"SHE THINKS SHE'S LIKE A MAN": MARRIAGE AND (DE)CONSTRUCTING GENDER IDENTITY IN COLONIAL BUHA, WESTERN TANZANIA, 1943–1960

Margot Lovett

This chapter had its origins in a conversation I had in the summer of 1989 with a male elder named Chaisaba Nkanda, who had worked as a career migrant on Tanzania's sisal plantations from the late 1930s to the 1950s. While discussing marriage, Mzee Chaisaba summed up the changes in relations between husbands and wives since World War II as follows:

> Today women are argumentative and fight with their husbands because couples marry without giving bridewealth. And so today a wife will talk back to her husband. She thinks she's like a man. But in the past, you gave bridewealth to marry. You couldn't take a woman for nothing. And then if your wife spoke back to you, you could beat her.[1]

It was in the absolute certainty of thought about (im)proper female conduct and gender identity expressed in that quote that this chapter was born. Mzee Chaisaba and other male elders with whom I spoke had definite ideas about what constituted appropriate gender relations, roles, and behaviors within marriage. A wife was supposed to be submissive, silent, and obedient in her interactions with her husband; she was supposed to act like a woman. This was contrasted with acting "like a man." That meant to think for oneself and challenge instructions with which one disagreed, to give directions and expect to have them obeyed without argument, to control wealth and direct labor—in short, to exercise power and authority not only within one's household, but within the wider society as well. And so, my investigations into the ways in which gender identity was socially constructed in postwar Buha, western Tanzania, emerged from those conversations. I was especially intrigued by two questions. The first was how gender identity not only serves to influence an individual's behavior, but often possesses the prior capacity to determine the range of behaviors s/he envisions as possible.[2] In other words, I sought to understand how gender functions as a mechanism of social control, initially by circumscribing thoughts and then by limiting actions.

The second question concerned the ways in which social institutions contribute to the maintenance of social control by inculcating and reinforcing what superordinate groups or classes view as "proper" gender roles and behaviors.[3] Marriage in Buha served as one of the most potent of these institutions, in part by delineating precisely what rights and obligations husbands and wives could claim from and owed to each other. Contained therein were clear efforts by Buha's political elite and dominant males to prescribe and institutionalize what they deemed to be appropriate gender identities and relations.[4]

This chapter focuses on male strategies to control women through marriage, and so it highlights the ways in which marriages were concluded and explores the efficacy of bridewealth versus non-bridewealth unions toward that end. It also analyzes women's responses to male attempts at control and to changes in the marital relationship itself occasioned by male labor migration. Finally, it considers the ways in which both the ideological underpinnings of marriage and the day-to-day lived realities of that institution, as experienced by the majority of Buha's women, served at once to buttress and to challenge—to construct and deconstruct—female gender identity. As such, the tension between the institution and the individual will be at the forefront of my analysis. It is undeniable that marriage had the power to mold female consciousness and behavior. But it is equally the case that Buha's women were able to think critically about their lives and pursue strategies to take control of them. They did this by managing, manipulating, or attempting directly to alter their life circumstances. At times, these maneuvers might have appeared on the surface as capitulation to the social order and ideology championed by dominant men. But I argue that in fact they were strategies of control pursued by relatively powerless individuals.[5] For such women, "establishing strategies to survive, when change is unlikely, needs to be recognized as acts of control."[6]

MARRIAGE DURING THE HEIGHT OF THE MIGRANT LABOR ERA

By the 1950s, marriage as a social institution in Buha had long been firmly intertwined with and so affected by developments in the wider colonial economy. The most important of these had seen Buha's emergence by the late 1930s as a major source area for migrant labor for Tanganyika's plantation sector. During the 1920s and 1930s, the overwhelming majority of migrants had been young, unmarried men who sought such employment primarily in order to acquire consumer goods for their personal use, move beyond the authority of their elders, or accumulate bridewealth to form a household. But three years of conscription for "essential civil production" during World War II had pushed significant numbers of married Tutsi and Ha men into the migrant labor force for the first time.

From this point on, labor migration became utilized by growing numbers of men as a means both of increasing their personal stores of wealth and of contributing to the reproduction of their households. During the 1950s, married men often sought employment as migrants to acquire cash to buy cattle to start or add to a herd; clothing for themselves, their wives, and their parents; and hoes, cooking pots, and other vital household and consumer goods.[7] Unpropertied unmarried men continued to make use of the migrant labor market to acquire the livestock and other goods they needed for bridewealth.

As it became common for husbands and fathers to depart for a period of waged work on distant mines and plantations in order to satisfy their need for cash, the very nature and meaning both of marriage and of the household changed. Marriage became transformed into a relationship of absences, consisting of lengthy periods during which husbands and wives lived and worked apart from one another. Concomitantly, with the removal of male labor, households progressively lost their identity as units of integrated production and consumption. Their daily reproduction now depended almost entirely on women (and older children, if there were any) and their labor, while many migrant husbands returned home after an absence of a year or two with little more than clothing for their wives.[8] Those men who succeeded in saving enough money to purchase cattle might use some of these to assist their sons to marry, or eventually pass the cattle down to sons as an inheritance,[9] and in this manner facilitate the formation of a new generation of households or the perpetuation of male-controlled and -identified wealth.

These shifts in the nature of marriage and the household largely resulted from the fact that the wives of virtually all Tutsi and Ha migrant workers stayed at home during the periods of their husbands' waged employment. They did so, not because they were forbidden by the state or capital to accompany their men to sisal or other plantations,[10] but primarily because their husbands insisted they remain behind. The question of whether or not the women themselves might have desired to go with their husbands simply was not an issue—the possibility of doing anything other than remaining at home never even occurred to the overwhelming majority of such women.[11] To behave like a woman in these instances meant to reside in your marital compound under the supervision of your husband's kin during the period that your spouse was away.

Men had specific reasons for proceeding to work alone. One ex-migrant explained, "We didn't take our wives with us to the plantations. If you went with your wife, someone might steal her from you. They might even kill you. No, we left our wives at home to look after our fields and cattle."[12] Similarly,

> Some men took their wives with them. It was up to the individual to do so if he liked. But if you took your wife, your house would be empty. There would be nothing there. And if you went with her, when you returned home, what would you eat? But if your wife remained at home, she'd farm.[13]

In the eyes of these men, there were distinct advantages to leaving their wives behind. Not only was a woman who remained in her rural home rendered safe from the advances of other migrants, but she would continue to tend her husband's livestock and, more importantly, cultivate his fields during his absence. By so doing, she would ensure both his uncontested claim to that land and his means of subsistence once he returned home.[14]

But leaving their wives behind was not without its drawbacks. Of primary concern for married migrants was the behavior of their spouses during the periods when the men were not in residence at home. Apprehensive that their wives might enter into adulterous liaisons, run away from their marital compounds, or even seek divorces, men attempted to more tightly regulate their women's movements and activities.

Migrants first relied on existing structures of social control, and particularly on prevailing residential patterns, to circumscribe women's freedom of action. A married couple typically lived with their children in the husband's father's compound, which meant that the parents, brothers, and unmarried sisters of an absent migrant could and did keep a watchful eye on his wife, monitoring and exercising control over her.[15] But migrants also relied on their neighbors to maintain surveillance over their wives, expecting that neighbors would question the wives if their conduct appeared out of the ordinary. Due to the efforts of both their families and their neighbors, migrants hoped that their wives would be prevented from running away from their marital compounds. As one ex-migrant claimed, we "weren't afraid [our wives] would run off somewhere. If she was your wife, where would she run away to? And she knew that her husband had gone to look for money. So why would she leave? And where would she go?"[16]

Indeed, the great majority of Tutsi and Ha women remained in their marital homes during the periods of their husbands' absences. Persevering as good wives should, and doing what was expected of them, they seemed to be waiting patiently and uncomplainingly for their men to return. But beneath the surface, these women were far from quiescent. Rather, they were actively developing and implementing strategies to ensure the survival of themselves and their children. They progressively abandoned millet for the much less labor-intensive cassava, with the result that by the mid-1940s, cassava had become the staple in the areas from which the heaviest concentration of migrants was drawn.[17] The women cultivated the bare minimum required to ensure their own and their children's subsistence,[18] and occasionally sold produce and/or farmed for better-off neighbors to secure cash to purchase needed consumer goods such as hoes or clothing if their husbands had failed to send them any.[19] Finally, women relied on female friends to replace their absent husbands' labor power by assisting with what had been the typically male tasks of cutting grass and clearing away brush to bring a new field into production.[20] The resourcefulness and self-reliance demanded of these women simply in order to survive were the antithesis of the docility and dependency publicly expected of them.

Often, too, migrants' faith that local structures and networks of control would render their wives immobile proved to be overly optimistic. During the 1940s and 1950s, sufficient numbers of women responded to their husbands' absences in ways other than those detailed above that they riveted the attention of Buha's Native Authorities and, through them, the colonial state. The institutionalization of migrant labor had drastically increased women's labor burden, compelling some to undertake what should have been male tasks. It had deprived them of the companionship and assistance of their husbands and, frequently, of the clothing and resultant public identity it was incumbent on the latter to provide: a woman quite simply could not leave her house unclothed.[21] These hardships eventually led a sizable minority of women to reject the passivity socially expected of them. Rather than behaving "like women," they acted instead "like men." Some abandoned their marital compounds in the middle of the night and returned to their natal families until their husbands' return.[22] Others ran away, sometimes with lovers with whom they took up residence, other times to the homes of relatives who lived in distant towns or villages.[23] Still others brought suit before the courts, secured divorces by reason of non-support, and contracted new, socially legitimated marriages.[24] Finally, some women whose migrant husbands had been absent for several years were permitted to dissolve their marriages on grounds of desertion.[25] In these ways, women forced the elite men who controlled the local courts to sanction new bases on which unhappy wives could gain divorces.

By the early 1950s, therefore, marriage and the oversight provided by migrants' kin and neighbors had increasingly failed to insure the immobility and, in male eyes, appropriate behavior of women. As migrants returned home to discover that their wives had left them,[26] wronged husbands themselves now began to use the courts to discipline their rebellious and disobedient wives. Punishment was deemed imperative, for men from the wealthiest and most influential of the political elite down to the poorest of migrants unequivocally laid the blame for adultery, divorce, and other instances of social upheaval squarely on the shoulders of women. The District Commissioner (D.C.) reported that Buha's *Bami* ("Chiefs") and *Batware* ("Sub-Chiefs") were "increasingly concerned about the loosening of moral sanctions" and so insisted that women found guilty of marital infidelity be punished by a fine or, in default thereof, by imprisonment.[27] This attempt to bolster men's waning ability to control their wives was justified on the grounds that "women are often the principal offenders [in adultery cases,] and if they can do as they like without fear of punishment, the evils likely to result will be far greater than any likely to result from a few going to prison."[28] While the degree of censure heaped on women surely was extreme, it does show that men were aware of the existence and power of women's agency. Underscoring the recognition that women were not simply passive beings was the grudging acknowledgment that they could not always be relied upon to act in the subservient, deferential way men expected of them.

While the proposal to imprison unfaithful women never was implemented, by the later 1950s they were publicly being held to account and punished for their behavior. It became common for a woman accused of adultery to be charged and fined, along with her lover as co-respondent, in the local courts.[29] The courts also showed a marked willingness to punish runaway wives and women whom they denied divorces because their reasons for desiring to end their marriages were considered insufficient.[30] The *Mutware* ("Sub-Chief") and court elders ordered these women to return to their husbands; should they refuse, they were fined for contempt of court, a punishment that was rationalized in part as serving to forestall similar behavior on the part of other women.[31] As the male-dominated courts understood, unruly women were dangerous and needed to be controlled, precisely because they showed other dissatisfied wives that they need not endure an intolerable situation.

It was hardly coincidental that male preoccupation with regulating women accelerated during the postwar era, for this was a time when social institutions were progressively challenged and rendered unstable. Male labor migration had altered the nature of marriage and created a new category of uncontrolled and potentially uncontrollable women. It had also significantly changed patterns of authority within households, sometimes sparking fierce male intergenerational antagonism. As Martin Chanock and other scholars who have analyzed the creation of "customary law" during the colonial period have shown, it is precisely at such times that norms are stated most forcefully and adamantly, particularly by those individuals or groups who are adversely affected by such change.[32] Confronted with what seemed to be the onset of social chaos, Buha's men responded by trying to reverse the pace of change. As discussed above, they turned to the courts and the local D.C. to bolster the institution of marriage and so to reassert their control over women. But they also had recourse to ideology toward that end. During the postwar era, threatened males more forcefully stressed the inculcation of proper gender relations within marriage. These were relations in which women were subordinate, deferential, and obedient, and the man was the unchallenged head of his household.

MARRIAGE AND CONSTRUCTING FEMALE OBEDIENCE AND SUBORDINATION

Socialization was a vital component in the creation of the ideal wife, and male reliance on it to mold female behavior was in itself nothing new. The values of respect for and obedience to one's father, and later, one's husband, had long been instilled in girls.[33] Older men had also imbued in boys and young men a sense of deference and inferiority to their elders, but the subordination of junior males had never been stressed as thoroughly as had that of females.

Boys and girls were socialized differently because of the varying degrees of autonomy and influence they one day would or would not wield within the larger society as a whole. Young men eventually would attain dominant status as heads of their own households, and as such were taught that their state of subservience, for however extended a period it might last, was ultimately transitory. But females never would shed their subordinate position. Regardless of age, women would perpetually be jural minors, subject first to the authority of their fathers, then to that of their husbands, and, eventually, to that of their sons. Thus, they learned that their subordination was a life-long condition.

By the postwar era, the gap between the ways in which the genders were socialized had widened considerably. The differential degrees of autonomy and dependency experienced by young males and females was particularly evident in changing customs pertaining to marriage. During the 1940s and 1950s, bachelors who returned home with cash and/or in-kind goods acquired through labor migration gained an increasing say not only in the choice of their wives, but also in determining the point at which they would marry and so attain a modicum of adult status.[34] This clearly marked an erosion of the authority that elder men had wielded over marriage, for the vast majority of these unions had previously been arranged by the fathers of the couple.[35]

Unlike the situation that obtained for young men, however, young women rarely, if ever, had a say in the selection of their spouses and the timing of their marriages. Young women were "supposed to behave in a passive way, to submit to the judgement of their parents . . . [and] accept the partner the latter have chosen."[36] Should a daughter refuse to marry someone her father had accepted as a suitable husband, for it was he who had the final say in the matter,[37] he might curse her by attacking her capacity to bear children, a vital part of what it meant to be a woman, thusly: "'You will die in childbirth,' 'you will never have any children,' 'you will remain sterile your entire life.'"[38] If she were adamant in her refusal to obey her father's wishes, she might face the threat of being disowned.[39]

Few young women dared court such possibilities. Pressure was brought to bear on them not only from their own families, but from the wider community as well. The presumption that a father had an almost unconditional right to select his daughter's husband was something that was not open to discussion, and the *Batware* and the courts safeguarded and strengthened that right.[40] The practical result of this pressure was that a girl might be compelled by her father to marry a man who in age was nearly his contemporary and already had several wives, for the sole reason that the suitor was wealthy and able to offer substantial bridewealth.[41]

> If your father liked cattle, he would force you to marry. If he got five bridewealth cattle, or ten for two daughters, and those cattle had offspring, he felt himself to be a real man. He was a man among men because he was rich.[42]

Daughters faced with such a situation almost inevitably capitulated to their fathers' wishes out of "respect" for their fathers. This was proffered out of a sense of daughters' own weakness, dependency, and profound lack of options, and it served both to highlight and to augment the authority of the male head of the household.

Elders of the past—the respect that they liked was if a girl was forced to get married to an older man, she'd agree. She'd go. If her father saw the cattle, he'd force her, saying, "go and get married so those cattle may come to me." They'd pull her like a goat until she'd agree to the marriage. But a child of today—if you tell her to go get married to an old man—there's no way. She won't agree. And that's why today parents complain that their children insult them and there's no respect like there was in the past.[43]

The constant rendering of "respect" reinforced and perpetuated female subordination and powerlessness. So too did giving a young woman's father the ultimate say in the selection of her husband. By effectively denying a daughter a voice in the arrangement of her marriage, this concentration of authority in male hands neatly foreshadowed what men saw as proper female behavior within marriage, where a wife was to be silent and defer to her husband's wishes.

Other customs, however, explicitly prescribed that behavior. One of these was the ritual parting of father and daughter on the day the new bride left her natal home for her marital compound. As the marriage party departed, her father announced to the groom and his escorts:

I give you my daughter. But care for her well. If later on some grave problems arise, come to speak to me about them. If she does not conduct herself as she should, if she wanders about where you do not want her to go, if she refuses the work that you give her, make her listen to reason: beat her and come to tell me about it. If she digs up someone else's cassava, if she steals cooked vegetables from the house, beat her, but in the inner chamber of the house, not in public.[44]

This pronouncement clearly emphasized that what was expected of a wife was obedience, industry, and honesty, and further buttressed a male-constructed gender ideology in which the husband had authority and was the decision-maker within the marital relationship. It also seems likely that the stress laid on beating a woman inside her house had little to do with preserving her privacy, but instead was intended to save her husband the embarassment of publicly demonstrating that he was unable to control his wife.

The version of marriage stressed by Buha's men in the 1950s thus held that before all else, a wife was required to show her husband respect through deferential behavior and gestures[45] and to acknowledge her subordinate status within the marital relationship. She was expected to concede that her husband was the head of their household and as such was her superior.[46] She was obligated to obey her husband, who claimed absolute rights over her labor: she was required to farm where he wanted, grow what he wanted, and perform whatever task he instructed her to perform.[47]

Throughout the 1950s, men attempted to secure female compliance with these desired norms of behavior, and availed themselves of a variety of options to enforce their authority over their wives. A physical beating was one of these options, and it was meted out in cases where, in her husband's opinion, a wife failed to show proper respect, by speaking back to him or disobeying him. Should she persistently refuse to obey and render respect, her husband could demand from her family reparation in the form of one of the cattle he had presented to them as bridewealth for her. The returned cow constituted the terms under which the husband would agree not to terminate the marriage and so demand restitution of all the bridewealth cattle.[48] "It's like this—you come to me saying, 'Your child has offended me. I don't want her. If she's to return to me, give me a cow. This is the fine that I'm claiming.' So you give him a cow."[49]

Much as a husband's daily claims to respect from his wife served continually to reaffirm female subordination, so too did the transfer of bridewealth. Indeed, by reinforcing female submissiveness and therefore the social control of women, bridewealth was central to structuring gender relations within marriage. As a male elder stated, "once bridewealth was given for a woman, she was like a slave. She had no freedom, because she could say nothing."[50] Similarly, in the words of a female elder, "if a husband beat his wife, she wouldn't defend herself or attempt to fight back because he had paid bridewealth for her."[51] Bridewealth simply strengthened the cultural expectation that Tutsi and Ha wives should exhibit a pronounced deference in their interactions with their husbands, and at times, some women experienced its transfer as deepening their own powerlessness.

It was possible to marry without bridewealth, but its absence could raise doubts about the freeborn status of the woman concerned, who also was snubbed for not having married in the "proper," socially accepted manner. Marrying without bridewealth also resulted in distinct social and legal disadvantages for men. A man who contracted a non-bridewealth union had no legal rights over his wife and children. He could not bring a claim for compensation in the event of his wife's infidelity, for it was the transfer of bridewealth that gave a husband exclusive access to his wife's sexuality.[52] Finally, any offspring of that union belonged to the wife's, as opposed to the husband's, lineage. The husband of a woman for whom bridewealth was not given

> never acquires full authority over his . . . wife and her children. Whenever it pleases her, she can go away and take her children with her, without her husband being able to stop her from doing so. Compared with other wives,

she is definitely in an advantageous situation. As one informant declared: "[Such a] wife does not have to submit to the insults an ordinary married woman often has to swallow."[53]

Nor could the husband demand respectful, obedient behavior from his spouse. In a non-bridewealth marriage, "the husband can say nothing to [his wife]. She will answer him: 'Be quiet, what did you give for me?' The result will be quarrels and she will return to her [natal] home."[54] By taunting her husband that, had he only married her in the proper manner, he would have gained the right to speak to her in any way he chose, a woman for whom bridewealth had not been received actively and successfully wielded the dominant ideology to her advantage.

Furthermore, to be married without the transfer of bridewealth meant that the union could more easily be dissolved. As interpreted by a male elder,

> Bridewealth marriages lasted longer. If a couple married without bridewealth, the marriage was only temporary. The wife would rule herself and the husband would rule himself. If the wife got tired of her husband, she'd just leave him and her father would welcome her home, saying it's better she lives with her [natal] family than with a man who gave nothing for her. But if the husband paid bridewealth, he knew he had to look after his wife, and she knew she had to respect him.[55]

Therefore, despite the potential social stigma, it seems that there were distinct advantages for women in non-bridewealth marriages. Unlike their counterparts who had contracted bridewealth unions, these women spoke up for themselves in their interactions with their husbands, and left the marital relationship if they considered it to be unsatisfactory. Their departures were facilitated by the fact that there were no cattle to be returned and so no paternal or familial objections to ending the marriage that might first have to be overcome.[56] In the eyes of men such as Mzee Chaisaba, with whose words I began this essay, women for whom bridewealth was not given quite simply thought they were "like men" and behaved accordingly.

The courts also treated these women quite differently from those whose families had received bridewealth for them. Preserved in the court records are numerous cases brought by women who had been married without bridewealth, but who nevertheless came to court to secure divorces. Once there, however, they discovered that the *Mutware* and court elders did not consider their unions to be genuine marriages, and so saw them not as wives, but as "lovers" who were free to leave their husbands should they so choose.[57] In one such case, heard before the Makere Ushingu court early in

1960, Kagufi Manamba sought a divorce from Ntaukilaka Ntayega. Ntaukilaka was opposed to terminating their marriage as he still loved his wife. But the court found that

> it is clear that Kagufi lived with Ntaukilaka as his lover and not as his married wife, for no bridewealth was paid for her. Thus, there is no way to compel her to continue with their relationship if her heart doesn't want to do so. One sided love can't build a relationship between a man and woman, and if it is ordered that Kagufi must return to Ntaukilaka, it may be dangerous for him. Kagufi will get the divorce she has asked for.[58]

The precise nature of the "danger" that possibly awaited Ntaukilaka was left unspecified, but it seems likely that the court feared that Kagufi might try to poison or bewitch him; perhaps, too, as occurred elsewhere in Tanganyika, she might have done him physical harm.[59]

Clearly, the degree of freedom and agency socially accorded to "lovers" was in stark contrast to that which could be exercised by "wives." Unlike husbands or "lovers," "wives" were required to show cause as to why the divorce should be granted, and had to successfully persuade the male-controlled courts to act favorably on their claims.

Bridewealth thus served the dual function of an ideological instrument through which the values of female subservience and respect were inculcated and women's behavior consequently was regulated, and as a practical means of binding women into marriage. By the 1950s, Buha's male population viewed marriage and the courts as indispensable tools for the policing of their women. The most blatant example of this came in Ushingu, where, in a meeting with the D.C. at the end of 1955, "the people of Ushingu" proposed that a tax be levied on all single women who "refuse for no good reason to get married."[60] The state also viewed marriage as a mechanism for social control, and shared the concerns of Buha's men about the dangers posed by unattached women. In 1949, the Native Courts Adviser had informed Tanganyika's Provincial Commissioners that "to make divorce too easy [for women] is definitely 'contrary to public morality and policy.'"[61]

CONCLUDING COMMENTS

For Africanists, asserting that marriage functions as a mechanism of social control is certainly nothing new or surprising. Indeed, recent work has convincingly demonstrated how and why colonial states, in partnership with African men, manipulated marriage practices with the intent of more strictly regulating women's behavior and curtailing their freedom of movement.[62]

But recognizing that marriage as an instrument of control is the historical product of conscious human endeavor has enabled us to examine which groups or classes benefit most from that institution, which attempt to define social reality through it, and accordingly whose interests are best served by supporting and preserving the status quo.

During the postwar period, Buha's men attempted to reinforce a version of marriage that most benefited them in their quest to augment their diminishing control over women. A vital part of that endeavor was persuading women to accept passivity and obedience as cornerstones of female gender identity. Virtually from birth, therefore, girls were socialized to be deferential and submissive and to acquiesce to male wishes and demands. The transfer of bridewealth upon marriage reinforced those values and expectations. Gender roles and identities therefore must be acknowledged as one product of "the historical constellations of social and political power" extant in any society.[63] As such, they have the capacity both to reflect and to perpetuate existing networks of social control. But just as the dominant ideology itself may never be fully accepted or internalized, so too may control be far from absolute and attempts at control fail to produce the desired consequences.

This failure was demonstrated when, to the frantic concern of Buha's men, a minority of Tutsi and Ha women refused to behave "like women," and responded to their life circumstances in ways whose meaning seems to us to be utterly unambiguous. Rather than waiting patiently and uncomplainingly in their marital homes, some wives of absent migrants returned to their natal compounds, sued their husbands for divorce, entered into adulterous relationships with men they then deemed to be their new husbands, or ran away to live with distant relatives. These women clearly rejected passivity as a component of female gender identity. But even the great majority of women who remained in their rural homes during the periods of their husbands' absences did not simply and uncritically comply with what was socially expected of them as women. Because they did not engage in actions that outside observers have categorized as resistance, they appear on the surface to have been thoroughly socialized, and to have internalized the dominant order's conception of what it meant to be a woman. But beneath the surface, these women were actively engaged in a process of constructing a more self-reliant female gender identity by developing and pursuing strategies for control and survival. These included eschewing the cultivation of millet in favor of cassava, planting the absolute minimum required for subsistence, and relying on female friends for practical and emotional support. Among themselves, they also indulged in a pointed critique of gender roles and relations within marriage. They outwardly demonstrated respect for their husbands when present, but then ridiculed them in front of other women as useless: unlike women, who bore the primary responsibility for ensuring their families' survival through the food they produced, "men's work was to sit and get drunk."[64] All of these actions were means of securing mastery over their lives. As Michelle Fine noted, Western social scientists and psychologists still do not comprehend how subordinated individuals take control of their lives. "We fail to understand how they determine what is controllable and what is not. We dismiss control strategies that look like 'giving up' but are in fact ways to survive."[65] We do not recognize that, in the face of power, apparent "surrender, in its place, was as honorable as resistance, especially if one had no choice."[66]

NOTES

1. Interview with Mzee Chaisaba Nkanda, June 13, 1989.

2. Here I have drawn upon the work of the feminist psychologist Rhoda Unger, particularly the introduction to her edited volume, *Representations: Social Constructions of Gender* (Amityville, NY: Baywood, 1989).

3. See, for example, Peter L. Berger and Thomas Luckmann, *Construction of Reality: A Treatise in the Sociology of Knowledge* (Garden City, NY: Doubleday, 1966).

4. Sondra Farganis has argued that marriage as a social institution has "rules and regulations which establish patterns of behavior, that is, which explain how the individual is to act. . . . Learning how to act or behave is learning how to play socially sanctioned roles, which . . . spell out the rights and obligations incumbent upon one." Farganis, "The Social Construction of Gender: The Turn to Fiction," in Unger, ed., *Representations: Social Constructions of Gender,* 310.

5. This seems to echo the actions of Rebeka Kalindile, a Tanzanian peasant woman, in her relations with her husband and in her work as a local organizer of women. See R. Kalindile and Marjorie Mbilinyi with Tusajigwe Sambulika, "Grassroots Struggles for Women's Advancement: The Story of Rebeka Kalindile," in Magdalene K. Ngaiza and Bertha Koda, eds., *The Unsung Heroines* (Dar es Salaam, Tanzania: WRDP Publications, 1991) 109–148, and particularly 143–145.

6. Michelle Fine, "Coping with Rape: Critical Perspectives on Consciousness," in Unger, ed., *Representations: Social Constructions of Gender* 188.

7. Laurent Sago, "A Labour Reservoir: The Kigoma Case," in Walter Rodney, Kapepwa Tambila, and Laurent Sago, *Migrant Labour in Tanzania during the Colonial Period* (Hamburg: Institut für Afrika-Kunde, 1983), 51 and 64; J. H. Scherer, *Marriage and Bride-Wealth in the Highlands of Buha (Tanganyika)* (Groningen, Netherlands: VRB Kleine, 1965), 126–127; and interviews with Mzee Chaisaba Nkanda, June 13, 1989; Mzee Kamlete Gwakila, October 2, 1989; Mzee Matai Magulu, June 13, 1989; Mzee Kamalo Nkulimba, December 14, 1988; Mzee Bera Lukema, June 4, 1989; and Mzee Ntibakula Ngomela, October 20, 1989.

8. Interviews with Bibi Magdalena Kilahunja, October 21, 1989; Mzee Charles Mbanguka, November 13, 1988; Bibi Marecelina Francis, May 28, 1989; Bibi Zilarusha Kagoma, May 26, 1989; Bibi Marecelina Geregola, December 8, 1988; Mzee Stephano

Migezo, December 18, 1988; Mzee Antoni Ruhanyula, October 21, 1989; and Mzee Patrick Mporogomi, December 23, 1988.

9. Interviews with Mzee Maulidi Mpanda, October 20, 1989; Mzee Kamalo Nkulimba, December 14, 1988; Mzee Matai Magulu, June 13, 1989; and Mzee Chaisaba Nkanda, June 13, 1989.

10. Government Circular No. 1 of 1952 instructed administrative officers that "Africans leaving their homes to seek work should be encouraged to take their families with them if they wished to do so." Labour Commissioner to Member for Social Services, May 30, 1953, Tanzania National Archives (henceforth TNA) 24693, vol. 3.

11. Interviews with Bibi Gulesi Simon, June 9, 1989; Bibi Ngoroye Kidohera, June 12, 1989; Bibi Magdalena Kilahunja, October 21, 1989; Bibi Zilarusha Kagoma, May 26, 1989; Bibi Marecelina Geregola, December 8, 1988; Bibi Bertha Charles, December 6, 1988; Bibi Marecelina Francis, May 28, 1989; and Bibi Denisa Eliadori, May 24, 1989.

12. Interview with Mzee Madabali Mkuyuba, October 19, 1989. Similarly, Mzee Bera Lukema and Mzee Rubati Kamangu concurred that migrants were reluctant to take their wives with them to the plantations because they were afraid that another man would steal them away and they'd be laughed at when they returned for having lost their wives. Interviews of June 4, 1989, and December 9, 1988, respectively.

13. Interview with Mzee Kamalo Nkulimba, December 14, 1988. Similarly, Mzee Mchakena Nkwakuzi stated that migrants left their wives at home to farm so that there would be something to eat when they came home. Interview of July 1, 1989. In an interview of October 20, 1989, Mzee Ntibakula Ngomela echoed that sentiment, as did Mzee Antoni Ruhanyula in an interview of October 21, 1989. Mzee Matai Magulu confirmed that "generally people from here left their wives at home. They saw it was better because when you came home you'd find your compound in good condition." Interview of June 13, 1989. Finally, Mzee Sadock Lilenga agreed that migrants' wives remained behind because "We went there to look for money. We couldn't break up our compounds." Interview of October 21, 1989.

14. *Wakili* [Shabani] Heru Juu to D.C. Kasulu, August 25, 1954, TNA 198/L4/4/vol.1, stated that unless a migrant laborer leaves his wife or mother on his land, he will lose it if he remains away a long time, and the land will revert to the *Mutware* to be reallocated as s/he sees fit.

15. Interviews with Bibi Denisa Eliadori, May 24, 1989; Bibi Marecelina Francis, May 28, 1989; Mzee Yoram Mapili, June 17, 1989; and Mzee Mchakena Nkwakuzi, July 1, 1989.

16. Interview with Mzee Kamalo Nkulimba, December 14, 1988.

17. Interviews with Bibi Bertha Atanasi, June 3, 1989; Bibi Magdalena Kilahunja, October 21, 1989; Bibi Zilarusha Kagoma, June 12, 1989; and Bibi Theresia Lazaro, June 7, 1989.

18. Interview with Bibi Magdalena Kilahunja, October 21, 1989; Bibi Zilarusha Kagoma, May 26, 1989; and Bibi Ngoroye Kidohera, June 12, 1989.

19. Interviews with Bibi Bertha Charles, December 6, 1988, Bibi Marecelina Geregola, December 8, 1988; Bibi Denisa Eliadori, May 24, 1989; Bibi Zilarusha Kagoma, May 26, 1989; Bibi Marecelina Francis, May 28, 1989; Bibi Ngoroye Kidohera, June 12, 1989; and Bibi Gulesi Simon, June 9, 1989.

20. Interviews with Bibi Ndakije Kamalo, May 25, 1989; Bibi Magdalena Kilahunja, October 21, 1989; Bibi Denisa Eliadori, May 24, 1989; Bibi Mpuniye Pius, June 29, 1989; and Bibi Mwanbilo Hwago, June 30, 1989.

21. In Case 70 of 1961, Munyegera Court Civil Case Files, 1961, TNA acc. 392, Chubwa Ntahuga sought a divorce from her husband "because he shamed her—he didn't give her clothing."

22. White Fathers, Kigoma Diocese, "Table d'Enquête sur les Moeurs et Coutumes Indigènes, Tribus des Baha et des Banyaheru," unpublished manuscript, 1951, 73–74.

23. See, for instance, D.C. Kasulu to D.C. Moshi, March 17, 1960, TNA 198/M5/21; Saving Telegram, Political Kasulu to Political Kigoma, December 17, 1943, TNA 180/20/68; *Wakili* Issa A. Luhinda, Makere to D.O. Kasulu, August 19, 1946, TNA 198/L5/9; and Case 389 of 1948, Extracts from Heru Chini "B" Court Case Book, 1948, TNA acc. 389; Case 251 of 1950, Munyegera "B" Court Case Book, 1950–51, TNA acc. 392; Case 20 of 1957, Manyovu "I" Court Civil Case Files, 1957, TNA acc. 393; and Sago, "A Labour Reservoir: The Kigoma Case," 77.

24. In 1952, for example, Marachira Muluga successfully sued her husband for divorce, arguing that he refused to provide her with any clothing and she could no longer bear such troubles. Case 112 of 1952, Munyegera "I" Court Civil Case Files, 1952, TNA acc. 392. See also Case 10 of 1948, Manyovu "B" Court Case Book, 1948, TNA acc. 393; Case 22 of 1950, Buhoro "I" Court, as cited in Local Courts Law Reports, Kasulu, n.d., TNA 63/L4/7; and Case 14 of 1953, Heru Chini Court Criminal Cases, 1953, TNA acc. 389.

25. At a meeting of the Buha "chiefs" held in 1952, it was "agreed that there was no objection to local courts granting divorces to wives who had been deserted by their husbands." Minutes of the Buha Chiefs Conference held at Kibondo, October 16 and 17, 1952, TNA 198/L4/9. See also Case 44 of 1954, Makere Bunganda "I" Court Civil Case Files, 1954, TNA acc. 396; Case 20 of 1957, Manyovu "I" Court Civil Case Files, 1957, TNA acc. 393; and Case 1 of 1960, Makere Ushingu "A" Court Civil Case Files, 1960, TNA acc. 398.

26. The District Officer (D.O.) highlighted this problem in the Annual Report for 1951: Kibondo District, TNA 202/R/J/A/2/1951.

27. Provincial Commissioner, Western Province, to Chief Secretary, April 21, 1949, TNA 180/20/41.

28. Provincial Commissioner, Western Province, to Chief Secretary, April 21, 1949, TNA 180/20/41.

29. Cases 13 and 28 of 1959, Makere Ushingu "B" Court Criminal Case Files, 1959, TNA acc. 398; and Case 6 of 1960, Makere Bunganda Court Criminal Case Files, 1960, TNA acc. 396.

30. Insufficient reasons consisted of infrequent, mild beatings, or unspecified intermittent quarrels. See Adequate Reasons for Divorce, as cited in the Local Courts Law Reports, Kasulu, n.d., TNA 63/L4/7; and Bishop J. van Sambeek, "Croyances et Coutumes des Baha," (unpublished manuscript, Kabanga, 1950), 68.

31. Cases 33 and 113 of 1959, Makere Ushingu "B" Court Criminal Case Files, 1959, TNA acc. 398.

32. See, for example, Martin Chanock, "Making Customary Law: Men, Women, and Courts in Colonial Northern Rhodesia," in Margaret Jean Hay and Marcia Wright, eds.,

African Women and the Law: Historical Perspectives (Boston: Boston University Papers on Africa, VII, 1982), 53–67; Chanock, *Law, Custom and Social Order: The Colonial Experience in Malawi and Zambia* (Cambridge: Cambridge University Press, 1985); and Elizabeth Schmidt, "Patriarchy, Capitalism, and the Colonial State in Zimbabwe," *Signs* 16, 4 (1991), 732–756.

33. Interviews with Bibi Kalinganila Nkayamba, September 29, 1989; Mzee Chaisaba Nkanda, June 13, 1989; and Bibi Mwanbilo Hwago, June 30, 1989.

34. Scherer, *Marriage and Bride-Wealth*, 48–49; van Sambeek, "Croyances et Coutumes," 64–65 and 82; White Fathers, "Table d'Enquête," 29; and interviews with Mzee Kamalo Nkulimba, December 14, 1988; and Mzee Rubati Kamangu, December 9, 1988.

35. Scherer, *Marriage and Bride-Wealth*, 48–49; van Sambeek, "Croyances et Coutumes," 64.

36. Scherer, *Marriage and Bride-Wealth*, 48.

37. van Sambeek, "Croyances et Coutumes," 65–66. A girl's father would accept a suitor, inform his wife of his decision, and leave it up to her to persuade their daughter to agree to the marriage.

38. van Sambeek, "Croyances et Coutumes," 64–67; and Scherer, *Marriage and Bride-Wealth*, 48.

39. Interviews with Bibi Mwanbilo Hwago, June 30, 1989; and Bibi Mpuniye Pius, June 29, 1989.

40. In 1940, a White Father, Mejean, calculated that in 90 percent of marriages in Kibondo, "moral force" had been brought to bear on the girl by her parents, sometimes backed up by the local "headman," an estimation with which the Assistant D.O. concurred. B. J. Dudbridge, Asst. D.O. Kibondo to the Administrative Officer in charge of Buha, Kasulu, October 25, 1940, TNA 180/A2/36. Scherer similarly found that "sometimes undue pressure is brought to bear upon rebellious daughters" to acede to their fathers' wishes. Scherer, *Marriage and Bride-Wealth*, 48.

41. Case 40 of 1954, Munyegera Court Civil Case Files, TNA acc. 392; van Sambeek, "Croyances et Coutumes," 65; and interviews with Bibi Mwanbilo Hwago, June 30, 1989; she was about sixteen in 1929 when she was compelled by her father to become the fifth wife of a much older man who gave two cows and one bull in bridewealth for her, a considerable sum at that time; see also Bibi Kilanganila Nkayamba, September 29, 1989; Bibi Magdalena Kilahunja, October 21, 1989; Mzee Mayekeyeke Ntumo, October 2, 1989; and Mzee Ntibiyagwa Chamangali, December 16, 1988.

42. Interview with Bibi Nyambele Rugiga, October 19, 1989.

43. Interview with Bibi Kalinganila Nkayamba, September 29, 1989.

44. van Sambeek, "Croyances et Coutumes," 99.

45. Gestures of deference included a wife bending her knees slightly while using both hands to present her husband with an object, or walking behind him when proceeding somewhere. White Fathers, "Table d'Enquête," 56.

46. van Sambeek, "Croyances et Coutumes," 171; White Fathers, "Table d'Enquête," 56.

47. White Fathers, "Table d'Enquête," 57 and 59.

48. Interviews with Mzee Kahehe Numvile, October 19, 1989; and Mzee Baregereje Birontse, October 23, 1989.

49. Interview with Mzee Sadiki Mpanda, October 20, 1989.

50. Interview with Mzee Antoni Ruhanyula, October 21, 1989.

51. Interview with Bibi Theresia Lazaro, June 7, 1989.

52. Case 133 of 1944, Heru Juu "B" Court Case Book, 1944–45, TNA acc. 388; Case 30 of 1953, Buhinga "B" Court Cases, 1947–57, TNA acc. 400; and Case 24 of 1959, Makere Bunganda Court Criminal Case Files, 1959, TNA acc. 396.

53. Scherer, *Marriage and Bride-Wealth*, 84–85.

54. White Fathers, "Table d'Enquête," 29.

55. Interview with Pastor Theo Vomo, July 3, 1989.

56. In cases where bridewealth had been transferred, the fathers or brothers of unhappy wives often pressured them to remain in their marriages on the grounds that they lacked the cattle to return to their sons- or brothers-in-law upon divorce. See Case 13 of 1943, Buhinga "B" Court Case Book, 1942–43, TNA acc. 400; Case 253 of 1948, Extracts from Heru Chini "B" Court Case Book, 1948, TNA acc. 389; Case 33 of 1953, Manyovu "I" Court Civil Case Files, 1953, TNA acc. 393; and Case 19 of 1960, Makere Bunganda Civil Court Case Files, 1960, TNA acc. 396; and J. H. Scherer, "The Ha of Tanganyika," *Anthropos* 54 (1959), 873.

57. Case 133 of 1944, Heru Juu "B" Court Case Book, 1944–45, TNA acc. 388; Cases 9 and 11 of 1958, Makere Bunganda "B" Court Civil Case Files, 1958, TNA acc. 396; Cases 2 and 4 of 1960, Makere Ushingu "B" Court Civil Case Files, 1960, TNA acc. 398. The greater freedom accorded urban women who contracted non-bridewealth marriages is discussed by Parpart, "Sexuality and Power on the Zambian Copperbelt, 1926–1964," in Sharon Stichter and Jane Parpart, eds., *Patriarchy and Class: African Women in the Home and the Workforce* (Boulder, CO: Westview, 1988), 141–160.

58. Case 2 of 1960, Makere Bunganda Court Civil Case Files, 1960, TNA acc. 398. See also case 9 of 1958, Makere Bunganda "B" Court Civil Case Files, 1958, TNA acc. 396.

59. See, for example, Marjorie Mbilinyi, "Runaway Wives in Colonial Tanganyika: Forced Labour and Forced Marriage in Rungwe District 1919–1961," *International Journal of the Sociology of Law* 16(1988), 1–29.

60. *Wakili* H. Kilato, Makere Ushingu, to D.C. Kasulu, December 14, 1955, TNA 198/L5/9.

61. J. P. Moffett, Native Courts Adviser to the Provincial Commissioner, Tanga, with copies to other Provincial Commissioners, December 23, 1949, TNA 29563.

62. James Ault, Jr., "Making 'Modern' Marriage 'Traditional,'" *Theory and Society* 12, 2 (1983), 181–210; Theresa Barnes, "The Fight for Control of African Women's Mobility in Colonial Zimbabwe, 1900–1939," *Signs* 17, 3 (1992), 586–608; George Chauncey, Jr., "The Locus of Reproduction: Women's Labour in the Zambian Copperbelt, 1927–1953," *Journal of Southern African Studies* 7, 2 (1981), 135–164; Marjorie Mbilinyi, "Runaway Wives," 1–29; Elizabeth Schmidt, "Negotiated Spaces and Contested Terrain: Men, Women and the Law in Colonial Zimbabwe, 1890–1930," *Journal of Southern African Studies* 16, 4 (1990), 622–648.

63. Farganis, "The Social Construction of Gender," 309.

64. Interviews with Bibi Marecelina Geregola, December 8, 1988; Bibi Ndalijanye Yongeze, June 30, 1989; and Bibi Magdalena Kilahunja, October 21, 1989.

65. Fine, "Coping with Rape," 189.

66. Maya Angelou, *I Know Why the Caged Bird Sings* (New York: Bantam Books, 1969) 212, as cited in Fine, "Coping with Rape," 195.

REFERENCES

Ault, James, Jr. "Making 'Modern' Marriage 'Traditional.'" *Theory and Society* 12, 2 (1983), 181-210.

Barnes, Theresa. "The Fight for Control of African Women's Mobility in Colonial Zimbabwe, 1900-1939." *Signs.* 17, 3 (1992), 586–608.

Berger, Peter L. and Thomas Luckmann. *The Social Construction of Reality: A Treatise in the Sociology of Knowledge.* Garden City, NY: Doubleday, 1966.

Chanock, Martin. "Making Customary Law: Men, Women, and Courts in Colonial Northern Rhodesia." In Margaret Jean Hay and Marcia Wright, eds., *African Women and the Law: Historical Perspectives,* 53–67. Boston: Boston University Papers on Africa, VII, 1982.

————. *Law, Custom and Social Order: The Colonial Experience in Malawi and Zambia.* Cambridge: Cambridge University Press, 1985.

Chauncey, George, Jr. "The Locus of Reproduction: Women's Labour in the Zambian Copperbelt, 1927–1953." *Journal of Southern African Studies* 7, 2 (1981), 135–164.

Farganis, Sondra. "The Social Construction of Gender: The Turn to Fiction." In Rhoda Unger, ed., *Representations: Social Construction of Gender,* 309–321. Amityville, NY: Baywood, 1989.

Fine, Michelle. "Coping with Rape: Critical Perspectives on Consciousness." In Rhoda Unger, ed., *Representations: Social Construction of Gender,* 186–200. Amityville, NY: Baywood, 1989.

Hay, Margaret Jean and Marcia Wright, eds. *African Women and the Law: Historical Perspectives.* Boston: Boston University Papers on Africa, VII, 1982.

Kalindile, Rebeka and Marjorie Mbilinyi with Tusajigwe Sambulika. "Grassroots Struggles for Women's Advancement: The Story of Rebeka Kalindile." In Magdalene K. Ngaiza and Bertha Koda, eds., *The Unsung Heroines,* 109–148. Dar es Salaam, Tanzania: WRDP Publications, 1991.

Mbilinyi, Marjorie. "Runaway Wives in Colonial Tanganyika: Forced Labour and Forced Marriage in Rungwe District 1919–1961." *International Journal of the Sociology of Law* 16 (1988), 1–29.

Ngaiza, Magdalene K. and Bertha Koda, eds., *The Unsung Heroines.* Dar es Salaam, Tanzania: WRDP Publications, 1991.

Parpart, Jane. "Sexuality and Power on the Zambian Copperbelt, 1926–1964." In Sharon Stichter and Jane Parpart, eds., *Patriarchy and Class: African Women in the Home and the Workforce.* 141–160. Boulder, CO: Westview, 1988.

Rodney, Walter, et al. *Migrant Labour in Tanzania during the Colonial Period.* Hamburg: Institut für Afrika–Kunde, 1983.

Sago, Laurent. "A Labour Reservoir: The Kigoma Case." In Walter Rodney, et al., *Migrant Labour in Tanzania during the Colonial Period,* 58–78. Hamburg: Institut für Afrika-Kunde, 1983.

Scherer, J. H. "The Ha of Tanganyika." *Anthropos* 54 (1959), 841–904.

————. *Marriage and Bride-wealth in the Highlands of Buha (Tanganyika).* Groningen, Netherlands: VRB Kleine, 1965.

Schmidt, Elizabeth. "Negotiated Spaces and Contested Terrain: Men, Women and the Law in Colonial Zimbabwe, 1890–1930." *Journal of Southern African Studies.* 6, 4 (1990), 622–648.

————. "Patriarchy, Capitalism, and the Colonial State in Zimbabwe." *Signs* 16, 4 (1991), 732–756.

Stichter, Sharon and Jane Parpart, eds. *Patriarchy and Class: African Women in the Home and the Workforce.* Boulder, CO: Westview, 1988.

Unger, Rhoda. "Introduction." In Rhoda Unger, ed. *Representations: Social Construction of Gender.* 1–10. Amityville, NY: Baywood, 1989.

Unger, Rhoda, ed. *Representations: Social Construction of Gender.* Amityville, NY: Baywood, 1989.

van Sambeek, Bishop J. "Croyances et Coutumes des Baha." Deuxième Partie. Unpublished manuscript, Kabanga, 1950.

White Fathers, Kigoma Diocese. "Table d'Enquête sur les Moeurs et Coutumes Indigènes, Tribus des Baha et des Banyaheru." Unpublished manuscript, 1951.

4

Wayward Women and Useless Men: Contest and Change in Gender Relations in Ado-Odo, S.W. Nigeria

Andrea Cornwall

I gave her N20 and she threw it back at me, telling me I was useless and if I thought she could cook soup with N20 then I should do it myself.

—Bayo, mechanic, 30s

I made up my mind not to get married as I realised men are such idiots. They are all useless. I told my father and he started to beg me, saying "what will people think?" That's how I came to be married and in the situation you see me in now.

—Iya Tunde, trader, 40s

Men in Ado-Odo, a small Yoruba town in the agricultural hinterland of metropolitan Lagos, have long expected subservience from their wives. But the women of today try their patience. Unlike wives of yesteryear, today's women are represented as wayward: rude, troublesome, and disobedient, and liable to run after other men and their money (see Cornwall 1996). While many women join in the clamor of dismay about wayward women, they also have to contend with husbands whose willingness and ability to give financial support to their families may be sporadic and uncertain: husbands whom they accuse of being no good to them, "useless."[1] Contemporary sexual partnerships between men and women are held up against the yardstick of an idealized former time, *igba atijo* ("the olden days"). In their commentaries on *igba atijo*, people offer not only versions of the past but perspectives on a troubling present.

Wayward women and useless men populate discourses on the present, but are completely absent from narratives about the past. *N'igba atijo* ("in the olden days"), so older people said, co-wives ate from the same pot, seniority formed the basis for relations of respect, husbands were chosen for women, and wives were found for men, who relied on their fathers' help too much to refuse. Order prevailed. These days there is no such certainty. The changes that people pinpoint in intimate relationships between men and women parallel other changes, in other relationships: those between men and their mothers, between co-wives, between parents and their children.

In this chapter, I take representations of these "good old days" as a starting point to explore changes and contests taking place in gender relations during the twentieth century. I focus on the two major areas for contemporary moralizing: the growth of economic opportunities for women and the decline in women's compliance with hegemonic notions of endurance and obedience. Looking at the emergence of "wayward women" and "useless men" in discourses on gender relations and intimate relationships, I examine the implications of change for female agency and autonomy in contemporary Ado-Odo.

PASTS IN THE PRESENT: REPRESENTING "THE OLDEN DAYS"

Reference to previous times forms a familiar part of everyday commentaries on life in Ado-Odo. Women and men who told me their life stories, chewed over promising pieces of gossip, or talked about current problems had recourse to this past, which served both to signify and to reinforce their own moral position. Sometimes, accounts of the "olden days" accompanied tales of lived experience in the past. More often, however, the phrase *n'igba atijo* ("in the olden days") was used to unleash a torrent of complaints about the present. So often were "the olden days" invoked in conversations about contemporary affairs that they acquired rhetorical resonance beyond a description of other times, serving less to inform about what things had actually been like than to provide a vivid contrast with whatever the speaker wanted to focus disapproval on.

Discourses on immorality frame the problem as one of the present and one in which female agency stands out as the prime cause for concern.

Two aspects of these discourses are particularly striking. First, women were as voluble as men on the subject of women's waywardness, and men as well as women bemoaned those "useless men" who failed to fulfill their obligations. Secondly, the insistent complaints about morally corrupt (*iṣekuṣe*) behavior were not merely those of "the older generation" about "the youth of today." The young frequently joined the old in an unlikely chorus. And all used the particular past of *igba atijọ* to focus their concern.

Older people drew on these "olden days" to tell cautionary tales, stressing the compliance with authority people of that time had shown, their assiduous attention to duty as mothers, wives, husbands, fathers, and workers. Recasting experiences of other times within the frame of a collective, contrastive *igba atijọ* submerged the particularity of their own pasts. By reclaiming a "traditional" past in their narratives, they were perhaps laying claim to a moral high ground that, in the wake of socioeconomic change and the exigencies of modernity, has slowly slipped out of their reach. For today's behavior is doubly troubling for those whose authority, livelihoods, and reputations are also at stake in the behavior of others. Their commentaries on change, then, also spoke about control and about agency and autonomy.

Younger people may have new opportunities and models of interaction to draw on, but their accounts of the present state of affairs were equally saturated with disquiet. Invoking the "olden days" in their accounts of change, younger people often replicated the moralizing rhetoric of their elders. Young women roundly blamed other young women for being "corrupt" and running after men for money; young men bemoaned the current state of affairs, blaming the greed of young women. These charges cast a shadow over the possibilities for negotiating sexual relationships.

Recourse to "tradition," to *igba atijọ*, frames some of the current uncertainties and conflicts over the allocation of rights and duties within a timeless order that is invested with a moral authority. There is no place for dissonance—let alone any disobedience—in hegemonic narratives spun as moral commentaries on the present. Tradition, as a contested resource (Hobsbawm and Ranger 1985), becomes the vehicle for expressing a dismay that is not merely *nostalgic* but is loaded with the emotive concerns of people concerned about the uncertainties the present heralds for their futures. Women's and men's stories of their own experiences of intimate relationships, as well as their accounts of the lives and times of others, reveal details that locate the recurrent themes of tales of *igba atijọ* within contests of the present.

ENDURING ARRANGEMENTS?
MARRIAGE IN THE "OLDEN DAYS"

Expectations of what a "husband" or "wife" should do or be have their own historicity, bound up in complex ways with changing notions of responsibility and of agency. Over the course of the twentieth century, competing discourses on masculinity have created complex arenas of contestation over men's obligations. Colonial notions of marriage, specifically of men as providers (see Lindsay 1996), and discourses on marriage and morality in the world religions have reconfigured the ways in which claims and contests over conjugal obligations may be played out.

For many of the elderly women I knew and for some elderly men, their first marriages were arranged for them by their parents or senior relatives. Dependent on their fathers for dowry and for land, young men were obliged to accept. Young women had little option to express a preference, let alone refuse a choice.[2] Iya Abiola, an Ado-Odo trader, spoke of her marriage as an interlude in her life that came and went, something she "endured" so as to bear and raise her beloved son. Like many of her peers, her marriage in the mid–1930s was arranged by her father. She told me:

> You would just be told, "Go and plait your hair, you're going to your husband tomorrow." You couldn't reject this, as you had no power. You had to obey the parents. I didn't know my husband at all before I married. I just carried my load on my head to Ilaro to find him there. When I got there I couldn't reject him. I was just happy to have a pregnancy. That's what everyone did.

Comfort, now in her 70s, told me of the pressure young women were under to remain and endure: "We just had to accept. But some ran away. If she ran away then people would come to beg the father to allow her to come home. But he would not yield. He would not be pleased. He would not accept for her to come back to the compound again as she had disobeyed her father, which she must not do." Women's options were limited. Only infertility, madness, or extreme maltreatment were recognized as reasons for women of reproductive age to extricate themselves from arranged marriages; the practice of the levirate left widows to be inherited by a relative of their deceased husband (Fadipe 1970). Older women told me that women who "misbehaved" would be brought into line by harsh punishment by their husbands, with the approval of their fathers. Those who fled home without a good reason might be sent straight back to their husbands. Parents would be reluctant to offend friends or patrons, or to tarnish their own reputations, by supporting a daughter who would not or could not endure.

In these and other accounts of *igba atijọ*, told in generalizing narratives or situated in versions of lived pasts, defiant women were almost completely absent. Yet they appeared, in numbers, in customary court records from nearby towns from 1874 onward.[3] Divorce cases provide vivid glimpses of female agency that is far from the image of the demure, obedient wife in accounts of *igba atijọ*. Records from the last decades of the nineteenth and the first decades of the twentieth century, the time that borders on *igba atijọ*, are replete with instances of claims for refund of betrothal payments ("a consideration that failed") and of women who had gone astray.

One case tried at the nearby town of Badagry in 1892 is especially revealing: it concerns one of these "wayward women" who had been promised to a Lagos trader, from whom money and assistance had been demanded by her parents. Having fulfilled his part of the bargain, the trader asked her to go to Lagos with him. She refused. He then took her to court for repayment of the amount spent on her, saying that she had become a "prostitute." The woman, Abesi, opened her testimony by cross-examining him: "When I agreed to be your wife did not my father tell you that I had had connection [i.e., sex] with a man? . . . When I returned to Badagry and you asked me to go back with you to Lagos, did I not tell you that I did not like your ways, so would not go with you?" Abesi, the "prostitute," had lost her virginity to another man and then refused to accompany her husband. For this, she was termed "wild."[4]

Abesi exemplifies a kind of waywardness that was to emerge in court cases from this period onward and reappear in narratives in the present: her recalcitrance, her sexual experience, her outspokenness, and her sheer defiance might be less shocking today, but it matches the chorus of complaints aimed at today's wayward women. Although cases like hers were unusual in the past, she was not alone. Court records reveal numbers of women who were clearly equally reluctant to enter into or remain in unhappy marriages. After spending years courting women, expending considerable sums of money—each item of which is faithfully listed and reclaimed in the records—men would find themselves rejected, passed over for another. Some women would just take the cash and go. In cases of extreme recalcitrance, force might be used. One Otta woman, for example, was kept in shackles for days until she eventually escaped.[5] Another, from Badagry, was tied up and taken to her fiancé by a despairing mother, after living what her mother termed "a rather dissolute life." The court heard how the young woman had a child before marriage and then wandered off "ostensibly on other business," never to return, only for her husband to hear that she was with another man.[6] As soon as divorce was formalized in customary law, in 1907 (Zabel 1969), women were able to make use of the courts to dissolve marriages so as to remarry. To do so, they needed only the money to repay their dowries. One case from Otta in 1908 is an example of how straightforward this quickly became. The woman simply said of the husband she had rejected, "I am tired of staying with him, I would like to get another husband."[7]

Images of obedient compliance, spun in stories of the first (often only) marriages of elderly women in Ado, evoke an era in which women endured their lot: out of fear of their fathers, the absence of alternatives, respectability, and resignation. Court records tell an entirely different story, invoking the agency not only of recalcitrant fiancées but also of scheming mothers. To reach the courts in a time where disputes were usually resolved by compound heads (*baale*) or by the *ọba* (king) himself, these cases may well represent the extremes that were shrugged off when I mentioned them to older men and women in Ado. But they give intriguing hints of the fracturing of control over women that was to become so much of an issue in the following decades. The wayward characters of the present appear to have had precedents, then, in cases from the distant past. The new opportunities provided by an increasingly monetized economy weakened gerontocratic controls (Peel 1983), opening up spaces for women—and younger men—to exercise their agency. Expectations and options had begun to change.

"MODERN TIMES"

Apart from a few enterprising women who made substantial gains from longer-distance trading in the early part of the twentieth century, most women in Ado-Odo did not generate sufficient money from their work to become effectively independent from their husbands until the 1940s, when women's opportunities for capital accumulation and diversification began to expand (Cornwall 1996).[8] Ado women learnt new trading skills from immigrants from central Yoruba towns and began to take advantage of improved transport opportunities and the expansion of trade that accompanied wider changes in the economy (Bauer 1954; Galletti et al. 1956). Meanwhile, the institutions of colonial governance placed an increasing premium on education, offered primarily by the Christian missions (Ajayi 1965). Younger, educated men had opportunities that took them into the expanding urban centers and away from the control of their elders. Men who, in previous decades, had become "big" through the acquisition of traditional titles and influence within the orbit of the town had to contend with a rising, younger, educated population of men who were not disposed toward demonstrating the kind of deference their elders expected (see Fadipe [1939] 1970; Peel 1983).

While the kinds of marriage patterns Mann (1985) describes for the Christian elite in early colonial Lagos only came to impinge much later on the marriages of men and women in Ado, by the early 1940s attraction was beginning to replace arrangement in marriages. And both "endurance" and "cooperation," the watchwords of *igba atijo*, resonate with Christian discourses on marriage. Conjugal arrangements in some marriages, especially those of educated Christians, came to be patterned on the ideal of the wage-earning breadwinner and his dependent spouse. Educated men began to assume positions as providers as the new masculinities modeled on colonial expectations during the 1930s and 1940s came to redefine male responsibilities (see Lindsay 1996); making regular payments of *owo onje* (feeding allowance) came to be equated with "being a man." The pervasive association of Christian ideals with modernity came both to encompass and to be deployed to oppose reconstituted traditions, offering competing frameworks within which some men, and fewer women, could articulate disagreement with the dictates of fast-crumbling gerontocratic structures.

Chief Ajuwon spent his early adulthood in the midst of these changes in the late 1930s and early 1940s. He contrasted his life and marital choices as an educated man with those of his brother, an uneducated farmer. While he had felt free to marry whomever he wanted, his father had chosen a wife for his brother and the couple had barely exchanged a word during three years of courtship. Chief Ajuwon noted: "They [our fathers] were not able to control us . . . if we liked things we did them in our own way." "Doing things our own way" meant that men like Chief Ajuwon could now select their own wives—and pay their own dowries if necessary. But it was not only educated men who were able to choose. Chief Basiru Ajose narrated the tale of his marital history, which began with a contest over the right to make such choices. It was not education but migration, to the expanding urban metropolis of Lagos, that gave him the freedom to assert himself.

Basiru Ajose began his working life as a farmer and started working on the roads, ending up in Lagos in 1942, where he built up a career in construction. He had been courting a woman in Ado. After he went to town he didn't see her again. Instead, he got to know a woman who lived nearby. He said, "That lady was grown up as I was, so I thought that she had been meeting other boys and was corrupt [i.e., not a virgin], but I started to be her boyfriend anyway." In 1946 they decided to marry. He still had not seen his fiancée in Ado, but had not ended the relationship: he'd just gone away. When he sent a message to his parents that he had someone he wanted to marry in Lagos, they said, "What of the one here?" They did not want him to marry a Lagos lady, he said; "Those ones were considered too free with themselves, *aṣewo* (prostitutes)." He ignored his parents, found an older couple to act as parents to make the arrangements, and soon afterwards he and his "Lagos lady" were married.

On their wedding night, he expected to find that she was sexually experienced. To his surprise—and that of the older couple—she was a virgin. "She was grown up," he said, "and they too thought that she must have gone after men." He was very pleased. His wife became pregnant immediately. When she delivered, he sent a message to Ado. His parents came to Lagos. When they arrived, they were surprised. They said, "We thought you had married an old woman!" People in Ado-Odo said at that time that when men went to Lagos they married "harlots" or old women.

Attitudes in small-town Ado-Odo to the women from the "big city" spoke not only of the changes in gender relations that had begun to impinge on women's options in urban contexts, but of the changes taking place in Ado-Odo itself. By the 1940s some women were beginning to choose for themselves—and to leave relationships if they were not satisfied. Few as they were, such women began to set an example and open up spaces for others. Able to seek and find work outside Ado-Odo, unmarried young men could now seek partners of choice elsewhere, abandoning wives arranged for them at home. Married men migrated to Lagos or beyond and left their wives behind. Some wives remained with their husbands' families, fending for themselves. But others moved on themselves, finding new partners. Their mobility was due, at least in part, to wider economic changes (see Galletti et al. 1956).

Expectations of marriage had begun to change, and with them the "conjugal bargain" (Whitehead 1981) that equated dependency with maintenance. Prior to the 1940s, most women made negligible gains from their work. As trade opportunities changed, younger women were able to generate their own capital (see Cornwall 1996). Trading offered other opportunities. At the night market, young women and men would meet under the cover of darkness. Travel around the area on public transport also brought new contact with men. Abiona, now in her 60s, told me of how she'd moved around the ring of markets in the area by lorry. On the way, she kept on coming across the same driver and gradually got to know him. Within a year, they were married. Her older sister noted that for her own generation, this would have been unthinkable.

As women began to establish trade that yielded more than simply subsistence, some realized that they no longer needed to obey their fathers. There were men around with their own money who wanted to marry these women, irrespective of what their parents had planned for them. Cases that were exceptional in Iya Abiola's time now became much more common, with women refusing to go to husbands and breaking off engagements made without their consent. Increasingly, marriages came to be contracted between individuals, often without reference to the desires or designs of their parents. As Mr. Akinwonmi, a retired teacher and former customary court judge, put it: "People saw themselves as entitled to rights. They started to make up their minds as to what they wanted and how they wanted it."

The education of women was seen by many as having the greatest direct influence on how women viewed themselves and their choices. Other factors also played a part in wider changes in gender relations. Subtle shifts in the balance of economic power between husbands and wives placed those women who had become involved in the distributive sector during the cocoa boom (Galletti et al. 1956; Bauer 1954) in a better economic position than many of their husbands when boom turned to bust. In the 1950s, market relations came to play a greater part in the processing sphere in the towns. Those farmers whose wives sought other means of generating income became "customers" for women engaged in food processing. Women could seek better deals and buy their raw produce elsewhere; others were no longer willing to labor for their husbands, devoting their time instead to their own trading careers.

These new opportunities meant greater autonomy for women; some were able to use their improved economic prospects to gain better bargaining positions within marriages, as well as to survive—and thrive—outside them. Iya Shina was one woman who gained greater autonomy. After some years of marriage, she realized that she was gaining little from the work she put into her husband's farm. So she started trading. Her husband was pleased that she was earning and feeding the family. But she soon realized that her lot was not much improved. She was working harder than ever. All her husband was going to do with the extra money she brought in, she thought, was to use *his* money—money he was saving due to her work—to marry more wives. So she secretly started saving, little by little, and laid the foundations of her own house in the late 1950s. Over the next two decades, many more women would follow suit: creating their own spaces where, as one woman put it, "as I am the owner, he cannot give me any instruction." Women who left to live in their own houses, as well as those who returned to their father's house when they had had enough, began to be known by the name of *ilemọṣu*, a label that came to be used to categorize and castigate any women who left their husbands (see Cornwall 1996).[9]

As women's opportunities expanded, they shouldered more of the responsibility of catering for the family. Some women, especially those married to polygamist husbands, had to cope without even the bare minimum of assistance toward household provisioning. Their husbands presaged the "useless men" of the present. But husbands' neglect was about more than simply being unable to provide. It was also about unwillingness to take responsibility. Some men, realizing that they could get away with it, continued to marry wives who effectively supported their hearth-holds themselves.[10] Iya

Safuratu, a petty trader in her 60s, told me, "some women will marry the husband and be responsible for their feeding and everything. That has been my fate." Her story is revealing.

> Iya Safuratu was initially engaged to a man who turned out to be a thief. She needed a way to repay her dowry and had no means of her own. A wealthy man, an associate of her brother, approached her parents, who gladly accepted him as a husband for her. He repaid her dowry and they were married. He married a string of wives, but gave them nothing at all to feed themselves or their children. Each wife used her own business to keep her hearth-hold going. Iya Safuratu struggled to make ends meet. But she endured. At first she was the youngest of four wives, but her husband went on to marry another seven. She stuck it out. It was only when he told her one day that from then onward his latest wife would be doing everything that Iya Safuratu had been doing on the farm that she decided she had to go. She went back to her parents and started trading, saving small amounts of money. And the day came, finally, when she could go to court and repay her dowry. All these years later, she proudly showed me a receipt dated 1963.

Like Iya Safuratu, women were now in a position where they could save some of the proceeds from their trading activities toward the amount needed to release themselves from marriages. Until then, women had needed another man in the wings before they could leave their husbands. By the late 1950s, they were gradually acquiring the means to free themselves. Character, family, and popularity had long been more important criteria than material wealth. As the 1960s dawned, money began to make more and more of a difference.

LOVE AND MONEY

By the 1960s it was fairly common for women to be pregnant before marriage, and by this time dowry was not paid if they were. The normative expectation of dowry payment remained.[11] Although arranged marriages still took place, the obligation to heed parents' wishes and the sense of duty were giving way to relationships formed through attraction and love—as well as money. Civil court records of the time contain several references to "love" in divorce cases, such as cases in which a woman testifies that "I have no love for him and I was asked to love him" or where a man talks of how he "fell in love" with a woman.[12] In several cases, women bringing suits had moved in with their husbands without parental consultation, or had been sent there by their fathers when already pregnant.

The meaning of marriage was changing. Once a functional bond wrought through links between families, marriage in the 1960s had become more of a relationship between individuals and as such a far less clearly defined "bundle of interactional possibilities" (Burnham 1987:50). Although families still influenced the shape of marriages, women had greater scope for making and breaking relationships on their own terms. Marriages were often not particularly close, let alone "intimate" in the sense of companionable. Still, the seeds of new kinds of conjugal arrangements, sown earlier, began to take root. These revolved around individual choice, women's desire for children, and the economic benefits that might accrue from relationships with wealthy men. Rather than marrying just to have children and enduring whatever came along as their mothers did, this generation of women had, and made, choices. They were also beginning to be able to exercise their rights: demanding that their husbands "provide proper care" [i.e., pay for their children's upkeep] and "packing out" [i.e., leaving] if husbands turned out to be "useless."

Women whose children had grown up had long been free to leave whenever they wished and set up home independently. Increasingly, parents came to acquiesce in their daughters' returning home earlier in their life courses and in their remaining non-married. Custody arrangements—which inevitably favored the father's family—provided a significant disincentive to the formal dissolution of marriages. The option of moving out and going home if there was trouble with a co-wife was one, however, that allowed some women to take their children with them as long as they did not set up home with another man. Those who did find themselves other lovers were gossiped about and treated with disdain: they were, people said, *aṣewo* ("prostitutes") and not to be trusted. Even those whose only wish was, as one put it, "to live in peace," were labeled *ilemoṣu* and cast as wayward women whose voracious appetite for men and money drove them out of marriages.

Ilemoṣu were seen as the harbingers of the "city ways" that began to be more prominent in Ado's social life in the late 1950s and early 1960s: the night parties, the finery and glitz of new fashions, and the broken marriages that began to fill the courts.[13] And it was no longer just younger women who were accused of "misbehaving." Joseph, now in his 60s, told me of the string of unfaithful wives he had married during this time, adding that his own mother was too fond of partying and had met an untimely end as a victim of love medicine. Joseph, like other men his age, had married at a time when traces of the old ways persisted. For them, the "new women" were almost by definition "wayward," simply for asserting their right to make any kinds of choices for themselves. But the men were to see more changes yet.

By the 1970s, numbers of women had secured personal livelihoods that left them completely economically independent of and sometimes wealthier than their husbands. Men reported their wives going to night parties, dressing extravagantly, and taking lovers. Such wives, they said, became rude and troublesome, refusing to obey their orders and answering back. It would be said of such women, *o ti di ẹja gbigbẹ ko ṣee ka* ("they have become like dried fish, you cannot bend them"): they are so set in their ways that they cannot be changed. Yet men's complaints, so redolent with bravado, fall rather flat in the face of their inability to provide. And those wives whose rudeness and waywardness so appalled husbands and relatives alike voted with their feet in response.

Enhanced prospects for regional trade as a result of the civil war, and the 1970s oil boom, provided further opportunities for enterprising traders. Of those who became successful through shrewd marketing of local commodities, and others who prospered from imported goods, building their own houses became not only an expression of that wealth but also a route to further autonomy. Like Iya Shina, women who owned their own houses could set the agenda for relationships with men, secure from the fear of their husbands bringing home a troublesome new wife or telling them to go. Others were able to leave earlier on in their life courses to set up trade in nearby towns, where they could enter into relationships outside the control of in-laws (cf. Sudarkasa 1973).

Yet while some women became wealthy and while most managed to make an independent income for themselves, for many the economic gains that accrued from this work were insufficient for accumulation on any scale (cf. Berry 1985; Dennis 1991). Children who might have worked for them were attending school in increasing numbers, leaching profits from trade. Some husbands not only scaled down their contributions, but began to resent women's spending power, creating further frictions (see Cornwall 1996). Women became increasingly unwilling to put up with being treated badly by husbands or with contests with co-wives, over access to a husband's resources, that were becoming more acute with the demands of educating their children.

The oil crisis of 1981 sent shock waves throughout the economy. By the time the Structural Adjustment Program (SAP) was inaugurated in 1986, the easy life fueled by the oil boom had started to collapse. As the economy lurched, cross-border smuggling from the nearby Benin Republic boomed in Ado (Asiwaju 1991). For the young men who were the principal beneficiaries of this trade, smuggling offered them the chance to take as many wives as they wished. People told me how unmarried and married women alike, impressed by the smugglers' conspicuous consumption, began to follow these men in droves. Marriage to Ado's farmers or craftsmen was far less glamorous than the chance these "*fayawo* boys" (smugglers) offered them for fancy clothes and a relatively easy life. Two retired customary court judges, Yele Akinwonmi and Chief Kuyebi, situated the spate of divorces in the later 1980s as directly driven by the disparities in wealth between ordinary workers and the *"fayawo boys."* Some of the marriages contracted in this period were very short-lived. Court records also reveal that longer-term relationships also petered out as women sought other husbands who would provide for them better—or simply left to live alone.

In the early 1990s, as austerity hit harder, people had become more cautious about marriage possibilities. For some men the economic austerity of the SAP era made them practically dependent on their wives, with a significant impact on their bargaining power within conjugal relationships. Others had wives who were earning as much as their husbands were. But although the balance of economic power shifted in favor of women, anecdotal evidence from a range of sources, including customary court judges, suggests that there has been a *decrease* in the divorce rate in Ado-Odo. Alhaja Oloruntosin, a worldly trader in her 60s, offered a revealing analysis of these changes:

> In the olden days, men were the producers and women just the consumers. Women in Ado didn't have much of an idea about making money. They depended on men to feed them. If men failed to cater for the children, they would move out to another husband who would give them feeding allowance, as they would be suffering too much. Out of necessity they would have to leave their children behind. These days, women do not expect their husbands to do much for them. They have many different jobs and greater skills in trading. They can face the children and use their money to educate them. This has meant that there are fewer divorces, as women just put up with men due to fear of losing their children.

Is a decrease in divorce necessarily a case of women-in-general putting up with their lot in life? Earlier this century, divorce came to represent an intention to remarry and it retains that primary purpose. There are still few women who divorce "just to be free," But there are other options. For some, changing ideas, opportunities, and practices have enabled them to stay in relationships that they might otherwise have left. As one woman in her 40s reflected, things are no longer so clear-cut. Women of her age these days, she said, pause to reflect:

> Once they [the children] have grown up, or left to marry or to work, she's got more time on her hands, is more comfortable with her business. That's the time she starts to ask herself questions and thinks about her relationship with her husband. It's a time when you'll see whether the love is

there, when you'll want to be petted by him and for him to pet you. And
if there's no love, then the woman can decide to pack out.

Deciding to "pack out," at whatever stage, is a choice that remains difficult
for reasons that go well beyond the viability of living alone. It is significant,
however, that shifts in circumstances have given women considerably greater
freedom to make these choices—and shifts in the meaning of intimate relationships have made those decisions all the more complex.

WAYWARD WOMEN?

What, then, are the implications of these changes for marriage and divorce? It seems plausible that it is precisely an intention to remarry, or even
to marry at all, that is on the decrease. A drop in divorce would certainly fit
with the kind of resignation expressed by those women who remained in
cohabiting relationships to look after their children. And it would fit with
the women who take lovers as "helpers," or seek satisfaction from men outside their marriages (cf. Orubuloye et al. 1993; Guyer 1994). But it would
also fit with the increasing numbers of women who have children without
cohabiting, or "pack out" of unhappy marriages to live without a husband:
those women who become *ilemoṣu*—wayward women despairing of those
"useless men."

Even though women have been building their own houses, leaving their
husbands after their children are grown, and returning home from abusive
relationships for decades, non-married women remain objects of popular
disdain. The figure of the *ilemoṣu* has become an ever more potent target for
abuse, acquiring new rhetorical dimensions in recent times: it has come to
be used to represent *any* woman living without a man, irrespective of
whether she has gone astray or simply gone away. In some respects, *ilemoṣu*
represents the inverse of the good wife. The use of the term for any woman
who steps out of line provides a powerful normative injunction to women of
all ages. For those women who do make it on their own without male partners represent more than simply a threat to conventional morality. They are
able to occupy the space left empty by "useless men" and provide for themselves, literally displacing their husbands (Cornwall 1996).

From what people in Ado told me, the "scourge" of *ilemoṣu* was represented as an epidemic growing more alarming by the day. Reports of the
numbers of *ilemoṣu* around the town implied an explosion of waywardness
of intriguing proportions. Yet here lies the twist. Having heard men and
women alike regale me with stories and complaints about these wayward
women, I asked a friend to name all the *ilemoṣu* in our quarter. He began
reeling off names. It was then that I finally began putting the picture to-

gether. Yes, these were independent women. Yes, they lived alone, and yes, I knew them to have left their husbands. But all they had in common was that they had chosen to leave marriages and not to remarry. One was 80 years old, driven away from her marriage by ruthless co-wives. She was fondly called "mother" by the people in her part of the quarter, a beloved old woman rather than a voracious temptress. Another had described her marriage to me: "I have been to the war front and returned peacefully. Enough is enough." Yet another had "endured" beyond endurance, sharing a room with her husband and his new wife until a mysterious sickness struck, one she attributed to that new wife. Yet another had moved out because after bearing six children she was desperate to avoid another pregnancy. The list went on and on. These were the *ilemoṣu* of the present. They all talked of seeking peace; they all survived without cohabiting male partners. They had no need for men, "useless" or otherwise. And the lack of any single distinguishing characteristic beyond their marital status was in itself significant: these were, in many respects, everywoman.

THE GOOD OLD DAYS? PERSPECTIVES ON CHANGE

N'igba atijọ, or so it seems, the idea of "useless" men was almost unthinkable. These days, it has become an everyday reality. And the image of women of the "olden days" as dependent, nurturing, and above all faithful wives and mothers, who managed and endured, embraces fewer and fewer of today's women in the eyes of those whose complaints focus on their behavior and choices. Encroaching into the spaces left by their disappearance are women who are cast as wayward and troublesome; women whose very desires, let alone their rights, had been totally passed over in those "good old days." The *igba atijọ* when co-wives ate from the same pot, a pot that was partially filled with food the husband provided, and when women knew their place, describe an ideal that today's times leave far behind. Marriage has acquired an entirely new complexion: from companionate relationships based on love, to emotionally distant cohabiting arrangements, to relationships existing only through the link a child provides between parents who have never lived together (see Cornwall 1996). The attention focused on those wayward women who appear to gain their upkeep from the wads of cash "sugar daddies" or "*fayawo* boys" offer them expresses more than moral disapproval. For those women have come to represent a means of getting things the "easy way." For the vast majority of women in Ado, life is by no means easy.

The emergence of categories of women who are cast as openly defiant and disobedient (the *ẹja gbigbẹ* kind of characters, who will not change their ways), who are unwilling to endure (the *ilemoṣu*) and who are unabashed about taking lovers (disparagingly referred to as *aşewo*, "prostitutes") has come to fill a disproportionate amount of space within discourses on change. These are categories of the present, although those who inhabit them can be imagined for the past. And these labels are deployed to attempt to restrict the space women in their reproductive years might enter. *Igba atijọ* serves as more than a moral caution to these women. It comes to represent not only the resentment of aging parents, but also their *own* longing: for a time when women could expect support from their husbands and knew that most women were sufficiently restrained from enjoying affairs to pose no threat to other women's livelihoods.

NOTES

1. References to men as "useless" are principally to men of being no use in terms of financial support, as well as other forms of domestic support expected of men. There is no local term as such; people just talk of men as literally "no good."

2. The term "dowry" is used in this context to refer to a series of payments made by a man or his parents to the parents of a woman to establish a marriage.

3. None of the customary court records prior to 1965 could be located for Ado-Odo: I draw here on customary court records from nearby Badagry (1874–1908) and Otta (1905 onwards), located in the archives of the Universities of Ibadan and Obafemi Awolowo respectively.

4. University of Ibadan archives: Badadiv 1/2/1: 2 August 1892.

5. University of Obafemi Awolowo Archives: Otta Customary Court records: Orisafunmi v. Akide, case 27/08, 21 August 1908.

6. University of Ibadan Archives. Badadiv 1/2/1: 21 November 1905.

7. University of Obafemi Awolowo Archives: Otta Customary Court records: Talabi v. Taiwo of Otta, case 7/08, 10 July 1908.

8. These changes came later than they came to larger towns in the region, such as Abeokuta, Ilesha, Ibadan, and Ijebu-Ode. As communications between Lagos and the interior improved and with the rapid growth of the cocoa economy, Ado-Odo fell from a position of comparative regional prominence to become a backwater. As a result, some of the social practices described here are in some respects decades behind similar changes in other towns (see, for example, Peel 1983 for Ilesha).

9. *Ilemoşu* refers to women who leave their husbands to return to their family home, or set up home alone.

10. I use the term "hearth-hold," following Ekejiuba (1995), as an accurate description of actual relations of consumption and production within Yoruba "households." Hearth-holds are units with women at their center and are composed of women and those for whose food women are responsible (Ekejiuba, 1995): men can be members of a single hearth-hold or can (and often do) belong to more than one hearth-hold.

11. This is evidenced by one revealing case from 1968 in which the petitioner claims that nothing had been paid, "with the excuse that she loved the respondent during that time" and that she had moved in with her husband without informing her parents. The court heard this with some amazement, arguing "how could it be

possible to pack there without receiving anything?" Ado-Odo Customary Court Records, Ado-Odo, Case 1/68.

12. Ado-Odo Customary Court Records, Ado-Odo, 1968.

13. Divorce had, by then, become the principal business of customary courts. Taking a snapshot from one year, 1965, around 91 percent of the cases dealt with by the local customary court in Ado were related to the dissolution of marriage arrangements: 70.4 percent were divorce cases, 15.6 percent dealt with "adultery"—cases that involved a woman becoming pregnant by another man without having first dissolved a previous marriage—and 5.4 percent dealt with the recovery of betrothal fees. Land, debt, and other civil cases made up the remaining cases. Source: Ado-Odo Customary Court Records, Ado-Odo.

REFERENCES

Ajayi, J. F. 1965. *The Christian Missions in Nigeria 1841–91: The Making of an Educated Elite*. London: Longman.

Asiwaju, Anthony I. 1991. *The Nigeria/Benin Transborder Trade, Border Control and the Nigerian SAP Programme*. Boston: Boston University African Studies Center Working Paper 155.

Bauer, Peter. 1954. *West African Trade*. London: Routledge and Kegan Paul.

Berry, Sara. 1985. *Fathers Work for Their Sons: Accumulation, Mobility and Class Formation in an Extended Yoruba Community*. Berkeley: University of California Press.

Burnham, Phil. 1987. "Changing Themes in the Analysis of African Marriage." In David Parkin and David Nyamwaya, eds., *Transformations of African Marriage*. Manchester: Manchester University Press, pp. 37–54.

Cornwall, Andrea. 1996. "For Money, Children and Peace: Everyday Struggles in Changing Times in Ado-Odo, S.W. Nigeria." Ph.D. thesis, School of Oriental and African Studies, University of London.

Dennis, Caroline. 1991. "The Limits to Women's Independent Careers: Gender in the Formal and Informal Sectors in Nigeria." In Diane Elson, ed., *Male Bias in the Development Process*. Manchester: Manchester University Press.

Ekejiuba, Felicia. 1995. "Down to Fundamentals: Women-Centred Hearth-Holds in Rural West Africa." In Deborah Fahy Bryceson, ed., *Women Wielding the Hoe*. Oxford: Berg.

Fadipe, Nathaniel A. [1939] 1970. *The Sociology of the Yoruba*. Francis Olu Okediji and Oladejo O. Okediji, eds., Ibadan, Nigeria: Ibadan University Press.

Galletti, R., K.D.S Baldwin, and I. O. Dina. 1956. *Nigerian Cocoa Farmers: An Economic Survey of Yoruba Cocoa Farming Families*. Oxford: Oxford University Press.

Guyer, Jane. 1994. "Lineal Identities and Lateral Networks: The Logic of Polyandrous Motherhood." In Caroline Bledsoe and Gilles Pison, eds., *Nuptiality in Sub-Saharan Africa: Contemporary Anthropological and Demographic Perspectives*. Oxford: Clarendon Press, pp. 231–252.

Hobsbawm, Eric and Terence Ranger. 1985. *The Invention of Tradition*. Cambridge: Cambridge University Press.

Lindsay, Lisa. 1996. "Putting the Family on Track: Gender and Domestic Life on the Nigerian Railway, 1935–1965." Ph.D. thesis, University of Michigan.

Mann, Kristen. 1985. *Marrying Well: Marriage, Status and Social Change among the Educated Elite in Colonial Lagos*. Cambridge: Cambridge University Press.

Orubuloye, I. O., John C. Caldwell, and Pat Caldwell. 1993. "African Women's Control over Their Sexuality in an Era of AIDS: A Study of the Yoruba of Nigeria." *Social Science and Medicine* 37(7):859–872.

Peel, J.D.Y. 1983. *Ijeshas and Nigerians*. Cambridge: Cambridge University Press, 1983.

Sudarkasa, Niara. 1973. *Where Women Work: Yoruba Women in the Marketplace and in the Home*. Anthropological Papers 53. Ann Arbor: University of Michigan.

Whitehead, Ann. 1981. "'I'm Hungry Mum': The Politics of Domestic Budgeting." In Kate Young, Carole Wolkowitz, and Roslyn McCullagh, eds., *Of Marriage and the Market: Women's Subordination in International Perspective*. London: CSE Books.

Zabel, Shirley. 1969. "The Legislative History of the Gold Coast and Nigerian Marriage Ordinances." Parts 1 & 2, *Journal of African Law* 13(2):64–79 and 13(3):158–217.

5

"GONE TO THEIR SECOND HUSBANDS": MARITAL METAPHORS AND CONJUGAL CONTRACTS IN THE GAMBIA'S FEMALE GARDEN SECTOR

Richard A. Schroeder

INTRODUCTION: OF MARRIAGE AND MARKET GARDENS

The phenomenon of cash crop production by African women is perhaps not quite so anomalous as was once assumed. This fact notwithstanding, a boom in market gardening by Gambian women in the late 1970s and 1980s stands as perhaps one of the more dramatic cases on record. Over little more than a decade and a half, hundreds of women's communal gardens sprang up in the Gambia River Basin, effectively replacing the male peanut crop as the primary source of cash income in many areas. By the early 1990s, for example, between 45 and 80 percent of the women in two highly productive horticultural enclaves on the North Bank earned more cash than their husbands (Schroeder 1999), this despite significant market constraints and competition with male orchard owners for land, water, and labor resources (Schroeder 1993, 1995, 1999; Schroeder and Suryanata 1996).

One of the offshoots of the surge in female incomes and the intense demands on female labor produced by the boom was an escalation of gender politics centered on the reworking of what Whitehead once called the "conjugal contract" (Whitehead 1981). Focusing on several Mandinka-speaking communities in one of The Gambia's premier garden districts along the northern Gambia-Senegal border, I outline below two phases of political engagement between gardeners and their husbands. The first phase, comprising the early years of the garden boom, was characterized by a sometimes bitter war of words. In the context of these discursive politics, men whose wives seemed preoccupied with gardening claimed that gardens dominated women's lives to such a degree that the plots themselves had become the women's "second husbands." Returning the charge, their wives replied, in effect, that they might as well be married to their gardens: financial crisis conditions during the early 1980s had so undermined male cash crop production and, by extension, husbands' contributions to household finances, that gardens were often women's only means of financial support during this period.

As the boom intensified, so, too, did intra-household politics. The focus of conflict in the second phase—which extended into the mid-1990s—was related to the use of cash crop income and the amount of time gardeners allocated to their complex horticultural enterprises. These struggles mirrored the image several authors have painted of "non-pooling" households in Africa (cf. Guyer and Peters 1987; Dwyer and Bruce 1988; Stichter and Parpart 1988, for reviews of this literature), except that Gambian women entered budgetary negotiations holding the economic upper hand. I document below the wide range of tactics gardeners and their husbands used to try and control household budgets, and demonstrate that the outcome of these struggles was that women in garden districts ultimately took over a wide range of unprecedented budgetary responsibilities from their husbands. I acknowledge that this outcome appears in some respects as a capitulation on the part of gardeners, but argue that it can also be read as strategic and symbolic deference designed to purchase the freedom of movement and social interaction that garden production and marketing made possible. I conclude that garden incomes did indeed win for women significant autonomy and new measures of power and prestige, but that these gains came only at a price.

MAPPING MARITAL METAPHORS

It is because wives had nothing to do before except sitting near their husbands. But now wives are running both day and night struggling for survival. That is why [relations between men and women] ha[ve] changed. If you want to do something for your husband, you must go to the garden.
—North Bank gardener

[W]hat they produce from the rice fields is meant mainly for home consumption. But what they produce from the garden goes directly to their personal use, that is why they are more concerned with gardening. Probably
that is why some of them are at odds with their husbands.

—Gardener's husband

The basic rationale for prioritizing horticulture over other development
objectives in The Gambia was developed under the auspices of Women in
Development (WID) programs following the 1975 UN declaration of the
International Decade of Women. These projects were characterized by a
strong underlying ideological conviction that women were motivated in their
economic activities in ways that differed fundamentally from men. Put simply, women were considered to be more attuned to the "bread and butter"
issues of food and family welfare than men; they were considered to be better parents because they were seen to be more responsible providers (Whitehead 1981; cf. Schoonmaker-Freudenberger, 1991).[1] Funding of women's
projects was thus a logical, direct, and cost-effective means of making in-
vestments "pay off" in terms of family well-being.

In the context of the mid–1980s, this rationale dovetailed neatly with the
mandate to intervene to save "starving African children" that emerged in the
wake of the devastating famines that swept the Sahel and the Horn. The
combined effect was a sharp upsurge in international aid, which targeted with
increasing specificity the African region, agricultural development and female producers (Thiesen et al. 1989; cf. Watts 1989).[2] The enactment of WID
strategies in The Gambia consequently translated directly into hundreds of
grants to women's garden groups for barbed wire, tools, hybrid seed, and
well-digging costs.

The significance of this investment pattern is that it fed into a dramatic intensification of the demand for women's agricultural labor. The
garden boom marked a fundamental shift away from predominantly
rainfed agriculture toward ground-water-based irrigated production. Not
only were gardeners required to mobilize for a second full production
season with the cessation of seasonal rains, but high evapo-transpiration
rates during the dry season gardening period necessitated a rigorous wa-
tering schedule. Gardeners irrigated their crops twice daily—in the morning and evening when evapo-transpiration rates are lower due to cooler
temperatures. These tasks took up to six hours a day depending on the
distance between village and garden sites and the extent of an individual
gardener's holdings.

During the first phase of the boom, the routine absence of women from
family residential compounds was widely criticized. Their husbands claimed
that no good would ever come from the gardens, and that women should

stop neglecting their marital responsibilities. A key complaint stemmed from the fact that women were no longer available to greet guests properly. As one male informant put it:

> Presently you are here talking to me but my wives are not here. They are not doing what is obligatory. If you had found them here, they would have given you water to drink, and perhaps you would need to wash as well. I am now doing . . . what they are supposed to do.[3]

Indeed, the work regime followed by women, extolled by developers as the embodiment of positive maternal values, very quickly became imbued with meanings associated with a failure to meet marital obligations. As one woman described the situation: "Some men, when they are asked about their wives, they will say, 'She is no longer my wife; she has a new husband.'" The phrase, "She's gone to her husband's" (Mandinka: *a taata a ke ya*), used by men to indicate that their wives were not at home, but working in their gardens instead, became a shorthand expression marking women's neglect of marital responsibilities; it demonized gardeners as bad wives.

When asked directly to interpret the metaphor equating gardens with husbands, men and women in the garden districts offered two distinct readings. One interpretation, common among men, reflected the frustrations they confronted in the garden boom, specifically the fact that gardens dominated women's lives to such a degree as the boom took shape that their husbands hardly saw them anymore on a day-to-day basis. According to this interpretation, which was widely acknowledged by gardeners themselves, gardens supplanted husbands' wishes as the primary ordering force in a woman's workday.

> A wife is brought home to fulfill her obligations to her husband. She should be around her husband all the time to render such services. When women are away from home almost the whole day gardening, they do not perform what is required of them. (Gardener's husband)

Vegetable growers "greeted" (*saama*) their gardens (and not their husbands) when they watered their vegetables first thing in the morning;[4] they spent their days "at the side of" their gardens; and they brought their gardens water at dusk, that is, at precisely the time when a man might expect his bath water to be delivered. Consequently, gardeners' marriage partners found themselves increasingly without companionship and forced, by default, to assume new domestic labor responsibilities. This was especially true of older men who had been economically marginalized due to age or ill health and who spent a great deal of time within the spatial confines of the family

Photo 5.1 Second husbands: Gardens in many parts of The Gambia now generate such substantial incomes for women that they have become largely self-sufficient in meeting their own financial needs. (From Richard A. Schroeder, *Shady Practices: Agroforestry and Gender Politics in the Gambia.* Copyright ©1999 The Regents of the University of California. Reproduced with the permission of the University of California Press.)

compound or in its immediate vicinity. Early in the boom, the loss of women's "prestige services" caused a great deal of bitter resentment.

By contrast, women often interpreted the phrase *a taata a ke ya* with an emphasis on the importance of garden earnings in meeting household budgetary obligations. For them, gardens had, for all practical purposes, replaced husbands as the principal source of cash for subsistence and other forms of consumption ("Women are doing what men *should* be doing"). Somewhat sardonically, they maintained that women might just as well have been married to their gardens. One grower underscored the point dramatically by asserting that not just her garden, but the well bucket that she used to irrigate her vegetables, was her husband, because everything she owned came from it:

> This [indicating her dress]; this [her shoes]; this [her earrings]; this [miming the food she put into her mouth]; and this [clutching her breast to indicate the food she fed her children, her voice rising in mock rage as a group of gardeners gathered nearby hooted with laughter]—they all come from this bucket! That's why this bucket [together with the garden] is my husband!!

Clearly, the Mandinka marriage system was placed under significant strain due to the changes accompanying the push toward commercialization. It is equally clear that the rhetorical struggle over marriage and market gardens had as its object the right to occupy the moral high ground vis-à-vis the conjugal contract. A variant saying promoted by men marked women's gardens as their "*second* husbands." Here the rhetoric invoked tensions and resentments that frequently accompany a man's taking of a second *wife*. This discourse reflected the fact that while first marriages are often arranged marriages, second marriages may be undertaken by choice. The usage echoed jealous charges that men give second wives preferential treatment because they consider them prettier and stronger, or because they are more fertile than their older co-wives. In seizing and using the "second husband" metaphor to castigate women, men in garden districts attempted to turn the tables on their wives and assume a superior moral position from which they could wield leverage in the renegotiation of conjugality that almost inevitably ensued.

RAISING THE STAKES

> Before gardening started here, if you saw that your wife had ten *dalasis* you would ask her where she got it. At that time, there was no other source of income for women except their husbands. . . . But nowadays a woman

can save more than two thousand *dalasis* while the husband does not even have ten *dalasis* to his name. So now men cannot ask their wives where they get their money, because of their garden produce.[5]

—Gardener's husband

In the first phase of conflict brought on by the boom, men openly expressed their resentment in pointed references to female shirking and selfishness. Their feelings were also made plain in actions taken by a small minority who forbade their wives to garden, or agitated at the village level to have gardening banned altogether (Schroeder and Watts 1991). In the second phase, men dropped their oppositional rhetoric, became more generally cooperative (cf. Stone, Stone, and Netting 1995), and began exploring ways to benefit personally from the garden boom. Seizing the opportunity, women, accordingly, began a prolonged attempt to win their husbands over and generate the goodwill necessary to sustain production on a more secure basis.

The key to vegetable growers' success in this regard lay in their strategic deployment of garden incomes. For reasons that I explain below, the disposition of garden income was often concentrated in the hands of older women who worked in tandem with their daughters. This is significant, insofar as an older woman's social obligations were likely to be broader than those of a younger woman. In deciding how much of the surplus generated by the work unit would be allocated to each individual member of the group, and what form the compensation would take, the unit leader shaped the complex politics of the horticultural boom. She chose, for example, whether to buy a bag of rice for her daughter and son-in-law's family, pay for the school expenses of a nephew or grandchild, disburse portions of the cash surplus at season's end to each work unit member, give a cash gift to her own husband, or simply keep the funds for herself. In making these choices, the woman accumulated a significant measure of power and prestige, elements that might well have been exclusively enjoyed by her husband or other male relative previously by virtue of their control over the groundnut cash crop.

Rural Gambian households were under significant economic stress in the late 1970s and early 1980s when the boom was initiated. Given the poor market conditions facing the male cash crop sector at the time, many men were forced into what might be called *legitimate default* vis-à-vis their customary obligations to feed or otherwise provision their families. Survey data show that both senior members of garden work units and women working on their own took on many economic responsibilities that were traditionally ascribed to men. Fifty-six percent of the women in a 1991 sample, for example, claimed to have purchased at least one bag of rice for their families.[6] The great majority bought all of their own

Photo 5.2 Reversal of fortunes: For the first time, Mandinka women's cash crop incomes outstrip those of their husbands. (From Richard A. Schroeder, *Shady Practices: Agroforestry and Gender Politics in the Gambia.* Copyright ©1999 The Regents of the University of California. Reproduced with the permission of the University of California Press.)

(95 percent), and their children's (84 percent), clothing, and most of the furnishings for their own houses.[7] Large numbers absorbed ceremonial costs, such as the purchase of feast-day clothing (80 percent), or the provision of animals for religious sacrifice.[8] Many paid for their children's school expenses. And, in a handful of cases, gardeners were responsible for major or unusual expenditures such as the roofing of family compounds, the provision of loans for purchasing draft animals and farming equipment, or payment of the house tax. There is, unfortunately, no baseline data that can be used to gain historical perspective on this information. Nonetheless, several male informants stated unequivocally that, were it not for garden incomes, many of the marriages in the village would simply fail on "non-support" grounds.

One category of income expenditure by gardeners in the 1991 study remains unexplained. Of the women sampled, 38 percent reported undertaking some measure of direct support of their husbands via cash gifts. Typically dispersed in small, regular amounts, these gifts occasionally amounted to hundreds of *dalasis*. Seeking to regain control over their own labor, gardeners used cash gifts to overcome their husbands' resentment and effectively buy their goodwill (see further discussion in Schroeder, 1999). In this regard, the effect of the gifts seemed quite decisive. Witness the following statements of two men married to North Bank gardeners:

> Today no one would say ["she's gone to her husband's."] . . . Every man who is in this village whose wife is engaged in this garden work, the benefit of the produce goes to him first before the wife can even enjoy her share of it. That is why those statements they used to say would not be heard now. . . . In fact some men among us, if it were not for this garden work, their marriages would not last. Because their [own economic] efforts cannot carry one wife, much less two or three, or even four. Women can [now] support themselves. They will buy beds, mattresses, cupboards, rice . . . from the produce of these gardens. . . . In fact I can comfortably say that gardening generates a greater benefit than the peanut crop that we [men] cultivate. Before you offer any help to people farming groundnuts, it is better you help people doing gardening, because we are using gardening to survive.
>
> At the moment, a man cannot get from his groundnut farm what a woman can earn from her garden. Not even two bags of groundnuts in some cases. In the whole of the village, you can [easily] count the number of men who have eight bags [the rough equivalent of D1000]. And out of that [you must subtract] seed [and] fertilizer. . . . it is only the women's sector that contributes greatly at this moment. When this is developed, the men will also develop.

The impression left by these comments is that the choices women made with regard to the disposition of their garden incomes, some motivated by compassion and others by more strategic considerations, met their mark. There is a third possible interpretation of these actions, however. According to some male informants, the disposition of women's garden incomes was not always such a clear-cut matter of *choice*. They pointed out that men also actively pursued opportunities to gain access to their wives' money. In other words, the cash gifts and in-kind contributions women made to their families could also be construed as a *"taking"* by men. This proposition requires closer inspection.

THE PRICE OF AUTONOMY

> They thought we were wasting our time in the bush, but when they realized the benefits they started praying for us.
>
> —North Bank gardener

Open admissions by men in Gambian garden districts that they consciously engaged in maneuvers to gain access to their wives' incomes were understandably quite rare. Those who did divulge information on this topic stressed the difficulty of generalizing about the strategies they were describing, and felt it important to emphasize that men only engaged in such practices when they knew that their wives could afford to share their assets. These caveats notwithstanding, the data shed a great deal of light on the process of negotiation and mutual accommodation precipitated by the boom.

The first set of strategies used by men can be loosely grouped under the heading of "loan-seeking." It consists of several different pretexts under which men asked their wives for money, each with its own degree of commitment toward eventual repayment, and its own threat of reprisal in the event that the funds were not forthcoming. The simplest scenario involved asking for a loan with no intention whatsoever of repayment. In this case, the crucial consideration for the husband was how much to request. If he aimed too high, his request might not be granted because his wife could legitimately say she did not have the means to meet his demands. Also, if she did give him a larger sum, she was much more likely to either insist upon repayment or refuse to grant him an additional loan in the future should he fail to make restitution. The ideal, then, was to ask for a substantial amount, in order to make the request (and its attendant loss of face) worthwhile, but to keep the request small enough so that the eventual financial loss could be absorbed or effectively written off by the woman without retribution. Informants indicated that a request for an amount slightly less than an average week's net earnings would be reasonable in most cases.

After defaulting more than once on repayment, or upon encountering resistance from his wife, a man might ask an intermediary to request the loan on his behalf. There were actually two or three different scenarios in which this might occur. In one, the man's wife realized that the third party was acting as a surrogate. She nonetheless participated in the transaction willingly, since she knew that, in the event of default, she could at least pursue the matter through the traditional court system. She would not consider taking similar recourse in the case of her husband's direct default, however, since the courts often presumed that intra-family loans were used for some form of joint family benefit, and would most likely decide against her.

A second type of loan-seeking via an intermediary often took place under conditions in which the wife was not aware that the loan was actually intended for her husband. This option presented itself when the husband had already exhausted his other more straightforward prospects, or in the event that he was simply too ashamed to ask his wife for cash directly. Since the wife had no knowledge of the fact that her husband would be the end beneficiary of the loan, this option retained the advantages of the first form of "indirect" loan: she more willingly acquiesced to terms because third party loans were more enforceable than direct loans between marriage partners.

Moreover, from the husband's perspective, his prestige was not sacrificed in the process. In practice, however, the husband was still required to meet the terms set by his surrogate for repayment.[9]

One other more casual ploy completes the list of loan-seeking behaviors. This strategy grew out of the regular battle between husbands and wives over everyday petty cash expenditures, or what I will refer to collectively as "fish money." These involved cash outlays for meat, fish, cooking oil, sugar, condiments, matches, candles, flashlight batteries, and laundry soap; in short, all the basic recurrent expenditures of everyday life in rural Gambia. Typically, the woman (or a small child sent on her behalf) would mention to her husband as he was about to leave in the morning that she needed money to buy fish so she could cook lunch. If for some reason she wanted to embarrass him, she might deliberately make the request in the presence of guests. For his part, the husband would then complain that he had no money and ask her to "help" him (*maakoi*) with a small loan so he could make the necessary purchases. The effect of this tactic was that the wife ended up paying out of her resources for something that should have, by custom, been the husband's responsibility.[10]

A woman's failure to provide a loan or pick up everyday expenses could result in a variety of sanctions being imposed upon her. Most common were the quarrels men initiated with their wives in order to raise the stakes in money matters. The basic strategy was for the husband to carefully select a pretext for picking a fight with his wife. As my informants explained it, the husband should not act immediately after the loan request was denied; nor, however, should he wait too long after the loan denial lest the meaning of his action be obscured altogether. My informants provided two hypothetical examples. In the first, the husband decides to return home unannounced from a firewood cutting expedition, or a hard day of work on the family's fields. He arrives at a time when he knows his wife is either in her garden, or has yet to draw the evening water supply from the town tap (in the village in question, the public taps were routinely closed between 10 A.M. and 5 P.M.). He then demands to know why there is no bath water waiting for him, complaining: "I came from the farm very tired and dirty, and this woman wouldn't even help me with bath water!" In the second scenario, he intervenes to chastise his wife as she reprimands one of his children for some obvious infraction: "How can you be so cruel to your daughter!"

A third scenario, an example of which actually occurred on the North Bank in 1991, involved a more extreme form of reprisal. As described by a group of women gardeners, a domestic dispute took place during the month of Ramadan, when practicing Muslims are expected to fast from sunrise to sundown. A row broke out at 6 A.M., when a man beat his wife, ostensibly because she failed to provide him with water to perform the pre-dawn ablutions that mark the opening of the day's fast. The women recounting the incident roundly condemned the man because they were convinced that the real motive behind the beating was retribution after the man's wife refused to honor a loan request.

It should be apparent from these examples that choosing a pretext for a fight in the context of the garden boom was a simple matter. With women routinely absent from family compounds, and cutting corners in order to juggle competing demands on their time, men were in a position to selectively invoke the abrogation of any number of traditional norms governing marriage relationships. The message, in any event, was quite clear: women who did not comply with requests for cash and acquiesce in the niceties of the loan-seeking charade were forced to pay a different sort of price. The number of beatings and shouting matches did not have to be terribly high before this point sank in.[11]

To be sure, the tactics men used to alienate garden income did not always poison social relations in this manner. Indeed, my informants produced a short list of strategies with the opposite effect, which they placed under the general heading of "sweetness" (*diya*). In the first hypothetical circumstance they mentioned, the husband is exceedingly nice to his wife—what might be called in English, "buttering her up." He supports her positions in public discussion, and acts as an advocate on her behalf on matters of substance having to do with her garden.[12] Alternatively, he might offer material support by (1) contributing labor; (2) lending her his donkey cart;[13] or (3) providing a small cash loan. He thus places himself in a position to benefit from his wife's good graces when she decides how to spend her garden earnings.

The final set of strategies employed by men seeking to control their wives' money entailed decisions over the disposition of their own cash crop returns. I have already alluded to the fact that men routinely defaulted on the financial obligations they were expected to fulfill ("If you tell your husband to buy you a shirt or a pair of shoes, he will say you are crazy, I have more important things to do"). Much of this behavior can justifiably be attributed to the generalized economic hardship that accompanied the economic trends of the 1980s. Above and beyond such "legitimate" default circumstances, however, were steps taken by men to *deliberately* default on their responsibilities. This they accomplished by quickly disposing of their own cash assets before the exigencies of everyday life ("fish money," third party loans) absorbed them.

The key consideration for a man in such circumstances was to choose an investment target that met with the tacit approval of his wife or wives. Examples of expenditures that would be fully sanctioned include the purchase of corrugated zinc "pan" or concrete for a construction project in the family living quarters, the acquisition of a horse or donkey or additional animal traction equipment for farming purposes, and the payment of costs associated with ceremonial occasions such as circumcisions or dependents' marriages. Likewise, investment in a seasonal petty trading venture was largely beyond reproach on the grounds that some joint benefit could potentially be derived from the income generated by the husband's sales efforts. Far less welcome was the purchase of luxury items such as a new radio, fancier furniture for the husband's personal living quarters, or expensive clothing. A woman's reaction to her husband spending money on other women depended on the circumstances. A middle-aged woman without a co-wife might not object strongly to her husband marrying again since she stood to benefit from sharing her domestic workload. However, when the husband already had more than one wife, and his money from groundnut sales or salary payments provided little or no apparent joint benefit, the women often rightly assumed that he was squandering his money on gifts to girlfriends, perhaps the most "illegitimate" expenditure of all. This and other deliberate default practices were not only frowned upon by women, but were actively resisted, as the next section demonstrates.

BUYING POWER

The description of men's budgetary tactics I have compiled establishes that women did not simply buy their husbands' goodwill outright. Men pushed their advantages wherever they could to shift the balance of economic power in the household (back) in their favor. Men were not in a position to leverage their wives' consumption choices at will, however. Indeed, there was considerable evidence that women were firmly resolved to protect their interests, as the following quotation demonstrates:

Our husbands stopped buying soap, oil, rice. . . . We provide all these things. Obviously our marriages would change. We do all this work while our husbands lie around home doing nothing. Whenever we return from gardening, we still have to do all the cooking, and all our husbands can say is, "Isn't dinner ready yet?" And then they start to shout at us. Remember, this is after we have already spent the whole day at the garden working. . . . A husband who has nothing to give to his wife—if that wife gets something from her own labor, she will surely find it more difficult to listen to him. We women are only afraid of God the Almighty. Otherwise we wouldn't marry men at all. We would have left them by themselves. . . . Men are always instructing us, you better do this or that for me, while they sit at the *bantaba* [the neighborhood meeting place] all day doing nothing. They describe us as foolish, but we are not, and we will not listen to them. (North Bank gardener)

Women used several different strategies to protect their cash incomes. The most basic was for a woman to prevent her husband from ever knowing how much cash she had on hand in the first place. This required that she adopt a "false face" of sorts within the family compound (Pred 1990; Scott 1990), as though she were not engaged in a complex, year-round production system involving perhaps a dozen different crops, grown in three or four sometimes far-flung locations, each generating its own seasonal pattern of income. In order to create and maintain this fiction, women rarely discussed garden matters with, or in the presence of, their husbands. This resolute silence stood in sharp contrast to the running discussion and debates women engaged in along the footpaths to and from, and in, the gardens themselves. A veritable stream of information concerning prices available at the different North Bank market outlets (*lumoolu*) was exchanged as women moved about and tended to their crops.

Many gardeners hid their income through the use of intermediaries to carry produce to market on their behalf. Survey results showed that well over half of the women in my research sample relied at least occasionally on someone else to carry produce to market for them. Others shipped produce to market directly from garden sites. In this way, their husbands were prevented from actually seeing the produce assembled in one place, which would have allowed them to develop a clearer sense of how much their wives actually earned. Women also sequestered their savings in such a way that they could not be touched by their husbands. This they accomplished in a literal sense by wearing "money belts" on a regular basis. With respect to larger cash sums, money was commonly given to older female relatives or trusted neighbors for management and safekeeping. In one village, for example, gardeners opened up savings accounts with a local shopkeeper (cf. Shipton 1995). Parallel records were kept by the shopkeeper and a trusted local civil servant indicating running balances in individual accounts. Assets were thus protected from seizure by the merchant, who was held accountable by the civil servant. At the same time, the shopkeeper paid no interest and was free to use the cash to capitalize his business or engage in money-lending. In exchange, women benefited from keeping their assets relatively liquid without exposing the extent of their accumulation directly to husbands.

Even with such diversionary tactics in force, the peak of the marketing season almost inevitably brought with it increased "loan-seeking" behavior on the part of men. Consequently, the second major area of attention for women concerned controlling the terms under which loan agreements were undertaken. Thus, if a woman's husband repeatedly defaulted on loans, she often chose to stop granting him loans altogether. Alternatively, she waited for, or insisted upon, the intervention of a third party in the loan transaction.

Photo 5.3 Discretionary income: Many men resent the fact that women gardeners can now afford to purchase personal items such as radios, jewlery, clothing, etc. (From Richard A. Schroeder, *Shady Practices: Agroforestry and Gender Politics in the Gambia.* Copyright ©1999 The Regents of the University of California. Reproduced with the permission of the University of California Press.)

Nyack College Library

In the relatively rare event that this failed to generate the desired outcome of a reasonable repayment rate, the woman might choose the risky route of public disclosure. Airing the dirty laundry of intra-marital finances was, however, a virtual invitation to divorce; moreover, the messiness of such a scandal would almost certainly damage the woman's reputation along with her husband's. Such a course was, nonetheless, at times preferable to enduring the repeated predatory demands of a greedy husband. An alternate tack involved the woman trying to strategically pre-empt her husband's loan requests by giving him cash gifts before he even asked for them. Such gifts constituted an attempt to carry out an increasingly obligatory transfer of assets under terms that the woman herself controlled: rather than suffer the whims of her husband, the woman determined both the amount and the timing of the gift, thus inoculating herself against unexpected and exorbitant loan requests that ran the risk of disrupting personal plans at inopportune moments.

Finally, when all else failed, women simply opted for the solution widely employed by their husbands—they tied up their cash assets by spending them as quickly as they received them:

> What happens is, some men would like their wives to loan them some money out of their garden sales. Many times women will grant the requests, but most of them will never be refunded. So women gradually limit, or refuse, credit to their husbands. We have a new tactic: when we go to market [with our produce], we simply spend all our money on things that we need, and come home with no money at all, to avoid the loan requests altogether. (North Bank gardener)

Among the items women bought under such circumstances were dowry items, such as dishes or pieces of cloth, for their daughters. While some of the men interviewed bitterly criticized their wives for assembling overly lavish trousseaus for their daughters, this tactic was at times a woman's direct response to her husband's own profligate spending habits. In cases where deliberate default was mutual, the family's financial security was obviously placed in jeopardy, and the marriage itself rested on quite shaky ground.

CONCLUSION

The Gambian garden boom produced dramatic changes in the normative expectations and practices of marital partners in the country's garden districts. In the context of climatic change, new foreign investment patterns, and structural economic adjustment (Schroeder 1999), the growth of a female cash crop sector virtually inverted the economic fortunes of rural men and women in many areas. As a partial consequence, men withdrew key financial support from their families. At the same time, the rigors of a double-crop (rainy/dry season) rice and vegetable production regime forced women to either default on, or otherwise finesse, a variety of domestic labor obligations. In short, both men and women responded to the garden boom in ways that led to a significant reconfiguration of customary marriage practices (cf. Carney and Watts 1990).

Discursive politics played a prominent role in the negotiations that accompanied those changes. The wielding of marital metaphors as weapons in a battle to seize and/or regain the moral high ground resulted in something of a stand-off: men used the charge that women had "gone to their husband's" to force their wives to transfer control of at least a portion of their assets or face continued verbal assault. Women gardeners, in turn, appropriated the metaphor to underscore the perpetual failure of their husbands to provide for their families, and used it to help win for themselves the freedoms necessary to complete their gardening tasks successfully. In short, the notion that women were "gone to their husband's" encapsulated the mutual default of *both* marriage partners on customary responsibilities.

Generalizing on societies with "a pronounced division into male and female spheres," Jane Guyer notes that "the specialization [of budgetary responsibilities] is never complete; it oscillates according to each sex's ability to cope with its own sphere, and its ability to tap into the other or to shift the responsibilities" (Guyer 1988: 171–72). The "ability to cope" in rural Gambia was directly tied to the capacity of individuals to earn cash incomes, and thereby to the respective fortunes of the separate crop production systems. These fortunes varied widely by household; they also hinged on factors such as climate and international market perturbations that were well beyond local control. By contrast, the "ability to tap into" another sphere or "shift responsibilities" was directly related to the localized power dynamics that took shape in the garden districts. These had to do with moral economic forces, strategies of deception, and the tactics of marital negotiation concerning property, income, and power relations.

Since "coping" strategies and ruses designed to shift responsibilities were in play at all times, it is extremely difficult, from an analytical standpoint, to prize the two apart. Negotiations over cash transfers between men and women became—quite literally—give and take situations. Loans were loans until men stopped paying them back. Then they either became "cash gifts," as described above, or the source of more serious struggles that led to divorce. By a similar token, gardens were "husbands" that controlled women's labor, until they became "husbands" that provided food for women's families. Such ambiguity inflects a final reading of women's "autonomy" in the context of the garden boom. While there is evidence that acts of accommodation undertaken by women on the North Bank softened the rhetorical stance their husbands once took against gardening, the achievement of this accommodation "plateau" did not alleviate the pressure on women entirely. They were still required to meet a rigorous set of financial obligations: not only were they forced to contend with the domestic financial squeeze engineered by their husbands, but they did so under the pressure of surplus extraction from traders and truck drivers. This double bind was exacerbated in drought years when the irrigated vegetable crop became one of the few bastions against generalized food shortage and extreme economic hardship.

The price of autonomy notwithstanding, women in The Gambia's garden districts succeeded in producing a striking new social landscape—by embracing the challenges of the garden boom, they placed themselves in a position to carefully extricate themselves from some of the more onerous demands of marital obligations. Indeed, in a very real sense, they won for themselves "second husbands" by insisting that the rules governing the conjugal contract be rewritten. Thus the product of lengthy intra-household negotiations brought on by the garden boom was not the simple reproduction of patriarchal privilege and prestige; it was instead a new, carefully crafted autonomy that carried with it obligations and considerable social freedoms.

NOTES

I would like to acknowledge the following funding sources for providing generous support during fieldwork: the Fulbright-Hays Doctoral Dissertation Research Award, the Social Science Research Council/American Council of Learned Societies International Doctoral Dissertation Research Fellowship for Africa, the Rocca Memorial Scholarship for Advanced African Studies, and the National Science Foundation Fellowship in Geography and Regional Science. Special thanks to Dorothy Hodgson, Sheryl McCurdy, Marjorie Mbilinyi, Susan Geiger, and Jane Guyer who read the manuscript and offered advice and encouragement.

1. Kabeer (1994: chapter 5) provides an excellent review of the literature devoted to "maternal altruism."

2. The industrious work habits of market gardeners also perfectly matched developers' agendas to promote entrepreneurism in remote corners of Africa. Judging from the inflow of capital directed at "gender equity"–oriented projects, including the $16.5 million invested in the Jahally-Pacharr rice project (Carney 1988), and a five-year (1990–94), $15.1 million Women in Development Project—at the time of its establishment, the only "free-standing" WID project in the world funded by the World Bank—it is clear that ideologically motivated gender programming was highly lucrative turf in The Gambia during this period. Indeed, struggles over the rights to control WID-oriented developmental largesse were being waged at all levels, from the level of individual marriages up to that of nationwide projects (Schroeder 1993, 1995; Carney 1992).

3. At least one North Bank community banned gardening altogether in the mid-1980s because of the irritation men felt at losing this highly symbolic service from their wives (Schroeder and Watts 1991).

4. It is a traditional sign of deference for a woman to go to her husband's sleeping quarters first thing in the morning and greet him with a curtsy before going about her daily affairs. This is especially the case when a large age differential exists between marital partners. Women interviewed on this topic admitted that garden work sometimes interfered with this practice: "Yes, it's true because a man may go [to the mosque] for dawn prayers and continue on some errands in the village. Before he comes back home, the wife may leave for the garden without seeing him." In most cases, however, women went out of their way to continue performing this highly symbolic gesture. A pattern of shift work evolved between women and their daughters in order to accommodate these emotionally charged demands (Schroeder 1995, 1999; cf. Clark 1994).

5. The Gambian *dalasi* was exchanged at a rate of D7.35=$1.00 in 1991 when these remarks were recorded.

6. This was a substantial contribution. Prices for rice were in the neighborhood of D200 per bag on the North Bank in 1991. By comparison, the annual rural per capita income in the Gambia as a whole was roughly D1500 and the average income for gardeners in my research sample was D1096.

7. Husbands and wives in the Mandinka-speaking communities where this research was conducted commonly occupy separate living quarters. Women sleep with their husbands on a rotational basis with other co-wives; typically a rotation lasts for two days and nights, during which time the wife "on duty" also cooks and cleans for her husband.

8. In an informal survey conducted in 1989 of mostly well-to-do gardeners, eight of thirty-five women surveyed had purchased the ram or goat for that year's major Islamic feast day of *Taboski (Id ul Kabir)*.

9. A variation on the strategy of loan-seeking via an intermediary occurred when a third party, typically a junior family member, or even a child, first approached the *husband* for a loan. In this situation, the man simply referred the would-be loan recipient to one of his wives. ("Presently if any child asks his/her father to buy anything for him/her, he will say to that child, 'go to your mother.'") It is worth noting that whether or not the husband had cash of his own at the time of the request was not necessarily an issue. Indeed, if he *did* have cash on hand his objective in diverting the loan request might revolve around that fact precisely: his aim was to protect his personal assets and shift the loan burden onto his wife's shoulders.

10. These sorts of domestic budgetary battles did not originate with the garden boom; nor were they unique to The Gambia (cf. Guyer 1988).

11. There is in fact little evidence that the incidence of domestic violence has risen since the onset of the garden boom. If anything, it may have declined. See the discussion of "sweetness" below.

12. For example, some men were instrumental in helping their wives negotiate access to land.

13. The loan of a donkey or ox cart was not an insignificant gesture. Since men controlled virtually all animal traction resources in The Gambia, vegetable growers would otherwise have been forced to carry hundreds of kilos of produce by headpan a kilometer or more to the village. Many women without the benefit of *diya* did so anyway.

REFERENCES

Carney, Judith. "Struggles over Crop Rights and Labour within Contract Farming House-holds in a Gambian Irrigated Rice Project." *Journal of Peasant Studies* 15, 3 (1988), 334–349.

———. "Peasant Women and Economic Transformation in The Gambia." *Development and Change* 23, 2 (1992), 67–90.

Carney, Judith and Michael Watts. "Manufacturing Dissent: Work, Gender and the Politics of Meaning in a Peasant Society." *Africa* 60, 2 (1990), 207–241.

Clark, Gracia. *Onions Are My Husband: Survival and Accumulation by West African Market Women.* Chicago: University of Chicago Press, 1994.

Dwyer, Daisy and Judith Bruce, eds. *A Home Divided: Women and Income in the Third World.* Stanford, CA: Stanford University Press, 1988.

Guyer, Jane. "Dynamic Approaches to Domestic Budgeting: Cases and Methods from Africa." In Daisy Dwyer and Judith Bruce, eds., *A Home Divided: Women and Income in the Third World,* 155–172. Stanford, CA: Stanford University Press, 1988.

Guyer, Jane and Pauline Peters, eds. "Special Issue: Conceptualizing the Household: Theory and Policy in Africa." *Development and Change* 18, 2 (1987).

Kabeer, Naila. *Reversed Realities: Gender Hierarchies in Development Thought.* New York: Verso, 1994.

Pred, Allan. "In Other Wor(l)ds: Fragmented and Integrated Observations on Gendered Languages, Gendered Spaces and Local Transformation." *Antipode* 22, 1 (1990), 33–52.

Schoonmaker-Freudenberger, Karen. "L'Intégration en Faveur des Femmes et des Enfants: Une Evaluation des Projets Régionaux Intégrés Soutenus par le Gouvernment du Sénégal et UNICEF." Unpublished report. UNICEF, Dakar, Senegal, 1991.

Schroeder, Richard. "Shady Practice: Gender and the Political Ecology of Resource Stabilization in Gambian Garden/Orchards." *Economic Geography* 69, 4 (1993), 349–365.

———. "Contradictions along the Commodity Road to Environmental Stabilization: Foresting Gambian Gardens." *Antipode* 27, 4 (1995), 325–342.

———. *Shady Practices: Agroforestry and Gender Politics in The Gambia.* Berkeley: University of California Press, 1999.

Schroeder, Richard and Krisnawati Suryanata. "Gender and Class Power in Agroforestry: Case Studies from Indonesia and West Africa." In Richard Peet and Michael Watts, eds., *Liberation Ecologies: Environment, Development, Social Movements,* 188–204. London: Routledge, 1996.

Schroeder, Richard and Michael Watts. "Struggling over Strategies, Fighting over Food: Adjusting to Food Commercialization among Mandinka Peasants in The Gambia." In Harry Schwarzweller and Daniel Clay, eds., *Research in Rural Sociology and Development: Vol. 5, Household Strategies,* 45–72. Greenwich, CT: JAI Press, 1991.

Scott, James. *Domination and the Arts of Resistance: Hidden Transcripts.* New Haven, CT: Yale University Press, 1990.

Shipton, Parker. "How Gambians Save: Cultural and Economic Strategy at an Ethnic Crossroads." In Jane Guyer, ed., *Money Matters: Instability, Values and Social*

Payments in the Modern History of West African Communities, 245–276. Portsmouth, NH: Heinemann, 1995.

Stichter, Sharon and Jane Parpart, eds., *Patriarchy and Class: African Women in the Home and the Workforce*. Boulder, CO: Westview Press, 1988.

Stone, M. Priscilla, Glenn Stone, and Robert Netting. "The Sexual Division of Labor in Kofyar Agriculture." *American Ethnologist* 22, 1 (1995), 165–186.

Thiesen, Albert, S. Jallow, John Nittler, and Dominique Philippon. "African Food Systems Initiative, Project Document." United States Peace Corps, Banjul, The Gambia, 1989.

Watts, Michael. "The Agrarian Crisis in Africa: Debating the Crisis." *Progress in Human Geography* 13, 1 (1989), 1–42.

Whitehead, Ann. "'I'm Hungry Mum': The Politics of Domestic Budgeting." In Kate Young, Carol Wolkowitz, and Roslyn McCullagh, eds., *Of Marriage and the Market: Women's Subordination in International Perspective*, 88–111. London: CSE Books, 1981.

PART II:

CONFRONTING AUTHORITY

6

DANCING WOMEN AND COLONIAL MEN: THE *NWAOBIALA* OF 1925

Misty L. Bastian

INTRODUCTION: THE (SELECTIVE) FORGETTING OF 1925

In a 1925 memo to the Owerri Province (Nigeria) Resident, entitled "Women's Purity Campaign,"[1] Kenneth Cochrane, then District Officer of Bende, reported a face-to-face confrontation with "several hundred" *Nwaobiala* dancers in the market town of Umuahia. The women had caused a series of disturbances in the area, beginning with the stripping of young women in the marketplace and continuing with the seizure of property belonging to Christian women and some unspecified men. Cochrane presided over several court cases resulting from the property seizures and fined the assembled women accordingly. Although he did not think they took their fines "seriously," he was content to write to his superior that the "Women's Purity Campaign" was no real threat to the government and should be treated as a civil matter rather than as a wholesale breach of the peace.

Four years later this same Kenneth Cochrane claimed, before a commission of inquiry set up to investigate the more widespread "Aba Riots" or Women's War (*Ogu Umunwaanyi*) of 1929, that Igbo and other southeastern women had never before made such a demonstration (Aba Commission 1930: 157). Since the early 1930s, there has been a similar selective forgetting of the *Nwaobiala* in the face of the more famous subsequent events of the Women's War. When it is mentioned, the *Nwaobiala* is quickly dismissed as a "prequel" to the *Ogu Umunwaanyi*, yet I would argue that the *Nwaobiala* was a more important event, with greater consequence, than either the colonial men who knew of it and forgot it, or the academics who followed them, have previously believed.[2] This chapter will not only show how the *Nwaobiala* was historically grounded but also that it is a mistake to differentiate the *Nwaobiala* completely from the Women's War that followed it.

Since most of what we know about the *Nwaobiala* comes from colonial documents, it might appear that any project seeking to explicate the movement fully is doomed to failure because of partialities set down sixty years ago by male colonial bureaucrats as they recorded southeastern Nigerian women's activities. I use these colonial documents, however, to explore the elusive quality of the dancers' alterity and to ask why it was so easy to forget that certain "others" (in this case resisting women) existed, until they returned in greater force and spoke in a language that colonial officialdom (perhaps incorrectly) recognized.

"CALLING MEN BULL DOGS": THE INEXPLICABLE IN OKIGWE, 1925

A Miraculous or Monstrous Birth

British official sources agree that the *Nwaobiala* began with a "miraculous birth" before October of 1925, somewhere near Atta in Okigwe district. The documents are otherwise silent on its beginning. Because the colonial administration did not inquire too closely into this miraculous birth, or because the details were not considered important enough for inclusion in the record, this is the extent of our information on how the *Nwaobiala* started. It does not, however, necessarily represent the extent of our potential knowledge. Inadvertently, the women dancers deposited a clue about the birth in the archives: their movement had a name.

Although the colonialists themselves repeatedly named the events of 1925—"Dancing Women's Movement," "Women's Purity Campaign," "Market Riots," and even "Anti-Government Propaganda" in Abakaliki— they recorded only two names that the women dancers gave themselves or their dance: *Nwaobiala* or *Obanjili*. The first carries the clue about the miraculous birth mentioned above; the second is most often ignored.[3] *Nwaobiala* could mean several things. Since British colonial convention was to ignore tone in Igbo orthography, it is impossible to say with absolute certainty what the term meant to the dancers in 1925. It seems to me that the term might be divided into three words: *nwa obi ala.*[4] This phrase can be translated as "child from the heart/center of Ala (the land)," or "child from the compound of Ala," depending on the tone of *obi*. Ala is the earth deity, also known in Igbo as Ani. Ala/Ani is represented throughout Igbo-speaking areas as female, and she is one of the most important Igbo deities. Ala/Ani is spoken of in general terms as the land. However, every village group in the Igbo-speaking southeast also has a shrine to the *ala/ani/ana* on which it stands. These shrines serve as foci for the local veneration of the land.

During the early colonial period, Igbo-speaking women owed purificatory duties to the more general aspect of the deity. In some areas women were responsible for the ritual opening and cleaning of pathways between villages or between villages and "bush" shrines. In other areas, like riverine Onitsha, women moved across the landscape with torches lit from their cooking fires, symbolically burning away the impurities or pollution (*alu*) that had accumulated over the course of a year (Henderson 1972: 403). Ala/Ani was called upon by women in their most intimate travail as well.

Ala/Ani was thought to contribute form (*onunu*) to the newborn child, just as other forces contributed other aspects of its physical being and personhood. Among contemporary Igbo-speakers who otherwise profess Christianity, children who are too perfectly formed or children who suffer deformity from birth are still associated with the earth deity, and these precautions may be taken as signs of her special notice. The earth's pleasure might be expressed by extreme beauty of form, but most cases I heard of during field studies were concerned with Ala/Ani's displeasure, and her punishment of the bodies of human beings whose parents had transgressed certain prohibitions. Children born with teeth or with too many (or too few) digits, for example, were said to be signs of the land's anger.[5] The "miraculous" birth of 1925 was thus probably seen as a portent sent from the earth to warn people of their transgressions.

The reaction to this warning took a familiar, indigenous form: Igbo-speaking women's long-established and public practice of "making" *egwu* (songs/dances). *Egwu* performances were used, prior to 1925, to shame local male authorities as well as to give voice to women's communal grievances and demands. Men did not usually take part in the creation of women's *egwu*—just as women did not overtly interfere with the political oratory of men. These songs/dances were formulated, practiced, and polished during women-only meetings and unveiled at public events like markets or town festivals. New *egwu* circulated by means of these performances, where nonparticipant women watched and learned the latest movements, words, and tunes.[6]

Although the British and subsequent Igbo historians have suggested that the women's movement might have been influenced by men, it seems rather unlikely. The lists of demands made during the *Nwaobiala* often ran counter to the interests of male authority, a fact recognized by at least some colonial administrators and "native authorities." The archives contain enough information on the *egwu* for a brief analysis that is female and locally centered rather than male-directed or provoked from outside. We must turn now to these documents for a view of women's interests and desires in 1925.

Sweeping up Pollution

Although existing descriptions of the *Nwaobiala egwu* are not detailed, colonial officials did collect lists of demands and noted the dancers' movement through southern Okigwe and Bende divisions into towns as far north as Enugu. The British first began to notice what they called bands of dancing women in November 1925, although later investigation showed that the movement was well underway in Okigwe during October. The bands would suddenly appear in a town, usually in the marketplace, and announce their presence by a prolonged and ritualized sweeping of public spaces. While sweeping pathways, market spaces, and shrines in the town, the women would evidently gather information from curious observers about the residences of important elders, warrant chiefs, and other colonially affiliated men.

It is not clear if local women would participate in this first sweeping, but it seems likely that they would gather to ascertain the identity of the strange sweepers. The purificatory symbolism of the dancers' actions was no doubt obvious to the women of the targeted town. Sweeping was (and still is) a quintessentially female task among Igbo-speaking peoples, often the first chore a young girl is assigned to do. During the 1920s, it was an integral part of Igbo women's daily routine within the marital compound, as well as an important part of their annual rituals of land purification. Igbo-speakers in this period used a hand broom that required them to bend at the waist, coming into closer contact with the ground than was allowed by long-handled Western brooms. This close-to-the-ground sweeping is one of the few motions we can connect with any surety to the *Nwaobiala egwu*. Sweeping thus associated the women dancers intimately with the ground/land, the material representation of the deity their song/dance's name evoked.

The first movement across the town landscape out of the marketplace was important and must be seen as part of the *egwu* itself. *Nwaobiala* dancers arrived in the central women's public space, the *afia* (market), and proceeded to work their way, sweeping, through most of the other exterior spaces of the town. Any town's market was a central gathering spot, used for age grade, rotating credit association, and other meetings as well as for buying and selling. The market was also a primary locus for the announcement of news and grievances. Women who came into the market were considered to be under the protection of the ritual market peace and should not be molested or physically harmed. Breaking the market peace was *nso ani* (an abomination against the earth).

Partially because the town's major shrine to Ala/Ani was within or on the fringe of the marketplace, the deity was thought to watch that space closely. The *Nwaobiala* dancers thus began their *egwu* by making a complex symbolic statement with their movements as well as their verbal displays. They associated themselves and their song/dance in one gesture, the sweeping of the marketplace, with the market peace, the earth deity, women's "useful" trading activities, and their purificatory responsibilities. All of these were aspects of female authority and power within Igbo-speaking towns, rarely invoked beyond calls to the earth for protection or revenge. By bringing these markers of female authority together in the first movement of their *egwu*, the dancing women represented themselves to their potential audience as agents of that authority.

Moving out from the market space into the *ama* (pathways) that fed into the market from all parts of the town, *Nwaobiala* participants signaled an engagement with the town as a whole by taking on purificatory duties usually reserved for townspeople. They may have seemed like spirits mysteriously appearing there, as spirits reputedly still do in Igbo marketplaces. Coming out of that special space, evoking its divine protection, and brandishing brooms, the bands of dancers must have appeared formidable. Indeed, after some district officers forbade the dance, their orders were "ignorned" [*sic*], and the local people excused themselves to the British "by saying they were afraid."[7]

It is possible that this sweeping *egwu* was meant as a representation of widespread and problematic pollution in Igbo areas during the mid-1920s. Under more ordinary conditions, it would be unusual for strangers coming out of the market to cleanse the public lands of a town. That was usually the task of those women who had married exogamously into local lineages, in their social personae as wives and mothers of the town. The sight of unknown women performing the intimate ritual work of the town must have mobilized townswomen to learn more about the reasons behind such an implied insult to their work. Perhaps they took up their own brooms to uphold town honor. The archival records are silent on whether the dancers sang or spoke to their observers during this ritual activity, but there can be little doubt that their actions drew attention. Offhand comments in the records reveal that some townswomen joined the dancers when they began the next stage of the *egwu*, the visit to chiefly or other male elders' residences.

The dancers' visits ultimately drew the attention of colonial officials, since they involved local men selected for positions of authority under Lugardian policies of indirect rule. After discovering where the warrant chiefs were housed, the *Nwaobiala* "band" would enter those compounds and begin another song/dance. The Assistant District Officer of Awgu, A. Niven, described this scene: "[They] proceeded to sweep and clean [the chief's] compound, as compound cleanliness is not customary in this division this not only caused an impression but also gave the neighborhood time to assemble, then the dance began."[8] Niven's editorial comment about compound cleanliness may be sarcastic, but it tells us something about colonial disregard of Igbo-speaking women's daily activities; which, in turn, tells us something about how women's organizational abilities could be so inexplicable to Niven and his colleagues.

To those administrators who did not take a very serious view of the proceedings, the *Nwaobiala* represented purity (meaning chastity) and its Victorian handmaiden, sanitation. K.A.B. Cochrane, who would deny that southeastern women were known for their organization in 1930, interpreted the entire *Nwaobiala* movement as a call to arms over prostitution: "It is realised that the diseases caused by prostitution are decreasing fecundity."[9] Cochrane did not speculate on why women would carry out a movement against prostitution by sweeping markets and other village spaces.

Sweeping was clearly viewed as incidental to this "Anti-Government Propaganda" by colonial authorities, even though its presence was dutifully noted in the memoranda. In the male-dominated, servant-filled world inhabited by British colonial officials, any domestic task was, by definition, mundane and unidimensional, worth little consideration. Nor did this literal-mindedness end with sweeping; Cochrane and his colleagues also extended it to their interpretations of the women's *egwu* within local authorities' compounds.

Unlike the British male administrators of the 1920s, however, I want to query this sweeping *egwu* further. Although groups of townswomen were required to sweep the public spaces as a purificatory gesture, they would have been unlikely, under normal circumstances, to enter the space associated with patrilineality and assert purificatory claims over it. Van Allen's (1976: 61) description of the Igbo practice of "sitting on a man" informs us that women used their pounding sticks, which were also domestic implements, against men who displeased them, but she does not note any use of brooms.

The women belonging, by birth or marriage, to a particular patrilineage's compound were the only people who would sweep it, even during the annual purification rituals. It was unheard of for women unattached to the patrilineage, or to the village-group, to enter these privatized spaces and clean them, much less set up the ground for an uninvited *egwu* there. Women from outside might come to any town's market, but they would not presume to enter the town's compounds without permission, especially if they had a grudge against the compound owners. Intervillage cases were more likely to

Photo 6.1 A well-to-do young Igbo woman of the 1910s. (From D. Amaury Talbot, *Woman's Mysteries of a Primitive People*. London: Cassell & Co., 1915. Also in edition reprinted by Cass, 1968.)

be settled on a neutral battlefield, in some area between the disputing towns, than by disturbing the privacy of particular compound spaces.

Following the women's *egwu* from its initial appearance in the marketplace, to its unusual sweeping of village public spaces, to its outright threatening sweeping of lineage spaces, we can trace a progression of the dance inward toward the very center of town life. *Nwaobiala* dancers seemed to be demonstrating how the need for purification could not be contained; how the contagion spread from the loci of public interaction into those most privatized places where powerful men held sway over their relations. By sweeping warrant chiefs' compounds, the dancers established their control over the space, as well as over those inhabiting the space. However, as anyone who has ever swept a floor knows, this represents only a temporary mastery. The broom offers only interim success in the war against dirt. The same was evidently true of the *Nwaobiala*'s compound sweeping: women took over the space, advised men, and made demands of them for a brief interlude before disappearing again, always on a note that assured the male audience of the potential for a stronger sanction. Sweeping was a prelude—a stirring up of the dust—for the identification of pollution. The actual songs women sang and danced to spoke directly to that pollution and its sources.

"Songs Which Might Not Be Considered Too Correct"

Colonial officials interested in identifying the sources of "Anti-Government Propaganda" took special care to collect information about *Nwaobiala* songs. The following lists provide the most detailed material in the archival record on the *Nwaobiala*. Assistant District Officer Niven provided the Senior Resident in Onitsha with what appears to be the most complete list of the women's complaints and demands (Nigerian National Archives, Enugu [NNAE] M. P. 62/1925). There is another list (NNAE, M. P. No. 18/1926), collected from dancers at some unknown location and apparently translated by an indigenous clerk at the District Office in Onitsha, that adds some intriguing information to Niven's memo. These lists appear below:

1. That they were sent by Chineke (God) to deliver this message and that it would help women to bear children.
2. That no dirt was to be allowed in houses and compounds and more sanitary cleanliness to be observed.
3. That no nuisance should be committed in [a] compound or under breadfruit trees or palm tree lest the falling fruit be contaminated.
4. That all the old roads were to be cleaned and reopened.
5. That old customs should be observed and not allowed to lapse.
6. That no girls or young married women should wear cloth until they were with first child, but go naked as in old days. (At Achi the "dancers" had actually torn the cloths off some girls they met.)
7. That men should not plant cassava but leave this as women's perquisite and that cassava should not be mixed with yams in the farms and that Aro coco yams (the big pointed leaved colocasia) should not be planted at all.
8. That women with child should not eat coco yams[,] cassava or stock fish as these resulted in birth of twins.
9. That poor men were often punished in native courts at instance of rich men, all cases in which poor men were concerned as defendants should be tried at chief's [*sic*] houses and only taken to native court if unsatisfactory. (It was obvious that people were not clear as to what this meant.)
10. Free born to marry free born and slave slave [;] Christian to marry Christian, pagan pagan.

11. In paying dowries for wives the amount should not be too much but brass rods or other native currency should be used for the first payment in preference to cash money.

12. More honesty should be shown in dowry disputes when stating amounts paid or claimed (very desirable).

13. Women should not charge too much for their services as prostitutes (from Lokpanta via Ngoda and Amuda in Okigwe district) and married women should be allowed to have intercourse with other men without being liable to be taken [to] the Native Courts.

14. That the message should be passed on at once to four other chiefs always in a Northerly direction.

15. That all chiefs visited must expect to be called to Okigwe soon to interview "Chineke" (God) personally.

16. The chiefs visited to dash the women dancers a goat or 10/-.

17. Fowls and cassava[,] eggs and other native produce to be sold in markets at fixed price (The price fixed varied from 3d. [for] fowls at Achi to 1/6 in other places, usually being lower than current market prices). (Niven's list, with his annotations in these parens.)

1. Brushing market-places and ones compound, the owner of the compound will only present them some yams[,] goats or fowl.

2. That English money should do away with entirely [*sic*] and that cowries must come more for use.

3. Fowls to be bought for 3d.

4. To pay only one bag of cowries for marrying young girls, and half bag for marrying a woman.

5. That roads made by English people should be destroyed[;] that the roads brought or causes death.

6. Calling men bull dogs.

7. That men must not go to market but women, that women must not do farm works but [these are] for men, and that cocoa yams should be cut off and no more in use.

8. That women must be kept naked so that privates must be kept warm by the sun.

9. When saluted, the answer will be, that Chineke got salutations. (Onitsha clerk's list)

From these complex lists, the British administration distilled a limited number of conclusions: that the *Nwaobiala* was "about" sanitation and the evils of prostitution, that it was an expression of native, specifically female, conservatism, that local men "in general were not at all in sympathy with it," and that it was not inherently political, and therefore it probably should not be seen as seditious.[10] The last point was the majority view, even though several officials expressed a belief that the *egwu* was conspiratorial or was instigated strictly from outside. The indulgent view that women were incapable of seditious behavior triumphed through its appeal to an image of African women's life experiences as inherently mundane, irrational, ahistorical, and apolitical. The District Officer of Owelli, MacGregor, gave the strongest statement of this perspective in the *Nwaobiala* files:

> I would add that the song was sung only by women—the most conservative part of the community, and the most influential who alone invariably sing at their dances and who once getting hold of an idea, in their feminine way cling to it tenaciously, without understanding, regardless of reason and sense. (from a letter attached to NNAE, Memo No. 124/M. P. 62/ 1925)

This discourse exonerated colonized men from any blame in the affair and kept the overworked administration from feeling it had to use (costly) force just when other policies were being developed for the peaceful exploitation of this hitherto "unpacified" part of the Nigerian colony. The colonialists' memos contained an implicit expectation that local men should keep better control of their womenfolk, an expectation that was surely passed along, by way of colonized intermediaries, to the men throughout the southeast who had "allowed" women to behave in such an outrageous fashion. This expectation would be expressed more explicitly after the events of 1929.

Without the dancers' own exegeses, and considering that the lists were filtered through at least two levels of interpretation—those of local memorization and translation from Igbo into English—before they were written down, these representations of the oral part of the *egwu* (song/dance) constitute a very partial expression of the poetics of the movement. Even so, they are extremely evocative, containing kernels of that alterity that colonial officials avoided by not questioning and considering insignificant. It might be profitable for us to do what the recorders of the lists never did; reconsider the lists and try to understand the cultural content of some of these "not so proper" *egwu* songs.[11]

Falling Fruit, Unclothed Girls, and Death on the Roadways

Both lists agree that a primary demand of the *Nwaobiala* dancers was for cleanliness in compounds and markets, and, as we have seen, the only motion we can definitely associate with the *egwu* is that of bending low to the ground and sweeping. Officials took these admonitions to mean that women felt southeastern towns were dirty and in need of a housewifely cleaning. But was the dirt women were determined to sweep away some literal dirt that they could sweep with their brooms? There are several clues in the lists that point to deeper contaminations and widespread pollution.

The dancers announced that Chineke sent them to deliver the *egwu*'s message, "and that it would help women to bear children." Here we see something interesting: they did not invoke the name of Ala/Ani in their demands, even if it was inscribed in their name for themselves. Igbo-speaking people in the late 1980s often described Chineke to me as "God." However, they also pointed out that *o* (he/she/it) was a spirit, and in some way an aspect of Chukwu (the name that has become synonymous in the Igbo-speaking southeast with the Christian God). I was told that Chineke is a creative spiritual force, usually positive in its interactions with human beings and invoked to ward off the *nso ani* (abominations) that bring sanctions from the earth deity. Women who wished to cleanse the land, and thus avoid Ala/Ani's anger, might well enlist the aid of Chineke.[12]

The connection between contamination and childbearing was well-known to Igbo speakers in the 1920s. As noted above, the birth of monsters or unearthly beauties was considered part of a communication system between the earth and the human beings living on it. Difficulties in childbirth were thought to be afflictions sent from Ala/Ani to signal her displeasure with human acts like adultery, having sex in inappropriate places (notably outside the village, lying directly on the ground) or at inappropriate times (e.g., during pregnancy or while nursing). Women involved in lengthy, increasingly dangerous birth travails were encouraged to confess their wrongful actions in order to ease their pain and bring out a living child. Bearing a dead child was extremely polluting; for the mother, for witnesses to the birth, and for the place where the birth occurred. Igbo-speaking women of the 1920s tried to give birth within their marital compounds, squatting outside the buildings in the *ilo* (courtyard) under the surveillance of senior women.

If both child and mother died in childbirth, their bodies would be disposed of, usually without burial, in the "bad bush" (*ofia ojoo*). Having one's body cast aside unceremoniously was tantamount to losing one's divinely created form, as well as one's human, social identity, and thus to losing one's opportunity for future incarnations in the human community. This evidently led to an unresolved, anomalous condition that people found dangerous and wished to avoid.

Since women's bodies and women's children might bear the initial brunt of Ala/Ani's anger, it behooved women as a group to take action and alert men to a communication from the earth deity, especially a communication visited on and through women, like a "miraculous birth." It also behooved women to pay closer attention to their purificatory responsibilities: keeping compounds, marketplaces, shrines, and pathways clean, unblocking or drawing attention to the potentially dangerous areas of contamination.

The third point in Niven's list is more generally directed. No one should allow a "nuisance" to be committed within compounds "or under breadfruit trees or palm tree lest the falling fruit be contaminated." Colonial officials took this demand to be about sanitation, and may even have seen it as proof that a decade of colonial and missionary sanitary campaigns was finally showing results. Reading this point in light of southeastern Nigerian women's rhetoric during the 1930 Aba Commission's hearings on the *Ogu Umunwaanyi*, however, calls this interpretation into question.

Since women in the *Ogu* are known to have expressed themselves in what was, for the British, a scatological fashion, a rendering closer to the spirit of this demand is that people should not shit beneath breadfruit or palm trees; the trees that Igbo-speaking people referred (and still refer) to rhetorically as "useful trees" or the "trees that bear fruit."[13] In 1929 women sang a very similar song to warrant chiefs and colonial officials. Enyidia of Mbiopongo gave this summation of the warring women's *egwu*: "We said, 'What have we, women, done to warrant our being taxed? We women are like trees which bear fruit. You should tell us the reason why women who bear seeds should be counted'" (Aba Commission 1930: 79). Women thus made a direct connection between themselves and "trees which bear fruit" only four years after the *Nwaobiala*.

This point thus appears as a highly metaphorical statement, asking its intended audience not to shit on (make conditions intolerable for) women, lest children, who belonged to their father's patrilineages, be besmirched. In other words, the problems of southeastern women had ramifications for the rest of the population; one group could not suffer without a more generalized suffering taking place. Whatever the proper exegesis for this set of demands, however, problems with purification, fertility, and power were clearly being acted out in the colonized Nigerian southeast in 1925, on and through the bodies of women.

The bodies of women were constantly and explicitly referenced by the *Nwaobiala* dancers, and were a major nuisance (in a more straightforward sense of the word) to their colonial chroniclers. Kenneth Cochrane, one of the few British officials actually to confront the *egwu* in progress, was first called in during early November 1925 to investigate rumors that young, unmarried girls were being stripped by senior women in the Umuahia market. On 12 November, he was met by "several hundred women" who were behaving in an orderly fashion. Umuahia residents agreed that girls had been stripped, but no official complaints were filed over the incident. Cochrane

Photo 6.2 Early twentieth century Igbo market scene, showing informal spatial arrangements and women's dominance. (From George T. Basden, *Among the Ibos of Nigeria.* London: Seeley, Service, & Co., 1921. Also in edition reprinted by Cass, 1966.)

therefore postulated that "the clothes had been taken away by their mothers who knew that the clothes were the price of their daughter's profligacy" (NNAE, M. P. No. 1538/128/1925).

From the point of view of the colonial administration, women stripping other women constituted a minor breach of the peace. For Igbo-speaking women, this activity could not be so easily shrugged off: it was purposeful and shocking. Girls appeared naked in the marketplace before 1925, so it was not their undress that impressed itself on onlookers. It was the actual act of stripping that was radical in its implications, and it was this act that was justified in the oral component of the *egwu.* Both lists record aspects of this justification. Niven was told that girls should not wear cloth "until they were with first child, but go naked as in old days." Onitsha District Officer Milne's African informant wrote that "women must be naked so that privates must be kept warm by the sun." A literate Igbo member of Achi Native Court, J. C. Iwenofu, wrote to his District Officer (M. MacGregor) and said that the demand was even more elaborate: "All girls to be naked as in the olden times and not to trade. [A]ny girl who offend this law to be taken to the god at Okigwe."[14]

As I have noted elsewhere (Bastian 1993a), nakedness in late 1980s Igbo marketplaces was considered a sign of madness or, in some areas, a preliminary to witchcraft confession. The idea of stripping someone in the market was extremely repellent. People told me that such behavior would signal absolute public humiliation for the person stripped. In the 1920s, Igbo markets were obviously different from their late twentieth-century counterparts. Women traders in towns like Umuahia probably did not wear the elaborate garments, many of them in Western styles, that contemporary traders affect, and markets were still used as meeting grounds for every town association and dance group. Markets were also different, at least before the 1920s, in that serious traders were not usually in their teens or twenties. *Afia* (market/ trade) was the business of women who were mature, had borne several children, or who, although married for several years, had no children of their own.

Young girls were not supposed to work in the marketplace. They had tasks to perform at home or were involved in various activities meant to beautify and strengthen their bodies in preparation for marriage and the bearing of children for their husbands' patrilines.[15] Within their natal compounds, girls were under the surveillance and supervision of senior women, as well as under the eyes of older men. Compounds enclosed (and protected) young women's productive and reproductive potential for their future husbands. In contrast, markets were open, freewheeling, and tempting spaces. Mature women would supposedly be less tempted, or else would be able to keep their temptations discreet. Their indiscretions would also be less damaging, since they had already produced children or gained personal fame.

Cloth, the symbol of work in the marketplace and hence maturity, was a form of wealth and a marker of status for men and women in the 1920s, but it was beginning, because of colonial trade practices, to be available to a larger number of consumers than ever before. Some of those new consumers were women who were considered too young and untried to wear cloth. As these young women became involved with the numerous Christian missions, they were exhorted to cover their nakedness and to engage in wage labor that would enable them to buy cloth to make "frocks" and undergarments.[16] As young women, under the twin pressures of Christianization and modernity, invested in clothing at an unprecedented rate, the social value of the cloth-wealth older women had accumulated over the course of their lifetimes seriously eroded.

Young women entered the cash economy through the auspices of small-scale trade, domestic labor for the missions or the administration, or through the sale of sexual services. All of these trades took female youth away from what was considered, by their elders, to be their more appropriate work: compound domestic chores and approved forms of beautification. As young women entered trade they competed with more senior, married women for places in the transforming economy of the southeast. Albeit an unintended consequence of missionization, young women's trade further propelled the imperial project of making the colony pay for itself.

Putting women's bodies into "modest dress" was close to the heart of every mission, and female missionaries specialized in teaching sewing and laundry practices to women interested in converting. Some young women who wore frocks or wrappers were demonstrating their allegiance to the missions—and, hence, they may have been seen as a threat to the *Nwaobiala* dancers' purification plans. Being stripped naked would have been, from the point of view of the affected girls, like having these new attributes—individualized Christian identities and powers of consumption—stripped away. Senior women, who were less likely to be involved in mission culture but whose trading skills were depended on to inject cash into their suddenly needy households, were under pressure from all sides. The sight of young girls walking about in the sign of senior women's former wealth and status must have seemed quite intolerable.

Many older forms of accumulation were devalued in this period, and women who had invested in those forms found themselves similarly devalued. For example, it had become difficult for women to divorce, or to assist their daughters in divorcing, because of the monetization of bridewealth. Bridewealth paid in pounds and shillings was hard to collect and even harder to refund, since most British currency immediately circulated back into mercantile capitalist or mission pockets and was soon to return to colonial treasuries as well, through male taxation.[17] Young women spending currency on clothing were implicated in foreign economic practices that did not take into account the interests of women and that worked actively against women's position in the southeastern Nigerian socioeconomic structure.

Beyond elder women's distaste for the effects of missionization and new forms of labor for young women, like sex work in the rapidly urbanizing areas of Onitsha, Aba, and Umuahia, lay indigenous notions about appropriate body conditions for fertile, "useful" women. The incorrectly clothed (and sexualized) young woman was perceived as a danger to the patrilineal system as a whole. Wrapped in purchased cloth and sold just like that cloth to any stranger, her "privates"/body would not see the sun, but would be kept shadowed and cooled, taking the edge off her fertility in much the same way as too little sunlight could ruin crops. Christian women's self-imposed rules on marrying monogamously, and only Christian men, also meant that Igbo exogamous and polygynous relations were subverted by the 1920s. This had its own chilling effect on women's and men's fertility, and on their political and social activities.

Instead of women moving across the landscape through exogamy and market trade, the period of high colonialism in southeastern Nigeria brought new forms of (masculinized) mobility. These androcentric movements were inscribed on the landscape in the form of roads, railbeds, and an attachment to the vagaries of global markets. As the interior was "opened up" by mercantilists, missionaries, and colonialists, Igbo women also discovered that the roads, railways, and transformed marketplaces could become a conduit for dangerously divisive forces.

The roads built by colonialists with the labor of the colonized made people "go missing," through death, servitude, or complete alienation from Igbo values; they did not bring people together for marriage or trade, as the women's pathways did. Worse, people who used these new roads returned to their towns, bringing a host of afflictions.

The use of women in road construction and even women's use of the newly constructed roads themselves were peculiarly sore points by the 1920s because of women's special ties to the earth and local market systems. Women were responsible for the pathways (*ama*) that linked periodic markets and insured alliances between towns. Government road construction, based on colonial needs, often ran counter to women's intervillage pathways or "bush roads." Sometimes the newly constructed roads ran across women's paths or obliterated them altogether (Ukwu 1967: 661–62). Lorry traffic could be heavy and dangerous for unwary pedestrians. Women on their way to nearby markets found themselves in peril, even though they were assured of safety by virtue of their status as *ndi afia* (people of the marketplace).

Women made the *ama* during their passage to and from neighboring towns. Their bodily connection to the paths, created by direct, physical contact with the earth, also made them responsible for any abomination that might find its way into villages through the *ama*. The advent of ungovernable, unpurifiable roads was therefore a direct challenge to women's power and interest in the southeast. Being forced to help construct "unnatural" roads, using the colonialists' technology, added insult to injury.

During the *Nwaobiala*, Ideani and Alo women militated against colonial constructions such as roads. In the words of Milne, "The women dancers of these towns collected together and placed obstructions on one of the main Provincial Roads, they then proceeded to Nobi Court, burnt the market and filled the Court with refuse" (NNAE, M.P. No. 18/1926). The women's main targets—the government road, court building, and market—all stood as reminders of women's waning influence within the country. By obstructing passage along the illicit road, burning the market to purify it of colonial, mission, and male contaminations, and throwing refuse into the court, Ideani and Alo women pointed to the loci of contamination and made a succinct, activist statement about overweening male ambition and colonial practices. In 1929 the same sorts of protests would occur, but with greater frequency and under the direction of thousands of southeastern women. When a number of women were killed in December 1929 after a demonstration sparked by a passing colonial motorist, the fears and insistences of the *Nwaobiala* dancers five years earlier had come to disastrous fruition.

SOME CONCLUSIONS

As the *Nwaobiala* dancers understood in 1925, mission Christianity was meant to displace indigenous religious and economic practice, just as the colonial administration was meant to undermine indigenous power structures. European practices of power did not simply affect Igbo-speaking people's formal institutions; they were inscribed upon the colonized landscape and the bodies of those who inhabited it. Women were not only forced out of processes of judgment and compensation; they literally had no access to official buildings or to the minds of those who sat in them. Senior women did not simply witness an abstract erosion of their authority over younger women; they watched as younger women iconically wrapped themselves in the fabric of colonial rule, mission ideologies, and economic exploitation. The flow of strange commodities, ideas, and people did not suddenly open up in Igbo-speaking peoples' midst; it was built gradually with mission bicycles, "native bearers," corvée labor for railroad and road construction, and finally the roads that brought afflictions as well as goods to so many.

The *Nwaobiala* and the *Ogu Umunwaanyi* that followed it were a single, lengthy, and historically continuous attempt to culturally reinscribe and re-embody the southeastern Nigerian landscape and the people who inhabited it. These movements were meant to decolonize southeastern Nigerian people by marshaling the material and imaginative tools inherent in *egwu*, a female performative mode already well-known and previously used for politicized protests in local contexts.

If the *Nwaobiala* dancers were guilty of a major oversight, it was that they did not fully recognize the presence of an alien and rival *egwu* in their country. This song and dance—the performance of colonialism, missionization, capital, and Western technologies—had its own potencies. One of these powers was the ability to ignore what the colonial *egwu* found inexplicable, while cataloging it for future reference and conserving it for the sake of "completeness." Yet in this conservation, however ill- or even unintended, something of the *Nwaobiala* dancers' intentionality, instrumentality and, indeed, aesthetics persists. It moves within the transcribed passages.

Beyond chronologies and "facts," events like the *Nwaobiala* need to be probed for what is left of their historically and culturally contingent meaningfulness; not only because "we" somehow need to know what "they" meant, but because the colonized others also transformed, however unconsciously, those who wrote about them. In turn, all of the actors' knowledge and the power of their (separate but not separated) performance—resistant to the imperial archive even as it resides within it—can continue to work their transformations on us, who are reading and writing about "dancing women" at the other end of the twentieth century.

NOTES

A number of people have, over a long period, read and commented on various versions of this chapter. Every comment has been a useful one, and I appreciate them all. I would especially like to acknowledge the assistance of Rosalind Shaw and the close reading of "the usual suspects," notably Adeline Masquelier and Brad Weiss. Nadia Abuelhaj, Michael Kevane, and Sean Malarney, once my colleagues at the Harvard Academy for International and Area Studies, gave me important notes at an early stage of the construction of this chapter. Richard and Helen Henderson have also discussed with me at great length many of the questions relating to gender and pollution among Igbo-speakers in this paper. I am, finally, indebted to the editors of this volume, Dorothy Hodgson and Sheryl McCurdy, for their insightful and (literally) incisive ideas for bringing the chapter under control at last.

1. This and most future references to the *Nwaobiala* of 1925 come from the Nigerian National Archives at Enugu (NNAE), OP. 391/1925 6/11/25 ONPROF 7/12/92, "Bands of Women Dancers Preaching Ideas of Desirable Reforms—Movement Of." Cochrane's memo is filed in M. P. No. 1538/128/1925, dated 9 December 1925.

2. For previous, brief discussions of the *Nwaobiala*, see Meek 1937; Afigbo 1966; Gailey 1970; Ifeka-Moller 1975; Mba 1982. There is also a discussion of other southeastern women's 1925 "disturbances," which may or may not have been associated with the *Nwaobiala*, in Akpan and Ekpo 1988: 18–20.

3. The other recorded name for the *Nwaobiala*, *Obanjili*, possibly has to do with yam (*ji*) cultivation and a return, from the new staple of cassava, to a yam-based cuisine (*jili*, yam-eating). On querying Igbo-speakers on the Naijanet listserv about possible meanings for *obanjili*, I received several responses. One older man suggested that this term had to do with the yam barns that once held one of the most visible components of men's wealth in southeastern Nigeria. Mba (1982: 45–46) argues that cassava offered southern Nigerian women a new economic independence and another staple crop to turn to during periods before the yam harvest. Cassava (manioc) was introduced to coastal West Africa in the seventeenth century by Portuguese traders, but internal evidence from the *Nwaobiala* suggests that it had only recently gained importance in the southeastern Nigerian interior. Senior women seem to have been demonstrating their distaste for the extra agricultural labor (as well as preparation requirements) that became their lot after cassava's arrival.

4. Ifeka-Moller (1975) uses an alternative term, *nwa obolia*, for these events. However, Mba (1982), who interviewed Women's War participants in the 1970s and therefore must be given credence for her knowledge of the women's own discursive practices, also prefers *Nwaobiala*. I have chosen to follow Mba's lead.

5. In pre- and early colonial times, twin births were also seen as *nso ani* (abominations against the earth). Multiple births supposedly too closely resembled those of animals. Prominent contemporary families with twins are still scrutinized for aberrant conduct, as are the families of albinos or other "abnormal" children.

6. During slack periods in the agricultural cycle, some women evidently went from town to town, seeking out new *egwu*. As women of Agbaja told Green (1964: 209): "if, in the dry season, they heard that the people of another place were doing a new dance, about ten of them would go off and learn it and they would then practice it in the moonlight."

7. NNAE, Memo No. 124/M. P. 62/1925, District Officer, Agwu to the Senior Resident, Onitsha.

8. NNAE, Memo No. 124/M. P. 62/1925.

9. NNAE, Memo M. P. No. 1538/128/1925.

10. Quotation from Milne, in NNAE, M. P. No. 18/1926.

11. If not pushed aside completely, then gossiped about in the Government Reserve Area of Onitsha, or kept for private journals, letters, or memoirs. Since this research is still preliminary, I have not yet found many of these officials' personal papers, nor have I seen any mention of the *Nwaobiala* in colonial memoirs of the period.

12. Chineke's ambiguous gender may also be involved in the women's poetical evocation of its name. Although most people I knew thought of Chineke rather uncritically as male (since he is somehow related to Chukwu, who has been constructed since mission times as God the Father), Rosalind Shaw informs me that Chineke is more complicated. People she spoke to in northern Igbo areas seemed unsure whether Chineke was male, female, both, or neither (Shaw, personal communication; see also Nwoga [1984:27–31] for a discussion of who or what Chineke might be).

13. See Green (1964: 201) for an example that is as graphic as she felt able to translate for the public record. She tells us that women only used this type of language when they were offended and making a communal statement of disapproval or when they were singing privately about women's business.

14. A copy of this 3 November letter was appended to District Officer MacGregor's memo to the Senior Resident, Onitsha, dated 23 November 1925 (NNAE, Memo No. 581/M. P. 62/1925). A number of Igbo-speaking men seem to have assisted colonial officials in their investigations of the *Nwaobiala*, although few were credited by name. It is possible that a good deal of information came from men, particularly as few colonial administrators were present at any of the *Nwaobiala* events and even fewer seemed to speak regularly with Igbo women.

15. Young women had their own dance groups and other associations. They also passed the time by working on complex, plaited and sculpted hairstyles and painting *uli* (intricate, sinuous designs) or making elaborate scarifications on each others' bodies. See Basden (1966: 337) for an early drawing of Igbo women's scarification. Even though young women did not wear cloth, their bodies were covered.

16. Part of an 1898 letter from Church Missionary Society Secretary Baylis to Archdeacon Dennis in Onitsha addressed this issue directly: "*Clothing for Girls at the Onitsha School.*—the Committee are still unprepared to make a grant for the clothing of the girls at the Onitsha school. They hold strongly that the natives ought to be encouraged to provide clothing for themselves. In the case of the girls already engaged to Christians, it would seem reasonable that they should take this matter up if the girls' parents are not able or willing to do so. In the event of there being special cases where provision by the natives seem impossible, then the Committee feel that private help should be sought by the Missionaries, and that there should be no impression given that the Committee were prepared to clothe the girls" (letter dated 28 October 1898, Church Missionary Society (CMS) Archives, University of Birmingham, G3 A3/L5, p. 74).

17. The place of mission Christianity in the monetization of African societies is often overlooked. In Bende and Okigwe divisions, the missions were an important channel for the accelerated use of British currency. More than a decade before the administration imposed its "head tax" in 1928, the Primitive Methodist mission under Reverend Fred William Dodds was collecting cash from its parishioners: "I have emphatically insisted that every church shall pay the whole of its expenses, salary of teacher, cost of materials, cost of church furnishings, indeed, that no cost whatever in respect of that school should be borne by the mission" (from a letter written by Dodds, dated 5 December 1916; quoted in Kalu, 1986: 52).

REFERENCES

Aba Commission of Inquiry. 1930. *Notes of Evidence Taken by the Commission of Inquiry Appointed to Inquire into the Disturbances in the Calabar and Owerri Provinces, December, 1929*. Lagos.

Afigbo, A. E. 1966. "Revolution and Reaction in Eastern Nigeria: 1900–1929 (The Background of the Women's Riot of 1929)." *Journal of the Historical Society of Nigeria* 3: 539–57.

Akpan, Ekwere Otu and Violetta I. Ekpo. 1988. *The Women's War of 1929: A Popular Uprising in South Eastern Nigeria (Preliminary Study)*. Calabar, Nigeria: Government Printer.

Basden, George T. 1921. *Among the Ibos of Nigeria*. London: Seeley, Service & Co.

————.1966. *Niger Ibos: A Description of the Primitive Life, Customs and Animistic Beliefs of the Ibo People of Nigeria*. London: Cass.

Bastian, Misty L. 1985. "Useful Women and the Good of the Land: The Igbo Women's War of 1929." M.A. thesis, University of Chicago.

————. 1993a. "'Bloodhounds Who Have No Friends': Witchcraft, Locality and the Nigerian Popular Press." In *Modernity and Its Malcontents*, edited by Jean and John Comaroff, 129–66. Chicago: University of Chicago Press.

————. 1993b. "Making the Market Strange: Gender and Spatial Transformations in the Onitsha Marketplace." Paper presented at the Harvard Anthropology Seminar, February 1993.

Cole, Herbert M. 1982. *Mbari: Art and Life among the Owerri Igbo*. Bloomington: Indiana University Press.

Gailey, Harry A. 1970. *The Road to Aba: A Study of British Administrative Policy in Eastern Nigeria*. New York: New York University Press.

Green, M. M. 1964. *Ibo Village Affairs*. New York: Praeger.

Henderson, Richard N. 1972. *The King in Every Man: Evolutionary Trends in Onitsha Ibo Society and Culture*. New Haven, CT: Yale University Press.

Ifeka-Moller, Caroline. 1975. "Female Militancy and Colonial Revolt: The Women's War of 1929, Eastern Nigeria." In *Perceiving Women*, edited by Shirley Ardener, 127–57. London: J. M. Dent and Sons.

Kalu, Ogbu U. 1986. "Primitive Methodists on the Railroad Junctions of Igboland, 1910–1931." *Journal of Religion in Africa* 14(1): 44–66.

Leith-Ross, Sylvia. 1936. *African Women: A Study of the Ibo of Nigeria*. London: Faber and Faber.

Martin, Susan. 1988. *Palm Oil and Protest: An Economic History of the Ngwa Region, South-Eastern Nigeria, 1800–1980*. Cambridge: Cambridge University Press.

Mba, Nina Emma. 1982. *Nigerian Women Mobilized: Women's Political Activity in Southern Nigeria, 1900–1965*. Berkeley: University of California, Institute of International Studies, no. 48.

Meek, C. K. 1937. *Law and Authority in a Nigerian Tribe: A Study in Indirect Rule*. Oxford: Oxford University Press.

Nwoga, Donatus Ibe. 1984. *The Supreme God as Stranger in Igbo Religious Thought*. Ahiazu Mbaise, Nigeria: Hawk Press.

Perham, Margery. 1937. *Native Administration in Nigeria*. London: Oxford University Press.

Ukwu, U. I. 1967. "The Development of Trade and Marketing in Iboland." *Journal of the Historical Society of Nigeria* 3(4): 647–62.

Van Allen, Judith. 1976. "'Aba Riots' or Igbo 'Women's War'? Ideology, Stratification, and the Invisibility of Women." In *Women in Africa: Studies in Social and Economic Change*, edited by Nancy J. Hafkin and Edna G. Bay, 59–85. Stanford, CA: Stanford University Press.

7

ROUNDING UP SPINSTERS: GENDER CHAOS AND UNMARRIED WOMEN IN COLONIAL ASANTE

Jean Allman

In March, 1933, the District Officer's "Quarterly Report" for the Mampong District in Asante contained a strange entry for the town of Effiduasi. "Becoming alarmed at the amount of venereal disease spread in the town by unattached spinsters," the officer wrote,

> the *Ohene* [chief] published an edict commanding that all unmarried maidens should forthwith provide themselves with husbands. This shook the Wesleyan Mission somewhat but only one complaint was received. In fact, the husband hunt seems to have been rather enjoyed by the girls than otherwise. The *Ohene*, however, was warned against the futility of publishing unenforceable orders and against advertising the frailties of his maidens. (National Archives of Ghana, Kumasi [NAGK], ARA 1286)[1]

Although the officer cast this so-called "husband hunt" as a minor incident in the town of Effiduasi, there is enough written evidence and ample oral testimony to suggest that it was anything but minor and to reveal that it was certainly not isolated. Between 1929 and 1933, in a number of towns throughout this region of the former Gold Coast, chiefs were ordering the arrest of women who were over the age of fifteen and not married.[2] As one of those who was arrested recalled:

We were arrested and just dumped into a room—all of the women of Effiduasi who were not married. . . . The *ahemfie* [palace] police [did the arresting]. The women were flirting around and so they became an embarrassment to the King. So, he decided that they should get married. . . . they announced it that on such a day all women should be able to show a husband. . . . When we were sent there, we were put into a room. . . . When you mentioned a man's name, it meant that was the man you wanted to marry, so they would release you. . . . You would go home with the man and the man would see your relatives and say, "I am getting married to this woman." (Fom 1993)[3]

The pattern, it seems, was similar in each town. A "gong-gong" was beaten to announce the arrest of unmarried women [*asigyafo*].[4] A woman was detained, usually at the chief's court, until she spoke the name of a man whom she would agree to marry. That man was then summoned to the court where he would affirm his desire to marry the woman and pay a "release fee" of 5/-. If the man refused to marry the woman, he was fined. In some cases, the fine was 5/-, in others it was as high as £5. After the woman's release, the man was expected to pay a marriage fee of 7/- and one bottle of gin to the woman's family (NAGK, ARA 1907).[5]

I have come across no earlier references to anything that resembles the rounding up of unmarried women in documentary sources for the eighteenth and nineteenth centuries. For the colonial period, the written evidence on the subject is limited to a small collection of correspondence, a Quarterly Report entry and a few customary court cases. Fortes made brief mention in his field notes from the 1945–46 "Ashanti Social Survey" of the fact that

periodically the political authority stepped in and decreed that all unmarried women must get married; in some cases they were placed in a cell and told to name their choice; theoretically the men could refuse, but in practice it appears to have been difficult for them to refuse. In order to facilitate marriages in this situation, marriage by registration was introduced, so that only a small fee (usually 5/-) [was paid]. (Fortes Papers, Centre for African Studies, Cambridge University, no date.)

In the more recent secondary literature, there are only two brief references to the detention of unmarried women in Ghana's colonial period—and these in sources not pertaining specifically to Asante. D. D. Vellenga, in her 1983 piece, "Who Is a Wife?" made general reference to chiefs' concerns about the number of women not properly married. "Some even went to the extreme measure," she wrote, "of locking up such women until their lovers would pay a fee to release them, thus legitimising the relationship" (Vellenga 1983:150).[6] P. A. Roberts discovered more detailed information on the arrest of unmarried women in Sefwi Wiawso—an area to the southwest of Asante, which was incorporated into the empire in the early eighteenth century as a tributary state (Roberts 1987:61). She found evidence of a 1929 "Free Women's Marriage Proclamation," which ordered that "such women . . . be arrested, locked up in the outer courtyards of the *omanhene*'s palace in Wiawso and held there until they were claimed by a husband or by any other man who would take charge of them. The male claimant was required to pay a fine of 5/- to release the woman" (Roberts 1987:61). For the most part, however, "husband hunts," or the "capture of spinsters," have escaped historical inquiry.

Based upon the reminiscences of women who were either among the "spinsters" caught or who bore witness to the "capture," the correspondence of British officials, and the records of customary courts, this chapter explores gender and social change in colonial Asante by dissecting and then contextualizing the round-up of unmarried women in the late 1920s and early 1930s. It seeks to understand this unusual episode in direct state intervention into the negotiating of marriage as part of the general chaos in gender relations that shook Asante in the years between the two world wars. Often articulated in the language of moral crisis, in terms that spoke of women's uncontrollability, of prostitution and venereal disease, this chaos was, more than anything, about shifting power relationships. It was engendered by cash and cocoa, by trade and transformation.[7]

This was not, however, how the arrests were explained in the early 1930s. British officials in Asante first expressed concern about the detention of unmarried women in 1932. In July of that year, the Chief Commissioner wrote a memo to his assistant requesting that enquiries be made and a report furnished. "I am informed," he wrote, "that there is a custom in Ashanti that young girls of 15 years of age upwards are ordered to marry. It is even alleged that any who refuse are placed in prison" (NAGK, ARA 1907). Shortly thereafter, the Assistant Commissioner, having sought information in Bekwai and Mansu Nkwanta, filed his response along with letters from the chiefs of both towns and from the District Officer resident in Bekwai. The officer wrote that the local Roman Catholic priest first informed him of the practice and that "no complaint was made . . . by any Ashanti or for that matter any african [*sic*], one or two africans [*sic*] rather took it as a joke." He added that he had heard of similar actions being taken in Adansi, Edweso, and even Kumasi a few years earlier, although he understood "the Kumasihene is not in favour of it" (NAGK, ARA 1907).

The chiefs confirmed the detentions of unmarried women and justified their actions by arguing that venereal diseases and prostitution were prevalent in their division.[8] In a three-page letter, the Bekwaihene and his councillors expressed their desire "to prevent prostitution which we have notice[d] to bring sterility and incurable venereal diseases." The solution, they argued, was to "encourage conjugal marriages among our womenfolk." If the chiefs were prepared to offer a concrete solution to the "problem" of unmarried women, they were far more equivocal in explaining why the "problem" of women not marrying existed in the first place. On the one hand, they argued that "the tendency . . . is attributable to the prevalent financial depression which renders the men incapable to conform with . . . the expenses of our native customary laws concerning marriage." On the other hand, the chiefs betrayed much concern about women's growing uncontrollability, fondly recalling "the good old days of our ancestors . . . [when] no girl or woman dared to resist when given away in marriage to a suitor by her parents and relatives as is the case now." Yet in their letter to colonial officials, the customary rulers of Bekwai were less intent on explaining the marriage crisis than with exposing its dreadful symptoms—immorality, prostitution, and disease. They assured officials that their intentions were "clean" and that they would continue the practice of detaining unmarried women "unless there is any justifiable reason to encourage prostitution and its attendant prevalence of sterility and venereal diseases" (NAGK, ARA 1907). As for the District Officer, he was not fully convinced by the chiefs' arguments. The idea of stopping "the spread of venereal disease is a good cloak," he wrote, "behind which to hide a money making proposition." The Bekwaihene collected a release fee of 5/- on every woman caught, the officer noted, and a fine of £5 on every man whose name was called but who refused to pay the fee and marry (NAGK, ARA 1907).

How women viewed these arrests in the late 1920s and early 1930s is far more difficult to reconstruct than the views of chiefs or colonial officers, but at least one woman's experience of being arrested has been preserved in a 1929 customary court case from Asokore. In *Kwaku Afram v. Afuah Buo* the plaintiff sought judicial relief for the defendant to explain her reasons for refusing to marry him after 5/- had been paid on her behalf "during the capture of spinsters in Asokore." The plaintiff claimed that he saw a "certain young man from Seneajah connecting with the girl . . . [and] upon the strength of that . . . found out that the defendant did not like to marry" him. Afuah Buo's defense was brief and direct:

> I live at Asokore. I am a farmer. Some years ago, a gong-gong was beaten that spinsters are to be caught. I was among (and previous [to] that I was told by Plaintiff that I must mention his name and he will clear me out). I did and he came and paid 5/- and discharged me. . . . About two weeks after Plaintiff does not care for me, nor subsist me. I informed one Attah Biom of the treatment and Plaintiff said because he was ill hence he did not do it. What I have to say is that because Plaintiff did not care for me,

nor subsist me, hence I connected with someone, to get my daily living. That's all I know. (Fortes Papers 1929)

In the end, the Asokore Native Tribunal ruled against Afuah Buo, fining her £5.9.0—£3.4.0 of which went to the plaintiff as costs and compensation.

Although brief, Buo's testimony raises a number of important issues. First, the fact that her case was brought before the court in 1929 and that the "capture" of spinsters in Asokore had occurred "some years" earlier suggests that the problem of unmarried women was not simply a by-product of the "financial depression." We therefore need to investigate social and economic changes and their impact on gender and conjugal relationships earlier to the depression if we are to understand the magnitude of the crisis. Secondly, Buo's testimony points to a serious contest over the very meaning of marriage in the late 1920s. It suggests that the crisis was not simply about marriage and non-marriage, as the chiefs' arguments imply, but about what constitutes a marriage and what responsibilities are incumbent upon each partner. For the plaintiff and, indeed, for the court, the payment of the release fee constituted "marriage" and entitled Afram to exclusive sexual rights in his wife. The marriage was a state of being; it either was or it was not; there could be no mitigating factors. For Buo, exclusive sexual rights were contingent upon a man's ongoing provision of minimal subsistence or "chop money." In her view, marriage was "a process," as Vellenga argued, "tenuous and fluid in nature" (1983:145).[9] Buo's definition of the marrying process allowed her to move in and out and between the categories of wife and concubine—a movement easily branded as prostitution by Asante's colonial chiefs.

Evidence suggests that the Asokore court's vision of marriage as "state of being" rather than "process" may be of recent origin and Buo's fluid interpretation more firmly rooted in Asante's precolonial past. Certainly R. S. Rattray's understanding of precolonial marriage was of ongoing negotiations between two groups of individuals. Fortes, though he did not historicize marriage customs, wrote that the conjugal relationship in Asante was "envisaged as a bundle of separable rights and bonds rather than as a unitary all-or-none tie." My own readings of customary court cases from this period lead me to conclude that chiefs and elders were articulating a new definition of marriage that upheld the husband's exclusive sexual rights in his wife, while discounting the husband's reciprocal obligations toward that wife.[10] This "petrified" vision of marriage as an "all-or-none tie" left women with little or no defense in countless numbers of cases heard in Native Tribunals during the colonial period (Rattray 1929:26; Fortes 1950:280).

In recalling the capture of those remaining unmarried, Asante women certainly do not speak with one voice.[11] Some echo the perspective of Afuah

Buo, others that of Asante's chiefs. Still others speak from a singular perspective that defies categorization. Yet these very contradictions bring the personal to bear on the structural relationships between economic and social change and, for our purposes, are fundamental to the process of disentangling charges of prostitution and concerns about "spinsterhood" from women's assertions of autonomy in a rapidly changing colonial economy. Interestingly, no one with whom I have spoken points to the depression or to men's inability to afford marriage payments as reasons for women's non-marriage. Akosua Atta certainly saw the root of the problem as men not proposing marriage to women, but she could point to no economic reasons for this. "I don't know why," she pondered, "things were not expensive then as they are now" (Atta 1992). Others saw the problem as a straightforward one of numbers. Women were not marrying because "the women outnumbered the men." From these perspectives non-marriage was not a *choice* that women made, it was something that happened through no fault of their own. Because of men's refusal to propose or simply because of the demography of the times, some women were left unmarried.

Most reminiscences of the period, however, cast the decision not to marry as a choice, though there is little agreement on how to characterize women's agency. Even Rosina Boama, who was sure that the main reason women did not marry was that there were not enough men, allowed that some women might have chosen not to marry. "I can't say," she recently recalled. "They were just roaming about. Whether they were not having [husbands] or were not getting [husbands], I can't say" (Boama 1992).[12] Other women were not so torn in their reasonings and echoed the sentiments expressed by chiefs in the early 1930s as they pointed to women's uncontrollability. "During that time," recalled Beatrice Nyarko, who was nearly forty years old during the capture of unmarried women at Effiduasi, "young girls were misbehaving" (Nyarko 1992). Jean Asare, who was a child at the time, remembered that "women were just roaming about, attending dances, sleeping everywhere. Some even went as far as Kumasi to sleep with boyfriends, so . . . it was a disgrace to the town and to the people here in the town" (Asare 1993). As Yaa Dufie explained, it was "because of the fear of contracting that disease [*babaso*, or venereal disease]. That's why they locked them up" (Dufie 1992). Indeed, several women did not hesitate to call those who had been captured "prostitutes." When asked if she were certain these women were prostitutes [*atutufo*] and not concubines of one sort or another [*mpenafo*], Beatrice Nyarko responded,

It was proper prostitution. If they see you as a waiting man, they will come to you and say the price, but it wasn't a bargaining thing. If she sees you, you can give her money and she will come to you. The next time, she may see another man, too, who can give her money, [and] she can go to him. (Nyarko 1992)

Many women, however, had more difficulty leaping to the assumption that those who had not married were prostitutes. As Akosua So reflected, "some girls don't want to marry. It's a personal thing. Some don't like it. Some don't want to lead good lives." When asked if they were prostitutes, she replied, "They can't openly declare themselves as prostitutes, but the ones who weren't married, people assumed they were prostitutes" (So 1992). Perhaps some were; clearly most were not. Eponuahemaa Afua Fom reported that both unmarried women and prostitutes were arrested. When asked why some women had chosen not to marry, she replied, "Each person had their own reason. Some were lazy. They didn't like to go to farm and to cook for the husband, so they wouldn't marry. . . . The men wanted to marry, but the women didn't want to marry and it's even worse now" (Fom 1992). In a subsequent conversation, Afua Fom would inform me that she was among the sixty spinsters caught in Effiduasi in the early 1930s.[13]

According to Afua Fom and her sister, Adwoa Addae, both of whom were in their mid-eighties when I met them, women were unmarried and were choosing *sigyawdi* (being unmarried or the state of non-marriage) for reasons that had more to do with the economics of conjugal obligations than with laxity in morals. Adwoa Addae has always lived with her sister in the family house (*abusua fie*). She had four husbands, but no children, and so helped raise her sister's eight children. The first time we spoke, Adwoa Addae explained the events behind the capture of unmarried women in this way:

> Men were not buying! That is why the women were saying that they would not marry. The men were not taking care of them. . . . The men were not serving us well. You would serve him, go to the farm with him, cook for him and yet he would not give you anything. . . . The man and woman may farm together, but the woman would do the greater part of it. . . . [The men] prefer to sit and do nothing. (Addae 1992)

Although Adwoa was not captured, she recalled those days as ones in which women asserted a great deal of autonomy and independence, much of it linked to the establishment of cocoa farms or to engagement in foodstuffs trade. Adwoa divorced at least one of her husbands because he refused to cultivate a cocoa farm for her:

> I got married to my husband because I had wanted some benefits from [him] . . . so that maybe, in the future, I would not suffer. . . . If the cocoa

is there, the proceeds—I will enjoy them. But my husband was not prepared to think that far, so I decided to divorce [him].

Adwoa Addae did not consider her actions unusual, and her reminiscences warrant extensive quotation. "In those days," she recalled,

women were hardworking, so we could live without men. The only thing we did not get were children, so we were forced to go in for these men. Apart from that, we were independent. We could work without the assistance of men. I don't know, but that might have accounted for what the chiefs did. . . . Those days are better than these days. In those days women could work hard and get a lot of things they wanted. But today it is not like that. Even if you try to assert some form of independence, you will see that it doesn't work as it used to work. In those days, even though women wanted to be independent, they still got married to men, but it was because they wanted to. . . . In those days, if you had a wife and you did not look after her well, she would just go. If you looked after her well, she would stay. (Addae 1993)

If Adwoa Addae remembered her years as a young woman as years of autonomy, she also remembered them as ones of broader social disorder. Not only were unmarried women arrested, she recalled, but women who were married were instructed by the chief to "buy cloths for our husbands, which we did, and even in some cases sandals and other things. . . . We really did not understand why the chief was saying that, but we had to do it" (Addae 1993). Rattray, in his extensive discussion of marriage, argued that one of the main liabilities that a husband incurred upon marriage was responsibility for his wife's maintenance (Rattray 1929:25–6), including the provision of large pieces of cloth (Rattray 1927:81–2). The order by the Effiduasihene that men need no longer provide cloths for their wives and that wives should provide cloths for their husbands thus undercut one of the fundamental obligations of marriage. Afua Fom remembered the order only as a "temporary measure that the King took. . . . It was not customary so it did not last long." When asked if she thought it was related to the capture of unmarried women, she replied, "We could not ask because, customarily, when the chief says something you cannot ask a question."

Although Afua Fom did not suggest a direct correlation between the capture and the order concerning cloth, her recollections point to a series of attempts to assert control over women. Not only were there the arrests of "spinsters" and the recasting, however temporary, of marital obligations, there was an attempt, according to Fom, to register girls upon passage of their first menses:

The King was also using another means [to determine who was unmarried, but eligible for marriage]. When the woman was old enough, when she starts passing the menses, you will go to a registrar who will register that this woman is old enough to marry. . . . [Women registered] at the court . . . so that they'll have a rough idea which people are not marrying but are eligible to marry. There are puberty rites, too. Because of the puberty rites . . . people got to know which girls are eligible for marriage. . . . By this they got to know who was married and who was not.

I have not yet come across any written documentation that provides details on the registration of girls at puberty in Effiduasi. Nonetheless, it does not appear to be outside of the realm of possibility in a world in which, for the moment, anyway, confusion reigned.

How can one make sense of these charges and counter-charges—of prostitution, venereal disease, immorality, and "bad girls," of captured "spinsters," wives clothing husbands, and chiefs registering girls at menarche? In short, how does one sort through the chaos that seemed to engulf the gendered world of colonial Asante in the late 1920s and early 1930s? Certainly, it is not a question of figuring out who was telling the "truth" or of ascertaining the precise number of prostitutes in a town like Effiduasi in 1929 (the town's population was estimated as 3,778 in 1931; National Archives of Ghana, Accra [NAGA] ADM. 52/5/3) in order to evaluate the veracity of the chiefs' charges. Even if it were possible to retrieve those figures, they would tell us nothing about how prostitution was defined in 1930 or the ways in which its meaning was contested. It is my contention that the reminiscences of women like Afua Fom and her sister point us in the right direction. Their repeated references to women's autonomy during this period—whether through complaints that men were "lazy" or through matter-of-fact statements like "in those days, the women were able to get money faster than the men"—highlight the importance of the economic and social context in framing the critical questions. In this case, we should not be asking whether the streets of Asante towns were overrun with prostitutes. Rather, we must ask: why were women perceived as being prostitutes, as being out of control, and why was that "uncontrollability" consistently articulated in terms of a moral crisis?[14]

These questions are certainly not unique to Asante. In recent years they have been posed quite dramatically in the growing body of comparative literature on gender and colonialism. As Nancy Hunt has reflected: "where women most often appear in the colonial record is where moral panic surfaced, settled and festered. Prostitution, polygamy, adultery, concubinage, and infertility are the loci of such angst throughout the historical record." (Hunt 1991:471). Hunt and a number of other historians concerned with gender issues, particularly in areas with sizable settler populations, have devoted much energy to exploring why this has been the case. Most have come to conclusions similar to Megan Vaughan, who has argued that

> "the problem of women" was shorthand for a number of related problems including changes in property rights, in rights in labour and relations between generations. . . . The real issue, of course, was that with far-reaching changes taking place in economic relations, so enormous strains were placed on both gender and generational relations. . . . these complex changes were described in terms of degeneration, of uncontrolled sexuality and of disease. (Vaughan 1991:144)

Asante, I would argue, provides no exception here, except that in Asante's equation there were no white settlers and cocoa was absolutely key.

The spread of cocoa farming in Asante, and throughout the forest belt of southern Ghana generally, has been well-documented by scholars over the past decades.[15] Several among them have been particularly concerned with gender and the exploitation of unpaid labor in the initial years of cocoa's expansion. Their writings provide material for constructing, at least provisionally, a gendered periodization of the development of the cocoa economy in Asante—a chronology that can provide a context for understanding not just the capture of unmarried women, but the crisis in morality and sexuality that engulfed Asante in the years between the two world wars.[16] Few would dispute G. Austin's contention that the labor necessary for the rapid spread of cocoa came "very largely from established, non-capitalist sources." Initially, these sources included the "farmowners themselves, their families, their slaves and pawns, cooperative groups of neighbors and, in the case of chiefs, corvée labour provided by their subjects."[17] However, with the abolition of slavery and the prohibition of pawning in Asante in 1908, wives' labor became increasingly essential because few men had the means to pay for hired labor.[18]

Wives' provision of labor in the creation of cocoa farms flowed logically from pre-cocoa productive obligations between spouses. Wives commonly grew food crops on land cleared by their husbands—crops that fed the family and provided a surplus wives could sell. Indeed, in the first three to four years of a cocoa farm's existence, the only returns from cocoa farms were the food crops—particularly crops like plantain or cocoyam—that were planted to shade the young trees during their first years. After that point, however, food crops (that is, the wife's only material and guaranteed return on her labor investment in the farm) diminished. Any labor invested by a wife after a cocoa farm became mature was directly compensated "only in the continued obligation of her husband," as Roberts writes, "to provide part of her subsistence from his own earnings" (Roberts 1987:54). Obviously, for wives, the investment of labor in a husband's cocoa farm did not provide for future economic security. For this reason, as C. Okali observed, "wives working on new and young farms were always aware that they were not working on joint economic enterprises. They expected eventually to establish their own separate economic concerns" (Okali 1983:170). The historical evidence suggests that this is precisely what many did *after* the initial establishment of cocoa in an area. As Austin has suggested, women's ownership of cocoa farms in Asante during the first two decades of the twentieth century was exceedingly rare. After that point, it became far more common and was directly correlated to the length of time cocoa had been cultivated in a given area. "The longer that cocoa-growing had been established in a given district," he writes, "the higher the proportion of women among the growing number of cocoa farmowners and among the increasing number of owners of bearing trees" (Austin 1994:141–2).[19]

Thus, by the third decade of the twentieth century, many Asante women were establishing their own cocoa farms in an effort to gain better long-term economic security than was promised from laboring on a husband's mature farm.[20] And the independent establishing of a cocoa farm was only one in a series of options that opened to women in areas where the cocoa economy was in place. "The growth of male cocoa income," according to Austin's account, "created economic opportunities for women in local markets, both as producers (for example, of food crops and cooked food) and as traders" (Austin 1994:142–3). Certainly Gracia Clark's work on Kumasi market women portrays this era as absolutely pivotal, with women moving in dramatic numbers into trading, especially in previously male-dominated commodities (Austin 1994:142–3; Clark 1994: esp. 316–8). That many women seized such opportunities in the 1920s may have stood them in good stead, at least vis-à-vis many subordinate males, when the cocoa economy contracted after 1928. While far more research is required, it is not improbable that while farming incomes fell, local trading incomes continued to expand. In other words, women who had moved into foodstuffs marketing may have been better placed to weather the economic drought of the 1930s than many of the small-scale male cocoa farmers who had entered the cocoa economy in previous decades.

It is in this confusing period of transition in the gendered development of Asante's cocoa economy that we must locate the strange episodes in which unmarried women were rounded up. It was during the period from 1920 to 1935, with cocoa well-established in many parts of Asante, that women's role in the cash economy was both changing and diversifying. Many wives were making the move from being the most common form of exploitable labor during cocoa's introduction to exploiting, themselves, the new openings for economic autonomy and security presented by the still-expanding cocoa economy. Their moves are evident not just in the statistics documenting the increasing number of women cocoa farmowners or in descriptions of the growing markets in foodstuffs, but in the crisis in marriage so well-documented in customary court cases and in life histories. Indeed, even when the cocoa economy began to contract at the end of the 1920s, at least some women were well-placed to endure the lean years that lay ahead because they had moved into the local markets as traders. Perhaps that is the resilience Afua Fom so succinctly captured when she mused that "in those days, the women were able to get money faster than the men." And in those days of disorder, women like Adwoa Addae were quite prepared to divorce husbands who refused to set up farms for them. Others turned to customary courts to challenge matrilineal inheritance, demanding portions of a divorced or deceased husband's cocoa farm in recognition of labor invested.[21] Still others sought to avoid marriage altogether or to insist on the mutuality of conjugal obligations.[22] These bits and pieces evidenced a crisis in conjugal obligations in Asante, a contest over the meanings of marriage. They were, more than anything, about the struggle for control over women's productive and reproductive labor in Asante—control at the very moment women were beginning to negotiate their own spaces within the colonial economy. That this was a struggle articulated in a discourse of "bad girls" and "lazy men" or of prostitution, venereal disease, and moral degeneration should come as no surprise. Women's economic alternatives were easily represented, as Roberts has argued, "as the removal of constraints upon their sexuality" (Roberts 1987:49).[23]

But how could constraints be reasserted? How could moral order be constructed out of the crisis? Indirect rule, I would argue, was key to the ordering process and must be understood in terms of its specific implications, during the interwar era, for mediating gender conflict and reformulating gender subordination.[24] While indirect rule served the obvious ends of providing administration on the cheap and legitimating colonialism, it also facilitated colonization of the domestic realm—the world of marriage, divorce, adultery, childbirth, and death. Asante chiefs, as the arbiters of "customary law," were empowered to manipulate meanings and redefine relationships. A good portion of their energy was thus focused on women's roles, women's sexuality, and women's challenges to definitions of marriage.[25] The capture of unmarried women, therefore, simply evidenced one set of efforts by Asante's indirect rule chiefs to intervene directly in the negotiation of marriage and to regulate women's productive and reproductive power.

And were those efforts successful? Many women remember the capture of "spinsters" as solving momentarily the crisis in marriage. As Beatrice Nyarko recalled, "People became afraid. It put fear in them" (Nyarko 1992). Rosina Boama agreed: "When the chiefs did that, they started getting married and things became calm" (Boama 1992). However, in the long run, many argue that "it didn't help at all" (Addae 1992), that its impact was short-lived. Certainly, the capture did not serve, as Grier writes of indirect rule generally, to "guarantee girls and women as unpaid sources of labor on the farms." Indeed, nothing in Asante politics from 1900 to the present has managed to guarantee that exploitation, only to facilitate it in the face of consistent and unrelenting challenge (Grier 1992:323–8).

But this particular form of coercion was unsuccessful in even minimally facilitating the exploitation of women's unpaid labor and one important reason for its failure was that the capture of unmarried women did not obtain the backing of the colonial government. In contrast to their support for various changes in the "customary" meanings of marriage, divorce, and adultery during the colonial period, the British authorities did not consider the arrest of unmarried women to be legitimate or to have "customary" precedents. This is not to suggest that the British were unconcerned with women's uncontrollability, but that the ways in which that control could be articulated were circumscribed by notions of what was deemed repugnant to "justice, equity and good conscience," or by a "repugnancy test," as Kristin Mann and Richard Roberts have termed it (1991:13–4, 21).

Yet perhaps far more important than the absence of British support in explaining the long-term failure of the round-ups was the success of many women in subverting the entire process from the outset. Afua Fom recalls that once women entered the room where they were to be kept, some would immediately mention a name—"any man's name." They had arranged with men in advance of their arrest: "'When I am arrested I will mention your name, so you will come.'" At times, a woman gave her release fee to a male accomplice; once arrested, the woman named that man, he came, he paid the fee, and she was set free, supposedly to marry her suitor. At other times, Afua Fom reported, women mentioned their brother's name. The brother paid the fee for his sister's release. Once the sister married, the brother would expect to be reimbursed by the husband. "He'll get some money," she recalled, "from whomever wants to get married to you" (Fom 1993). Afua Fom's recollections of how women circumvented the aim of the capture is certainly corroborated by Afuah Buo's testimony in the 1929 Asokore trial. Buo, it will be recalled, testified that the plaintiff had told her, prior to her arrest, that he would "clear [her] out" if she were arrested.

Women's circumvention of chiefs' efforts to regulate their productive and reproductive labor with the assistance of male accomplices underscores women's ability to shape actively the emerging colonial world. There is certainly no shortage of evidence on this score. Once the cocoa economy was established, many challenged their roles as unpaid productive labor and sought economic autonomy in the rapidly expanding cash economy as cocoa farmowners in their own right, or as foodstuff producers and traders. The chaos unleashed by this movement of women into the cash economy, combined with a host of other factors—urbanization, Western education, Christianity, and British colonial courts—warranted drastic action by those empowered to restore order out of chaos. But the actions of Asante's chiefs in this particular case—the wholesale arrests of all unmarried women—appear to have been easily circumvented by the women concerned. Granted, chiefs still collected 5/- for every woman captured, thus making the exercise a "money-making proposition," but they did not succeed in securing control over women's productive and reproductive labor, or, in their own words, encouraging "conjugal marriages among our womenfolk." At best, the chiefs had succeeded merely in implementing, and for a very short time, a kind of "non-marriage tax" by making women pay 5/- for not marrying. This is not to suggest that women simply walked away from episodes like the "spinster round-ups" as long-term victors in the struggle for control over their labor, particularly their labor as wives. The spaces women negotiated for themselves in the colonial economy were narrow at best, fleeting at worst and required constant, ever-evolving forms of defense. But it is to argue that women made history in colonial Asante, they were not just victims of it. The story of the capture of unmarried women thus stands as testament not simply to the power of chiefs under indirect rule, but to the success of at least some Asante women in negotiating the harsh terrain of cocoa, cash, and colonialism.

NOTES

Research for this chapter was supported by the National Endowment for the Humanities, the Fulbright-Hays Research Program, the Social Science Research Council, the Institute of African Studies, University of Ghana, and the University of Missouri Research Council. I wish to acknowledge this support and the generous assistance of the staffs of the National Archives of Ghana, Manhyia Record Office, and the Centre for African Studies at Cambridge. A longer version of this chapter appeared in the *Journal of African History* 37:2 (1996). I wish to thank the journal editors for permission to reprint it here.

1. It is worth underscoring here the wide-ranging autonomy enjoyed by Native Authorities in Asante and other parts of the Gold Coast, compared to the limited powers allotted to chiefs by colonial authorities in areas with a substantial white settler population and/or a large migrant labor force. See Rathbone's discussion of the "remarkably indirect Indirect Rule" that characterized the State Council in colonial Akyem Abuakwa (Rathbone 1993:54–67). Also see Allman (1991:179–80). Cf. Chanock (1985:25–47 and passim, 1982).

2. To date, I have found written evidence of arrests occurring in the Asante towns of Adansi, Asokore, Bekwai, Edweso, Effiduasi, and Mansu Nkwanta.

3. Most interviews were conducted by the author with the assistance of N. O. Agyeman-Duah. Ivor Agyeman-Duah and Selina Opoku-Agyeman assisted with some of the 1993 interviews. Copies of interview transcripts are on deposit in the Melville J. Herskovits Library, Northwestern University, and the Institute of African Studies Library, University of Ghana.

4. Christaller defines *osigyani* (pl. *asigyafo*), as "an unmarried person, i.e. a man or women who has either not been married at all, or a man who has sent away his wife, or a woman who has forsaken her husband, in general one who is not in the state of regular marriage" (Christaller 1933:456).

5. The fees involved in these arrests, though not exhorbitant, were not inconsequential.

6. Vellenga's references were to a sub-file in the "Ghanaian archives" entitled, "Forced Marriage of African Girls, Prevention of, 12 June 1939," and a letter to the editor, *Gold Coast Independent*, 15 January 1930.

7. I am not alone in associating chaos with cocoa. Gwendolyn Mikell (1989) has used "chaos" to describe the broader economic, political, and social turmoil associated with the spread of cocoa production throughout Ghana in her book. My use of "chaos" here is more circumscribed than Mikell's, in that it is meant to capture the specific disorder in gender relations that occurred in Asante as a result of the expanding cash economy.

8. The Mansu Nkwantahene reported that "the object of beaten gong-gong is to prevent venereal diseases and etc. prevalent within the Division" (National Archives of Nigeria, Kumasi [NAGK], ARA 1907).

9. Lovett has discussed the fluidity of marriage arrangements in the urban townships of the Copperbelt during the same period (1989:31). For a discussion of marriage in Asante today, see Clark (1994), chapter 9, but esp. 344–8.

10. See also Tashjian (1995) and Allman and Tashjian (2000).

11. Since 1992, I have been collecting life histories and reminiscences from older Asante women as part of a broader project on gender and social change in the colonial period. These efforts have focused on the Ashanti Newtown district of Kumasi, on suburban Tafo and on the rural towns of Effiduasi and Asokore. While none of the women with whom I spoke in Kumasi and Tafo recalled the capture of unmarried women, many in Effiduasi and Asokore could remember the episode in some detail.

12. Again, we are hampered by the dearth of demographic information for this period. Certainly, no such imbalance appears in the 1948 *Census,* and the *Censuses* for 1921 and for 1931, although admittedly unreliable, in fact suggest that the male population in Asante was growing faster than the female population during this period as a

result of immigration from the Northern Territories. See Gold Coast (1948), Engman (1986), esp. 92 and 100–5 for data on sex ratios.

13. It is difficult to retrieve the numbers involved in these arrests. Most of the women whose reminiscences I have recorded talked of "many" or "not many." The written sources provide no statistics. Afua Fom recalled that there were "maybe sixty. . . . But there may be more than that because they were going to the farms. The sixty is what I saw. But we were more than sixty because they went far" (Fom 1993).

14. Jeater's recent study (1993) underscores the importance of disentangling women's economic agency and independence from moral discourses regarding promiscuity and perversion.

15. Among the more easily accessible sources are Austin (1987); Dunn and Robertson (1973); Grier (1992:304–28); Hill (1963); Okali (1983); Mikell (1989); and Vellenga (1986).

16. Implicit in Roberts' discussion of cocoa in Sefwi Wiawso is such a "gendered chronology," though it differs in important respects from the chronology proposed here for Asante. See Roberts (1987:53–5).

17. Austin (1987:260–2); Grier (1992:314); Mikell (1989:107). See also Austin (1994).

18. Many of those wives, in fact, were pawns to their husbands, despite the 1908 abolition. While male pawnage decreased dramatically after 1908, wives-as-pawns were quite common well into the 1940s. As Austin has argued, "The pawning of women was relatively safe from prosecution by the colonial authorities, as long as the loan could be presented as a marriage payment, that is as *tiri sika*." He demonstrates quite convincingly that pawnage was not simply abolished, but declined in uneven, ambiguous, and very gendered ways that profoundly impacted conjugal relationships. See Austin (1987:264–5; 1994:137–43).

19. Women's entry into cocoa farming did not mirror men's. Most significantly, women's plots were generally smaller than men's, their size being limited, as Grier argued, "by the labor [a woman] . . . could spare, by the willingness of her kin members and spouse to help her out, and by her ability to acquire a pawn or hire a laborer" (1992:322).

20. Austin notes the special case of pawn-wives who had to share some of their proceeds with their "creditor-husbands" and thus had less incentive to acquire farms in their own right as a means of security and autonomy (1994:142).

21. Countless numbers of such cases can be found in the record books stored at Manhyia Record Office, Kumasi. See, particularly, the records of the Kumasihene's Native Tribunal, 1926–35, the Asantehene's Divisional Native Court B, 1935–60, and the Kumasi Divisional ("Clan") Courts, 1928–45 (consisting of Kyidom, Kronti, Gyasi, Ankobia, Oyoko, Benkum, Akwamu, and Adonten).

22. Roberts noted a similar pattern in Sefwi Wiawso (1987:54–5).

23. See also Allman (1991:176–89); Hunt (1991; 1990: esp. 155–6); Summers (1991); Schmidt (1992: esp. 98–106); and Jeater (1993: esp. 119–69).

24. Vaughan (1991), esp. 129–40, and Parpart (1994), esp. 244–49, make important contributions to our understanding of the gendered implications of indirect rule. Unfortunately, most scholars addressing this question work in areas with sizable settler populations, in former colonies where indirect rule institutions bore little resemblance to precolonial political organizations. (Roberts' pioneering work on Sefwi Wiawso is an important exception here [1987, esp. 48–57].)

25. For example, chiefs and elders refused to consider allowing wives to inherit from their husbands for fear that Asante women would simply poison their husbands at the slightest provocation in order to inherit the farm. See Asante Confederacy Council, *Minutes of the Third Session*, 7–23 March 1938.

REFERENCES

Interviews:

Adwoa Addae, Effiduasi, 28 August 1992; 30 June 1993
Akosua Atta (a.k.a. Sarah Obeng), Asokore, 26 August 1992
Akosua So, Effiduasi, 28 August 1992
Beatrice Nyarko, Effiduasi, 24 August 1992
Eponuahemaa Afua Fom, Effiduasi, 1 September 1992; 30 June 1993
Jean Asare, Effiduasi, 30 June 1993
Rosina Boama, Effiduasi, 24 August 1992
Yaa Dufie, Effiduasi, 25 August 1992

Archival Sources:

Fortes Papers. Centre for African Studies, Cambridge University. "Marriage Prestations," no date, and *Kwaku Afram v. Afuah Buo*, 13 August 1929, Native Tribunal of Asokore, mimeo.
Manhyia Record Office, Asante Confederacy Council, *Minutes of the Third Session*, 7–23 March 1938.
National Archives of Ghana, Accra (NAGA): ADM.52/5/3, *Mampong District Record Book, 1931–1946*.
National Archives of Ghana, Kumasi (NAGK), Ashanti Regional Administration Files (ARA) 1286: Report on Native Affairs: Mampong District for Two Quarters Ending the 31st March 1933 and ARA 1907: Assistant Chief Commissioner, Ashanti, to Chief Commissioner, Ashanti, dd. Kumasi, 19 July 1932; District Commissioner, Bekwai, to Assistant Chief Commissioner, Ashanti, dd. Bekwai, 23 July 1932; Bekwaihene to District Officer, Bekwai, dd. Bekwai, 23 July 1932; Mansu Nkwantahene to District Commissioner, Bekwai, dd. Mansu Nkwanta, 26 July 1932; Chief Commissioner to Assistant Chief Commissioner, dd. 18 July 1932.

Published Sources:

Allman, Jean. 1991. "Of 'Spinsters,' 'Concubines' and 'Wicked Women': Reflections on Gender and Social Change in Colonial Asante." *Gender and History* 3: 176–89.
———. 1994. "Making Mothers: Missionaries, Medical Officers and Women's Work in Colonial Asante, 1924–1945." *History Workshop Journal* 38: 23–47.
———. 1996. "Adultery and the State in Asante: Reflections on Gender, Class and Power from 1800 to 1950." In J. O. Hunwick and N. Lawler (eds.), *The Cloth of*

Many Colored Silks: Papers on History and Society. Evanston, IL: Northwestern University Press, pp. 27–66.

Allman, J. and Tashjian, V. 2000. *"I Will Not Eat Stone": A Women's History of Colonial Asante*. Portsmouth, NH: Heinemann.

Austin, G. 1987. "The Emergence of Capitalist Relations in South Asante Cocoa-Farming, c. 1916–33." *Journal of African History* 32: 259–79.

———. 1994. "Human Pawning in Asante, 1800–1950: Markets and Coercion, Gender and Cocoa." In T. Falola and P. E. Lovejoy (eds.), *Pawnship in Africa: Debt Bondage in Historical Perspective*. Boulder, CO: Westview Press, pp. 119–60.

Chanock, Martin. 1982. "Making Customary Law: Men, Women, and Courts in Colonial Northern Rhodesia." In M. J. Hay and M. Wright (eds.), *African Women and the Law: Historical Perspectives*. Boston: Boston University Papers on Africa, VII, pp. 53–67.

———. 1985. *Law, Custom and Social Order: The Colonial Experience in Malawi and Zambia*. Cambridge: Cambridge University Press.

Christaller, J. G. 1933. *Dictionary of the Asante and Fante Language Called Tshi*. Basel: Basel Evangelical Missionary Society.

Clark, Gracia. 1994. *Onions Are My Husband: Survival and Accumulation by West African Market Women*. Chicago: University of Chicago Press.

Dunn, J. and A. F. Robertson 1973. *Dependence and Opportunity: Political Change in Ahafo*. Cambridge: Cambridge University Press.

Engman, E.V.T. 1986. *Population of Ghana, 1850–1960*. Accra: Ghana Universities Press.

Fortes, Meyer. 1950. "Kinship and Marriage Among the Ashanti." In A. R. Radcliffe-Brown and D. Forde (eds.), *African Systems of Kinship and Marriage*. London: International African Institute, pp. 252–84.

Gold Coast 1948. *Census of Population, 1948*. Accra: Government Printer.

Grier, Beverly. 1992. "Pawns, Porters and Petty Traders: Women in the Transition to Cash Crop Agriculture in Colonial Ghana." *Signs* 17: 304–28.

Hill, Polly. 1963. *The Migrant Cocoa-Farmers of Southern Ghana*. Cambridge: Cambridge University Press.

Hunt, Nancy Rose. 1990. "Domesticity and Colonialism in Belgian Africa: Usumbura's *Foyer Social*, 1946–1960." In J. O'Barr, D. Pope, and M. Wyer (eds.), *Ties That Bind*. Chicago: University of Chicago Press, pp. 149–77.

———. 1991. "Noise over Camouflaged Polygamy, Colonial Morality Taxation, and a Woman-Naming Crisis in Belgian Africa." *Journal of African History* 32: 471–94.

Jeater, Diane. 1993. *Marriage, Perversion, and Power: The Construction of Moral Discourse in Southern Rhodesia, 1894–1930*. Oxford: Clarendon Press.

Kyei, T.E. 1992. *Marriage and Divorce among the Asante: A Study Undertaken in the Course of the "Ashanti Social Survey (1945)."* Cambridge: African Studies Centre.

Lovett, Margot. 1989. "Gender Relations, Class Formation and the Colonial State." In Jane Parpart and Kathleen Staudt (eds.), *Women and the State in Africa*. Boulder, CO: Lynne Rienner, pp. 23–46.

Mann, Kristin and Richard Roberts. 1991 (eds.), *Law in Colonial Africa*. Portsmouth, NH: Heinemann.

Mikell, Gwendolyn. 1989. *Cocoa and Chaos in Ghana*. New York: Paragon House.

Okali, C. 1983. "Kinship and Cocoa Farming in Ghana." In Christine Oppong (ed.), *Female and Male in West Africa*. London: George Allen and Unwin, pp. 169–78.

Parpart, Jane. 1994. "'Where Is Your Mother?': Gender, Urban Marriage, and Colonial Discourse on the Zambian Copperbelt, 1924–1945." *International Journal of African Historical Studies* 27: 241–71.

Rathbone, Richard. 1993. *Murder and Politics in Colonial Ghana*. New Haven, CT: Yale University Press.

Rattray, R. S. 1927. *Religion and Art in Ashanti*. Oxford: Clarendon Press.

———. 1929. *Ashanti Law and Constitution*. Oxford: Clarendon Press.

Roberts, P. A. 1987. "The State and the Regulation of Marriage: Sefwi Wiawso (Ghana), 1900–40." In H. Afshar (ed.), *Women, State, and Ideology: Studies from Africa and Asia*. Binghamton: State University of New York Press, pp. 48–69.

Schmidt, Elizabeth. 1992. *Peasants, Traders and Wives: Shona Women in the History of Zimbabwe, 1870–1939*. Portsmouth, NH: Heinemann.

Summers, Carol. 1991. "Intimate Colonialism: The Imperial Production of Reproduction in Uganda, 1907–1925." *Signs* 16: 787–807.

Tashjian, V. 1995. "It's Mine and It's Ours Are Not the Same Thing: A History of Marriage in Rural Asante, 1900–1957." Ph.D. thesis, Northwestern University.

Vaughan, Megan. 1991. *Curing Their Ills: Colonial Power and African Illness*. Stanford, CA: Stanford University Press.

Vellenga, D. D. 1983. "Who Is a Wife?" In Christine Oppong (ed.), *Female and Male in West Africa*. London: George Allen and Unwin, pp. 144–55.

———. 1986. "Matriliny, Patriliny and Class Formation Among Women Cocoa Farmers in Two Rural Areas of Ghana." In Claire Robertson and Iris Berger (eds.), *Women and Class in Africa*. New York: Holmes and Meier, pp. 62–77.

8

"MY DAUGHTER . . . BELONGS TO THE GOVERNMENT NOW": MARRIAGE, MAASAI, AND THE TANZANIAN STATE

Dorothy L. Hodgson

INTRODUCTION[1]

To maintain their hegemony,[2] patriarchies[3] in different times and places define gender relationships and roles like "wife," "mother," "daughter," or even "woman" in ways that seem natural, self-evident, unchangeable. Women who defy these dominant representations by challenging patriarchal control of their sexuality, fertility, or autonomy disrupt the status quo and threaten patriarchal hegemony by exposing the possibility for alternative, non-normative meanings and practices. To defuse the subversive potential of these "wicked" women, patriarchies must stigmatize the women's actions or persons as "wicked" or morally corrupt. Paradoxically, these same women serve as the moral foil patriarchies need to sustain their dominant conceptions of "appropriate" gender roles and relations: the threat of being labeled and ostracized as "wicked" keeps other women in line.

To help us theorize about the relationship between patriarchies and "wicked" women, I would like to examine one moment when a patriarchy, or rather layers of patriarchy, was directly challenged by an unlikely antagonist. In 1992, a young Maasai woman in Tanzania took her father to court rather than marry according to his will. By directly challenging her father's authority, and by implication, the authority of local elders, her suit disrupted local gendered relations of power. Her father and elder Maasai men were therefore compelled to scramble, both inside and outside of the courtroom, to defend their "legitimate" authority, an authority premised on a certain configuration of "naturalized" and "proper" gender roles and relations. And ultimately, by challenging the dominant meanings of "daughter" and "father," this one "wicked" woman reconfigured, however slightly, local gendered relations of power. Set within the shifting, gendered landscapes of power of the individual, family, community, and nation-state, the case provides a window onto the strategies—the ongoing and complex negotiations, contestations and collaborations of power—required for patriarchies to maintain their dominance by silencing and ostracizing "wicked" women.

THE CASE OF THE DISOBEDIENT DAUGHTER

The facts of the case are complicated. Almost twenty-five years ago, Aladala kicked one of his wives, Nayieu, out of his homestead (*enkang'*) after her first three children died in infancy. She moved to her brother Ronda's homestead where she eventually gave birth to four healthy children, two boys and two girls. Ronda cared for her and her children as a husband should have—he helped Nayieu to feed, clothe, and care for her children, financed the children's primary education, and contributed cattle and small stock for slaughter on the required ritual occasions.

Aloya, one of her daughters, became involved with Masierr, a young, educated Maasai man who lived nearby and was a successful farmer and livestock trader. They soon had a son, and Masierr made several bridewealth payments to Aloya's mother and uncles. Simultaneously, however, Aladala arranged a marriage for Aloya with another man named Shongon, then negotiated a settlement with the elders to re-establish his rights over Aloya—he gave Ronda five head of cattle and bridewealth rights over another daughter, then took Aloya, her son, and Nayieu to his homestead to prepare for Aloya's marriage to Shongon.

On the same day that Aladala moved Aloya to his home, Masierr made plans with his brothers to recover her. That evening they walked to Aladala's homestead, quietly woke Aloya, and escorted her and her baby to Masierr's homestead. The next morning they hired a car, and Masierr, Aloya, and the baby drove away to hide with a relative of Masierr's.

When Aladala woke up that morning and realized what had happened, he was furious. He sent a man to the police to report that Masierr had "stolen" his daughter, then quickly called a meeting of the elders of his Lukumai clan.

That same afternoon, the elders of the clan walked together to a neighboring homestead where a woman from their clan was married to one of Ronda's brothers. They forced the woman and all her children to pack immediately and come with them—even though she and her husband were completely uninvolved in the elopement, she was now the Lukumai clan's "hostage" until Ronda helped return Masierr and Aloya. The elders were pleased by her calm submission to their demands, and promised her a sheep as a reward for her good behavior as a clan daughter.

While the hostage woman and her children lived at Aladala's homestead, the search for Masierr and Aloya continued. In about two weeks they were found and forced to return to their village. Masierr spent the night in police custody, on charges of "stealing" Aloya, but was released the next morning. A few days after they were found, Aloya and her son returned to Aladala's homestead. Preparations were renewed for her impending marriage to Shongon. But that night Masierr again came with his brothers and took Aloya; this time they went directly to the police station in Monduli. At the station, Aloya swore a statement in fluent Swahili accusing Aladala of forcing her to marry against her will, and threatening to kill herself by drinking cattle dip if he persevered. And so began the court case of Aloya versus Aladala, daughter versus father, the law of the Tanzanian state versus current patriarchal renditions of Maasai cultural "tradition."[4]

By directly challenging the authority of elder Maasai men, Aloya's suit threatened local gendered relations of power. As the events recounted so far attest, elder men met on various occasions to make decisions that affected the lives of men and especially women not in attendance, decisions that were to be heeded without hesitation, without questioning, and certainly without direct confrontation. And, most people obeyed, thereby acknowledging and reinforcing the authority of the elders. Nayieu packed her belongings and moved back to her husband's homestead for the first time in over twenty years; the daughter of the Lukumai clan, called from her farm, calmly changed her clothes, gathered her children, and walked away from her husband and house. And the elders, accustomed to having unchallenged authority, expected no less.

But Aloya wanted more—knowing that she had no voice in the decisions of the elders, she sought a forum where she could speak her position and confront her father as an equal—and the legal system of the Tanzanian state, unlike the meetings of Maasai elders, provided her such an opportunity. Rejecting the passive role of silent assent expected of her as a "daughter" in Maasai society, she reached outside to the encompassing system of the Tanzanian state. Within the structure of the Tanzanian state she was not a daughter but a citizen, and she knew that citizens—male or female, old or young, wealthy or poor—ideally had an equal voice before the law.

Of course, ideals rarely correspond with reality. As numerous feminist scholars have shown, nation-states like Tanzania are inherently gendered in their constitution, objectives, and practices (Parpart and Staudt 1988). Comprised mainly of elite men with a history of excluding women from political power and economic resources, and promoting political and development agendas that reinforce their own authority, the Tanzanian nation-state, despite its former socialist rhetoric and practices has been and still is profoundly patriarchal (cf. Geiger 1982, 1987, 1997; Mascarenhas and Mbilinyi 1983; Swantz 1985; Tanzania Gender Networking Programme [TGNP] 1993).

As an important arena for the exercise of state power, the Tanzanian legal system is similarly patriarchal. Modeled on the British system, it uses both British and Tanzanian laws and case holdings as precedents. Like the earlier colonial legal system, however, it defers to "customary law" when possible. But, as Chanock (1982) has shown for Northern Rhodesia, "customary law" was collaboratively produced by colonial administrators and elder men. Eager to achieve the "neutrality" and "consistency" essential to the Western, "rational" legal model, colonial administrators searched for the normative rules in each "culture," which they could learn, record, and then apply to the specifics of the various cases. They turned to elder men, who, as the recognized "authorities" on "culture" and "tradition," used the opportunity to strengthen their control over women and younger men by offering partial, interested, versions of "customary" law. Recording and codifying the elders' decisions in diverse cases as "law" reified what were actually specific decisions made according to the particular details of each case, details that often included extenuating circumstances like previous exchanges or kinship relations. Once customary laws were codified, elder men were accustomed to invoking them and having them enforced by colonial administrators (Chanock 1982; see also Moore 1986; Hay and Wright 1982; Schmidt 1990; Mann 1982; Mann and Roberts 1991; Mbilinyi 1988).[5]

The alignment between the parallel patriarchal legal systems of the elders and the state continued into the postcolonial period. Increased agitation and activity by Tanzanian women and others did, however, produce legislative changes, such as the enactment of the Marriage Law of 1971, which held, among other things, that "No marriage shall be contracted except with the consent, freely and voluntarily given, by each of the parties thereto" (Law of Marriage Act, 1971, section 16[1]). Of course, despite explicit pronouncements that the Marriage Law and other national laws took precedent over "customary" law when they directly conflicted, it was still left to the discretion of the local magistrates to decide which law to invoke and how to interpret its application.[6]

News of Aloya's accusations against her father and her threat of suicide quickly reached the village. Most people I spoke to were shocked, astonished that a young woman would have the audacity to take her father to court. They claimed that it was the first such case they had heard of. Village elders, especially those of Aladala's close-knit Lukumai clan were furious, recognizing in Aloya's actions a direct challenge to their authority: If, as fathers, they could not control their daughters, then whom could they control? A somber mood infused the villagers as they observed the elders' frequent meetings. Almost immediately, the Lukumai elders threatened to curse Aloya if she pursued the court case against her father. Their prompt threat revealed their anxiety over the failure of their "legitimate authority" to elicit respect and exert control. As their ultimate weapon, the curse would both stigmatize and ostracize Aloya in a single act.[7]

The elders also moved quickly to reassert their control over their other daughters. After a flurry of meetings, they nominated an elder man to serve as the *Laigwenani lo Mila* ("Chairman of Tradition/Customs") for the three villages in the area. His power was to settle debates within Maasai "customary" law—such as Aloya's case—before they went to the government court. The office was clearly a compromise solution by the local Maasai patriarchy as it tried to reconfigure itself to accommodate the postcolonial shifts in the structures of the state, shifts evident in the local magistrate's willingness to hear Aloya's case. The novelty of the office and its intermediary position between Maasai and state authorities were clearly marked by the merging of the local and national language in its title: *Laigwenani* means chairperson or leader in Maa, while *Mila* is a Swahili word meaning culture or tradition. And state administrators were complicit in this reconfiguration of the parameters of Maasai patriarchal authority: local Chama Cha Mapinduzi[8] officials and area elders attended the improvised blessing ceremony, and a document detailing the ceremony and the new Chairman's duties was quickly carried to the District Officer for endorsement. With the agreement of the state, the elders had quickly regained their authority to decide their own "customary" affairs, such as the marriages of their daughters. They were too late, however, to regain jurisdiction over Aloya's case.

Other reactions were diverse. Humiliated by his daughter's actions, Aladala assured the elders that no matter what the court decided, Aloya would marry Shongon as promised. As the bereft suitor, Shongon was furious. I met him a few days later at a ceremony, and he coldly told me that if Aloya had been his daughter, he would personally have handed her the cattle dip to drink rather then suffer such insolence. Only two extended families, that of Masierr and that of Aloya's maternal uncles, overtly supported her. A few educated men and women with whom I spoke privately told me that they admired and supported Aloya, and disapproved of the institution of arranged marriages. But they all said they would never voice such opinions in public, as they were afraid the elders would accuse them of having assisted and advised Aloya. Like most villagers, they too feared the anger and curses of the elders.

Despite the lack of overt help and encouragement and the looming threat of the elders' curse, Aloya pursued her case. On the first day of the trial her confrontation with different layers of patriarchy was strikingly visible: she stood quietly in her witness box, across from her father standing in his, both boxes a symbolic equal distance from the elevated platform where the male magistrate sat between his two elder male advisors. Both her witnesses and Aladala's witnesses would be men; no women would speak for or against her. The magistrate did ask Aladala if Nayieu, Aloya's mother, would testify, but Aladala replied that she would not come, and he was satisfied with the two witnesses he had, both elder male members of his clan. Despite her disadvantage as the lone woman in an intensely male space, Aloya had one advantage: the courtroom space was configured not only by gender but by the politics of the nation-state. Unlike Aladala, she had attended a government primary school and spoke fluent Swahili, the national language of Tanzania. She could therefore address and understand the court directly, while Aladala had to use an interpreter throughout the proceedings.

First the magistrate read, in Swahili, the charge against Aladala—that, contrary to Marriage Law 5/71, which forbids forced marriages, he had tried to force Aloya to marry against her will. Then Aloya, quietly but firmly, in fluent Swahili, told her story to the court:

> It was on May 5th, 1992 that the accused tried to force me to marry another man when I was already married. He tried to force me to marry [Shongon]. I am already married to [Masierr]. But [Aladala] told me that I had to marry the man he wanted, not [Masierr]. But Masierr and I were married in 1985 in Monduli Juu. The accused knows that I am married to [Masierr]. [Aladala] is my father, my parent, but since I was born I have grown up at my uncle's homestead. When I was married, my mother received my bridewealth. During all of my life I never knew that the accused was my father since I was not born and was not raised by his hand. I only ever knew my uncle. . . . I was told that my father had banished my mother a long time before I was born. . . . That is all. I just don't want to be forced to marry someone I don't want. (OCT, pp. 2–3)

In answer to questioning from her father, she replied:

> I told you that I didn't want you to force me. One day you came to my uncle's homestead. You didn't hit me, but you told me that you didn't want

me to marry [Masierr] because he was snot (*kamasi*). You tried to force me to marry that other man. My uncle had already married me to [Masierr]. My uncles drank the bridewealth beer. I didn't know that you were my father. (OCT, p. 3)

Under further questioning from the magistrate's two advisors, she added:

[Aladala] never came to my uncles before I was married. My mother told me my father was around but I didn't know he was the accused. My uncles were always there as well as other elders who were neighbors. . . . My father never came to slaughter for my mother, and when I was circumcised I didn't see him. My uncles slaughtered for my mother. I have given birth to one child with my husband. [Aladala] tried to force me to marry after I had given birth. I asked him what would happen to my child and he told me my child would be taken by my new husband. It is not good to give the blood of one person to another person. If I had given birth outside of marriage, the child would have been paid for, but I gave birth while I was married. (OCT, p. 3)

Masierr testified next, repeating and confirming much of Aloya's testimony. He explained that Aloya was his wife, that he had begun courting her in 1985 after she had finished school, and had paid bridewealth to her mother and uncles for her, marrying her in the "traditional" Maasai way. He told the court that he could have taken Aloya to his homestead after she was circumcised, but usually a man waited until his new wife had given birth to her first child at her parents' home. So when Aloya gave birth, he began to arrange her move, which was when Aladala appeared and began to make trouble. Masierr did add some new information, however: that Aladala had threatened to whip Aloya if she refused to marry Shongon. During questioning, Aladala and the advisors to the magistrate all asked Masierr if he had known at the time who Aloya's father was. He repeatedly denied that he knew about Aladala, explaining that that was why he had given the engagement beer to Aloya's uncles.

In questioning the remaining witnesses, the court concentrated on three main issues: eliciting the details of "traditional" Maasai marriage; clarifying the rights and obligations of a "father"; and determining whether Ronda or Aladala should be properly regarded as Aloya's father. Their questions probed the parameters of patriarchal authority, its constitution and expression.

In determining the details of "traditional" Maasai marriage and bridewealth, the magistrate and his advisors, like their colonial predecessors, deferred to the authority of the male elders. They asked Aladala's two witnesses, elder male members of his Lukumai clan, to describe how Maasai marriages were arranged, focusing on the issue of consent. "According to the traditional customs of the Maasai," asked one advisor, "does a girl have the freedom to be able to search for a man that she likes?" "She is not able," answered the first witness. The advisor continued, "So you are saying that the accused used that traditional power to tell [Aloya] you WILL be married by that man?" The witness replied, "She wasn't forced. . . ," but the magistrate badgered him until he admitted that Aladala had the ability to use his "traditional" power to force Aloya to marry. "So," the magistrate said, "we can say that this girl had no choice?" "A long time ago yes," the witness replied, "but these days. . . ." "I am asking about a long time ago," interjected the advisor. "In the past," continued the witness, "she couldn't have chosen the person, . . . [but these days] she is told that a certain person is her fiancé, but if she doesn't want him she should say something before his wealth is sent." "So when," continued the magistrate, "did [Aladala] receive the [bridewealth] cattle? . . . He didn't tell her, did he, that he had accepted the wealth of a person?" "No, he didn't tell her." Similar questions were asked of Aladala's second witness: "If a father has decided to give his daughter to someone, does his daughter have a voice [in the decision]?" "According to Maasai custom," the witness replied, "she has none" (TT, pp. 50–53, 71).

In his testimony, Aladala asserted his "traditional" right to arrange Aloya's marriage without her knowledge in accordance with the version of Maasai "customary" law described by his witnesses. He claimed that both he and Aloya's mother Nayieu had known that Shongon was Aloya's fiancé, but that "with us, a child does not ask who she is engaged to." As to Aloya's accusation that he tried to force her to marry, he claimed that she had never said that she did not want to marry Shongon: "If she had told me at home that she didn't want him, I would have let it go. But she never said anything at home, she came straight to this courtroom" (TT, pp. 26, 29).

Several themes emerged from this discussion. One was the ambiguous role of "consent" in determining the difference between a "voluntary" marriage, an "arranged" marriage, and a "forced" marriage. Aladala's witnesses and Aladala himself argued that Aloya's marriage to Shongon was merely arranged, and that, unlike the custom in the past, she had the right to consent or not to consent to the arrangement. But Aloya's and Masierr's testimonies, and even part of Aladala's, disproved such claims: First, Aladala admitted to having received a substantial amount of bridewealth before Aloya was ever aware of her proposed spouse—was he really planning to ask her for her consent? Secondly, Aloya claimed several times that even after she told her father that she did not want to marry Shongon, he insisted that he would force her to. She was not going to marry Masierr, as she wished, but Shongon, as he wished. And finally, Masierr mentioned that Aladala had threatened to whip Aloya if she did not comply—surely the threat of physical violence implied that consent was not "freely and voluntarily" given?

A second theme was the legitimacy of her marriage arrangements with Masierr. For Aloya, Masierr, and Ronda, the marriage was legitimate—the proper permissions requested and granted, gifts paid and received, and now a child was born of the union. But in Aladala's eyes, it was not a legal marriage because he, as Aloya's father, had not made the arrangements, and had not received the bridewealth: "If there is someone who has deceived [Aloya] into believing that he would take her, then he has deceived me because I am her father, and that girl does not have two fathers, only me" (TT, p. 4). Aladala said that he first saw Masierr, "the one who deceived Aloya," on the day that he brought the five cattle to Ronda, and that very night Masierr stole Aloya. So, since, in his opinion, Aloya's relationship with Masierr was not a legitimate marriage, he felt free in arranging a "real" marriage for Aloya.

The payment and receipt of bridewealth was crucial to both parties in determining the legitimacy of the marriage. Masierr had paid Ronda several head of cattle in bridewealth for Aloya. But Aladala had received thirty-five head of cattle from Shongon for Aloya. And, according to all accounts in the village, Aladala, a once wealthy man turned poor, had already "eaten" them, used them all up. So Aladala offered the court a deal: he would let Aloya marry Masierr if Masierr agreed to reimburse the thirty-five cattle that Shongon had paid Aladala. And if Masierr refused, then Aloya could return "home" with Aladala, and stay with him until she found a man she liked who was willing to pay the full number of cattle (TT, pp. 3–4). The magistrate, shocked at the number of cattle ("thirty-five!"), registered Aladala's offer, but continued the investigation. When the court probed Aladala later about "traditional" Maasai bridewealth, he claimed that thirty-five cattle was the customary amount of bridewealth—the amount he had paid for his wife and that Shongon had promised to pay for his daughter (TT, p. 22).

But these definitions of "traditional" Maasai marriage and bridewealth now raised another issue before the court: If Maasai "tradition" allowed a father to arrange his daughter's marriage, as Aladala and his witnesses testified, then who was the father in this case—Aladala or Ronda? If bridewealth was crucial to both parties in determining the legitimacy of the marriage, who, as Aloya's father, should have been the recipient?

The court's probing exposed at least two competing definitions of fatherhood: a jural definition based on rights established through marriage and bridewealth, and a more "social" definition, based on the duties and responsibilities of a "father." For Aladala, it was enough that Nayieu, despite over twenty years of separation, was still his wife, making Aloya, as her child, his daughter. The elders had affirmed his rights when they decided that he could take Nayieu and Aloya to his *enkang'* if he gave Ronda five cows and bridewealth rights for his other daughter. And, by Maasai "customary" law, he was right—since the bridewealth he had paid for Nayieu had never been returned by her parents or her brothers, she was still, legally, his wife. And any children she conceived, whoever their genitor, or biological father, would therefore be recognized, legally, as the children of Aladala. For these Maasai elders, their patriarchal authority as husbands and fathers was constituted and expressed through the exchange of bridewealth.

The court, however, found Aladala's definition of "husband" and "father" and, by implication, the constitution of Maasai patriarchal authority, unconvincing. Their disbelief was evident in a question they asked Aladala's second witness: "According to Maasai custom, once you have married, even if your wife stays apart at her family's for forty years and you never go there, she is still your wife? Because your name is there? Even if you never took care of her and you just left her?" (TT, p. 63) "Yes," replied the witness, "she is mine" (TT, p. 63).

The court was less interested in such jural definitions and more interested in the duties and obligations entailed in being a "father." For the magistrate and his advisors, patriarchal authority and rights were established through the fulfillment of patriarchal obligations and duties; such authority was not bought but earned. During cross-examination of Ronda, Aladala, and Aladala's two witnesses, the court probed for the answers to the following questions:

- Where did Nayieu and her children, including Aloya, live during the past years?
- Who helped to feed and clothe Nayieu and her children?
- Who sponsored and paid for Aloya's schooling?
- Who provided animals at ritual occasions such as the name-giving ceremony (*orokiteng' le ntomonon*) and Aloya's circumcision?
- Had Aladala ever visited Nayieu and her children before the meeting with the elders?
- Had Aloya ever seen Aladala before the meeting?
- Who did Aloya consider to be her father?

Ronda testified that he fulfilled most of the above duties: he provided Nayieu and her children with a place to live and helped them meet all their food, clothing, schooling, and ritual needs. As a student, Aloya had used his name, "Ronda," as her "family" name.[9] He claimed that Aladala had never visited, coming only when Aloya reached marrying age. Furthermore, Aladala had never contributed anything to the family's maintenance, "not even tea leaves, much less a goat" (OCT, p. 6). Finally, neither Aladala nor Ronda had provided the animals for Aloya's circumcision ceremony; Masierr, as her fiancé, had.

Sensing the importance of these matters to the court, Aladala disputed Ronda's testimony. Awkwardly, he tried to characterize himself as fulfilling the court's definition of "father." He claimed that he had visited and slept with Nayieu while she lived at Ronda's, and that Aloya and the other children had known for many years that he was their father. He admitted that he knew that Aloya had used "Ronda" as her second name at school, but said it had not bothered him. The court remained unconvinced: "So here you are confirming for us that you had nothing to do with your child, but now when she is 'sweet' you remember her?" Aladala disagreed: "That's a lie, . . . I have fed her since she was little until now" (TT, pp. 19–20).

The ambivalence in trying to satisfy both definitions of "father" was evident in the contradictory testimonies of Aladala's two witnesses. Their allegiance to Aladala and desire to protect the legitimacy of elder male Maasai authority took precedence over their oaths to tell the truth, and they tried desperately to give the answers to the above questions that they thought the court wanted to hear. Both began their testimony with strong statements that Aladala had in no way forced Aloya to marry. The first witness supported Aladala's argument that Aloya had not been forced because she had never told her father she did not want to marry Shongon. Both witnesses claimed that Aladala had given food and animals to his family, although neither could clearly remember the details of such transfers. But the magistrate and his advisors soon caught them lying in their eagerness to help Aladala—the first witness claiming at first that Aladala was present at Aloya's circumcision, then later that Aladala would have been there except that he was in jail at the time; the second witness claiming to know the most intimate details of Nayieu's house, by virtue of being her neighbor, including the details of conversations he had not been part of.

The meaning of "father" was thus the source of much disagreement and confusion in these testimonies. A distinction was made between a "father" as a male person with a legal right obtained through marriage, and a "father" as a male person who actively performs the duties and obligations expected of the father role. While clearly distinguished in Ronda's and Aladala's accounts, the meaning of "father" was a source of ambiguity in Aloya's and Masierr's testimonies. When Aloya and Masierr said they didn't know that Aladala was Aloya's father, that was untrue. Like all the villagers and the local anthropologist, they knew that Aladala was the husband of Nayieu and thus the legal father of Aloya and Nayieu's other children. What they meant was while they knew about Aladala, they did not recognize him as fulfilling the role of Aloya's father since he had neglected his wife and children for so long. It was Ronda who had performed the fatherly duties that the court explored, so it was Ronda who was therefore recognized and treated like Aloya's father. And in his role as father, he had dutifully arranged his daughter Aloya's marriage and accepted bridewealth from his future son-in-law. For Ronda and the court, patriarchal authority was not bought, but earned.

In rendering his judgment, the magistrate first discussed the conflict evident between the marriage laws of the Tanzanian state and the "traditional" marriage laws of the Maasai. According to the magistrate, Marriage Law 5/71 clearly states that "anyone involved in any way with a marriage who knows that the permission of one of the parties to the marriage was not given, or was given only under force or by coercion; that person is guilty, and deserves a sentence of three years in prison" (D, p. 3). The magistrate continued:

> But this law contradicts the customs and beliefs of the Maasai which give the power to decide about marriage to the parents of both parties. Even if the party to the marriage is male or female, he or she has no choice about the marriage other then to obey the decision of his or her parents. Since these customs directly conflict with Marriage Law 5/71, we will follow the Marriage Law in our decision. (D, p. 3)

The magistrate then asked each of his two advisors to give their views on the guilt of Aladala. Both the advisors agreed that Aladala was guilty, as accused, of trying to force Aloya to marry against her will. The first advisor said he believed Aloya's testimony, and he understood how Aladala's actions had forced her to run away to her fiancé and finally bring this case. He thought that Aladala's guilt was clear—"instead of refuting the accusations against him, Aladala had tried to argue that his actions were OK. He proved his guilt by saying that [Aloya] should pay the thirty-five cattle so he could return them to [Shongon]" (D, p. 4). The advisor stated that he thought Aladala, not Masierr, should return Shongon's bridewealth.

The second advisor agreed with the comments of the first one, and added that he found the evidence that Aloya had already borne a child with Masierr compelling. Her suicide threat was also strong evidence that she was being forced to do something against her will; he worried that "the accused could lose her life from taking poison." He agreed that Aladala should return Shongon's payments, and thought Aloya should marry the man she wanted, following the customary marriage process.

The magistrate agreed with the recommendations of both advisors. Then he gave the courtroom a long lecture about the "evils" of forced marriages:

The accused knows the results of forcing his daughter to marry another man, but still, disdainfully, he does it. The harm done won't affect him but his daughter; she who is to be married will carry the burden of the house, even though she won't like it. She won't be patient, and a marriage of this kind will only be a marriage of misery, with the following likely results: (1) hate; (2) suffering; (3) death.

A person who has been forced to marry another person she doesn't like because of the greed of her parent over bridewealth must confront such misery, such hate in the marriage house, and finally she will take poison to remove herself from such a life. So that this affair is able to be understood in the community, I must openly pronounce that it is a very bad offense to force a person to marry another person she or he doesn't like. I find [Aladala] guilty as charged. (D, pp. 4–5)

Aladala was outraged. From his box, he yelled at the magistrate in Maa: "Take my daughter then, she is yours, she belongs to the government now. You take care of her, you marry her off, you receive her bridewealth. I disown her here and now." Then he sat down, bitter with anger, humiliation, and confusion. How could a magistrate deny him his rights as a father over his daughter, rights recognized by the Maasai elders themselves? How could the court support the accusations of a daughter against a father? What kind of legal system and government was this that could say that certain Maasai laws and customs were wrong?

The magistrate did consider the conflicts between the marriage laws of the Tanzanian state and those of the Maasai when he sentenced Aladala ten days later. First Aladala stood, pleading for leniency: "I am an old, sick man. My family depends on me. My children have no food" (D, p. 5). Then, after listening to the punishments suggested by his advisors, the magistrate said that since this was Aladala's first such offense, and since he recognized that Aladala had been acting according to Maasai custom, he would reduce the punishment recommended by the Marriage Law:

[Aladala], as a first time offender, will pay a fine of 5,000 shillings or go to jail for six months. . . . He will pay all the court costs. Furthermore, he will not continue to force [Aloya] to marry another man. As to the bridewealth of thirty-five cattle that he received from another man, Aladala is responsible for returning that bridewealth himself. That bridewealth will not be part of the marriage of [Aloya] and [Masierr]. (D, p. 5)

The sentence sounded lenient to Aladala's accusers, severe to his supporters, but all were happy that the case was over. Most of the villagers were surprised at the outcome, and worried that the case set a bad precedent for future marriages.

CONCLUSION: RECONFIGURING GENDER

As many Maasai realized, this case was more than the story of the true love of a young couple or the greed of an old man. By confronting her father, by challenging the very definitions of father and daughter, Aloya shifted, however slightly, the existing gendered relations of power. A daughter was no longer silent and obedient but outspoken and even confrontational. And a change in the definition of daughter necessarily created changes in other, related definitions—like father. An assertive daughter implied a father whose authority was no longer absolute, no longer unquestioned.

As a moment at which dominant representations of "proper" gender roles and relations were directly challenged by a "wicked" woman, this case has illuminated how certain gendered relations of power in one patriarchal society are maintained and might be changed. Aladala and his fellow elders used several strategies to defend their "legitimate" authority against Aloya's attack: outside of the courtroom, they threatened to curse her; inside, they appealed to "tradition" and "custom," argued that being a "father" was established through bridewealth payments, and articulated the rights of fathers and deference of daughters as "natural" and immutable. Like patriarchies elsewhere, the Maasai elders tried to vest relationships of family and kinship with certain meanings, rights, and obligations that seemed "natural" and self-evident. To speak of these duties, rights, and obligations as "culturally" determined, as based on "tradition," and therefore as normative and natural, served their interests by obscuring the possibility for change.

In Aloya's case, the Maasai elders failed to convince the state "authorities," who sided with Aloya and alternative notions of "fatherhood" and "legitimate" patriarchal authority. For Aloya and the magistrate, "fatherhood," and, by implication, patriarchal "authority," was not a matter of kinship or bridewealth, but a status acquired through the fulfillment of certain obligations and responsibilities. Furthermore, the court narrowed the parameters of a father's rights: despite the elders' version of Maasai "tradition" and "culture," fathers could not force their daughters to marry against their will. The rights of Maasai fathers were circumscribed by the rights of Maasai daughters as citizens of the nation-state.

Infuriated by the denial of his rights, Aladala, as the representative of the elders, wielded their ultimate weapon: he cursed Aloya in the courtroom, both stigmatizing and ostracizing her in one verbal act. If Aloya could not be a proper Maasai daughter, then she could live outside of Maasai society as the daughter of the government. By morally and physically marginalizing

Aloya as a "disobedient" daughter unwanted by her family, Aladala's curse warned other daughters, tempted to follow her example, about the dire consequences awaiting them as "wicked" women.

Aloya's encounter with the multiple layers of patriarchal authority—her father, elder Maasai men, the nation-state—illustrates the complex collaborations and clashes involved in maintaining or transforming any gendered configuration of power. Not only did she challenge and ultimately reconfigure Maasai elders' definitions of the roles and relationships of "daughter" and "father," but she compelled Maasai elders to reforge their patriarchal structures of authority to accommodate changes in the state legal system and case law: to prevent similar cases from being heard in the Tanzania court, they installed one of their own as a "Chairman of Tradition/ Customs." Their tactic exposed the ambivalent role of the state in the maintenance of local patriarchal authority. At the same time the state undermined the power of the elders in the court case, it reinforced their power by endorsing the creation of this new intermediary legal institution. As these Maasai elders learned, patriarchies must recognize and accommodate the shifting structures of power within and through which they operate in order to maintain their hegemony.

EPILOGUE

Let me conclude with a brief epilogue. Aloya is presently living with Masierr and their child in his father's homestead. Nayieu, her mother, has left Aladala and moved back to her house in Ronda's homestead. Shongon, disgusted with Aloya's actions and the outcome of the case, told Aladala that he did not want Aloya or any daughter of Aladala's seed, so Aladala has promised to give him another young woman instead, the daughter of a fellow clan-member. And the "hostage" Lukumai woman, after living at Aladala's *enkang'* with her children for several months, finally returned to her husband and home, without the permission or blessing of the elders, and without her promised sheep.

NOTES

References to primary materials are abbreviated in the text as follows:

D: Official court decision. *Ladala Kisika v. Aluya Ladala.* Case No. 100 of 1992 in the Primary Court of Kisongo, Monduli District. 5 pp.

OCT: Official Court Transcript of the case (provides written summaries of the proceedings as recorded by the court reporter). 10 pp.

TT: Transcription of my unofficial tape of the proceedings. 75 pp.

All quotations from the above materials are my English translations of the Swahili originals.

This chapter is a slightly revised version of an article that first appeared in the *Canadian Journal of African Studies* 30(1). With the kind agreement of both Heinemann and Avebury presses, the original version is also reprinted in Colin Creighton and C. K. Omari, eds., *Gender, Family and Work in Tanzania*. Aldershot, Hampshire, U.K.: Ashgate Press, 2000.

1. The research upon which this chapter is based was carried out from 1991 to 1993, and supported by a Fulbright-Hays Fellowship, the Joint Committee on African Studies of the Social Science Research Council, and the American Council of Learned Societies, the National Science Foundation (BNS #9114350), Andrew W. Mellon Fellowships, and a Rackham Fellowship from the University of Michigan. I am indebted to the Tanzanian Commission for Science and Technology for permission to carry out the research, and to Professor C. K. Omari and the Department of Sociology at the University of Dar es Salaam for research affiliation. Special thanks are also due to Neil Smith and the Center for the Critical Analysis of Contemporary Culture at Rutgers University for providing me with an Associate Fellowship (1994–95), and, more importantly, a warm, vibrant intellectual community in which to work, write, and laugh. Earlier versions of this chapter were presented to the Department of Sociology at the University of Dar es Salaam (1992), and the annual meeting of the African Studies Association (1994). I am grateful to participants in the Dar seminar, especially Marjorie Mbilinyi, for their detailed comments and criticisms, as well as Susan Geiger, Rick Schroeder, and Sheryl McCurdy for insightful criticisms of earlier drafts.

2. Antonio Gramsci's notion of *hegemony*, and particularly Raymond Williams' subsequent elaboration of it, illuminate the machinations of patriarchies. For Gramsci, hegemony is distinguished from domination in that hegemony is a form of indirect power constituted and exerted through the cultivation of consent, while domination is direct power predicated on coercion (Gramsci 1971). Key to Gramsci's concept are his insights that hegemony and the consent on which it is premised are always products of history, and that prestige and power are fundamentally interlinked: a dominant group's prestige enables its power (Gramsci 1971:12). Williams' discussion of hegemony not only incorporates these notions, but further clarifies how hegemony embraces the interlinked cultural and social dimensions of power, its meanings and practices: "[Hegemony is] a whole body of practices and expectations, over the whole of living; our senses and assignments of energy, our shaping perceptions of ourselves and our world. It is a lived system of meanings and values—constitutive and constituting—which as they are experienced as practices appear reciprocally confirming" (Williams 1977:110).

3. As numerous feminist scholars have shown, patriarchies are rarely comprised just of men: it is in the interest, at times, of certain women or categories of women to collaborate with patriarchal projects, especially women whose interests/prestige/power are most vested in the hegemonic system. And not all men participate—some silently excuse themselves, others are oppressed by the system, and some join forces combating it.

4. Since the case is in the public record of the Primary Court of Monduli, I will use the real names of all involved.

5. For examples of codifications of Maasai "customary law" on marriage and bridewealth by colonial administrators in Tanganyika, see "Sheria la Mahari za

Kimaasai" [Maasai Bridewealth Laws], undated; "Sheria za Ndoa ya Maasai" [Maasai Marriage Laws], 20 July 1950; "Masai Marriage Law," 15 May 1952; and "Maasai Custom to be Followed in the Hearing of Cases," undated; all in Tanganyika National Archives (hereafter, TNA) 17/250/1. The July 1950 document was written by a young Christian Maasai man, whose lament about the current state of affairs suggests a common reason for codifying "customary" law: "Customary marriage law these days is very similar to that of the past. But now the laws have become useless (*ovyo ovyo*), because [Maasai] women are seeing the customs of other tribes, including the ways of whores (*umalaya*) and living alone without men. Furthermore, many women these days are refusing to marry elderly men, and chasing young men instead" (my translation from Swahili original).

6. Almost all magistrates are men, and their patriarchal prejudice is often quite evident in their legal discussions and holdings. For example, "The Law and You," a popular column in the English-language newspaper, the *Sunday News*, insisted in an article entitled "Bridewealth and the Law" that bridewealth was a payment from the "bridegroom" to his prospective "father-in-law"—women neither gave nor received bridewealth (Kaniki 1989). A year later, another column on "Bridewealth in Customary Marriage" described, in explicitly gendered terms, the different reasons that either a wife or a husband could use to terminate their marriage: "Experience has shown that in the case of [a] wife the marriage can terminate when she behaves contrary to the customary behaviour or standard expected of a wife or when she becomes so disobedient to her husband. In the case of the husband the marriage contract can come to an end when the husband treats his wife cruelly or in some unbecoming behaviour which are contrary to the standard required of a husband" (Komba 1990). Husbands could divorce their wives for merely being "wicked"; wives could sue for divorce only if harshly treated by their husbands.

7. For a detailed ethnohistorical exploration of gender, age, and ethnic relations in this area, and in this village specifically, see Hodgson (1997, 1999, 2000).

8. Chama Cha Mapinduzi, or CCM, was still the sole political party in Tanzania at the time.

9. It emerged during the trial, however, that Nayieu and Ronda had only partly subscribed to Maasai tradition—they had given Nayieu's two sons the second name "Aladala" and recognized them as members of Aladala's Lukumai clan, but the daughters used "Ronda" as their second name and were counted as members of Ronda's clan. While the court did not explore this issue further, there are at least two related explanations for this situation. This division of sons and daughters between the two men and the two clans could partially be explained by the importance of patrilineality for clan, sub-clan, and lineage membership among the Maasai. To deny Aladala his sons would have been to deny him a continuing branch of his clan, as all the legal children of his sons would be Lukumai clan members. His daughters, however, even if recognized as members of his clan, as would usually be the case, would not provide the clan or lineage with descendants. Instead, the daughters' children, according to the patrilineal principle, would belong to the clan and lineage of their husbands.

A second, possibly related reason, has to do with wealth. As legally recognized sons of Aladala, the young men would be entitled to inherit part of his livestock and land when Aladala died. In accordance with Maasai "tradition," however, no inheritance would pass from the father to his daughters. But the daughters themselves were a source of wealth. By completely identifying Aloya and her sister as his daughters, through their second name and clan membership, Ronda strengthened his claims to their bridewealth, a bridewealth he felt entitled to as reimbursement for his expenses in helping his sister Nayieu raise her children. But Aladala, through his continuing rights in Nayieu, his wife, and the reimbursement cattle paid to Ronda, considered himself to be the father of all four children, sons and daughters alike.

REFERENCES

Chanock, Martin. 1982. "Making Customary Law: Men, Women, and Courts in Colonial Northern Rhodesia." In Margaret Jean Hay and Marcia Wright, eds., *African Women and the Law: Historical Perspectives*. Boston: Boston University Papers on Africa, VII, pp. 53–67.

Geiger, Susan. 1982. "Umoja wa Wanawake wa Tanzania and the Needs of the Rural Poor." *African Studies Review* 25(2/3): 45–65.

———. 1987. "Women in Nationalist Struggle: TANU Activists in Dar es Salaam." *International Journal of African Historical Studies* 20(1): 1–26.

———. 1997. *TANU Women: Gender and Culture in the Making of Tanganyikan Nationalism, 1955–1965*. Portsmouth, NH: Heinemann.

Gramsci, Antonio. 1971. *Selections from the Prison Notebooks*. New York: International Publications.

Hay, Margaret Jean and Marcia Wright, eds. 1982. *African Women and the Law: Historical Perspectives*. Boston: Boston University Papers on Africa, VII.

Hodgson, Dorothy. 1997. "Embodying the Contradictions of Modernity: Gender and Spirit Possession Among Maasai in Tanzania." In Maria Grosz-Ngate and Omari Kokole, eds., *Gendered Encounters: Challenging Cultural Boundaries and Social Hierarchies in Africa*. New York: Routledge, pp. 111–129.

———. 1999. "Pastoralism, Patriarchy and History: Changing Gender Relations among Maasai in Tanzania, 1890–1940." *Journal of African History* 40(1): 41–65.

———. 2000. *Once Intrepid Warriors: Gender, Ethnicity and the Cultural Politics of Maasai Development*. Bloomington: Indiana University Press.

Kaniki, Abdulrahman. 1989. "Bridewealth and the Law." [Tanzania] *Sunday News*, 17 and 24 September 1989.

Komba, Kenan. 1990. "Bridewealth in Customary Marriages." *Tanzania Daily News*, 11 March 1990, p. 8.

Mann, Kristin. 1982. "Women's Rights in Law and Practice: Marriage and Dispute Settlement in Colonial Lagos." In Margaret Jean Hay and Marcia Wright, eds., *African Women and the Law: Historical Perspectives*. Boston: Boston University Papers on Africa, VII, pp. 151–171.

Mann, Kristin and Richard Roberts, eds. 1991. *Law in Colonial Africa*. Portsmouth, NH: Heinemann.

Mascarenhas, Ophelia and Marjorie Mbilinyi. 1983. *Women in Tanzania: An Analytical Bibliography*. Uppsala, Sweden: Scandinavian Institute of Development Studies.

Mbilinyi, Marjorie. 1988. "Runaway Wives in Colonial Tanganyika: Forced Labour and Forced Marriage in Colonial Rungwe District 1919–1961." *International Journal of Sociology of Law* 16(1): 1–29.

Moore, Sally Falk. 1986. *Social Facts and Fabrications: "Customary" Law on Kilimanjaro, 1880–1980*. Cambridge: Cambridge University Press.

Parpart, Jane and Kathleen Staudt, eds. 1989. *Women and the State in Africa.* Boulder, CO: Lynne Rienner Publishers.

Schmidt, Elizabeth. 1990. "Negotiated Spaces and Contested Terrain: Men, Women, and the Law in Colonial Zimbabwe, 1890–1939." *Journal of Southern African Studies* 16(4): 622–648.

Swantz, Marja-Liisa. 1985. *Women in Development: A Creative Role Denied?* London: C. Hurst & Co.

Tanzania Gender Networking Programme (TGNP). 1993. *Gender Profile of Tanzania.* Dar es Salaam, Tanzania: Tanzania Gender Networking Programme.

Williams, Raymond. 1977. *Marxism and Literature.* Oxford: Oxford University Press.

PART III:

TAKING SPACES/MAKING SPACES

9

GENDER AND THE CULTURAL CONSTRUCTION OF "BAD WOMEN" IN THE DEVELOPMENT OF KAMPALA-KIBUGA, 1900–1962

Nakanyike B. Musisi

Let me tell you what causes women to desert. . . . it isn't clothes and it isn't money and it isn't kindness: it's the penis. If that is unsatisfactory no woman will stay with her husband.
                                                        —Southall and Gutkind 1957:91

In 1957, a woman would be labeled as "wicked" or "bad" for such a statement, yet women still made such comments. Indeed, the number of women considered bad increased during this period, despite social censure. Although Aidan Southall and Peter Gutkind reported such voices in their sociological study of Kampala, they did not invoke them in the title of their book, *Townsmen in the Making*. Nonetheless, the voices of such women suggest an answer to Gayatri Spivak's (1988) rhetorical question: "Can the Subaltern Speak?" With the exception of Southall and Gutkind (1957), Southall (1960), Gugler (1972), and Obbo (1980), the lives, activities, and problems of

Kampala's urban underclass of women has not been fully studied nor subjected to historical analysis.

Although such concepts as immorality, iniquity, or badness may be sociological terms of reference, they are also historical constructs. Bad women in Kampala have a history and several Luganda terms can be employed to describe them. Three of the most common terms are *Empala kitale*, *Bikazikazi* and *Banyanyagavu*. *Empala kitale* refers to unruly girls, *Bikazikazi* is used to denote undesirable women, and *Banyanyagavu* is the label of choice for women who are "bad in all respects." This chapter examines the histories of bad women by relying on Southall and Gutkind (1957) as a source for the women's voices it seeks to interpret. Southall and Gutkind conducted a two-year socio-anthropological study in Kisenyi and Mulago, two pockets of Kampala-Kibuga.[1] Drawing on the voices of ordinary women recorded in their study, this chapter has four main objectives. First, to investigate the historical and cultural construction of bad women in the emerging urban space of Kampala during the colonial era. Second, to critically analyze how women who reclaimed their own bodies and voices and constructed spaces for themselves came to be labeled as bad. Third, to draw attention to the processes through which the normative image of Baganda women was constructed and contested. Finally, to interrogate the construction of knowledge about women and the deployment of power over them so as to illustrate the role of "bad women" in the construction of the notion of the "good woman."

The application of moral labels to women in the urban space of Kampala-Kibuga emerged only after a long process of defining normative feminine behavior to establish what actions were respectable and permissible. I argue that the historical moments that gave birth to the new forms of stigmatization were periods of cultural uncertainty, the result of social, economic, and political changes that had begun around the middle of the nineteenth century. The ambiguities of this situation enabled people to borrow selectively from both indigenous culture and foreign norms of behavior associated with modernity in order to produce cultural hybridity.

As early as the first decade of the twentieth century there were new tensions in the relationship between the sexes (Musisi 1991b). And even though they might not have expressed it privately or acknowledged it publicly, most Baganda (especially men), colonial officials, missionaries, and, to a certain extent, later anthropologists were all aware of these struggles and the difficulty of consistently maintaining normative rules of respectable behavior (Musisi 1999). Labeling women's actions as socially deviant took place during this moment of social explosion and served to protect and reinforce the interests of an "imagined" [2] stable and established order.

THE HISTORICAL CONSTRUCTION OF "GOOD" AND "BAD" WOMEN

Before the middle of the nineteenth century, Buganda was a highly stratified society along lines of social status, clan, and gender (Musisi 1991b). Through a process of differentiation, members of a social group could be distinguished from non-members—commoners from royalty and the elite, women from men, wives from sisters, and one clan from another. Fallers has argued that the value system of the Baganda took account of these distinctions "by providing not merely an image of the 'admirable person,' but also of the 'admirable woman'" (Fallers 1973:7).

Evidence suggests that people understood what was morally expected of them through the internalization of wider Kiganda norms, socialization within their families and clans, and an understanding of their individual social positions (Musisi 1999). Several examples illustrate this point. First, from a political perspective, royalty were exempted from the laws and regulations that the kingdom imposed on commoners. The sexual behavior and customs of members of the royal household created an aura of freedom that served to distinguish them from commoners (Musisi 1991a). Second, the status of "wife" defined women's relationships to the means of production and shaped their social and sexual lives in Buganda's hierarchical structure (Sacks 1979). Karen Sacks has argued that women were economically and politically marginalized within the state (1979:208). I argue that there was an intimate connection between women's marginalization through economic dependence and control of their sexuality (Musisi 1991b). In a mutually reinforcing manner, women's sexuality and reproductive powers were central aspects of their productive relations and directly shaped their movements and behavior (Southall and Gutkind 1957:211). Additionally, it was inconceivable that women's sexuality could be deployed outside the private household sphere for any productive or monetary gain (Southall and Gutkind 1957:212).

According to John Roscoe, there was a double standard of sexual morality along gender and clan lines in Buganda. While extramarital sex was the norm for royalty and permissible for commoner husbands, it was forbidden for wives regardless of social status. If a husband suspected his wife of committing adultery, he was permitted "to tie her up and torture her until she confessed her guilt" (Roscoe 1966). Roscoe argues that the "husband would not be legally held responsible even if he killed his wife under such circumstances" (1966:263). Men who seduced married women were subject only to court fines, while female adulterers faced death and mutilation (Roscoe 1966:20, 23; Mair 1934:97). Men were only subject to death and mutilation if they seduced married women of royal households. From the perspective of the law and state prerogatives, a husband had the right to put his wife in the stocks for disobedience. Worse still, a husband could kill his wife without suffering any serious consequences (Roscoe 1966:20, 23; Mair 1934:97). Murder (apart from that committed by royalty) was a serious crime worthy of the death penalty, but manslaughter (perhaps more appropriately understood as woman-slaughter in this instance) was sanctioned if it was provoked by a wife's disobedient behavior. Differential norms also existed at the clan level. For example, members of the Mamba clan could intermarry, but sexual intercourse with a member of the same clan or with a woman of the mother's clan was considered *ekive* (an abomination) and was punishable by death (Roscoe 1966:261).

Moreover, the legal ideology of precolonial Buganda established sharp legal differences between men and women, decreeing that a woman did not constitute a legal entity in her own right. Instead, she was assigned a male guardian who controlled her and was responsible for her behavior both legally and socially.[3] Roscoe (1966:7) stated that "women were not free to move about without the consent of their husbands or masters, and in the capital every girl had some guardian from whom she had to obtain an escort when she wished to visit a friend or relative." The household sphere became the prime vehicle through which the state observed, controlled, and supervised what were deemed to be the proper forms of behavior for women. Even in the privacy of the "traditional" family (natal and extended), which was defined as the women's place, men exerted authority and dominance over, as well as responsibility for, women. According to Roscoe (1966), Kagwa (1934), and Mair (1934), women were expected to be submissive to men, an aspect of subordination emphasized in girls' traditional education (Mair 1934:67).

The distinction between the two sexes went further, even imposing separate diets for men and women. In peasant households, men rather than women enjoyed all of the available high protein foods. Taboos prohibited married women and those of a marriageable age from eating poultry, eggs, mutton, fish, grasshoppers, and several other nutritious foods. Even sitting positions were gendered. Women were always required to sit with their legs placed together and folded back from the knees so that the feet were together under their hips—*okufukamira*. To sit otherwise, such as with their legs straight in front of them or apart, was considered very unbecoming (Roscoe 1966:48). In sum, precolonial Buganda constructed a "good woman" as one whose freedom of speech and movement, sexual and reproductive labor, productive labor, comportment, diet, and residence were controlled by and needed approval from those who had power over her.

Bad women contravened some or all of these patriarchal codes. As such, women who ate poultry, eggs, mutton, fish, or grasshoppers; did not have homes, husbands, or children; avoided male control; cohabited or changed lovers rather than marrying; were available for illicit sex; accepted or demanded money for sexual services; or openly manifested evidence of sexual desires and feelings stepped outside their prescribed roles, challenged established power relations, and disturbed male hegemony. They aroused the resentment and disapproval of most men and good women. Later, their behavior provoked negative labeling by the Buganda state, inspired missionary and church discourses on morality, forged the creation of new colonial regulations, and elicited social stigmatization.

PROCESSES OF NORMALIZATION AND STRATEGIES OF CONTROL

In the 1870s, changes in ideologies regulating relationships of power began to shift discourses on sexual morality from the control of clans and men—husbands, brothers, fathers, and elders—into the hands of the Lukiiko,[4] native courts, missionary churches, and native schools. Most secular and religious proposals for the material, intellectual, and spiritual improvement of "natives" lives in Buganda depended heavily upon assumptions about the desirable form of family life: a stable, life-long commitment of spouses in a monogamous union (Obbo 1980; Southall and Gutkind 1957:66). The proposals were based on a fundamental fear on the part of the missionaries and colonialists that the Baganda as a "race" were about to become extinct.[5] These assumptions produced discourses that intricately joined knowledge and power over women. Some argued that decreasing control over women spelt disaster for Buganda as it meant a decline in the country's morality (Musisi 1991b). This in turn was perceived to have significant, disruptive social, economic, and political consequences: a spread of venereal diseases, a rising infant and maternal mortality rate and population decline, a decline in food production, and a reduction in the number of marriages registered by both church and state.[6] According to Sir Harry Johnston, the first Governor of Uganda, "the exhaustion of men and women by premature debauchery" was at the heart of population decline. He wrote to the Marquess of

Landsdowne that the Baganda through missionary teaching "are now becoming ashamed of marrying girls who have led a bad life before marriage" (1902:624).[7]

Early in 1899, the Lukiiko, which was largely influenced by the missionaries and by certain Christian chiefs, passed a law prohibiting married women and men from unnecessarily moving through areas of the capital inhabited by foreigners. The law was meant to prevent married women from moving to urban areas and having sexual liaisons with Arab and Swahili traders, Nubian soldiers, and other foreign men.[8] Equally important, the missionaries urged the Lukiiko to increase bridewealth rates in hopes of impeding customary marriages and thereby encouraging more people to marry in the church. In 1899 the Lukiiko fixed a minimum amount of bridewealth according to social status.[9] But the new levels of bridewealth prevented some young men from getting married and enabled the bride-wealth paying husbands to have greater control over their wives' productive and reproductive capabilities. By 1901, many Christian women were reacting to this control. They described themselves as "prisoners" (basibe) of their husbands (Waliggo 1976:283). To express their dissatisfaction with their husbands and their marital situations, women changed their names and gave their children similar names to show their new hardships. Names such as Samanya (I never knew . . .or If I had known I would not have), Sirinagyendida (I will have no where to return), Bwakwegayirira (marriage is a struggle of begging) and several others became very popular among Christian married women. In 1910, the women missionaries of the Church Missionary Society (CMS) responded to the widespread use of such loaded names by convening a conference to discuss the practice of married women using their husband's name.[10] In 1913, the Anglican Synod passed a resolution that newly married women should take their husband's name. Calling women by their husband's name was also meant to distinguish them from unmarried women who were presumed to be morally loose.

Happy that converts were willing to become monogamous, missionaries were troubled by the plight of the marginalized women, many of whom became "bad women." Their anxiety went so far as even to question the relevance of monogamy, given its social effects. By 1912, this had resulted in disagreements among missionaries at Mengo, the CMS headquarters.[11] In 1918, colonial officials blamed the Christian insistence on monogamy for women's "deplorable" social situation—being "free," unmarried, and not cared for.[12] They also noted that government policies aimed at stimulating economic growth were having an adverse impact on women's reproductive and productive labor (Roscoe 1922–23:104–5). According to Roscoe, the imposition of hut tax on men complicated the matter for women, as "chiefs found that they could not afford to pay for the huts of those women of their clans who had been discarded as wives, . . . The huts were therefore destroyed and the women were turned adrift by their relatives" (Roscoe 1922–23:104–5). But the imposition of hut tax was only part of a larger problem. By the end of the nineteenth century, more agricultural laborers were needed to farm the new tracts of land added to Buganda after the defeat of Bunyoro. And although most women did not own land, they were the primary producers of food and were central to the production of cotton in Buganda before the 1920s (Powesland 1973:20). Thus the traditional social and economic roles assigned to women and their centrality to the proper functioning of the church, the Buganda kingdom, and the colonial state made it imperative to place more restrictions on women's freedom of movement and association (Mbilinyi 1988).

Nonetheless, there was evidence that a gradual but threatening change in the status of women was taking place. In 1908, C. W. Hattersley, a CMS missionary, attributed this change to the emergence of "suffragettes" in Buganda (1908:109). Judging by Hattersley's observations, women were at least succeeding in resisting further additional work. The missionaries and Baganda men, however, attributed the shortage of agricultural labor and the resulting food crisis to a decline in the country's morality, unnecessary female migration from rural areas, and a decline in marriages (Roscoe 1921:170). Convinced that the old system of "bondage" in non-Christianized polygynous unions assured the nation of an adequate food supply, Roscoe (who influenced early colonial circles regarding Buganda customs) called for stricter control of women (1921:170). Women's freedom was diagnosed as the source of most of Buganda's troubles. The supposed erosion of morality was attributed to the breakdown of old Kiganda marriage laws, which, according to Roscoe, had "restrained society by fear" (1921:179).

In addition, the belief that the changing status of women was having a negative impact on population growth was emphasised in a dispatch of 30 September 1930 from the Acting Governor to the Secretary of State for Colonies (cited in Kucyzynski 1949:277). In the same year, the Acting Governor reported to the Secretary of State for Colonies the chiefs' concerns that "the growth of motor bus services on all the main roads is having bad effect on the birth rate." According to the chiefs, "a woman who is tired of life in a rural community and has three or four Shillings at her disposal can easily abandon her home and disappear in the towns, where she adopts a life of prostitution" (Kucyzynski 1949). The chiefs asked the colonial government to take steps to counteract what they saw as a "growing evil by controlling the acceptance of women as passengers." Although the Acting Governor was reluctant to legislate women's movement, he stated: "the problem is not a simple one, and . . . complete emancipation of native women from all forms of tribal control will not necessarily promote the physical welfare of the people" (Kucyzynski 1949; also see Mbilinyi 1988).

Women's freedom of movement, with its potential for sexual autonomy, caused fear among elite Baganda men, Christian missions, and colonial officials alike. All parties adopted a highly moralistic tone in dealing with women, particularly those who gained material benefits from the exchange of sexual services–otherwise labeled "prostitutes." The "prostitutes" were not only "dirty," they could also make one "sick" (Southall and Gutkind 1957:158). Short of advocating for the return of pre-Christian days, Dr. A. R. Cook of the Church Missionary Society, for example, argued in 1908 that the abolition of harsh deterrents to adultery and illicit sex (such as enslavement or death) had left the Baganda confused amid moral anarchy (Cook 1908:44–50).

THE GROWTH OF KAMPALA-KIBUGA: TRANSGRESSING THE "IMAGINED" MORAL ORDER

In 1906, Kampala was gazetted as a township, incorporating much of the *kibuga*, the capital of the Kingdom of Buganda.[13] This change was preceded by multiple, complex, social and political transformations. For example, in the second half of the nineteenth century, Kiganda culture and society encountered Islamic traders and clerics, Protestant and Catholic missionaries, and representatives of the Imperial British East Africa Company. Each of these encounters produced significant cultural, economic, political, and social changes, which resulted in conflicts over religious and political affiliations, strains in social and gender relations, realignments of relationships between wives and husbands as well as ruled and rulers, a synthesis of indigenous and foreign ideas, and changes of patterns of land ownership. Like other colonial cities, Kampala-Kibuga provided an early site for the significant confrontation of capitalist and pre-capitalist social relations, interactions between representatives of widely different ethnicities, "races," religions, and cultures, and, probably for the first time, unsupervised gender relations. As a result of these changes, the hegemonic control of the Kabaka, the ruler of Buganda, was weakened. And since the home was a microcosm of the state, the crisis in the hegemonic control of the Kabaka precipitated a corresponding crisis at the domestic level. Patriarchal control over women was challenged just as patrimonial control over all of Buganda had been weakened (Musisi 1991b).

Since Kampala-Kibuga experienced unprecedented growth in the 1910s, the 1920s, 1930s, and particularly 1940s were decades of cultural and political confrontations between the colonial and Buganda governments as township regulations were applied to significant parts of the *kibuga*.[14] After the Second World War, the urban space of Kampala-Kibuga expanded physically and demographically, at a time when major changes in employment and transportation were occurring. The introduction of motor transportation and bicycles in the 1920s revolutionized travel and movement in Buganda, as did the extension of the railway line from Mombasa to Kampala in 1931. At the same time, the colonial government was expanding its labor demands as government hospitals and public works departments needed more workers for cleaning jobs, sanitary assistance, the upkeep of roads, construction, and labor in a variety of industries (Southall and Gutkind 1957: 23, 27). Yet, despite having presided over these developments, colonial policy in Uganda operated with the view that town life was injurious to the traditional culture of "natives" (Southall and Gutkind 1957: 44; also see Schmidt 1990; Parpart 1994). Under these circumstances, problems of governmentality, confusion of boundaries and functions, sexual roles, and other social roles, all combined to open up spaces for contradiction, ambiguity, and a questioning of all colonizing authorities (Bhabha 1990).

The first concerted effort to control "prostitutes" in Kampala-Kibuga began in 1915 in the form of petitions from Kibuga residents (possibly property owners), many of whom, according to Gutkind (1963), were women. In 1917, the Buganda Prime Minister, Apolo Kagwa, ordered officials to "arrest all women who do not live with their husbands."[15] In a 1918 memorandum, both Catholic and Anglican bishops called upon the government to restrain "the present unrestricted liberty by which all are free to travel as they will and under which large numbers of women leave their husbands and their country for immoral purposes."[16]

The Buganda Lukiiko followed up the arrests by fully endorsing the bishops' recommendations. In addition, during 1920, the Lukiiko took it upon itself to curb the spread of venereal disease, to fight migration from rural Buganda as well as the decreasing marital and birth rates, and to prevent the frequent escape of wives from their husbands.[17] A year earlier, the bishops had proposed that people's movement, especially that of women, be further restricted. Moreover, the missions urged the government to uphold the "sanctity of home life" by introducing steps to encourage marriage, such as making the charging of exorbitant bridewealth a penal offense.[18] In its bid to enforce collaborative hegemony, the Lukiiko gave in to the bishops' demands thereby reversing the 1899 law that had set fixed bridewealth prices according to social status.

In the 1920s the Church Missionary Society, whose headquarters were located in the center of the *kibuga*, revived the campaign to rid the *kibuga* of "those women who live as prostitutes and have so commercialized the relationship between men and women that even the clan can do nothing for them" in terms of restraining them (Gutkind 1963:154). Emphasizing the need for legislation, a CMS representative remarked that "it is a minor feat to resist the soliciting by these women."[19] From the missionaries' moralistic point of view, as indicated by the language in their petition to the Provincial Commissioner during 1922, Kampala-Kibuga was polluted by the presence of these "bad women." They inquired of the Commissioner: "how best to clear the street?" To their disappointment, the Provisional Commissioner, who was not equally alarmed by the prostitutes, declined to take any firm action on the issue. In 1929, he retorted that "the subject is best dealt with by the Baganda themselves."[20] In 1925, the Deputy Director of Medical (Native) Services joined the missionary campaign because of medical concerns. During 1926 and 1927, the apprehensions of the Medical Department were further heightened. The Governor minuted on 26 June 1926 that he had "lately been considering the desirability of shutting down completely recruiting (immigrants—men) from the South-West until conditions in Kampala improved" (quoted in Richards 1973:32).

Gutkind (1963:154) has argued that during the colonial period, "Prostitution [in the *kibuga*] has not been considered as serious a problem, and hence received less official attention, as the brewing and consumption of liquor." But given the preoccupation with the potential medical danger of "bad women," this argument is hard to accept at face value. Rather it could be argued that although from about 1920 onwards the colonial government was less concerned about sexual morality, it was increasingly concerned with the general issue of legality and public hygiene. The government was very concerned that prostitutes could infect their partners with disease (Vaughan 1991; Summers 1991), thereby reducing the population of Buganda at the most crucial political, social, and economic moment of the colonial enterprise.[21]

By 1936, ministers of the Buganda government had joined the church campaign to petition the colonial government regarding "young girls who are in the *kibuga* as prostitute . . . living . . . near the Government Township" (Gutkind 1963:155). The ministers strongly objected to the presence of these women, urging that steps must be taken, otherwise "the whole of Buganda nation will be ruined" (Gutkind 1963:155). The colonial government's stalling on the issue forced the Buganda government to enact its own law against prostitution in 1941.[22] The new law provided for the deportation of non-Ganda women suspected of being prostitutes (Gutkind 1963:155). It also stipulated that it "was an offense for young girls under 20 years to be employed unless they can return to their homes at night." The persecution cooled off after World War II and it was not until 1956 that the Omukulu we Kibuga[23] was ordered by the Lukiiko to enforce the 1941 law. As a result, parish chiefs rounded up a number of women, returned them to rural areas, and only allowed those who could give proof of approved occupations to remain (Gutkind 1963:156).

The roots of this response emerged out of the economic contradictions produced by the emerging capitalist economy and the threatened/embattled patriarchy (White 1988; Schmidt 1990, 1992; Hansen 1992). Negative labeling, moralizing discourse, and state control were political responses to political and social protest that used legal and non-legal forms to regulate, control, and put down social unrest. Despite this legislative machinery, it was not unusual for senior members of the Buganda Government to interfere in efforts by the Omukulu we Kibuga to curb prostitution. Gutkind (1963:156) cited one example when in 1957, "The Omukulu we Kibuga had arrested a large number of women known to be prostitutes; he was forced to release a number of them because they were the mistresses of important officers in the Buganda Government." Lamenting his lack of power, the Omukulu we Kibuga wondered why the Buganda government wasted its energies requiring permits to "move about cattle in the *kibuga*" when it would not concern itself more effectively to restrict entry into the *kibuga* by those he considered "not gainfully employed"—women (Gutkind 1963:156).

"BAD WOMEN": SUBJECTS OF POWER

Baganda women in Kampala-Kibuga created new ways of being that seriously threatened patriarchal control. While women were able to reconceptualize their status and position because of emerging alternative discourses of being, they were becoming not only *objects* but *subjects* of power in their own right (White 1988). In spite of the dilemma the politics of being Muganda[24] posed, some women still responded as actors to threats to their autonomy. In one example, Southall and Gutkind noted that in the midst of a scorching exchange between two men over their female "object," one man challenged the other: "Let me tell you that she is not your wife and I love her and she loves me too. Remember that you have a wife at home and that this is a *public* woman" (Southall and Gutkind 1957:74–75; my emphasis). The woman in question immediately contested this patronizing and possessive remark: "I am not a *public* woman, but I love men who love me, and I am now telling you both to go away" (Southall and Gutkind 1957:75).

In the heat of the moment, such self-identification/knowledge was possible. And although women did not always provide a positive identification for themselves, they clearly rejected the labels they were given and implied that they considered themselves "free" individuals. A space for subversion was opened up, as in the case of a woman who abandoned her husband to forge a new life with an Indian lover. As she stated:

> [W]hen I left my husband he (the Indian lover) brought me here and rented this room for me. . . . I never asked him his name; I call him "bwana." He gives me 2 shillings a day for food and brings me . . . other things. He also gives me clothes. He has a wife at his house, but I never go there. . . . I now prefer Indians because I don't dig and I get money every day. My Ganda husband did not give me money for me to use. (quoted in Southall and Gutkind 1957: 78)

About her lover she commented: "I love him but not very much. I do not now take African lovers because he told me to stop doing so." And how did she get him? "I was able to love this man because he was a friend of my husband and he used to come to visit our house. He used to take me to a Ganda friend of his. . . . He used to give me ten shillings every time." And did she have a frank assessment of her condition? "I love him because he gives me money and the things he gives me. I also love other Indians who pay me five to ten shillings. I can receive them whenever my lover is not there." And for self-identification? "I am not a prostitute. I told you that I love other Indians, but that does not mean that I am a prostitute. I shall have African lovers after this Indian. He told me that Africans have venereal disease." And did she believe him? "Not only Africans but also everyone has it. Many Indians have it. I had . . . gonorrhea (*nziku*) when I was a young girl, but never had syphilis (*kabotongo*). Many Indians have both of these like Africans. I never had a European lover, but I should like to get one" (Southall and Gutkind 1957:78–79).

In the ambivalent space of Kampala-Kibuga, some women invoked the values of the past or of rural areas to critique unacceptable situations. Culture was manipulated as a tool for their own liberation. After a lengthy confrontation between a wife and husband of nearly three years, the wife declared:

> I tell you that I am not your wife, because you never gave my parents any beer and you never sent them salt or anything. I am here as your lover

only and you have no right to stop me doing anything when you don't give me good treatment. I will go back and call Luka to come to my parents and I will introduce him to them. He is ready to do so but I did not like to do that as I love you well, but your treatment is bad and because of that I will separate from you. As you know that you don't like me to love men, I don't like you to love women. But I will give you one more chance and if you will observe it, I will not love Luka anymore. (Southall and Gutkind 1957:174)

When making these demands and similar comments, such "bad women" challenged the boundaries of discourse and subtly changed its terms by setting up another space for negotiating cultural authority (Schmidt 1990).

It is evident that in Kampala-Kibuga, no single pattern controlled women's behavior and ideas. The dynamic of the emerging space did not permit adherence to old cultural controls and symbols. Instead, these same symbols were appropriated, translated, and renegotiated (White 1990). Although it was impossible for them to completely distance themselves from customary practices, women did recognize that within the urban space they could be in charge of their own destiny (White 1988, 1990). And they were not oblivious to the fact that this situation considerably threatened and undermined the established male order.

Although men and women "needed each other," a number of women voiced the opinion that it was better not to be too firmly attached to just one man whose position in the wage-earning economy did not seem to be secure (Southall and Gutkind 1957:187). They claimed that "only by going from one man to another can you get food because immigrants individually are poor and can never give you a lot of gifts" (Southall and Gutkind 1957:164). A significant sign of the power that these women wielded was that the men they associated with did so on these women's own terms—they had to please them (White 1988, 1990). The urban space provided "bad women" with the terrain for elaborating strategies of selfhood, singular or communal, that created new forms of identity and innovative sites of collaboration and contestation, in the act of defining the idea of an urban society itself. By adding materialist or commercial tenets to their sexual and other services/activities, otherwise known as "domestic skills," "bad women" gained access to male wages (White 1990; Robertson 1984).

CONCLUSION

The political economy of the colonial period privileged male labor and led to women's economic marginalization. As missionaries and colonial officials attempted to control the movements and practices of urban women, they labeled those who refused or failed to conform to their expectations as bad women. In their unauthorized occupation of urban space, what these women did or did not do, said or did not say, threatened colonial and missionary ideologies, policies, and programs. Urban Baganda women's actions revealed the ways power is negotiated between different groups of people and helped formulate Baganda ways of being.

Bad Bagandan women scorned patriarchal authority. Their recurring transgressions against African, colonial, and missionary attempts to control them underscore the diffuse nature of power. None of the parties involved was in complete control of the situation. "Bad women" fractured colonial, missionary, and Baganda impositions against them through their creative and subversive re-articulation of discourse and practice. Although not wholly representative of all Bagandan women, the history of "bad women" as captured by Southall and Gutkind helps us understand what they and other women faced in emerging colonial cities.

NOTES

I am grateful to Dr. Kate Parry, Hunter College, City University of New York, Dr. Sean Hawkins, University of Toronto, Dorothy Hodgson, and Sheryl McCurdy for their constructive criticism and for editing the earlier version of this chapter.

1. Kampala-Kibuga was a space that comprised the pre-existing urban space of the capital of the Buganda state (the *kibuga*) and the surrounding colonial city of Kampala.

2. I borrow this term from Benedict Anderson (1983).

3. A father, married brother, or husband could be a woman's guardian (Roscoe 1966:12, 55, 74, 232, 264; Mair 1934:41, 220; Richards 1966:93–94; Mukasa 1946:139).

4. This was the Buganda Parliament.

5. For a discussion of this fear, see Vaughan (1991), esp. chapter 6; Summers (1991).

6. See for example, Entebbe Secretariat Archives (ESA), Secretariat Minute Paper (SMP)5368, Joint letter by J. T. Willis, J. B. Biermans and John Forbes to Governor, 19 April 1918. Also see Vaughan (1991); Summers (1991).

7. Emphasis is mine.

8. ESA File 991/09, Law of 4 September 1899.

9. Church Missionary Intelligences, May 1900:339ff., Walker, Annual Letter November 1899; ESA, Colonial Office (CO)536/6–21 72, also in ESA SMP No. A 23, Wilson to Tucker, 26 February 1906.

10. Church Missionary Society Archives (CMSA), University of Birmingham Library, Minutes of Central Women's Conference, Mengo 17 January 1910.

11. CMSA A7/G3 Letter 337, Walker to Family 25 October 1896; Roscoe (1921:170, 179, 181).

12. SMP 5368, Provincial Commissioner Buganda, P. W. Cooper to Chief Secretary, 17 May 1918.

13. Official Gazette, 15 December 1943, 151. Kibuga could be described as the African city that could be compared to the Kampala, the colonial city.

14. For example, Mengo, Wandegeya, Mulago, Kisenyi, and Makerere Katwe.

15. This order was given to Mr. Balintuma, the *kibuga* tax collector (Gutkind 1963:154).

16. ESA File 5368, Protestant and Catholic Bishops to Governor, April 1918.

17. ESA File 46621, Lukiiko Resolution 5 January 1920.

18. Makerere University Library Archives (MULA), Bishops' File Mac-Mar. Marriage Questions 1912–1940, Archdeacon Baskerville, Memorandum December 1919.

19. Ibid.

20. Ibid.

21. Official Gazette, January 31 1916, 73–74.

22. Legal Notice No. 101 of 1941: 10203, The Buganda Law for Prevention of Prostitution.

23. The chief of the sub-county of the Buganda capital.

24. Buganda is the kingdom, the Baganda are the citizens of Buganda, and Muganda is the singular of Baganda. Luganda is the language of Buganda; Kiganda refers to things such as culture, customs, etc. that belong to the Baganda. All stem from the basic unprefixed root Ganda, often used for simplicity.

REFERENCES

Anderson, Benedict. 1983. *Imagined Communities. Reflections on the Origin and Spread of Nationalism.* London and New York: Verso.

Bhabha, Homi. 1988. "The Commitment to Theory." *New Formations* 5: 5–23.

———. 1990. "The Third Space." In Jonathan Rutherford (ed.), *Identity Community Culture Difference.* London: Lawrence and Wishart.

———. 1994. *The Location of Culture.* London and New York: Routledge.

Cook, A. R. 1908. "An Urgent Need in Uganda." *Mercy and Truth* 12: 44–50.

Fallers, Lloyd A. 1973. *Inequality: Social Stratification Reconsidered.* Chicago: University of Chicago Press.

Foucault, Michel M. 1980. *Power/Knowledge.* London: Harvester Wheatsheaf.

———. 1984. *The History of Sexuality, Vol. 1, An Introduction.* London: Penguin.

Gugler, Josef. 1972. "The Second Sex in Town." *Canadian Journal of African Studies* 6 (2): 289–301.

Gutkind, Peter W. 1963. *The Royal Capital of Buganda: A Study of Internal Conflict and External Ambiguity.* The Hague: Mouton and Co.

Hansen, Karen Tranberg (ed.). 1992. *African Encounters with Domesticity.* New Brunswick, NJ: Rutgers University Press.

Hattersley, C. W. 1908. *The Baganda at Home.* London: Religious Tract Society.

Johnston, Sir Harry H. 1902. *The Uganda Protectorate, Vol. 2.* London: Hutchinson.

Kagwa, Apolo. 1934. *The Customs of the Baganda.* New York: Columbia University Press.

Kucyzynski, R. R. 1949. *Demographic Survey of the British Colonial Empire, Vol. II.* London: Oxford University Press.

Little, Kenneth. 1973. *African Women in Towns: An Aspect of Africa's Social Revolution.* Cambridge: Cambridge University Press.

Mair, Lucy. 1934. *An African People in the Twentieth Century.* London: Routledge, Kegan and Paul.

Mbilinyi, Marjorie. 1988. "Runaway Wives in Colonial Tanganyika: Forced Labour and Forced Marriage in Colonial Rungwe District 1919–1961." *International Journal of Sociology of Law* 16 (1): 1–29.

Mukasa, H. 1946. "The Role of the Kings of Buganda." *Uganda Journal* 10: 136–143.

Musisi, Nakanyike B. 1991a. "Women, Elite Polygyny, and Buganda State Formation." *Signs: Journal of Women in Culture and Society* 16: 757–786.

———. 1991b. "Transformations of Baganda Women." Ph.D thesis, University of Toronto.

———. 1999. "Morality as Identity: The Missionary Moral Agenda in Buganda. 1877–1945." *Journal of Religion in Africa* 23 (1): 51–74.

Obbo, Christine. 1980. *African Women: Their Struggle for Economic Independence.* London: Zed Press.

Parpart, Jane. 1994. "'Where Is Your Mother?': Gender, Urban Marriage and Colonial Discourse on the Zambian Copperbelt, 1924–1945." *International Journal of African Historical Studies* 22 (2): 241–271.

Powesland, P.G. 1973. "History of Migration in Uganda." In A. I. Richards (ed.), *Economic Development and Tribal Change.* Nairobi: Oxford University Press.

Richards, Audrey I. 1966. *The Changing Structure of a Ganda Village.* Nairobi: East African Publishing House.

———. 1973. "The Problem and Methods." In A. I. Richards, (ed.), *Economic Development and Tribal Change.* Nairobi: Oxford University Press.

Robertson, Claire. 1984. *Sharing the Same Bowl.* Bloomington: Indiana University Press.

Roscoe, John. 1966. *The Baganda: Their Customs and Beliefs.* New York: Barnes and Noble.

———.1921. *Twenty Five Years in East Africa.* Cambridge: Cambridge University Press.

———. 1922–23. "Uganda and Some of Its Problems." *Journal of the African Society* 22: 104–105.

Sacks, Karen. 1979. *Sisters and Wives: The Past and Future of Sexual Equality.* Urbana: Illinois University Press.

Schmidt, Elizabeth. 1990. "Negotiated Spaces and Contested Terrain: Men, Women and the Law in Colonial Zimbabwe, 1890–1939." *Journal of Southern African Studies* 16 (4): 622–648.

———. 1991. "Patriarchy, Capitalism, and the Colonial State in Zimbabwe." *Signs: Journal of Women in Culture and Society* 16 (4): 732–756.

———. 1992. *Peasants, Traders, and Wives: Shona Women in the History of Zimbambwe, 1870–1939.* Portsmouth, NH: Heinemann.

Southall, Aidan. 1960. "On Chastity in Africa." *Uganda Journal* 24: 207–216

Southall, Aidan and Peter W. Gutkind. 1957. *Townsmen in the Making: Kampala and Its Suburbs.* Kampala: East African Institute of Social Research.

Spivak, Gayatri. 1988. "Can the Subaltern Speak? Speculations on Widow Sacrifice." In Cary Nelson and Lawrence Grossberg (eds.), *Marxism and the Interpretation of Culture.* London: Macmillan.

Summers, Carol. 1991. "Intimate Colonialism: The Imperial Production of Reproduction in Uganda, 1907–1925." *Signs: Journal of Women in Culture and Society* 16 (4): 787–807.

Vaughan, Megan. 1991. *Curing Their Ills: Colonial Power and African Illness.* Stanford, CA: Stanford University Press.

Waliggo, J. M. 1976. "The Catholic Church in the Buddu Province of Buganda." Ph.D thesis, Cambridge University.

White, Luise. 1988. "Domestic Labour in a Colonial City: Prostitution in Nairobi, 1900–1952." In Sharon B. Stichter and Jane L. Parpart (eds.), *Patriarchy and Class: African Women in the Home and the Workforce.* Boulder, CO: Westview Press.

———. 1990. *The Comforts of Home: Prostitution in Colonial Nairobi.* Chicago: University of Chicago Press.

10

YOU HAVE LEFT ME WANDERING ABOUT: BASOTHO WOMEN AND THE CULTURE OF MOBILITY

David B. Coplan

INTRODUCTION

In seeking to introduce some "wicked women" from South Africa's rural heart, I assumed that the editors meant the label ironically. They were, I supposed, less interested in women who played Basotho[1] Bonnies to their African Clydes than in accounts of those who refused to accept the hegemony of gender subordination, and thereby subverted regimes of patriarchy whether pre-, mid-, or postcolonial. The appellation "wicked" would then of course be both ironic and rhetorical, inviting an exposition of the ways domination has attempted to contain African female strategies of resistance through moralizing discourse. The scholarly liberation bestowed by postmodern critical languages should, however, as Maliq Simone has argued, "relieve cultural critics from the moorings of a certain moralism or theory that condemns the oppressed to being nothing more than signs of their oppression" (Simone 1991:162). And, I realized, on occasion even out of ironic wickedness and into just wickedness, literally. Lesotho's women, driven like their men from rural peasant life into wage labor, have for some four generations now been constrained to perform as social actors in situations of extreme structural and material stressfulness and legalistic limitation. Under such conditions a great many, often quite publicly, have simply gone "bad." A remarkable number, however, somehow have seemed to survive the battlefield of African migrant female life in South Africa with at least the core of Sesotho[2] behavioral values aspirationally, if not practically, intact. In my fieldwork among them I heard no apology for what they did, their insouciance a fortress like the mountains of their homeland. They rather took pride in what they might have preserved of their social ideals, surrounded as they were by devils male and female, foreign and domestic. My analysis of the *longue durée* of Basotho women's struggles, however, seeks not simply to portray a one-dimensional disruption of an indigenous patriarchal political economy by settler colonialism and racial capitalism. Rather I wish to reveal the changing conditions, obstacles, and forms of oppression that forced these women, in successive generations, to constantly rethink and reinvent their strategies for survival, facing unforeseen uncertainties through the creation of always insecure but nonetheless original lives.

MIGRANT LABOR AND THE DISCOMFORTS OF HOME

A woman's early years of marriage in colonial Basutoland were often hard and demanding. The bride would move from her natal home to the homestead of her in-laws, where for a period she occupied an extremely marginal position. She was expected to work hard, to be dutiful to her in-laws and to observe a special language of avoidance (*hlonipho*) in respect of male seniors. Only once her first child was born did her status improve from that of daughter-in-law (*ngoetse*) to mother (*motsoetse*). A measure of personal autonomy was only acquired once her husband built her a house, which her in-laws were inclined to resist because they lost the labor of their daughter-in-law and, where the son was a migrant, the remittances that he sent home. Indeed Basotho themselves compared the experience of a young bride to the arduous training endured by boys during initiation (Gay 1980b:93, 100–5, 122–3; Thetela 1987:54).

Resistance to this regime was certainly regarded by a young woman's elders, male and female, as wicked, and her options were in any case few. Alternatives, and hence the emergent wickedness of Basotho women, were intimately tied to the labor migrancy of Basotho men. Following the disasters of the Orange Free State (*Seqiti*) Wars of 1865–1868, Basotho trudged the 200 kilometers to Kimberley to dig in the newly opened diamond fields. By the 1870s, Basotho female camp followers had joined the migrant army, providing them with what Luise White has termed "all the comforts of home" (White 1990) and assisting the male diggers in the rampant illicit diamond buying that has so concerned DeBeers from that time to this. Most important were the commercial brewing and sexual services that provided an economic base for independent Basotho women's life and have set the pattern for their urban enterprises ever since. Then as now, the life of honky-tonk women was no easy business. As newly arrived evangelist Gwayi Tyamzashe wrote of Kimberley in 1874: "The life then of both Coloured [black] and Whites was so rough that I thought the place only good for those who were resolved to sell their souls for silver, gold, and precious stones, or for those who were determined to barter their lives for the pleasures of a time" (Wilson and Perrot 1973:298).

As early as 1892, the Basutoland authorities recognized the problem of women fleeing to the Orange Free State, a process accelerated by the South African War of 1899–1902 (Maloka 1995:58). In 1898 a full-scale rebellion was triggered when Chief Masupha seized a runaway wife from the Free State and the British sought to discipline him for his misdeed (Phoofolo 1980; Kimble 1983:14). As land shortage intensified, junior wives of polygynous men found themselves less assured of retaining access to fields. Upon the death of a husband they became increasingly vulnerable to being driven off their lands by the sons of senior wives (Thetela 1987:54). Junior wives then fled to relatives or friends in the Free State farms or small towns, or even pre-empted such marriages by eloping with their lovers. This practice, known as *chobeliso*, was to become increasingly common in Lesotho (Maloka 1997:106, 108). As a result of all this, the rates of polygamy declined sharply from an already much reduced 18.7 percent in 1911 to 8.4 percent in 1946 (Murray 1981:127).

The dependency on labor migration that followed from and exacerbated the gradual underdevelopment of Basutoland subjected women to growing economic and social stress, driving them into the labor recruitment centers at the colony's western border, and into the towns and mine shanties of the Free State and Transvaal. There is an extensive literature exploring the nature and consequences of this dispossession of Basotho female peasant producers from Basutoland, later Lesotho (Eldredge 1993; Coplan 1994; Bonner 1990; Murray 1981; Gay 1980b; Maloka 1997). Serially, it involved the compounded losses of arable lands and grazing, access to stock for ploughing and accumulation, male labor and conjugality, capital inputs, affinal solidarity, security of tenure and residence, and ultimately even of food security in the transformation of Basutoland from "granary to labor reserve" (Murray 1980). Women bore the brunt of agricultural labor and household management in the absence of the migrants, and while this severely reduced productive capacity, migrant earnings did not necessarily increase the flow of cash into rural homesteads, as men often overstayed and spent their money at the mines. Women left at home suffered, as dramatized in Azael Makara's poem of 1936:

I have nobody to plough for me, I am suffering!
Poor women who are left alone in Lesotho,
They are crying, their cry is a touching one!
There is no food, there are no children at home!
Who is to give a woman a child
While her husband lives with prostitutes?
I, the mother of the children feel the pain! (Maloka 1995:57)

Among the consequences of this situation was the virtual institutionalization of not only male but also female adulterous relationships. Basotho married women had long been accustomed to taking clandestine lovers (*linyatsi*; Spiegel 1991), a practice perhaps more developed among the Basotho than any other group, and an early indication of their women's greater autonomy. *Bonyatsi*—adultery—for men had been condoned on the basis of the once-normative institution of polygyny, forbidden by the Christian denominations to which the vast majority of Basotho nominally belonged. Adultery among women had probably become no less common, at least since the advent of labor migrancy, but might be overlooked in the desperate collective effort to prevent human weakness from threatening the crucial marital partnership between migrant and spouse. Women pointed to accepted notions of a universal human need for emotional and sexual satisfaction, and to beliefs about the harmful physiological and mental effects ("stagnant blood") of celibacy in justifying adultery for themselves. There have long been clear socioeconomic motivations for female adultery, however, since the cattle paid as bridewealth for a woman by her husband go to her father and other consanguineal relatives, while the secret but mandatory gifts from a lover are hers alone, free even from the restrictions that a husband may place on the disposition of other family income (Spiegel 1991:5–6). On the other hand, a wife's lover could be a significant drain on an absent husband's income, since her emotional attachment made her generous. As one woman said to me frankly, "You have to give the man something if he's doing 'the work' [sex]." As early as 1897, the missionary Jacottet transcribed the following comic song performed by two choruses of Basotho girls during initiation rites:

First group:
  "Listen, thus! The adulterer, it's the woman."
Second group responds:
  "Listen thus! The adulterer, it's the man."
First group responds:
  "And the woman also."
              (Jacottet 1896/1897:128; translation by Coplan)

Indeed, among the secret lore taught to girls during these rites are instructions in how to conceal adultery from their future husbands and, in the event their transgressions are discovered but tolerated by an understanding or equally guilty spouse, how to keep their affairs from causing him intolerable public embarrassment. Marriage is a social and economic partnership, preserving the male migrant's investment and entitlements in his home community and providing identity and security for women and children. And so adultery, a social practice more prevalent than marriage itself, has virtually never been discussed in public.

The severe strains of early marriage were compounded by widowhood, divorce, or desertion, which demanded the creation of new lives. A return to the wife's natal home was not an attractive option, as such a woman reverted to a dependent position with no automatic rights to either a site for a residence or a field (Thetela 1987:59). From the early 1910s, a growing number of women resorted to beer brewing and prostitution in the nascent urban centres of Basutoland, known then as government "camps." In the 1930s, these women became increasingly defiant. Many openly plied their trade at labor depots, and traveled around with the rough young sports fresh from the mines. Some men spent all their money on these women, and neither returned home nor sent money to their families (Maloka 1995:330, 333). Efforts at repression, half-hearted at best, were blocked by women's brazen resistance. Chief Sempe Nkoebe, for example, had a policy of fining prostitutes, chasing them from the town of Mafeteng, and confiscating their property, but in 1936 one such woman petitioned the local assistant district commissioner, complaining of this treatment and demanding the return of her property (Maloka 1995:334). Her application did not, however, succeed. Prostitution thrived on a system that kept male workers away from home for long periods, and likewise expressed the social disintegration set in motion by migrancy itself (Maloka 1995:334). All local and cross-border efforts to restrict female mobility failed, even when the South African Government began serious repatriation efforts in the 1930s.

During the Great Depression, many women shifted their base of operations to the gold-bearing Reef. So, between 1936 and 1946, the actual female population of Basutoland dropped by 5,623 (Murray 1981:4). Women's continuing social connections and travel to their places of rural origin, however, were still valued and even crucial to the operation of urban (im)migrant networks. Indeed, virtually every formal or informal activity that engaged African men was aided and abetted by female associates and dependents, many of whom established notoriously individualistic lifestyles. These women were loosely and prejudicially lumped into the category *matekatse*, from *ho teka teka* ("to wander aimlessly about"), and indeed many who crossed the border headed off without knowing where they were heading, guided to likely places of employment by those they met on the way (Thetela 1987:61). Others utilized their limited literacy to write letters to female friends and relatives living in the Free State towns or on the Witwatersrand (Thetela 1987:67). By the early 1930s, over 75 percent of Basotho girls, almost double the percentage of Basotho boys, could read and write some Sesotho (District Officer 92/3/1–6, Annual Reports of the Director of Education, 1919–1936 Office of Education, Basutoland), thanks to primary education in mission schools. Some Basotho men railed against the educational and other activities of the missions, depicting them as the cause of Basotho women's independence (Edgar 1987:69, 78).

In the Free State towns, Basotho women took up work as domestics, laundry women, beer brewers, and petty traders (Wells 1982:61–2; Ulrich 1997:16–21, 47). Basotho men were liable to label all those who made a living in this fashion as *matekatse*, but Basotho women did not, for the most part, engage in straight cash-for-sex transactions. Some entered into the adulterous arrangements already common in rural Basutoland. Others established longer-term relationships, in which men provided a monthly stipend in return for domestic and sexual services. In the early 1900s the Free State capital, Bloemfontein, became a powerful magnet for Basotho women when the British garrison there during the Anglo-Boer War created a concentrated market for domestic and sexual services (Wells 1982:64). For this and other reasons, Bloemfontein's black population climbed from 1,302 in 1890 to 18,383 in 1904, of which 44 percent were women (Ulrich 1997:19–20). Such even sex ratios were unparalleled in other South African towns until the 1940s. By the First World War most other Free State towns had followed suit (Temilton 1995:8).

The exodus of Basotho women alarmed Basotho patriarchs and the British colonial authorities alike. In 1915 a proclamation was proposed by the Basutoland National Council and issued by the colonial administration, making it an offense for a woman to leave the territory without the permission of her husband or father, and enabling a man to obtain a warrant and secure an absconding woman's return. Basotho women, however, found little difficulty in evading this restriction. Passes to visit border towns in the Free State for shopping or medical services were freely available, and in the last resort it was easy to pass undetected across the lengthy border (Bonner 1990:229; Kimble 1983:4–5). In the early 1930s, the combination of the Great Depression and drought had a catastrophic impact on rural economies, black and white alike. The drought, which peaked in 1932–1933, was especially severely felt in Basutoland and the Orange Free State. Thousands of Basotho streamed out of the colony to escape the deepening economic distress. The gold mines, which had experienced a near continuous shortage of labor since the start of the 1920s, were now overwhelmed by a glut. White farmers laid off their black farm tenants in the thousands, and found themselves unable to furnish food in kind let alone a wage in cash to those that remained. Small towns in the Free State were inundated with new arrivals, quickly saturating both the formal and informal labor markets.[3]

Closed off from their normal sources of employment and income, Basotho women had yet again to find alternative means of subsistence. The African newspaper *Bantu World* reported in February 1934 that "one result of the famine in Basutoland is that a large amount of pottery is being made by Basotho–with very lifelike images of snakes, elephants, etc." (17 February 1934). Many looked for opportunities further afield. Virtually the only areas of economic activity untouched by the Great Depression were the gold mines on the Witwatersrand. Here, a quarter million single male migrant workers were herded together in single-sex compounds, forming the largest market for the services Basotho women could offer anywhere on the subcontinent. By 1930 the South African Secretary for Native Affairs was reporting a steady stream of new female arrivals from Basutoland,[4] which swelled over the next several years. The end of the drought and the burst of mining and industrial expansion in the mid-1930s did little to arrest this trend. Basotho male migrants now quit the mines in growing numbers to take up higher-paid employment in secondary industry, and simultaneously sought out accommodation in the Goldreef's African locations. This shift in employment and residence frequently encouraged them to enter into longer-term relationships with African women in the towns, and either to neglect or to abandon their wives and families at home. Basotho women left Basutoland in even greater numbers to seek out missing husbands or to establish an independent living on the Witwatersrand. By 1956 an estimated 41,992 women were reported as being absent from Basutoland, more than half of them on the Reef (Murray 1981:4).

These successive migrations and transitions profoundly altered gender relations and family structures. Once women accepted that their marriages were finally ruptured they were often loath to submit again to the authority of men. Questioned by the Vereeniging Riots Commission in 1937, Albert Mduli remarked: "They do not stick to the men through whom they get their lodgers' permits. When a woman thinks she has sufficient money, she drives the man away and gets another" (Central Archives Depot, Pretoria, Department of Native Affairs 6671, File 87/332). As Simon Majara wrote in his Sesotho novel, *Liakhela* (1972:17), "When a man is not bringing money home he is left and she goes to a new man." Upon departing Basutoland, most women left their children behind them at their parents' homes. This radically reshaped the rural Basotho family, so much so that the social anthropologist Vernon Sheddick writing in the 1950s could describe the typical homestead cluster as consisting of "parents, with children of broken families and young marrieds" (Sheddick 1954:161).

Once established on the Rand, Basotho women successfully competed in illicit brewing and in the retailing of a range of domestic and sexual services to single men, enterprises previously dominated by women from Mozambique. Basotho women quickly became identified by the local and central authorities on the Witwatersrand as the principal source of social disorder and moral degeneration in the black urban population. In Nancefield in 1930, the local authorities alleged "weekend disturbances" were "almost invariably" caused by Basotho women.[5] Conflict intensified after the municipal monopolization of beer brewing in 1937, and by 1938 had reached such a pitch as to prompt an urgent appeal from the Witwatersrand Compound Managers' Association and Gold Producers' Committee. The uncontrolled supply of liquor and prostitution in the African locations, they asserted, was the cause of "considerable lawlessness during the weekends resulting in a large number of casualties." All these casualties were "directly attributable" to the uncontrolled supply of "skokiaan" and "women" (Gemmill to Secretary for National Affairs, 8 November 1930, Native Affairs Department, Pretoria).

These views were shared by many black people in rural areas as well as in the towns, who simply condemned these women as "prostitutes." Chiefs of the Sibasa region of the Northern Transvaal articulated similar concerns in a meeting with the Native Commissioner of the area, complaining that "our sons are taking advantage of leaving, go away, forget parents and wives, and take Basotho women."[6] African urban women from other ethnic groups felt equally threatened. Laura Longmore reports Nguni women from Johannesburg's Eastern Native Township as averring, "If your husband is in love with a Shoeshoe [Basotho] woman he will certainly leave you. Don't you know they have 'traps' for men," a reference to their artifically elongated labia minora, *hoa ikula* (Longmore, 1959:40–1).

Both local and central government made efforts to suppress the activities of Basotho women, and regain control of the situation through repeated weekend raids for permits and illicit liquor. Basotho women evaded arrest by burying liquor on public land outside their houses, devising elaborate warning systems, and having a man available whom they could claim as their husband. Even once arrested, the collective solidarity of beer-brewers was difficult to dent. In Benoni, "these women, under the inspiration of solicitors raise innumerable difficulties, e.g. they produce reported husbands, allege the only place they belong to is the location; they will not state where they originally came from and it is practically impossible to lead [provide] convincing evidence." Not only fees but fines "were paid collectively by the amalgamated liquor interests of the location."[7] As an exasperated location manager, G. C. van der Merwe, explained to the Vereeniging Riots Commission of 1937: "I could not make a plan to get these women out of the location because they all had a man and unless I could show two or three previous convictions you could not get them out. If you arrest a girl with the name of Maria, tomorrow she is Jane."[8]

Under pressure, the tactics of evasion often gave way to open defiance. In Bloemfontein, Basotho women responded to intensified police raiding in the mid-1920s by holding beer parties provocatively in the open and stoning police when they tried to make arrests; this in turn provoked police retaliation, a riot, and a mass stay away, which left five dead and eight wounded (Ulrich 1997:48–59). In Vereeniging a concerted attack on a police van in 1937 by Basotho women and young men, followed again by a police counter-attack, sparked the most serious riot of the decade, leaving two white constables dead and four others seriously injured (Bonner 1990:221–2; Ulrich 1997:57–9). In both scale and intensity, these and similar riots that erupted elsewhere signal a major departure in the popular politics of the black urban areas. Later, when the riot and the stay away were harnessed to black nationalism, the mass nationalist politics of the 1950s assumed their characteristic form. The same tradition of protest was later imported into the pre-independence nationalist politics of Basutoland. Policemen attempting to control an anticolonial riot in Maseru (the capital of Basutoland) in 1961 recorded that they "did not notice any men there, only a lot of women screaming and throwing stones" (Emprecht 1992:20).

Both the South African government and the British colonial authorities made repeated efforts to staunch this hemorrhage of Basotho women, but only with the extension of passes to women in the later 1950s were they able to prevent at least some from smuggling themselves over the border and merging with the Union of South African's population. The "Malan Pass," as it was called, reinforced in 1963 by the Bantu Laws Amendment and the Aliens Acts, greatly narrowed Basotho women's room for maneuver. Further entry into South Africa was banned, while women identified as born in Lesotho were compelled to return there. Thus after a half century of contestation, one of Basotho women's principal lifelines was almost cut off (Thetela 1987:25, 29–30, 98–103, 107–8).

RUSSIANISM, RHYTHM, AND REBELLION

While male authorities of every color and stripe deplored the "immorality" of the *matekatse*, it is clear that it was their literal physical mobility and independence that most concerned Basotho and white paternalists alike. In practice, proletarianized Basotho men were in the best position to attempt to control and exploit such women in the urban areas, a factor in the emergence of the famous Basotho "russian" gangs. Their violent conflicts with urban gangsters, other ethnic groups, and the police, and among themselves have been chronicled elsewhere (Coplan 1994:187–99, Bonner 1993; Thabane and Guy 1983). Arising during the Second World War, their name was inspired by the paranoia the white government and media expressed over the new, postwar Soviet threat.

"Russianism" was far more than a distorted and violent by-product of African proletarianization and urban social dislocation; it had roots deep in the combative rural male Basotho experience and ethos. The night before a battle, faction members would gather for a dance party called *famo* at their favorite shebeen, where their women would brew, cook, sing, and dance for them in encouragement. The term *famo* comes from *ho re famo*, "to flare the nostrils; to throw up one's skirt." Molefi Malefane, a retired russian, described the competitive ribaldry of these occasions in the late 1950s:

> A *famo* is like a [church] "tea meeting" with an accordion (laughter). The women are there. And the men are naked under the blankets, and we are in a circle, and there is a command: "*Likepi!*"[9] Then we lay out our pricks on the table. And the women are not wearing any panties under their skirts. When the *famo* dance is done, there shouldn't be any laughter; it's quite serious. They display themselves to the men. They even shave their vulvas, and put some lipstick, called "stoplight," around them. The man who is the good dancer and a good stick fighter is the one who the women want, and he gets whatever woman he wants. (Coplan 1994: 188)

Basotho commented that, in the old times of their independent chieftaincies, it was customary for women to disrobe flamboyantly before the troops, flinging off their blankets to inspire, excite, or shame their men as circumstances required. As Alinah Tsekoa, a veteran observer of many russian battles, sang in her Maseru shebeen:

> When it's [a russian battle] fought it is fearsome:
> I can fling off my blankets. (30 July 1988)

At dawn the men would take up their formation outside the bar and begin their dance, supported by women singing the following chorus, whose words illustrate the cross-gender solidarity among the besieged nascent urban Basotho proletariat:

> My boy [lover] when I get out of here, I will depart,
> Leave carrying you on my back [like a baby],

Photo 10.1 Nthabiseng Nthako, dancing at a tavern in Lower Thamae, Maseru, Lesotho, 1988. Courtesy of David B. Coplan.

> Boy, when I get out of here, I will depart,
> Fearful for you of the thief-men [*tsotsis*]. (Coplan 1994: 189)

Some russians emphasized that gaining the admiration of women was a major reason for their participation. Not only did women lavish their favors upon russians as protectors and heroes, but a russian could live quite comfortably on the proceeds of a woman's economic activity based in the shebeens or in the legal informal sector: a preferred alternative to migrant laboring.

Bonner (1993) notes that control of independent women was a central focus of competition among russian gangs, and the immediate cause of many a murderous encounter. This control, however, was predicated upon the re-establishment and defense of "normative" conjugal standards, notwithstanding the common-law nature of the majority of russian domestic relationships. Russians and their women were mutually supportive and independent counterparts. When hiding from the police, russians often gave their guns to their women, who brought the men food when they were arrested and jailed. Identification with the russians and their marginal position led female bar singers to express admiration for these stout-hearted men and to appropriate images of male battles to express their own existential struggles.

> Hae oele oele! You, child of 'MaKhalemang [a male russian, friend,
>   and fellow bar singer],
> Blow the whistle so the russians may fight oe!
> When's fought is fearsome,
> When's fought is fearsome,
> I can fling off my blankets.
> Hee! I, the child 'Ma'tsepe oe!
> The loafers' [russians'] whistle blower, Khalemang,
> Whistler of loafers, Khalemang, you, man of Mokotane's,
> Makotane's at Mantsonyane,
> Lead them into the way [of battle]; they know [well].
> Hee! [so] I seize the black [heavy] fighting stick;
> I'm fighting,
> I cannot be stopped; I am fighting.
>   (Alinah Tsekoa, "Malsepe," 30 July 1988)

Nevertheless, women singers are almost universally critical of russian *likoata* (uncultured ruffians; cf. Maloka 1995:333), and of the domineering, rude, egotistical, and violent behavior that they see as the anti-Sesotho side of russianism. A verse appearing in many shebeen songs runs:

What kind of people are you russians?
Each time you meet one another, you fight.
After greeting one another, you fight.

Other songs invoke the folk character of Satan as the embodiment of russianism, as in a 1950 recording, *Famo Ngoanana* ("Famo, Young Girl!") by Mamapetle Makara koa Famong (Gallotone GB2012):

Aoelele, manchild!
Heaven should have a place [for you]:
Who is the eldest son of God?
Hey! The very first of the first born is Satan;
At first he was allotted a small village;
Hey! Then he was given the pit of hell.
Hey! There he is, caught up in town;
On him are a knife and an ax,
Hey! He is in full funeral attire;
Hey! The cattle are burned with fire,[10] Satan;
If they are raw, they'll make you vomit.

Mamapetla's song plays on the biblical legend of Satan as God's original favorite among the angels, who, like a firstborn son of a chief, is given his own village to rule over. Rejecting his father and his patrimony, the song's migrant Lucifer ends up in the social hell of the townships. Now a proletarian gangster, the absconder is warned that "the cattle are burned." This expression means that "the cattle are stolen goods," but also serves as a metaphor for the dangerous, diseased town women that will bring him only misfortune and sickness.

Among the most renowned of all singers was 'Malitaba, now deceased, who for decades ran a shebeen in Moletsane, Soweto, Johannesburg, and attended her husband Sanaha, a russian faction leader, at numerous battles in the Johannesburg area during the 1950s and 1960s. Asked what role women played during the actual fighting she replied, "Why, to carry on singing, to give them courage to win the fight":

I'm not afraid of a muscle man,
    even one full of cunning.
Knives they can miss me,
Sticks swing over my head,
Cracking [together] over my head, Madoda jo!
The fighting sticks of men. ('Malitaba, 8 August, 1988)

The russians' women sing about the men's battles in detail, praising the valorous and handsome, mourning the fallen, projecting themselves into the

Photo 10.2 Unidentified informal tavern singer, Mohale's Hoek, Lesotho, 1989. Courtesy of David B. Coplan.

fray. These gangsters' molls also often quite literally fight with one another over the men. One even sang in the bar of how she had straightened one of the oversized safety pins used to fasten blankets at the shoulder, making it a murderous needle, and shoved it up the nostril of a rival, killing her on the spot. But the point (no pun intended) is that these fellow migrants, male and female denizens of the social wild(er)ness, identify with one another. Like their male fellow travelers, the migrant women sustain themselves and their "partners in crime" with songs in which their misfortunes are lamented but their care for true friends and lovers never dies:

Mr. Kapa 'Muso, my husband, he comes on his own account.
They slander me as a prostitute,
I am not a prostitute;
I [simply] narrate the causes [of my circumstances]:
At my home, girls,
At home eating is difficult;
Yes! I am a prostitute.
My father looked away to the kraal,
My mother looked away, deep inside the hut;
But why? [because] I am a prostitute.
I still think I shall go wandering;
Hardship piles up, quietly higher. . . .
. . . I can leave my man and cry, Sir, or Sello,
It is Sello and Fosa,
They ask where I am married,
It's Matitissi the Letebele
Helele, my girl child!
You have left me wandering about,
You have left me wandering about,
Helele, little girl of Lioling! [Teyateyaneng, a border town]
You will not see me married [yet];
I get married [fall in love] daily,
Daily my heart is long [hopeful],
You will never see me surly. (Nthabiseng Nthako, 29 January 1984)

Risking arrest and daily harm to remain physically and socially mobile, these women exposed yet another, painfully ironic gender contradiction of the migratory labor system. For men, South Africa has been the land of wage slavery; for women, it represents relative choice, opportunity, and independence. For them, "traveling" provides resources for domestic social power. The shebeen operator and the barmaid live in willful defiance of the identity that Basotho society and the migratory labor system prescribe for them. This "independence," however, came at such a price that many such women would gladly have exchanged it for stable conjugal life in Lesotho, were this only available. Mpho Nthunya recalls not only relentless and violent persecution by police in Benoni's African location in the 1950s (Nthunya 1996:39), but the extreme level of social conflict among Africans themselves:

The town had too many people, too much noise all the time, no peace. *Tsotsis*, gangsters were everywhere stealing things, fighting; . . . Basotho were fighting with Maxhosa; men were fighting with wives and girlfriends; men were drinking joala and fighting with anybody they see. Every day we saw some people dying in the streets, and when they were fighting, . . . when they found you on the way they could just kill you. (Nthunya 1996:44)

TRAVELING WOMEN

The attempts of local authorities to prevent women from crossing the Caledon River, and to repatriate them when they do, have little effect except to keep female migrants on the move, wherever they are. While more securely placed Basotho might label them *matekatse*, the women themselves protest that they go to *itsebeletsa* ("work for myself"), or *phelisa bana ba ka* ("support my children") (Gay 1980b:275). As the renowned 'Malitaba complained:

> I, 'Malitaba of Mphoso oe!
> They call me a vagabond,
> But I am not a vagabond; I am taking care of business.
> Should I mind when they wink at me?
> They spread evil of me in secret whispers,
> Yet they fear to speak out. (8 August, 1988)

Until 1962, 27 percent of known Basotho migrants were women (Gay 1980b:40), but the legislation in 1963 and 1979 that mandated their repatriation reduced the total to about 7 percent (Gay 1980a:24). Until the 1990s, younger women could only resent the restrictions and envy their mothers who had the opportunity for legal migration. A strong recent trend among younger women is internal migration to Lesotho's border towns, where in certain quarters females between the ages of twenty and thirty-four outnumber their male counterparts by four to one (see Wilkinson 1985:136–61). A town is the only place where a woman's chief might be herself, rather than her husband. Brewing and entertaining in a shebeen is one of the best available ways for independent women to extract some money from the migrant labor system, not only illegally in South Africa but in Lesotho as well (Gay 1980a:26–27). Money can be demanded from regular migrant boyfriends without forgoing the rewards of moonlighting among the local leftovers or, even better, with *ma-week-end* migrants living it up on a four-day pass. One of the Maseru neighborhoods formerly most notorious for shebeens was named after this social scene: Thibella, "Prevent," refers to the ways bar girls catch hold of returning migrants as soon as they re-cross the border, preventing them from ever reaching their rural homes and families. Conversely, women who accompany their husbands to the border are not simply saying goodbye but also making sure their husbands really go, and don't slip back to the shebeens for a few days instead. Once a woman is sure her husband is gone, of course, she may not fear to spend his earnings with a boyfriend at a shebeen herself.

Since the mass retrenchments of Basotho mineworkers that began with more than 5,000 sent home during the massive strike of 1987, swelling to an additional 50,000 in the 1990s, women have begun to reverse the pattern, migrating to work while their men stay home. In Lesotho, my recent ethnographic observations revealed a new social phenomenon: the male-headed, single-parent rural household. Unemployment in Lesotho itself now exceeds 40 percent. Men, without jobs or the legal right to seek work for more than two weeks across the border are forced to extract what subsistence they can from the land. Women, however, can often find jobs—however poorly paid—in domestic service, the informal sector, or light industries in Maseru and other border towns. Most male respondents said that they readily helped with housework and child-minding, but they could not help but feel some embarrassment and diminished self-esteem over turning over the role of breadwinner to their wives. Some indeed did not want their wives to work, fearing that such independence would lead to the break-up of their marriages. At the very least, they wished for their wives to come home every evening and not live out, or take up labor migrancy as the men had done. Talking with me in Ha-Mafefoane, Roma district, one ex-miner worried:

> I wouldn't like my wife to go to South Africa to work because I think she will get a rich man and she will forget all about me. I don't like my wife to work as a domestic because the pay is not good and also her employer will make her his lover. If she refuses she gets sacked and so sometimes, because we have so many problems, she will agree. Then this guy will be using my wife. She said to me that was all right, because there is nothing else we can do.[11]

To disappear into South Africa's swelling peri-urban slums, all a woman really requires is to find a man, or a series of men, usually migrants from within South Africa or perhaps from Mozambique, to provide accommodation, protection, and a little working capital. Hence many a wife who has told her retrenched and despondent husband that she is going off to look for work to support him and their children has not been heard from again. Others make no such promises but simply inform their husband that now that he has lost his job he is losing his wife and the mother of their children as well: "She went to the Free State and shacked up with a Shangaan," as an abandoned ex-miner ruefully told me. Young women are especially prone to leave, since they can most easily find housing and support from other men and unlike older, long-married women, they rarely have land or livestock (Thoahlane 1994).

It would be misleading, however, to suggest that the above is the dominant pattern. While the women I spoke to in Lesotho were by their very presence those who had not abandoned their husbands, they gave a variety of reasons for their constancy. Among these were love for their husbands and the desire to be loyal in an hour of need, and unwillingness to abandon young children, some of whom were chronically ill. Among their greatest worries was the provision of school fees. At a time when Basotho parents are increasingly aware that education and training are the only route to a potentially secure future for their children, thousands of children of ex-migrants are being forced to drop out of school. In the end, many women simply preferred facing life's hardships in the familiar social landscape of home, where forms of mutual assistance, however minimal, could be called upon as a last resort, though most denied receiving any contributions from relatives. Very few fought with their husbands over money. Without exception they desired the right to seek and take up employment freely in South Africa.

If a woman's life in Lesotho is a rock, for a woman migrant South Africa has always been a hard place. Some women are driven by broken relationships into migration and others choose it as their one chance to earn an independent livelihood, but they all leave homes where they are someone and travel long distances alone to seek work. As migrants they live independently but in constricted circumstances in bleak hostels, rented rooms, mine shanties *(mekhukhu)*, or servants' quarters. Domestic service is the most popular form of employment among Basotho women migrants, but many prefer a dangerous mobility to the "degrading subservience required in working for a white 'madam'" (Gay 1980b:285). Migrant women are much more on their own than male contract migrants, and their patterns of self-reliance are much more extreme than those of women who remain as wives of migrant workers living near affines and agnates in the rural areas. Male migrants visit home more often, spending more weeks at home and fewer uninterrupted months at work every year than do women migrants (Gay 1980b: 290–3). Women, unlike male migrants, hardly ever get to see their children, because they cannot risk trips home. They enjoy far more autonomy in their relationships than do actively married women, but their frequently unromantic "romances" are often simply mutually exploitative, and many are confirmed in a view of men as by nature unreliable, as "a resource which could be used to meet their immediate needs, but not as dependable partners with whom they could hope to build close conjugal relations and stable homes" (Gay 1980b:294).

Under such conditions, female networks, based as much on friendship as kinship, become as important as they are to rural women. Networks in South Africa help a woman with advice, housing, food, employment, men, and entertainment, while rural networks look after interests and property at home and provide the all-important service of childcare in a mother's absence. The reality of female migration alongside that of men has abolished the residential linkages among kindreds and lineages. Families in the Lesotho lowlands will commonly have some members giving migrant-subsidized mixed pastoralism a try, along with others who are effectively permanent emigrants to South Africa. Just as Sesotho transcends Lesotho, the Basotho are a borderland and cross-border people. With bureaucrats on both sides of the current political border dedicated to stopping the flow of Basotho work-seekers across it, the answer from Sesotho is that this is impossible: the experience of migrants, women as well as men, knows no boundaries:

> Chabane, I am going away.
> I am a person living in difficulties:
> I live by cheating workers [migrants],
> I'm not working; I'm a wandering divorcer [philanderer];
> I, a little girl of Lesotho.
> Give me a ticket, gentlemen, a ticket and my stick,
> When I leave, I wander about,
> I am going home, home to Lesotho yonder.
> When I leave, I move fast. . . .
> . . . Hele helele my sister Anna,
> The misfortunes that have seized me!
> Why am I going?
> I am the mother of marriages [I have many men]. . . .
> . . . These women, they speak about me,
> They speak about me girl, about me at the house corners.
> I look at them; they look away, yonder.
> He-e you, my girl child, my father or Nthako,
> I abandon my sisters [fellow barmaids];
> Here they are at Hlotse camp [town], girls,
> In whose trust do I leave them?
> I have entrusted them to God ee! [having no husbands]
> I have left, pray for me,
> Yes, because I am a prostitute.
> They ask of me, where am I ruled [staying]?
> I know where I live, girls:
> At Hlotse, the camp [town], . . .
> . . . My heart fights with my understanding,
> Me, a little girl of Masupha's. (Nthabiseng Nthako, 29 January 1984)

Nthabiseng Nthako, whom I recorded singing this song in Leribe town, northern Lesotho, was twenty-two years old, an unmarried barmaid afraid that the miner who paid the rent for her tiny ramshackle bedroom might forsake her, but confident of attracting a replacement when he did so. The male dimension of her stance is exemplified by the rhetorical request: "Give me a ticket, gentlemen, a ticket and my stick," referring to the train ticket and heavy wooden fighting stick that symbolize the intrepidity of the male migrant.

CONCLUSION

On 21 September 1998, armed forces of the South African Development Community under the leadership of the South African Defense Force invaded Lesotho, supposedly to restore order following an ill-defined "coup" by opposition parties dissatisfied with the results of the May national elections. The death and destruction that occurred in Maseru simply serve to demonstrate, tragically, the incapacity of Lesotho's post-independence leadership to provide stability and security, or indeed anything at all of value, to the majority of its working people. This incapacity has always had particularly unfortunate consequences for the women and families "left behind" by migrants (Murray 1981:171–7). Today, previous forms of Basotho women's wickedness, driven by rural poverty, landlessness, proletarianization, and the problems of their role within the migrant labor system, are being supplanted by new and previously almost unimaginable strategies as that system itself disintegrates. Previously, scholars wrote of the material underdevelopment and social costs imposed by the migrant labor system. Basotho adaptations to its conditions have been termed a "culture of migrancy" (Coplan 1994, 1995), in which Sesotho, Basotho language and culture, became a movable feast of social network formation and reciprocal practice wherever displaced Basotho sought to place themselves. Even those like the urbanized russians who gave up effective, if not ideological, economic connection to their rural homes sought to reproduce, in however distorted or inverted a form of practice, the patriarchal militancy of the chieftaincies. But one plain if unpalatable truth that this ethno-nationalist sociological discourse did not acknowledge was how much worse the situation would be if there were no South African jobs to which Basotho might migrate. In the 1990s, the Basotho and those who write of them have had the frightening and entirely unwanted opportunity to experience or observe what the decline of migrant employment means for a "culture of migrancy." From a high of over 120,000 in the late 1980s, the number of Basotho mineworkers has now fallen to less than 75,000, and the number is still falling. The second reality that the collaborative fiction of Lesotho, the country of the "nation of Basotho," refused to address was the massive *uprootedness* imposed by the collaborative policies of colonial underdevelopment on one side of the border and white settler expropriation on the other.

Despite its woeful appearance, the knight-errantry of migrant labor provided, for a hundred years, some kind of foundation for family, community, and national life. The women's errantry it fostered was, at its most admirable, sacrifice in the service of home and children, and even at its least admirable it largely reflected the human inability to cope with an ever-changing series of attacks and misfortunes that the stoutest of hearts might quail at. Today, with the "end of migrancy," I have encountered in my field observations women who have not simply left to seek work and men in South Africa but who in so doing have effectively abandoned their jobless husbands and starving children in Lesotho. In this ironic "masculinization of poverty," characterized by male-headed, single-parent households, feminist commentators might well find, sadly, further confirmation of the fragility of the naturalistic concept of the "maternal instinct" and the social construction of gender.

To strike a braver, more hopeful note, what we can see both in retrospect and in continuing development is a culture not of migrancy but of *mobility*, in which Sesotho, reflexively conceived, is not merely transported but in its concept and practice formulated amidst the experience and organization of multi-sited, mobile networks of kin, homeboys/girls (from the same town or district), and reciprocal friendship. So today, for example, a woman migrant may have a husband or siblings of either sex at home in Lesotho, children born in or out of wedlock there in the care of a mother, aunt, or older sister, and a man or men in the South African black township near the urban area where she works in commerce or domestic service.

The present South African government, be it said, has a genuinely sympathetic attitude towards the country's poor and dispossessed. Even the visible and much remarked-upon xenophobia toward struggling African noncitizens among these same poor does not affect Basotho immigrants as adversely as it does those from Zimbabwe, Zambia, or Mozambique, let alone those from Congo or Nigeria. Basotho are after all only nominal foreigners indistinguishable by language or custom from South African Sesotho-speakers, and easily able to nullify immigration controls with a ready mobility and a banknote. But the structurally driven predilection for control, identification, and *settlement* of the uprooted African proletariat of necessity works contrary to the post-apartheid survival strategies of the culture of mobility. It may be that, not only in the case of the Basotho, but in those of all of the region's rootless poor, such mobile cultures may have to be not only recognized but even supported if these women—and men—are not to internalize permanently ideas and forms of social action that are proving to be very wicked indeed.

NOTES

I want to acknowledge the invaluable contribution of Philip Bonner to this chapter as well as his own superb scholarship on Basotho women over many years, which has much inspired and informed my own present efforts.

1. "Basotho" is the accepted contemporary spelling. "Basuto" and "Basutoland" are colonial spellings that specifically refer to the pre-independence period prior to 1966.

2. "Sesotho" is the cognate term, referring at once to the language and the customary ideology and practice of the Basotho; a self-identifying means of behaving as well as a way of life.

3. University of Witswatersrand Library, Evidence to the Native Economic Commission, Box 3, 4635–6, 4708–9.

4. Central Archives Depot (CAD), Pretoria, Department of Native Affairs (NTS) 7725, File 166/333, SNA to Government Secretary, Maseru 8 October 1930.

5. CAD.NTS 7725, File 166/133, D.N.L. to SNA 20 October 1930.

6. CAD.NTS 6813, Minutes of meeting 10 January 1930.

7. CAD.NTS 7725, File 166/133, DNL to SNA 20 November 1930.

8. CAD.NTS 6611, File 87/332, Evidence to the Vereeniging Riots Commission, pp. 150–1.

9. A *kepi* is a steel pick or chisel used by herbal healers to pull medicinal plants and roots out of the ground. Here it is a euphemism for a man's sexual "magic wand."

10. A question often asked of Basotho in the rural areas who suddenly possess cattle for sale is, "Are they burning?" meaning, "Are they stolen?"

11. Interview with Ntate Makune, Maseru, January 1994.

REFERENCES

Bonner, Philip. 1990. "Desirable or Undesirable Women? Liquor, Prostitution, and the Migration of Basotho Women to the Rand, 1920–1945." In C. Walker, ed., *Women and Gender in Southern Africa to 1945.* Cape Town: David Philip.

Bonner, Philip. 1992. "Backs to the Fence: Liquor and the Search for Social Control in an East Rand Town, 1929–1942." In Jonathan Crush and Charles Ambler, eds., *Liquor and Labor in Southern Africa.* Athens, Ohio: Ohio University Press.

Bonner, Philip. 1993. "The Russians on the Reef, 1947–1957: Urbanization, Gang Warfare, and Ethnic Mobilization." In P. Bonner et al., eds., *Apartheid's Genesis 1935–1962.* Johannesburg: Ravan Press.

Coplan, David B. 1985. *In Township Tonight! South Africa's Black City Music and Theatre.* New York and London: Longman.

———. 1994. *In the Time of Cannibals.* Chicago: Chicago University Press.

———. 1995. "Motherless Households, Landless Farms: Employment Patterns among Lesotho Migrants." In J. Crush and W. James, eds., *Crossing Boundaries: Mine Migrancy in a Democratic South Africa.* Cape Town: IDASA/IDRC, 139–150.

Edgar, Robert. 1987. *Prophets with Honour*. Johannesburg: Ravan Press.

Eldredge, Elizabeth. 1993. *A South African Kingdom: The Pursuit of Security in Nineteenth Century Lesotho*. Cambridge: Cambridge University Press.

Emprecht, Marc. 1992. "Women's 'Conservatism' and the Politics of Gender in Lesotho, 1965–1992." Paper presented to the African Studies Association Conference, Boston, MA.

Gay, Judith. 1980a. "Basotho Women Migrants: A Case Study." *Institute for Development Studies Bulletin* (Sussex University, Brighton, UK) 11, 3:19–28.

Gay, Judith. 1980b. "Basotho Women's Options: A Study of Marital Careers in Rural Lesotho." Ph.D. thesis, Cambridge University.

Gay, Judith. 1980c. "Wage Employment of Rural Basotho Women: A Case Study." *South African Labour Bulletin* 6, 4:40–53.

Gunner, Elizabeth. 1979 "Songs of Innocence and Experience: Women as Composers and Performers of *Izibongo*, Zulu Praise Poetry." *Research in African Literatures* 10, 2:239–67

Heap, Marion. 1989. *Health and Disease in South-Eastern Lesotho: A Social Anthropological Perspective of Two Villages*. Cape Town: Centre for African Studies, Communications, No. 16.

Jacottet, E. 1896/1897. "Moeurs, Coutumes, et Superstitions des Ba-Souto." *Bull.Soc. Neuchateloise de Geographie* 9:107–51.

Kimble, Judy. 1982. "Labour Migration in Basutoland, c. 1870–1885." In Shula Marks and Richard Rathbone, eds., *Industrialisation and Social Change in South Africa*. London: Longman, 119–41.

Kimble, Judy. 1983. "'Runaway Wives'; Basotho Women, Chiefs and the Colonial State, c. 1890–1920." Paper presented to the Women in Africa Seminar (17 June), School of Oriental and African Studies, University of London.

Longmore, Laura. 1959. *The Dispossessed. A Study of the Sex-Life of Bantu Women in Urban Areas in and around Johannesburg*. London: Jonathan Cape.

Majara, Simon. 1972. *Liakhela*. Mazenod, Lesotho: The Catholic Centre.

Maloka, Edward Tshidiso. 1995. "Basotho on the Mines: Towards a History of Labour Migrancy, c. 1890–1940." Ph.D. thesis, University of Cape Town.

Maloka, Edward Tshidiso. 1997. "Canteens, Brothels and Labour Migrancy in Lesotho." *Journal of African History* 38:100–22.

Murray, Colin. 1980. "From Granary to Labour Reserve: An Economic History of Lesotho." *South African Labour Bulletin* 6,4:3–20.

Murray, Colin. 1981. *Families Divided: The Impact of Migrant Labour in Lesotho*. Cambridge: Cambridge University Press.

Nthunya, M. M. 1996. *Singing Away the Hunger*. Durban: University of Natal Press.

Phoofolo, Pule. 1980. "*Kea Nyala! Kea Nyala!* Husbands and Wives in Nineteenth Century Lesotho." Mohlomi Seminar Paper No. 3, National University of Lesotho, Roma.

Seidman, Gay. 1993. "If Harmony Closes, Will the Last One to Leave Turn out the Lights? Down-Scaling in the Free State Goldfields." Unpublished ms.

Sheddick, Vernon. 1954. *Land Tenure in Basutoland*. London: H.M.S.O.

Simone, T. M. 1991. "Between the Lines: Responses of African Civil Society to Ambiguous Rule." Centre for African Studies, Africa Seminar, University of Cape Town, 31 July.

Spiegel, Andrew. 1991. "Polygyny as Myth: Towards an Understanding of Extra-Marital Relations in Lesotho." In P. MacAllister and Andrew Spiegel, eds., *Tradition and Transition*. Johannesburg: Witwatersrand University Press, 145–66.

Temilton, Elvis. 1995. "African Protest Politics in the Context of the Socio-Economic and Political Conditions of the 1920s: The Industrial and Commercial Union in Bloemfontein 1925–1930." Honours dissertation, History Department, University of the Witwatersrand.

Thabane, Motlatsi and Jeff Guy. 1983. "The Ma-rashea: A Participant's Perspective." In Belinda Bozzoli, ed., *Town and Countryside in the Transvaal*. Johannesburg: Ravan Press.

Thetela, Puleng. 1987. "Basotho Women's Migration to South Africa, 1930–1963." B.A. and Ed. dissertation, National University of Lesotho, Roma.

Thoahlane Thoahlane. 1994. "The Changing Patterns of the Migrant Labour System in Lesotho." Unpublished ms.

Ulrich, Nicole. 1997. "The Making of Black Urban Culture and the 1925 Riot in Bloemfontein." Honours dissertation, History Department, University of the Witwatersrand.

Wells, Julie. 1982. "The History of Black Women's Struggle against Pass Laws in South Africa, 1900–1960." Ph.D thesis, Columbia University.

White, Luise. 1990. *The Comforts of Home: Prostitution in Colonial Nairobi*. Chicago: University of Chicago Press.

Wilkinson, R. C. 1985. "Migration in Lesotho." Ph.D. thesis, University of Newcastle upon Tyne.

Wilson, Monica and D. Perrot, eds. 1973. *Outlook on a Century: South Africa 1870–1970*. Lovedale, South Africa: Lovedale Press.

11

URBAN THREATS: MANYEMA WOMEN, LOW FERTILITY, AND VENEREAL DISEASES IN TANGANYIKA, 1926–1936

Sheryl A. McCurdy

Our elders advised us to stay away from Manyema women when I was in the Ujiji seminary. They said that if a man fell in love with a Manyema woman, she would take over his life.
> —Tanzanian friend and colleague,
> personal communication, November 1992

Such warnings about Manyema women have a long history. During the colonial period, British concerns about independent women loomed large in the rumors and anxieties circulating about Manyema women's sexuality. For Europeans, Manyema women's sexuality represented the evils of African urban living that threatened the economic and political security of the state. At moments of instability in the political economy, independent sexually active women who controlled their fertility became the focus of attention, fascination, scandal, and attack. In 1930, British colonial officials fueled existing rumors about Manyema women's sexuality and beauty when they published newspaper articles cautioning men not to attend Manyema women's dance competitions; the festivities and drink threatened their ability to think and act clearly. The authors hoped to alert young men to the dangers independent women (re)presented and place the responsibility for the failure or success of the colonial program at women's feet. This colonial narrative of female African sexuality and immorality probably masked a larger colonial fear: the possible failure of indirect rule, which did not include the townships, and the demise of the colonial project.

When the British colonial administration gained control of Tanganyika in 1921, actions and behavior that had served women well during the ivory and slave trade era—their intentional means of fertility control— were construed as evil and immoral. In the colonial mind, low fertility and high infant and child mortality proved that venereal diseases and immorality ran amok in Tanganyika Territory. This hypothesis lent credence to the colonial administration's campaign to rein in the sexuality of African women and improve their mothering capacities. Colonial administrators ignored the ways women and men transformed social relationships, roles, and obligations in response to the changing political economy introduced by colonialism. In reality, women's fertility reflected women and men's responses to the constraints and opportunities afforded by the political, economic, environmental, religious, and social changes. The eradication of venereal diseases alone would not guarantee high fertility.

British colonial officers hoped to reform or control the behavior of Manyema women, whose legendary beauty and sexuality was the subject of continuous speculation, envy, and intrigue along the Swahili Coast and the corridor of the former central ivory and slave trade route of East Africa. If they could not influence Manyema women's behavior, they hoped to inculcate in other African women behaviors they found more acceptable. Just who were the Manyema? What political economy, environmental circumstances, and social conditions forced, encouraged, and enabled Manyema women to act as independent agents, leading colonizers to agonize over their fertility and sexuality? This chapter explores Manyema women's survival strategies during the ivory and slave trade period and proposes that venereal diseases explain only a part of their low fertility. In this chapter, I suggest that Manyema women's low fertility emerged largely out of their responses to caravan commerce, high mobility, cholera and smallpox epidemics, and the lack of stability and security in their lives. I examine how late nineteenth-century memories, intrigues, and rumors circulating about Manyema women's sexuality fed into Victorian notions of the dangers independent women posed to their communities. I discuss the ways in which the British colonial administrators stigmatized once appropriate behaviors and actions that Manyema women used to control fertility. Finally, I examine the ways in which Manyema women's behaviors and practices came under attack during the late 1920s and early 1930s.

ENVIRONMENTAL THREATS AND MANYEMA MOBILITY AND FERTILITY

During the 1860s, when Zanzibari traders and *waungwana* extended the central route of the ivory and slave trade west of Lake Tanganyika, they attacked villages in what is now the northeastern area of the Democratic Republic of the Congo. After they killed adult men and captured adult women, adolescents, and children, they established new settlements and began sending slaves and ivory east. During the late nineteenth century, the term *waungwana* became synonymous with gentlemen. Some of these men affiliated with the ivory and slave trade had become Muslims, spoke Swahili, wore Swahili clothing, lived in towns, and considered themselves more cultured than most rural Africans (Becker 1887, 40; Glassman 1995, 61–64). When the dispossessed, the slaves and the *waungwana* of this area moved east across Lake Tanganyika in the ivory and slave caravans, or in small groups by canoe, they became known as, and came to call themselves, Manyema. When they arrived between the 1860s and 1880s, Ujiji was an outpost of the Zanzibari sphere of influence, which it served as a slave and ivory market and supply post for caravans, with residences for the Zanzibari traders owing allegiance to the Sultan of Zanzibar.

Wealthy Zanzibari traders and *waungwana* in Ujiji kept some female Manyema as concubines, forced other female slaves to work as domestic servants and fieldhands, and made other women, girls, and boys march east in caravans. Male slaves who remained in Ujiji could be domestic servants or fieldhands, but they also worked as boatmen, porters, caravan leaders, and trade agents. Masters generally provided female slaves residing in Ujiji, other than concubines, with a fixed weekly amount of beads or cloth to trade for their food and other essential items (Stanley 1878, 2).

Because of wildly fluctuating market prices, Manyema slaves and the *waungwana* frequently could not pay for food or clothing, and resorted to a variety of strategies to survive. Some slave women attached themselves to *waungwana* men and exchanged domestic and sexual services for food and clothing (Hutley 1976, 106). Slave men, who did not have this option, frequently engaged in direct contests for goods and produce and pitted themselves against the Jiji and Lakist traders (longer-term residents of the area) in market riots, which were common during the late

1870s and early 1880s.[1] Conflicts increased when cholera and smallpox
epidemics made day-to-day activities even more difficult to negotiate
(Livingstone 1875, 331; Christie 1876, 236, 246, 258).[2] During the latter
half of the nineteenth century, people traveled in and out of Ujiji from
all directions and many brought, while others took, diseases along with
them. No doubt venereal diseases accompanied, and followed in the wake
of, the cholera and smallpox outbreaks.

The smallpox and cholera epidemics did more than wipe out part of
the community; they caused ruptures in the social fabric by stressing relationships to the breaking point. Some people lost their kin support networks while others felt theirs had let them down. The following smallpox song, collected during the 1890s, was popular among women on the
Swahili Coast:

> I am leaving you, I am leaving,
> Never shall I return.
> I went down with the pox,
> Both the maize and the sorghum.
> You thought that I would die,
> And you would eat my flesh.
> But now I have recovered
> By the power of the Lord. (Mtoro bin Mwinyi Bakari 1981, 134)[3]

All of these epidemics disrupted people's lives and led them to consider and
embark on other ways of living.

In addition, Manyema women limited their fertility in response to the
multiple threats to their survival posed by increased mobility, the movement
of new groups of people into towns, the crowded and unsanitary conditions,
the caravan trade, and the disruption and slavery. During the latter half of
the nineteenth century, women lost their husbands through epidemics,
porterage, and slavery, others left partners, and many others never bothered
to contract a public long-term relationship of any sort.[4] Burton noted that
the Swahili (and Manyema) women on Zanzibar had small families (1872,
436). During the late nineteenth century, numerous women from slave communities living in trading centers along the upper Zaire River in the eastern
Congo had few or no children:

> Visitors were astonished by the lack of children in the trading towns . . . .
> there were a hundred children to be seen in a fishing village for every
> child to be seen in a trading village of the same size. A survey made by
> missionaries at Tchumbiri in 1899 revealed 384 adults and only 50 chil-
> dren. (Harms 1983, 105)

These women may have been either experiencing subfecundity or infertility or practicing contraception, abortion, or infanticide to suppress their fertility (Mtoro bin Mwinyi Bakari 1981, 18, 59; Scully 1996). It is possible that childlessness and low fertility became an adapted life strategy that passed from one slave generation to the next, creating an anti-natality mentalité among women whose support networks had been decimated by epidemics and the ivory and slave trade.

MEMORIES AND RUMORS ABOUT MANYEMA WOMEN'S SEXUALITY

When the Zanzibari traders and *waungwana* forced many Manyema women into their harems, and brought them east across Lake Tanganyika, they provided them with slaves, beautiful clothing, perfumes, jewelry, and the time to apply makeup and braid elaborate hairstyles. Furthermore, Zanzibari traders encouraged Manyema concubines to perform music publicly and allowed them to walk freely about town in groups and in pairs (Hutley 1976, 184). As highly visible members of the community in the towns of Tanganyika, privileged Manyema women enjoyed a certain amount of prestige and power for several decades before the British arrived in Tanganyika.

According to some travelers' accounts, Zanzibari men sought Manyema slaves because of their reputed beauty. Manyema women formed the core of most Zanzibari traders' households and in Ujiji some slave women translated their beauty into privilege and wealth. During the 1880s, in the compound of a Zanzibari trader, Rumaliza (Mohammed bin Halfan al Barwani), some seventy women engaged in various domestic projects designed to keep the household running smoothly as well as entertain guests and the wives and concubines themselves (Hutley 1976, 293, 294). Jane Moir, a European missionary based in Nyasaland, visited Ujiji in July 1890 and was a guest of Rumaliza, at the time the most successful Zanzibari trader of the area. She reported that he had twenty "slave wives" who each had five or six slaves of their own (Moir [1891] 1991, 31–32). In her letters home, Moir complained about the impudence of the slave girls assigned to care for her needs and the loud animated conversations the wives and slaves conducted in the courtyard.

Writing about his trip during 1893, a European traveler, Decle, also noted the beauty, wealth, and privilege of some Manyema women:

[The Zanzibaris'] wives are the most elegant women of Africa. . . . They are mostly Manyema women, generally slaves taken very young. . . . The richest bedeck themselves with collars of coral, interspersed with large silver beads, and bracelets of silver and glass beads alternating. They walk

Figure 11.1   A *waungwana* Manyema woman of the early 1890s. (From Lionel Decle, *Three Years In Savage Africa.* New York: M. F. Mansfield, 1898, p. 306.)

barefoot, not without a certain grace, and are heavily perfumed with musk. Nobody will be surprised that these magnificent beauties are very vain. They can make eyes at the passer-by against any women in the world. (Decle 1898, 306–307)

Fascinated by Manyema women in Ujiji, Decle devoted a couple of pages to describing their beauty, clothing, hairstyles, and jewelry. He also included a profile sketch to illustrate their delicate features, earrings, and braiding techniques.

Decle was not the only European to note the attractiveness of Manyema women. Other Europeans, Africans, and Zanzibaris valued Manyema women for their beauty and sexual allure (Stanley 1878, 118; Parke 1891, 344; Livingstone 1875, 259, 283). Livingstone recorded the comments of *waungwana* in the Manyema area northwest of Ujiji:

The Manyuema [*sic*] are far more beautiful than either the bond or free of Zanzibar; I overhear the remark often, "If we had Manyuema wives what beautiful children we should beget." (Livingstone 1875, 275)

Even African women on the Swahili Coast sang songs about Manyema women's beauty and sexuality:

Bwana mkubwa [the influential man] says,
"I want a woman from Manyema that has firm breasts."
Sembo's hands are gathering the fruits.
The nipples are decorated, made beautiful for in the bed.[5]

The anonymous author who recorded the song noted that it was sung by groups of women along the road. Apparently, Manyema women raised quite a stir on the Swahili Coast. They influenced earring and clothing styles and probably provoked jealousy among coastal men and women.[6]

Manyema women brought more than fashion with them when they moved east; they also brought rituals, dances, and associations. During the late nineteenth century in Ujiji, along the Swahili Coast, and in Zanzibar, Manyema women formed *unyago* puberty associations, Rua, Bisa, and Songye spirit possession associations, and popular dance groups.[7] Manyema concubines, slaves, and other dispossessed homeless women also shared the practice of stretching the labia that purportedly made them more desirable sexual partners. By the late nineteenth century, being Manyema afforded women a certain amount of *uwezo*, whether she was slave, concubine, or free. Here I use *uwezo* to refer to social capital. While Manyema women spoke Swahili, dressed in Swahili costume, practiced Swahili customs, and at varying levels identified themselves as Muslim; they did not identify themselves as Swahili. The Manyema remembered their place of origin and celebrated the rituals and practices they chose to transform to fit their new environments and circumstances (cf. Fair 1994; Strobel 1979).

Manyema women's reputed ability to captivate and control men, combined with their tendency to seek independent lives, created a mystique about them. These ideas fed rumors—among African women and men who were not Manyema—that Manyema women, while beautiful and sexually alluring, were dangerous. Whether Zanzibari traders originated rumors about Manyema women in order to keep their concubines to themselves, or men from other ethnic groups developed these stories to explain the types of relationships Manyema women and men formed, or Manyema men told the stories in order to reduce competition from outsiders is not important. The rumors that surrounded the sexuality of Manyema women reveal that some men and women desired and envied them and that some people considered Manyema women to be dangerous. The chaos Manyema experienced during the ivory and slave trade, in addition to the uncertainty of impending colonial rule, epidemics, and the threat of famine, certainly laid the foundation on which all sorts of explanations and types of social relationships could be built.

The 1891 depression in Ujiji followed the beginning of German colonial rule and the closing of the Congolese border. Soon afterwards, the Zanzibari traders lost their power and wealth and the ivory and slave trade dwindled. The 1892 rinderpest epizootic and the subsequent loss of cattle further strained the economic, environmental, political, and social conditions in Ujiji (Iliffe 1979, 130). Children and pregnant women, the most vulnerable groups in the population, probably died in the greatest numbers. Surveys conducted by the German colonial administration during the first decade of the twentieth century suggest the toll of famine on children was enormously high.

Following the Manyema rebellion in the eastern Congo during 1899, the Manyema presence in Ujiji increased. More arrived in 1908, when eager German colonial officials arranged for 2,000 Manyema associated with the "*Wahuni* Mutineers" to immigrate to Ujiji.[8] Notions of difference, based on slave and free statuses, between Manyema and Lakists (prior residents) declined after 1905, when the German colonial administration declared that all children born in Tanganyika after 31 December 1905 were free. The manumission of slaves in Ujiji gave former slaves, as a class, the opportunity to avoid manual labor. After manumission, from 1905 through the 1920s, the Manyema of Ujiji employed Ha laborers from the countryside to perform field and domestic work.[9]

The extension of the railway to Kigoma in 1914 provided an efficient communication and transportation network for the Manyema and the spread of Islam (Moravian Mission 1915, 56–57). Using the railroad, Manyema women and men increased their speed of travel; the circular movement of ideas, practices, and rituals between the Swahili Coast, Ujiji, the Congo, and Usumbura intensified during colonialism. It was not unusual, for example, for a young Manyema girl born at the beginning of the twentieth century in Ujiji to be sent to live with her maternal aunt in Dar es Salaam while she was a child. Her aunt might arrange her *unyago* celebration at puberty and select her first husband. After marriage, she might move to Tabora, have a child, divorce, and move back to Ujiji, with or without the child, depending on the child's age, the mother and father's relationship, and the woman and her partner's economic and social circumstances. At some point, she would probably remarry in Ujiji. She could live there with or without her husband, whose work probably included some traveling, or the pair might live in any of the towns on the perimeter of Lake Tanganyika.[10] At any point, a woman might be called on by an extended family member to attend a ritual or perform a duty or obligation in any one of these towns. The time she spent there could range from a few days to several months depending upon the situation.

GERMAN AND BRITISH POPULATION SURVEYS

During 1914, German colonial administrators worried about, "the great lack of growth in the middle district of Ujiji. . . . a complete failure of descendants to appear" (*Deutsches Kolonialblatt* 1914, 441).[11] The German colonial medical officer assumed that syphilis caused the miscarriages of many Manyema women ("as many as fifty percent of the residents have become infected") but he also suspected that the Manyema women and *askari* (police), in particular, induced abortions:

> Without doubt, however, it is more frequent that the native abortions are artificially caused, although the execution and other actions pertaining to the abortion are kept a secret if possible. For the most part, it is unquestionable that the *askari* [Manyema police] and [Manyema and Swahili] Swahili women are most included here. (*Deutsches Kolonialblatt* 1914, 441)[12]

The Germans blamed the low numbers of children on mothers' induced abortions, spontaneous abortions caused by syphilis, and early weaning practices, as well as on children's experiences of intestinal diseases and malaria. They believed that a woman's practices, behaviors, physical health, and relationships, as well as the environment, diseases other than venereal diseases, and the changing political economy, interacted and influenced her reproductive experiences.

German colonial administrators planned to combat the low birth rate through education, inspecting the population more closely to ascertain who might be practicing abortion, discouraging abortion, and promoting Christian values (*Deutsches Kolonialblatt* 1914, 440). But they learned that trying to change African sexuality and fertility would not be a simple process when the *askari* garrison at Bukoba demanded "to be circumcised *en bloc*" because the "arabized [*sic*] prostitutes" refused to have sex with them (Raum 1965, 167). Cultural and religious practices influenced social relationships and fertility and the choices that the Germans made as they began to establish their regime. While German colonial administrators were concerned with the low fertility of certain sectors of the African population, like the residents of Ujiji and the Swahili Coast, they focused their early medical efforts on large-scale disease eradication campaigns meant to improve health at a national level. What they might have accomplished in Tanganyika is unknown, for after World War I they lost their colonies. The Belgians administered the northwestern region of Tanganyika until the British took over the Protectorate in 1921. The British colonial officers, continuing the policy of the German colonial administration, conducted population surveys. They too found that certain groups of women in the population experienced low fertility.

When British colonial officers became aware of the high overall infant mortality in Tanganyika and the low fertility of Manyema women, they declared these women's conduct immoral, and held them accountable for population decline and the spread of venereal disease. The fact that some of these women chose to have fewer children or preferred living on their own to marriage fueled the European myth of the dangers of African women's "hypersexuality." In response to low fertility and concerns about the need for more laborers to ensure the success of the colonial state's economic endeavors, British colonial administrators prepared medical and education policies and programs designed to promote motherhood and family betterment, based on the interventions directed at working-class mothers designed during the 1900s back in England (Weeks [1981]1989, 126–127).

During the 1920s, the British colonial medical administration launched an anti-yaws and anti-syphilis campaign and established maternal and child health clinics to improve fertility and ensure infant survival. Beginning in the mid-1920s, maternal and child health campaigns encouraged hygienic deliveries and healthy babies. By 1930, British colonial attempts to reduce venereal diseases targeted the urban women deemed responsible—independent Manyema women who performed in dance competitions and owned their own houses. Public song and dance performances conducted by independent African women threatened European notions of proper female behavior, sexuality, and motherhood. Many Manyema women had few children, divorced frequently, and often lived independently. In Swahilized Muslim communities, Manyema women often married older men at puberty, then returned to their mother's homes as divorcées or widows. Later, when (and if) they remarried, they married whom they liked (Swantz 1970; Bujra 1968; Strobel 1979; Landberg 1986; Le Guennec-Coppens 1987; and Mirza and Strobel 1989). Many colonial administrators felt that the reproductive health of African women reflected the health and the future of the nation and worried that immorality, polygyny, and venereal disease among urban women threatened the survival of the state. With the mechanisms of indirect rule largely in place, a propaganda effort aimed at educating adults began with the publication of a special series of articles in the Swahili newspaper, *Mambo Leo*, that linked alcohol use to immorality and venereal disease and condemned all three.[13]

VENEREAL DISEASES AND MATERNAL EDUCATION

British colonial officials expressed their concern over labor productivity in terms of morality and targeted alcohol abuse and sexuality. Men suffering from the effects of alcohol or venereal disease often failed to report to work or adequately perform their duties. The reputed role of venereal disease in limiting the economic, social, and biological health of the nation continued to loom large in European colonial debates and plans of action. The concern was heightened for British administrators because of European racist and sexist attitudes rooted in nineteenth-century scientific notions of race, gender, and sexuality, and the emerging eugenics movement.[14] Scientific tracts of the period claimed that the "immoral hypersexuality" of the European prostitute was due to some genetic connection to Africans or even to chimpanzees.[15] By the beginning of the twentieth century in many middle- and upper-class European minds, both African women and European prostitutes represented a dangerous sexuality. Many British colonial officers believed that controlling African women's sexuality was the key to decreasing venereal diseases and increasing fertility.

Because of financial and staffing constraints and differences in philosophical approaches to disease eradication (e.g., curative v. preventative), colonial efforts to improve African health attempted quick-fix campaigns targeting specific infectious diseases. The sanitation and hygiene programs initiated by the Medical Department of the British colonial administration in Tanganyika during the 1920s served a two-fold purpose. First, in accordance with the British concept of "indirect rule," these programs allowed the most extensive health interventions with the least possible investment. Secondly, they contributed to colonial economic goals by promising to promote a healthy labor force. J. B. Davey, appointed the first postwar Medical Director in 1920, wrote that "more than 32 percent of the total estimated revenue is expected from house, hut and poll taxes. The development of the country . . . depends upon the labor of the native" (Davey 1923, 26).

Although the Contagious Disease Acts, enacted to control prostitutes and venereal disease in England, had been repealed decades earlier, the link between venereal disease, prostitution, and immorality remained emblazoned on Europeans' minds (Weeks [1981]1989, 84–95, 122–128). Furthermore, the European idea that there was a need for improved mothering capacities, rooted in the recent memory of the infant welfare campaigns in Europe and North America, led administrators to create similar programs in the colonies (Meckel 1990, 102–104, 133). In England and the United States, however, the infant welfare campaigns relied on nurses visiting and teaching poor and immigrant women at home. British colonial authorities would not and could not provide such an intensive initiative in Tanganyika. However, by focusing on women, British colonial officers in Tanganyika hoped to ensure that mothers would prevent particular groups of Africans from "dying out" and provide healthy and moral laborers for the future.[16]

Based on scanty evidence, colonial medical officers heightened European concerns about venereal diseases by claiming they were widespread. Extrapolating from 92 clinical cases he diagnosed in Kigoma, Dr. J. McClark, the Medical Officer during 1922, reported that venereal diseases were common among the 6,023 adults living in Ujiji.[17] During 1922, health care workers at Kigoma hospital treated 24 African cases of gonorrhea (16 African government employees and 8 non-governmental) and 68 cases of syphilis (McClark 1923, 126). Men, most of them in the government service, formed the core of the patients seeking treatment. British colonial administrators noted that most Africans were not voluntarily seeking biomedical treatment for venereal disease. It is possible that those men who sought treatment felt compelled to do so for fear of losing their jobs.

Between 1925 and 1929, health workers injected 99,962 Tanganyikan men and women with the bismuth solution of sodium tartrate (Sobita) to treat syphilis (Medical Department 1930, 65). Unfortunately, syphilis treatment required weekly injections over a two-year period and most patients did not complete the full course. Furthermore, bismuth treatment did not cure syphilis; treatment simply rendered patients non-infectious. Both Africans and Europeans wanted mothers to be able to deliver babies without transmitting syphilis to their newborns, but the lack of consistent treatment and follow-up resulted in constant reinfections and limited the success of the program. Undoubtedly, many mothers, unaware of their infectious state, passed their infection on to their newborns. Whether or not their infection actually was syphilis, or yaws—a non-venereal disease with similar lesions—is difficult to know. By World War II, many colonial physicians recognized that they had mistakenly identified yaws as syphilis (Davies 1956).

In addition to the anti-syphilis campaign, the colonial Medical Department designed the Maternal and Child Health Program "to accustom the native women to western medicine and to provide for the practical training of native midwives" (Medical Department 1934, 100). The Medical Department opened the first maternity clinic in Dar es Salaam in 1925, then others in Tabora, Kahama, Tanga, and Machame (Kilimanjaro) (Clyde 1962, 127). Manyema lived in Dar es Salaam, Tabora, Tanga, and other towns in Tanganyika and they circulated between these cities frequently. They may well have spread information about their own or others' experiences as they traveled from one place to another for one of their longer-term moves or short visits.

Initially, some clinics offered weekly child welfare clinics to which women were invited for afternoon tea. Women were encouraged to bring their infants and toddlers to the clinics for health assessments and vaccinations; in some places mothers could take sewing lessons (Clyde 1962, 127, 129). British colonial administrators claimed that the Tanga child health program was such a success that after a flood destroyed the clinic in 1933, officials immediately found another building so that a planned baby show could be held according to schedule.[18] Clinics held baby competitions to ascertain who had the "healthiest" baby and more importantly, to promote healthy habits. Refreshments were served and sometimes a school band played. Health workers encouraged mothers to bring their infants or toddlers to baby shows where judges would assess the children's health and awards would be distributed to the prizewinners. Baby shows or healthy baby competitions were not everyday or even weekly occurrences; they were special events that promised entertainment, refreshments, and prizes.

After the colonial medical staff decided that these initial clinics were successful, they created a territory-wide maternal and child health program. We may wonder whether among British colonial administrators a "successful clinic" simply meant one at which women appeared for special events. Women were at first reluctant to attend the antenatal and child health clinics, and initially it was difficult to find any women who would agree to deliver their babies at the clinic so that midwives could be trained during their deliveries. Finding suitable candidates to train as "native midwives" was in itself a never-ending process for the colonial medical staff. An "acceptable candidate" had to be literate, be able to move to a new location after training, and be accepted by the local population, and these rigid and unrealistic standards required continual reevaluation and reconsideration on the part of administrators (Medical Department 1935, 119; 1936, 123; 1938, 21).

During the late twenties and early thirties, maternal and child health care programs provided women with some entertainment, allowed them to gain familiarity with clinics and clinic staff, and offered some health care for their children. While some Manyema women may have delivered their babies in clinics in Dar es Salaam, Tabora, or Tanga before World War II, the clinics played a minimal role in influencing women to change their behavior and practices. The local midwives, herbalists, and spirit possession leaders continued to care for pregnant women and children and "a great deal of the [maternal and child health] work consist[ed] [solely] in the treatment of minor illnesses in mothers and children" (Medical Department 1937, 29).[19] As late as the mid-1930s, maternal and child health clinics in Tanganyika did very little pregnancy-related work. African women found many of the family betterment schemes amusing at best (Allman 1994; Odinga 1997), and intrusive at worst (Clyde 1962).

IMMORAL AND DISEASED WOMEN
DURING THE DEPRESSION

Community tensions increased in late 1929 when the colonial administration removed Ujiji's township status, further limiting the resources available to the largest urban African community in Tanganyika and bringing the residents under the jurisdiction of the Native Authority. The tax basis for town residents changed from house tax to hut and poll tax, which meant that men no longer paid one flat fee for a house, but instead had to pay a hut tax and a plural wives tax (Bagenal 1930, 12). For the first time since the beginning of British rule, Ujiji men were expected to pay full tax for their houses and one-half of that tax for each wife.

As taxation and the worldwide depression threatened people's livelihoods, Manyema and Lakists became increasingly antagonistic and vocal in their opposition to each other. Women expressed the animosities between the two groups in their rival dance competitions (McCurdy 1996). As early as 1930 the Provincial Commissioner of Kigoma worried about female dance competitions in Ujiji. He noted that

> there have been occasions quite lately where friction between the various "Bani" (Dancing Clubs) in Ujiji has almost led to rioting. Being apprehensive of the danger which rioting might mean to non-native shopkeepers the Native Administration have temporarily, at any rate, forbidden these Band Performances.[20]

Seven months after this ban on women's *ngoma* competitions was declared, the Acting Commissioner of Tanganyika Police and Prisons assured the Chief Secretary that since the prohibition, the Ujiji *Jumbe* (local administrator) had "experienced no difficulty in controlling the native inhabitants."[21] The temporary banning and the surveillance for "trouble" in Kigoma revealed the anxiety Manyema women provoked in British colonial administrators. The continuation of *ngoma* performances, however, showed the lack of influence the colonial officials had with Manyema women.

Although British colonial officers recognized that this was primarily an oral society where information and memory passed quickly by word of mouth through people's networks as they traveled by foot, bicycle, boat, rail, or bus, the colonial officers began a morality campaign among the literate population in hopes that changes in sexuality and morality might trickle down to the masses. The colonial administration used print media to get out their message about the evils of promiscuity, alcoholism, and the spread of venereal disease.

In 1930, *Mambo Leo*, a national monthly Swahili newspaper sponsored by the colonial administration, introduced a four-part propaganda series focusing on the three evils allegedly destroying the nation: syphilis, gonorrhea, and alcoholism. The articles warned of the evils of promiscuity, prostitutes, and alcohol and of their consequences: infertility, miscarriages, stillbirths, insanity, handicaps, blindness, etc.[22] In the July 1930 article, an anonymous author proclaimed that "drunkenness is a slave to syphilis and gonorrhea" and that "prostitutes reap the profits of drunks."[23] Perhaps more disturbingly for the female dance competitors of Ujiji, the article singled out *ngoma* performances as a menace to society because they brought together many people who, after drinking themselves into a stupor, engaged in "scandalous acts."[24] The article's focus on the *ngoma* as a primary source of corruption was a direct attack on an African cultural activity that was a significant basis for women and men's associational life.

Women used *ngoma* competitions for social commentary, to provide entertainment, and as a leisure activity. *Ngoma* were potential political rallying points, a fact that eventually became apparent to colonial officers. The diatribe against the *ngoma* was in progress at exactly the same time that administrators were discussing a proposal for stringent measures to control venereal diseases. By locating the disease in prostitutes, rather than in men, propagandists promoted an age-old idea that women were disease vectors. The image of the prostitute reaping profits was meant further to vilify independent unattached women. The *Mambo Leo* anti-venereal disease and anti-alcoholism campaign promoted negative stereotypes of women as prostitutes as a scare tactic in an attempt to uplift the morals and change the behavior of literate Africans. The messages of the articles were the following: women were dangerous disease vectors, free women were prostitutes, and women took advantage of men to reap profits. By tying the idea of lost profits to women and disease, the articles gave a message to a new class of wage earners that the proceeds of their work could be lost if they drank alcohol and associated with prostitutes. At the same time the implicit message was that unattached women in towns were diseased profit-mongers.

The *Mambo Leo* anti-venereal disease and anti-alcoholism articles situated the *ngoma*, the women who performed them, and the people who frequented and acquired sexual partners at these performances as being at the center of an immoral cultural act of debauchery that was sending the country on a downward spiral to certain disaster. Manyema or Swahili women performed the majority of *ngoma* in towns like Dar es Salaam, Tabora, and Ujiji, where many of these women were house owners in their own right.[25]

Propagandists publicly condemned and stereotyped them, declaring their behavior and practices immoral and diseased.

Readers of *Mambo Leo* necessarily had some education. Most were Christians, since missionized areas had the largest number of schools, but many Muslim men and women also were literate. In 1925, C. J. Bagenal, Senior Commissioner, noted that *Mambo Leo* was "well received" in Kigoma and Ujiji, indicating that a wide audience knew about the messages it contained.[26] The 1930 articles targeted the dangers of urban African dance performances for male wage earners. A *ngoma* could be any song and dance performance, but in urban settings *ngoma* often were organized associational activities of men and women. In the July 1930 *Mambo Leo* article the author warned urban male wage earners that *ngoma* performances were a dangerous phenomenon because of the temptations of alcohol and prostitutes, which, if sampled, could lead a man not only to contract venereal disease, but also lose his hard-earned wages.

I suspect most readers of *Mambo Leo* understood that the government published the articles therein for its own purposes. For example, one reader's letter to the editor began by referring to "your newspaper, that is written to tell us about happenings from around the country."[27] The negative comments about *ngoma* competitions and the evils of prostitution, and its effects of infertility, miscarriages, and stillbirths, reveal clearly that women were the focus of the government campaign to change African morals. The tactics included ostracizing "free" women and cautioning others to "change their evil ways" lest their reproductive capabilities be impaired if not destroyed.

Four years after the *Mambo Leo* morality campaigns, a decade into the anti-syphilis and anti-yaws campaign, and just nine years after the first maternal and child health clinics opened, Western Provincial Commissioner F. J. Bagshawe acknowledged that Manyema women still controlled their fertility:

> . . . the liwali [local Muslim judge] to see me. We talked about town women, the "wives" of boys, police, etc. why they had no children. He said the reason is that the boys, etc. as they are always on the move, don't marry respectable girls, but pickup older women, the castoffs of others of the same kind. These take on anyone they like "two or three a day." These women are afraid to have children as they may be cast off and saddled with the rearing of them which will prevent "reemployment." They prevent children by abortion. . . . He also said the women have a contraceptive. . . . He says that if 2 or 3 [seeds] are swallowed whole by a women she cannot conceive for a long time and may never conceive again. . . .[28]

Bagshawe's 1934 inquiry into Manyema women's childlessness and refusal to marry reveals at the very least that some of the single women associating with the police preferred not to have children. Manyema women overall did not heed European suggestions for restructuring their behaviors or sexual relationships. British intentions and programs to change Manyema women's behaviors and sexuality failed. Rumors about their sexuality and ability to dictate the actions of their partners endured. As one European, who lived in Ujiji between 1935 and 1939, remembered, "Manyema women were not shy and they were very charming" (Bishop Holmes-Siedle, personal communication, 16 March 1993).

CONCLUSION

The experiences of dislocations, epidemics, environmental change, and famine during the ivory and slave trade period and the early German colonial period also contributed to the ways in which Manyema men and women formed, and did not form, relationships. The strategies a Manyema woman employed in response to the changing political economy and changing environmental, religious, social, and cultural practices primarily determined what risks she, her fetus, and her children, might experience, and, in turn, partly explained her reproductive history. Victorian-informed maternal and child health education and mass injection campaigns may have educated women about the risks associated with certain behaviors, but the programs did not provide women with much in the way of alternatives or teach them anything new, except, possibly, the benefits of basic hygiene. During the 1930s, there was no cure for syphilis. African women's skepticism about the benefits of hospital-based medicine for maternal and child health care probably served them well before World War II and the advent of penicillin.

The morality campaign's attack on Manyema women's dance competitions linked colonial fears of independent women to colonial concerns about the survival of the labor force. When they blamed dancing women for creating a space for drinking and immoral, illicit, and diseased acts of sexual debauchery, British colonial administrators simultaneously accused them of spreading venereal diseases. While the British colonial officers hoped their propaganda would make the dance competitions less inviting and discourage wage-earning men from spending their time and money on independent women, they underestimated the immense cultural and social value of dance associations. Furthermore, colonial projects and campaigns presented no competition to the larger social and political processes that emerged during the late precolonial ivory and slave trade economy. The increased mobility of the Manyema after the introduction of the railroad, and their urban lives encouraged the creation of households and relationships the British abhorred, but could not prevent. There is no evidence that any of the colonial projects altered Manyema women's sexuality or marital practices. Instead, Manyema continued to have few children and several marriages.

NOTES

The research for this chapter was supported by an International Doctoral Research Fellowship, funded by the Joint Committee on African Studies of the Social Science Research Council and the American Council of Learned Societies, with funds provided by the Rockefeller Foundation. Additional funding for writing up the chapter was provided by the "Behavioral Science Education Cancer Prevention and Control," National Cancer Institute/NIH, Grant #2R25CA57712–06. The Population Research Institute at the Pennsylvania State University and the University of Texas-Houston Center for Health Promotion Research and Development, provided financial assistance and office support. I thank the Tanzanian Commission for Science and Technology for permission to carry out the research, as well as Professor Kapepwa Tambila and the History Department at the University of Dar es Salaam for research affiliation. I also thank Dennis Cordell, Rita Elliot, Susan Geiger, Dorothy L. Hodgson, Gregory H. Maddox, Pamela Scully, Carole S. Vance, Marcia Wright, and the members of the Houston Area African Studies Seminar Group for their comments on earlier versions of this paper.

1. Cooperative Africana Microfilm Project (hereafter CAMP), Center for Research Libraries, Chicago, CWMA/IL/CAA, Hore to Mullens (9 December 1878), Ujiji, section entitled, "An Ujiji Row," 40–45. Hutley to Whitehouse, Ujiji (19 October, 1879): "There is constantly something or other occurring in the daily market here, between the Arabs' slaves and the Wajiji."

2. CAMP, CWMA/IL/CA, Hore to Whitehouse, Ujiji (20 July 1880), 6, 7, fiche 41–42.

3. "Maize" and "sorghum" were types of smallpox that were less fatal than the one referred to as "sesame."

4. Strobel noted that in Mombasa, Kenya, of the eighteen slave women attached to one household, nine women never married and never had children; another four did marry but did not have children. The remaining five slave women who were not concubines, as a group, only had seven children. The two concubines had a total of five children between them (Strobel 1983, 120–21).

5. Geheimes Staatsarchiv, Preussischer Kulturbesitz, I92 Nachlass Schnee, No. 70 (hereafter GS, PK, I92 NS, 70), *Asili ya uzuri wa karatasi kulia masikioni, wanawake wa kiswahili*, 8. I thank Thaddeus Sunseri for sharing these documents with me. The pages of the documents in this archive are not numbered sequentially. The documents, written in Swahili in Roman script by someone familiar with the Swahili coastal culture, are not dated. Since the documents are from a German archive and speak of life on the Swahili Coast after the Manyema arrived, it is likely the author wrote sometime between 1850 and 1916. Most likely, he or she wrote for the German colonial adminis-

tration before World War I, which would narrow the time frame of authorship to the years between 1890 and 1914.

6. GS, PK, I92 NS, 70, *Asili ya uzuri wa karatasi kulia masikioni, wanawake wa kiswahili*, 8.

7. GS, PK, I92 NS, 70, *Ngoma zao za furaha, Pepo wa Kibisa, Pepo wa Kisonge*, 18–21; fieldnotes, 1993; Craster (1913, 82–85); and Fair (1994, 277–279).

8. CAMP, Tanganyika District Books, Reel No. 21, Kigoma District Book, Volume III, W. Ronayne, 1923, *"Wahuni* or Congo Mutineers," 4–5.

9. Fieldnotes, 1993, Recording No. 1, Kassim Hassan Benge and Husseini S. Lukanda, 28 November 1992, Majengo, Ujiji; Iliffe (1979, 131).

10. This paragraph is based on Recording No. 12, Mwanaidi Husseini, 8 January 1993, Ujiji; Recording No. 21, Shindo Haruna Selemani 27 January 1993, Mwanga; Recording No. 26, Zahura Shobani,* 1 February 1993, Ujiji; Recording No. 51, Issa Kitenga, 14 May 1993, Bangwe; and 1993 fieldnotes. An asterisk indicates a pseudonym.

11. Thanks to Marcia Wright for bringing this document to my attention and to Thaddeus Sunseri for translating it.

12. German and British colonial officials generally used the term Swahili to refer to any urban Muslim woman regardless of her identity or place of origin.

13. *Mambo Leo* was an African "newspaper supplied by the Government." Tanzanian National Archives Dar es Salaam, Tanzania (hereafter TNA), Secretariat File (hereafter SF), 15232/12, D. J. Jardine, Chief Secretary (hereafter C.S.), Dar es Salaam (hereafter DSM), 26 January 1932, Confidential Circular No. 1 of 1932, to all Provincial Commissioners, "The African Association." The national Maternal and Child Health (MCH) campaign began in 1925. No maternal and child health clinic existed in Ujiji until 1939.

14. For a detailed and eloquent discussion of this topic, see Vaughan (1991, 129–154).

15. For an introduction to the discussion of the racist nineteenth- and twentieth-century attempts to compare Africans to apes, see Marks (1998) and Schiebinger (1993).

16. Larsson uses this term in her discussion of Haya sexuality (Larsson 1991, 162). British colonial administrators had created similar projects in Uganda (Summers 1991) and Ghana (Allman 1994), as had the Belgians in the Belgian Congo (Hunt 1992).

17. CAMP, Tanganyika Territory, Kigoma District Book, Vol. 1, "1920–21 Census, Ujiji Sub-District."

18. TNA, SF 21725, "Native Maternity and Child Welfare Clinic, Tanga," Vol. I, Provincial Commissioner (P.C.), Tanga telegram to C.S., DSM, 9 February 1933, 1, and internal notes, 9 August 1933, 14. By 1930 British administrators hoped to establish a similar program in Bukoba. TNA, SF 19067, "Maternity and Child Welfare Bukoba Province, Secretary of Native Affairs, Tour Report," 5 June 1930, 1.

19. Recording No. 26, Zahura Shobani*, 1 February 1993, Vamia, Ujiji; Recording No. 27, Hawa Abdallah*, 2 February 1993, Busaidi, Ujiji; Recording No. 47, Asia Omari*, 7 April 1993, Gungu; and Recording No. 48, Neema Hassani*, 7 April 1993, Gungu. I have changed all the healers' names because their activities today require a license to conduct "cultural activities," and I do not want to jeopardize their activities by opening them up to government scrutiny.

20. TNA, SF 12218, "Native Administration, Kigoma Province," C. J. Bagenal, P.C., Kigoma Province to C.S., DSM, 28 January 1930, 31.

21. TNA, SF 12218, "Native Administration, Kigoma Province," Acting Commissioner of Tanganyika Police and Prisons, DSM to C.S., DSM, 22 July 1930, 73.

22. TNA , SF 19153, "Venereal Diseases, Anti-Venereal Measures," *Mambo Leo*, April 1930, 63–64, May 1930, 79–81, June 1930, 97–99, July 1930, 113–115.

23. TNA, SF 19153, "Venereal Diseases, Anti-Venereal Measures," *Mambo Leo*, July 1930, 114.

24. Ibid.

25. TNA 180/KG/B.1, 180/KG/B.1g, 180/KG/B.2g, "Ujiji Township, Tax Files," and Leslie (1963, 168–169).

26. TNA 1733/3/45, "Annual Report of Kigoma District, 1924," 28.

27. TNA, SF10690 "Payment of Hut or Poll Tax by Women," 31–33. P.C., Songea to C.S., DSM, 16 May 1935. A woman in Songea, Binti Zena Mwechande, allegedly wrote this letter during 1935 to complain about the tax on unattached females. I say "allegedly" because the District Commissioner claimed that she did not exist. He suspected that a hospital dispenser, "who kept several women" and avoided paying plural wives tax by not marrying them, was the author of the letter.

28. Rhodes House, Oxford University, Colonial Officials' Documents and Memoirs, MSS F. J. Bagshawe, Diaries, Vol. XV, 23 March 1934, 92–93.

REFERENCES

Allman, Jean. 1994. "Making Mothers: Missionaries, Medical Officers, and Women's Work in Colonial Asante, 1924–45." *History Workshop Journal* 38:23–47.

Bagenal, C. J. 1930. "Kigoma Province." *Annual Reports of the Provincial Commissioners, Tanganyika Territory, 1929*. Dar es Salaam: Government Printers.

Becker, Jérôme. 1887. *La Vie en Afrique*. Volume 2, Second edition. Paris.

Bujra, Janet. 1968. "An Anthropological Study of Political Action in a Bajuni village in Kenya." Ph.D. thesis, University of London.

Burton, Richard. 1872. *Zanzibar: City, Island, and Coast*. Volume 1. London: Tinsley Brothers.

Christie, James. 1876. *Cholera Epidemics in East Africa : An Account of the Several Diffusions of the Disease in That Country from 1829 till 1872*. London: Macmillan.

Clyde, David F. 1962. *History of the Medical Services of Tanganyika*. Dar es Salaam: Government Press.

Davey, J. B. 1923. *Annual Medical Report, 1922, Tanganyika Territory*. Dar es Salaam: Government Printer.

Davies, J.N.P. 1956. "The History of Syphilis in Uganda." *Bulletin of the World Health Organization* 15:1041–55.

Decle, Lionel. 1898. *Three Years in Savage Africa*. New York: M. F. Mansfield.

Deutsches Kolonialblatt. 1914. "Famillien-Nachwuchsstatistik uber die Eingeborenen von Deutsch-Ostafrika."

Fair, Laura. 1994. "Pastimes and Politics: A Social History of Zanzibar's Ng'ambo Community." Ph.D. thesis, University of Minnesota.

Glassman, Jonathon. 1995. *Feast and Riots: Revelry, Rebellion, and Popular Consciousness on the Swahili Coast*. Portsmouth, NH: Heinemann.

Harms, Robert. 1983. "Sustaining the System: The Middle Zaire." In Claire Robertson and Martin A. Klein, eds., *Women and Slavery in Africa*. Madison: University of Wisconsin Press.

Hunt, Nancy Rose. 1992. "Negotiated Colonialism: Domesticity, Hygiene, and Birth Work in the Belgian Congo." Ph.D. thesis, University of Wisconsin-Madison.

Hutley, Walter. 1976. *The Central African Diaries of Walter Hutley, 1877 to 1881*. James B. Wolf, ed., African Studies Center, Boston University, African Historical Documents Series, No. 4.

Iliffe, John. 1979. *A Modern History of Tanganyika*. Cambridge: Cambridge University Press.

Landberg, Pamela. 1986. "Widows and Divorced Women in Swahili Society." In Betty Potash, ed., *Widows in African Societies*. Stanford, CA: Stanford University Press.

Larsson, Birgitta. 1991. *Conversion to a Greater Freedom: Women, Church, and Social Change in Northwestern Tanzania under Colonial Rule*. Uppsala, Sweden: Acta Universitatis Upsaliensis Studia Historica Upsaliensia, 162.

Le Guennec-Coppens, Françoise. 1987. "L'Instabilité conjugale et ses conséquences dans la societé swahili de Lamu (Kenya)." In David Parkin and David Nyamwaya, eds., *Transformations of African Marriage*. Manchester: Manchester University Press.

Leslie, J.A.K. 1963. *A Survey of Dar es Salaam*. London: Oxford University Press.

Livingstone, David. 1875. *Livingstone's Last Journals*. Hartford, CT: T.W. Bliss and Co.

Marks, Jonathon. 1998. "Replaying the Race Card." *Anthropology Newsletter* (American Anthropological Association) 37(5):1, 4.

McClark, J., Dr. 1923. "Kigoma and Ujiji: Extracts from a Report." *Annual Medical Report, 1922, Tanganyika Territory*. Dar es Salaam: Government Printer.

Meckel, Richard A. 1990. *Save the Babies: American Public Health Reform and the Prevention of Infant Mortality, 1850–1929*. Baltimore: Johns Hopkins Press.

Medical Department, Tanganyika Territory. 1921–1940. *Annual Medical Report, Tanganyika Territory*. Dar es Salaam: Government Printer.

Mirza, Sarah and Margaret Strobel. 1989. *Three Swahili Women: Life Histories from Mombasa, Kenya*. Bloomington: Indiana University Press.

Moir, Jane. [1891] 1991. *A Lady's Letters from Central Africa: A Journey from Mandala, Shire Highlands to Ujiji, Lake Tanganyika and back in 1890*. Blantyre, Nyasaland: Central Africana Ltd.

Moravian Mission, Society for Propagating the Gospel. 1915. *Report of the Mission Board to the General Synod 1914*. Bradford, PA: H. J. Gledhill & Co.

Mtoro bin Mwinyi Bakari. 1981. J.W.T. Allen, ed. and translator. *The Customs of the Swahili People: The Desturi za Waswahili*. Berkeley: University of California Press.

Odinga, Agnes A. 1997. "Women and the Anti-Venereal Disease Campaign in South Nyanza, 1920–45." Paper presented at the African Studies Association Annual Meeting, Columbus, Ohio.

Parke, Thomas Heazle. 1891. *My Personal Experiences in Equatorial Africa: As Medical Officer of the Emin Pasha Relief Expedition*. London: Sampson Low, Marston & Company.

Raum, O. F. 1965. "German East Africa: Changes in African Life under German Administration, 1892–1914." In Vincent Harlow and E. M. Chilver, eds., assisted by Alison Smith, *The History of East Africa*. Volume 2. Oxford: Clarenden Press.

Schiebinger, Londa. 1993. *Nature's Body: Gender in the Making of Modern Science*. Boston: Beacon Press.

Scully, Pamela. 1996. "Narratives of Infanticide in the Aftermath of Slave Emancipation in the Nineteenth Century Cape Colony, South Africa." *Canadian Journal of African Studies* 30(1): 88–105.

Strobel, Margaret. 1979. *Muslim Women in Mombasa: 1890–1975*. New Haven, CT: Yale University Press.

———. 1983. "Slavery and Reproductive Labor in Mombasa." In Claire Robertson and Martin A. Klein eds., *Women and Slavery in Africa*. Madison: University of Wisconsin Press.

Summers, Carol. 1991. "Intimate Colonialism: The Imperial Production of Reproduction in Uganda, 1907–1925." *Signs* 16(4):787–807.

Swantz, Marja Liisa. 1970. *Ritual and Symbol in Transitional Zaramo Society with Special Reference to Women*. Lund, Sweden: Gleerup.

Tanner, R.E.S. 1962. "The Relationships between the Sexes in a Coastal Islamic Community." *African Studies* 21(2):70–82.

Vaughan, Megan. 1991. *Curing Their Ills: Colonial Power and African Illness*. Stanford, CA: Stanford University Press.

Weeks, Jeffrey. [1981] 1989. *Sex, Politics and Society: The Regulation of Sexuality since 1800*. Second edition. New York: Longman.

12

NEGOTIATING SOCIAL INDEPENDENCE: THE CHALLENGES OF CAREER PURSUITS FOR IGBO WOMEN IN POSTCOLONIAL NIGERIA

Philomena E. Okeke

INTRODUCTION

This chapter examines the changing gender relations of power in a specific African case: that of university-educated Igbo women in Nigeria, who in various ways have significantly informed, contested, and co-opted the process of social transformation to advance their status. Women interviewed for this study reveal the re-definitions of their place in society; their actions transgress normative gender dictates and threaten the existing social order. Although these women gain power and status through education and wage employment, they must still negotiate the constraints of family and societal gender expectations. Furthermore, persistent gender inequalities in education and wage labor shape the opportunities for social mobility at the same time that they perpetuate internal and foreign sexism. As a result, some elite women have been accused of using "bottom power" to circumvent these obstacles. "Bottom power," a common phrase in elite Nigerian circles, refers to any use by women of their sexuality to gain favor from men both as individuals and as authorities with access to social opportunities and privileges. Despite their awareness of the gender inequities structuring contemporary society, both men and women are deeply ambivalent about bottom power.

Elite women's options have improved over time, but the social status of individual women is still inextricably linked to their relationships with men and the male ruling class (Fapohunda 1983; Fatton 1989). Nigerian women have made more strides as consorts to men in power than as political figures in their own right. For example, the past three military regimes placed women's well-being under the office of the First Lady. The First Ladies for the 1985–1993 and 1993–1999 regimes propelled women into the limelight, initiating welfare programs, dispensing favors, and organizing alliances that supported and were supported by their respective regimes.[1] Such precedents advertise "bottom power" as a crucial tool for women who are well positioned to use it. But their achievements notwithstanding, women in such prominent positions only reinforce rather than challenge existing relations of gender, obscuring glimpses of women's resistance (P. E. Okeke 1999).

Nigerian women's increased representation in paid work over the past two decades has also highlighted "bottom power" as a viable female weapon. Women interviewed for this study confirm that the decline of the wage economy in recent times has not only reinforced the endemic politics of ethnicity and class, but also certain gender hierarchies. But the association of women's progress with bottom power ignores the challenges elite women must confront in both the wage economy and the larger society, and their efforts at evading or challenging social control. It is therefore important to examine the context in which the link between bottom power and women's progress has gained such significant social expression, by assessing women's schooling and employment in terms of policy, content, and prospect, especially in light of current economic realities. The analysis of elite women, in particular, draws attention to the specificities of a largely ignored minority group whose lives influence the female majority.

The first section of the paper traces the evolution of the Nigerian female elite class into contemporary society. The second section focuses on the structure of gender relations in elite Igbo circles as reflected in the lives of the women in this study. Their stance on and social interpretation of marriage/family and procreation/polygynous ties establish a strong basis for analyzing the challenges paid work presents to them. The third section moves away from the intense public gaze on bottom power and critically assesses the "wicked" acts of these elite women and their implications for gender relations of power in the future. The final section provides a brief look at the prospect of Nigerian women's career pursuits as one major avenue to social mobility.

THE RISE OF A NIGERIAN FEMALE ELITE CLASS: EDUCATION AND WAGE EMPLOYMENT

The Nigerian female elite did not emerge directly from any precolonial social formation, and their historical progression into today's society has not produced a monolithic group. Women's social status in many precolonial African societies was largely mediated by their relationship with men, although other factors such as age, status in natal family, royal ancestry, and religious affiliation assigned them to different ranks. These factors may have conferred power on certain women, but not necessarily an equal status with males (Robertson 1986; Afonja 1990).

Of the numerous ethnic divisions within Nigeria, the Hausas in the northern region, the Yorubas in the southwestern region, and the Igbos in the southeastern region are the dominant groups. Southern Nigeria embraced change much faster than the Muslim north. The elites have often concentrated around Lagos, which was the seat of both commerce and government (Fafunwa 1974). Britain succeeded in its gradual consolidation of power among Nigerian ethnic groups by utilizing the local authority structures controlled by men. By the turn of the twentieth century, the colonial government had established an indigenous male ruling class to work with. From this ruling class, a select group of educated Nigerians began to constitute an indigenous elite. While wealth, family connections, and political status afforded individuals entrance into the various colonial circles, education and paid work, by all indications, provided the greatest access. Despite the ethnic and religious heterogeneity within the elite group, members shared an "interest in issues, places, and ideas beyond the awareness of the masses [which] draws them together and gives them common ground for understanding and fellowship" (Smythe and Smythe 1960:93).

In terms of their access to economic opportunities, social prestige, and political power, Nigerian female elites followed a path clearly different from men's. Women's profiles in colonial elite circles were largely dictated by their subordinate status to men. Beside its racist undertones, British colonization invoked its own patriarchal conventions, which in many instances found an ally in the indigenous culture. The British introduced new avenues to social mobility, but disregarded many aspects of traditional female autonomy. Legitimized by Christian ideologies, the new social arrangement also undermined women's traditional economic niches (Mann 1985). While the missions encouraged the enrollment of both male and female children in schools, training for females was meant to help them become "modern housewives and helpmates" to the growing number of male civil servants (Pittin 1990:13). Over time, far more boys than girls pursued formal education, with gender inequality most pronounced at the higher levels. By 1900, the sex imbalance in primary and secondary school enrollment was grossly in men's favor (Taiwo 1980). The oil boom, which erupted in the early 1970s, and the inception of the Universal Primary Education (UPE) Scheme in 1976, boosted female enrollment considerably. By 1984, the national female primary and secondary school enrollment rates had risen to 44 percent and 35.5 percent, respectively (E. Okeke 1989:51–52). But despite this progress, men maintained their lead at all levels of education, particularly in technology and science (E. Okeke 1989:51–52; Fapohunda 1988).

Gender inequality in formal education carried over into the labor market. The oil boom financed the expansion of higher educational facilities and opened up employment opportunities in both the civil service and the private sector. With public subsidies, higher education was fairly affordable and economic prospects equally attractive. Many graduates sought employment in the lucrative and rapidly expanding private sector. Although these developments have greatly improved women's representation in paid work, the gender imbalance is still in place. And now the worsening economic situation threatens even these gains.

Elite women, in general, enjoy a higher status than women in the rural or urban informal economy. Although many non-elite women may secure some personal autonomy through their economic activities, men usually control their access to land and credit. In contrast, formal education gives Nigerian women access to waged labor, a strong economic base outside the direct control of men. Hence, women's pursuit of higher education represents a fundamental threat to male authority. But this threat is to a great extent counteracted by the structure of gender relations, which has tended to shape women's training and labor market opportunities. In these hard economic times, bottom power is considered a strong means of leverage for women in dealing with the challenges the current wage economy presents.

THE STRUCTURE OF GENDER
RELATIONS IN IGBO ELITE CIRCLES

Although marriage to elite men, education, and paid work give women access into elite circles, great diversity exists among the female elite. In addition to ethnic, religious, and political differences, elite women have different levels of schooling and labor market status. Women from the south benefited from missionization and an emphasis on education, and therefore constitute the majority of women at all levels in both education and the workplace. However, even among these southern female elites considerable differences emerge. This study analyzes the experiences of elite Igbo women. During the 1990s, Igbos constituted about 15 percent of the estimated total national population of 105,212,677 (Annual Abstract of Statistics 1998:27). Igbo women represented 14, 23, and 29 percent of total national female enrollment at the primary, secondary, and university levels (Annual Abstract of Statistics 1998:185, 195; National Universities Commission 1997).

This section explores gender relations in Igbo elite circles through a series of in-depth, semi-structured interviews with eighteen female Igbo wage-earners conducted between September 1991 and February 1992. Enugu, where the research was carried out, was originally the capital of eastern Nigeria, one of the three colonial regions. This sample is purposive in a number of ways. Foremost, I chose university-educated women, who are considered to be in the best position to tap the full potential of schooling, especially in light of the declining wage economy. I wanted to make visible the conditions under which Nigerian women are allowed to gain and maintain status in a competitive sphere dominated by men. I focused largely on women from my own ethnic group, with whom I shared similar qualifications and experiences. Through snowball sampling methods (I met my respondents[2] through my research assistants, friends, and relatives), I gathered a representative sample of university-educated female wage-earners.[3]

The interviews revealed the structure of gender relations (marriage/family and procreation/polygynous ties) within which the respondents negotiated their paths to social mobility. Their experiences clearly show that despite the serious social consequences involved, some elite women have pushed the boundaries of acceptable social behaviour.

Marriage and Family

Marriage in Igboland secures the right of passage to adulthood. Women are usually encouraged to marry earlier than men. Most men and women view women in their roles as mothers, housewives, and companions as subordinate to men. As Christie Achebe (1981) pointed out, women who have planned to pursue a career outside the domestic arena have had to adjust their aspirations to suit the dictates of their primary role as wives and mothers. Igbo society frowns on women contracting intimate relationships outside marriage. Being single raises suspicions and accusations about a woman's respectability, health, and suitability for marriage that can become burdensome as relatives and neighbors constantly question a woman about her behavior, practices, intentions, and interests. It is the institution of marriage, however, that actually burdens women; Igbo society expects women to accept responsibility for sustaining the marital union. In Safiya Muhammed's (1985:30) view, "the Nigerian society sees to it that marriage is much more of a commitment for women than it is for men. Our society does not only tell a woman that she is a failure if she fails to lure a male into marriage, it also cuts off most lines of escape from that inevitable path by barring her from other forms of social success." While this remains a commonly shared predicament, the personal circumstances of each woman I interviewed reflected the differing impacts of social pressure on their lives. Their responses clearly portrayed an understanding of and sensitivity to social expectations and boundaries. Erimma, thirty-five and single, a chemistry teacher, quoted an Igbo adage:

> In Igbo culture every woman "must" marry. Must in quotes because as the Igbos say, initially people ask, "Who is the father of this girl?" but after some time they begin to ask, "Who is the husband?" If you allow them to keep asking who your father is, then you have not "arrived."

Ogechi, thirty-six and single, a vice-principal in a mixed school, put it quite succinctly: "The ultimate ambition for every [Nigerian] woman is to get married at some point in her life . . . . No matter how hard you work, no matter how forward looking, how upwardly mobile, if you're not married, [people] still look down on you."

The social stigma attached to being single is, to some extent, shared by relatives, whose interference often heightens the pressure experienced by unmarried women such as Uzoamaka, a thirty-five-year-old school teacher who lived with her parents. Her father had retired a few years earlier from the civil service. Her mother was a housewife and barely literate. The family maintained very close links with many relatives. Against her initial convictions, Uzoamaka finally gave in to the pressures coming from all sides:

> They [relatives] are so much bothered about your single state that you wonder if it is really your business or theirs. [For example], my aunties would visit and stay overnight so as to have a heart-to-heart talk with me and to find out whether there was something wrong with me or it's a problem of suitors not coming at all. After some time, I realized that, like the Igbo man would say, there is actually an age you get to in this society and you have to get married, at least, to live among them [your own people].

When women do not marry, regardless of their beauty or social skills, Igbos suspect something is either wrong with the single woman herself or with her social background. They identify her as immoral, stigmatized, or simply unlucky.[4] Elite women may question the basis of these accusations, but no one would want to become the target of social attack or ridicule.

Procreation and Polygynous Ties

Children are the primary expectation of any Igbo marriage. As she ages, a single woman often experiences enormous pressure from her family to marry. They fear for her procreative ability. The unmarried *ada*, or first daughter, experiences the most pressure, for she is expected to marry first and may be "blocking the way [marital path]" for her younger sisters.[5] Although women who pursue higher education can delay marriage for a while, being single is considered a temporary situation.

The importance attached to procreation is also reflected in social attitudes toward modern contraceptive methods. Traditionally, women practiced abstinence or prolonged breast feeding between births. Many Igbos believe modern contraception enhances women's sexuality and is a threat to women's chastity. Girls do not study sex education in school and abortion is illegal in Nigeria, except when the life of the mother is threatened. Family planning organizations such as the Planned Parenthood Federation of Nigeria (PPFN) work mostly with married women in the cities, who often need their husband's permission to access such services (Pittin 1986). In his study of patterns of conjugal decision making in Nigerian families, Wambui Karanja (1983:237) noted that even among the elites, "substantial support was reported for the husband deciding alone such issues as those pertaining to children (family size, birth control use . . .)."

The stability of Igbo marriage depends on procreation, and the pressure exerted on a wife depends on the couple's social background and the degree of attachment to immediate and extended family relatives. Forty and divorced, Mma, a lawyer and chartered company secretary, shared with me a painful experience still fresh in her memory. She and her husband, a medical doctor, married in 1978, a year after they graduated from university. They left the next year for further studies in Britain. When she was still not pregnant by the end of the second year, her husband's family became impatient:

> You know what they do to us [women] in Igboland. Without children they don't think there is any hope for the marriage. I went to various hospitals

and the medical report showed that there was nothing wrong with me. Of course, it is often assumed that the fault is with the woman. I can't remember my husband going for any medical tests. I was the one who was worried.

The marriage lasted for only three years. After she and her husband separated, Mma returned to her parents' home where she lived for a few years before returning to the professional world.

Preference for sons exacerbates the pressure to bear children. Male heirs are important to men, not only for the continuation of their lineage, but also as proof of their manhood. The man who has no children cannot really lay claim to male status in society, and the man who produces only female children is simply not man enough. Although formal education significantly narrows the difference in the economic value attached to male and female children, son preference still exerts a remarkable influence on elite marriages. Given the conflicting loyalties that exist in Igbo marriage, women often turn to their children, especially sons, as their natural allies. Even a professional woman with a secure financial future appreciates the way a male heir secures her marital stability and social acceptance.

Procreation, son preference, and polygyny are inextricably linked. A childless marriage is highly vulnerable to divorce. Additionally, the woman who has only female children can expect a future co-wife. The Igbo consider a woman directly responsible for the sex of her offspring (Achebe 1981; Obikeze 1988). Thus, the Igbo view not having a male child (or indeed any child) as a woman's personal failure. The pressure exerted on single women as they age is society's attempt to ensure that a woman not only bears a child but has time to have more children if her first child is not male. Even in elite circles where education might have dispelled such myths, the perception that women determine the sex of the child prevails.

A number of legal ordinances introduced to regulate polygyny during the colonial period not only failed, but introduced alternative marital arrangements that enabled elite women to retain their autonomy (Elias 1958; Kasumu and Salacuse 1960; Ekong 1986). These include the case of "inside" and "outside" wives described by Karanja (1987); some women prefer to marry well-established men with other wives rather than to remain single or in an undesirable monogamous union. This arrangement guarantees an elite woman a respectable social status and the freedom to pursue a career, even as she chooses (as most such women do) to live away from her husband's main residence. By arranging such loosely organized, autonomous marriages, women bend Igbo expectations and may be accused of wielding bottom power to advance their status.

For All the Consequences: Women Taking a Stand

The views of the respondents vividly portrayed the structural constraints surrounding their lives and raised a number of pressing questions. If being single carries such a heavy social price, why do some women choose to remain single? Why do some women cling to socially unacceptable behaviors and practices in the face of enormous societal pressure? The single women I interviewed knew what they wanted in a husband and refused to simply accept any suitor in response to family and social pressure. Their stance signified a bold departure from social dictates. These single women redefined existing social expectations with values and normative patterns very different from the existing standard.

The views of young women about polygyny also indicated new trends in values and beliefs. Married or single, young women were strongly against polygyny. None of them was involved in a polygynous relationship. Despite their personal choices, however, they were not overly critical of the "outside wife" arrangement as an option for other professional women. The changing practice of polygyny now provides more social and economic freedom for elite women than ever before.

Elite Nigerian women are gradually breaking with certain norms of social acceptability, a brave and confrontational step afforded by their position. Their status as university-educated working women has given them more options, allowing them to push the boundaries of normative gender behavior. As the analysis in the next section conveys, however, the gender dynamic of wage employment, however socially construed, is only one of the many challenges elite women confront.

BOTTOM POWER AND THE
GENDER DYNAMIC OF WAGE EMPLOYMENT

Job structures in the public and private sectors are similar.[6] Both evolved from the colonial model, although the private sector offers a more attractive remuneration package. What is especially noticeable about both sectors is the pronounced difference in remuneration between the lower and higher job ranks. As Janet Bujra (1983) argued in her review of capitalist expansion in Africa, this pattern is traceable, in part, to racial inequalities embedded in the colonial civil service. Women's differential access to occupations allowed men to benefit from their long-term access to waged labor.

Although a number of changes in the post-independence era (e.g. wage harmonization and maternity leave) remedied some of the gender discriminatory patterns inherent in wage employment, overt gender discrimination still exists. For instance, men receive child allowance payments although women bear direct responsibility for their children's well-being. Still, much of the discrimination Nigerian women face in formal employment remains hidden.[7] The problem is not merely one of under-representation. Job descriptions and wage scales, structured to suit male candidates, reinforce male preserves in many establishments. One of the women I interviewed claimed female applicants had little or no chance of being recruited into the middle and higher ranks in the Cabinet Office because of its strong male culture. Covert gender inequalities also exist in the authority structure, policies, and practices of labor unions. Generally, trade unionism involves men, even in female-dominated occupations such as nursing. Apparently, these organizations neither promote women's representation nor address their concerns about the hardships of combining domestic and wage work. Hence, trade union movements rarely elicit women's interest (Okoronkwo 1985; Shettima 1989).

The country's mounting foreign debt, which led to the introduction of Structural Adjustment Programs (SAP), forced a down-scaling of the public service. During the 1970s, the government, with its buoyant resources, was able to stem the rise in unemployment, at least among higher education graduates. Since the 1980s, as Nigeria's unemployment rose and the formal sector shrank, large numbers of graduates have failed to secure employment.[8] The crisis in the labor market only strengthened the corruptive networks endemic in the formal sector. As Dan Agbese (1992:14) remarked, Nigeria found itself in economic decline facing a situation where the "opportunities for competition are circumscribed by unfavourable social and economic development." It was almost inevitable that many people found themselves resorting to informal short cuts to secure employment.

The sharing of knowledge about employment opportunities along ethnic and religious lines further complicates gender politics in the labor market. The interviewees' statements revealed a recent trend in the ethnic and class politics of "Who You Know." Uju, a thirty-eight-year-old French teacher, married with five children, explained the situation in Nigeria during the nineties: "More people than required are qualified. So if you have a godfather, an uncle, brother, or guardian who is highly placed or if you know any such person . . . that may help push your case." For women in the higher classes, bottom power may not be the first alternative. Ijeoma, a single, thirty-year-old bank accountant, conceded that her father's influence helped her secure her present job: "He was a former director of the bank. . . . So even though I went through the interview . . . and all, I think I had an edge over the other candidates." Nnenna, a legal manager in a commercial bank and mother of two young children, explained:

> Since the employment embargo from the mid 1980s, most of those who got employed had relations or godfathers there. Officially, they will advertise the positions, but it is those who know people that will be considered. The result is that merit rarely comes in. You find that a lot of [the staff] are mediocre. . . . Of course, there are basic qualifications, beyond which one's prospect lies with "Who You Know."

Chika, thirty-eight and mother of three children, recently transferred from the teaching field to the board responsible for teacher recruitment and placement, shared her personal observations:

> Somebody just shows up with a letter from the government house with the instruction "recruit this person." The person is automatically hired. Getting into teaching now depends on . . . who you know. They give you a piece of paper and you start work while those who graduated years before are still hanging around. In fact, the letter may even stipulate that the new teacher be posted to a school of his or her choice.

Many of those who have no "godfathers" resort to paying bribes. As Erimma, the chemistry teacher, remarked, "You know Nigeria. No vacancy, but vacancy may exist if you 'grease a few palms.'" Christie, forty-nine, an assistant deputy with the education board, agreed, revealing some of the negotiations taking place in the corridors of power:

> [Who You Know] comes in at some point. . . . If we're hiring and our director is interested, there is no way we can stop him from sending his candidate. . . . Of course they [directors] do sponsor candidates. Some may even write to the chairman of the panel or give the candidate a note the day before the interview saying, "I'm interested in this candidate.". . . That is where the lowering of standards comes in. You have to oblige the director.

In the more lucrative and fiercely competitive private sector, the stakes are much higher. According to Mma, who is the legal adviser and company secretary of her bank, "Members of the board or the management sometimes indicate their interest in certain candidates. Such candidates will definitely be considered as long as they sail through the written tests. The oral interview is where the bigwigs have the chance to use their position."

Who You Know is also crucial for a worker's advancement, especially in the private sector. The *en masse* promotion of teachers limits the need for a godfather to initial recruitment and transfers. Often, however, teachers use some form of influence to avoid being placed in or transferred to the rural areas. Similarly, other civil servants expect to be promoted every three years, except when accused of a gross dereliction of duty. In the latter case, the individual seeks intervention from a highly placed advocate to clear his or her name. A more rigorous evaluation process in the private sector makes the competition for promotion stiffer.

What happens to those who have neither godfathers nor the financial means to grease the palms of the powers that be? The politics of gender and sexuality provide women with another option. According to the women I interviewed, many women feel compelled to give sexual favors in return for a job or promotion. As Ngozi, an accountant, pointed out: "Things are no doubt rough for men who have no [one to intervene on their behalf], but when it comes to numbers, they are at an advantage. Who are the military officers, directors, commissioners, and managers? Men of course. [Bottom power] evens things out to some extent."

Although most of the interviewees argued in defense of women who resorted to this option, none of the respondents admitted to ever using it themselves. Nigerian women constantly deal with sexual harassment on the job. The interviewees claimed sexual harassment was not a major concern of theirs; it simply permeated the working environment. The women I interviewed perceived other women's strategy of using sex to get ahead in the workplace as a weapon in a world where they were greatly disadvantaged. Those without "godfathers" were considered the most likely to seek this survival strategy in the workplace. Onyeka, who was thirty-two years old, married, and the mother of two young children, was an economist in the Ministry of Finance. She gave the following example of promotion in the civil service: "In borderline cases . . . women who are not well qualified and who ordinarily will not be promoted, but who have over-established relations with the boss will definitely be promoted along with others." Christie, forty-nine and married with two young children, agreed with Onyeka. Drawing from her experiences in the civil service as a deputy director, she argued that organizational lapses often encouraged bottom power. She claimed that

[influence peddling] breeds indiscipline in the [civil] service because the person that came into the ministry through the director may flout rules as long as that man is still at the helm of affairs. You know that bureaucracy is based on rules and regulations, but they may not for instance come to work early most of the time. There are people here who are regarded as

sacred cows. These people have either godfathers or some big shots behind them. When they flout rules nothing happens, but when you do the
same, you're in trouble. These days many young girls are getting away
with such behavior.

The women in this study, married and unmarried, perceived bottom power
as a powerful force in the gender dynamics of formal employment. They
argued that marital status, social class, and moral codes influenced an individual woman's decision to use or not to use bottom power. Among the
women interviewed, the married ones had more to say about bottom power
than the single women. The interviewees targeted single female workers as
the most likely to resort to bottom power. While the single women interviewed admitted to the presence of bottom power in workplace relations,
they emphasized that there were legitimate ways of getting ahead in their
careers, which they would rather take.

The current social significance of bottom power is connected to the
strides this new generation of elite professional women has made in the
wage economy. Increased accusations of bottom power accompanied their
expanded ability to resist or escape the social pressures that kept previous generations of women down. Compared to an older generation of paid
workers, most of the single women interviewed had a higher academic
profile and a faster career track record. Those making their way up from
the lower ranks viewed young university-educated women with superior
credentials as a threat. During the 1990s, women in the lower echelons
found themselves in a changing work environment where the cultural
assertions afforded by age and gender were seriously being eroded by
young, highly educated, and ambitious women. Most single women managed to resist the pressures of marriage, procreation, and other social
expectations while climbing the career ladder. It was also clear from
interviewees' statements that they were not ready to bow to social pressures at the expense of their advancement.

Placed in the context of the worsening economic situation, the social
flurry surrounding bottom power makes women's progress in the wage
economy a target for social attack. The hard economic times stripped
many Nigerian men of their traditional breadwinner status. Many lost
their previously firm economic foothold in paid work or private business.
Waves of mass retrenchments in both the public and private sectors created an uncertain future for both the employed and the unemployed. Yet,
in the midst of this economic chaos, some women moved ahead, especially young women with new academic credentials on fast career tracks.
In defiance of social codes, many of these women held their ground, even
as they competed with male peers. Accusations of "bottom power" pro-

vided both men and women with a convenient, familiar, and unpopular target, educated elite Igbo women, on whom to blame their economic woes.

CONCLUSION

Igbo concern with the career profiles of highly educated young women is related to the economic security and social prestige that comes with their status. Elite educated Igbo women's status, despite its vulnerable elements, provides them with some leverage to flout certain social dictates and an ability to co-opt others to their advantage. For instance, the outside wife is not totally dependent on her husband, and what she may have lost in settling for marriage with an older man she makes up for with the freedom to pursue her career with the support of a powerful ally. Those who reject the "outside" wife option for life as single working women have fewer domestic obligations to balance against their career goals. Such women are also better placed to compete with men in the workplace. In fact, an elite professional woman can afford to maintain her status as single, divorced, or separated, taking on motherhood on her own terms with an informal marital relationship on the side.

In their professional and private lives, these women have forced others to reconsider the social codes, rules, and conventions governing contemporary social relations. Their actions bring to the fore the largely taken-for-granted social problems that old codes, rules, and conventions no longer address. Their defiant stance sends a very important message: "things cannot go on as they used to." For all the controversy elite educated Igbo women generate, accusations that they use bottom power divert attention away from the important questions their behavior raises. Their experiences also call for a re-examination of the value of education and wage employment, per se, as assets for Nigerian women's social mobility. Economic decline not only means fewer opportunities than ever before; it also diminishes the value of education. Schooling, even as a prerequisite, must become more specialty-focused with specific and limited training. Nigerian women must diversify their educational options in preparation for the challenges of a changing labor market.

Regardless of these challenges, in many ways elite women have not only changed the face of formal employment, but also shaped the confines and contours of contemporary gender relations. It remains to be seen whether society interprets these strides as "wicked" acts or gradually comes to confront and negotiate the unavoidable questions such women raise about future goals, behaviors, roles, obligations, expectations, and relationships.

NOTES

1. Shettima's (1995) review clearly shows that women's visibility in Nigerian politics has been for the most part minimal. Maryam Babangida initiated the program referred to as "Better Life for Rural Women" during her husband's 1985–1993 regime. The program was meant to improve the conditions of rural women's lives by expanding the economic opportunities available to them in agriculture, petty trading, and cottage industries. Despite initial accolades (e.g., Alarape 1992), the program soon degenerated into a social forum for army officers' wives and their elite female consorts. With the change of regime, General Abacha's wife, Maryam Abacha, took over the program and renamed it "Family Support" with some modifications. Both programs were fully financed from the public coffers. Odu (1994) unveils the charades involved in these programs.

2. Pseudonyms are used in place of participants' real names.

3. Of the eighteen respondents, twelve are public sector employees, eight of whom teach in secondary schools. The six private sector employees include two accountants, three lawyers, and an economist. Twelve of the women are married (all of them with children) while six of them are single. To reflect the proper historical contexts, I selected respondents from two major groups: women with more than ten years' working experience, whose education and employment status may have been shaped by the oil boom, and those with less than ten years' working experience, who joined the labor market after the oil boom.

4. Generally, women, far more than men, are expected to comport themselves in a socially acceptable manner. But historically certain families and clans bore social stigmas that could render their children, especially girls, highly unacceptable as marriage partners. For instance, a history of mental illness in a lineage could jeopardize the marriage prospects of female members more than the prospects of their male counterparts. The fate of *Osu* families in Igboland may even be worse. The *Osu* stigma often completes the social ostracization of families who flaunted very serious social taboos and embraced (in exchange for their freedom and rights) an oracle for protection. The significance of such cultural "mutations" may have lessened with social change, but it has not completely disappeared. See Ekiyor (1989).

5. Every girl is a daughter (*ada*), but the first girl in the family is referred to as *the ada*.

6. The formal sector may be narrowed down to a range—from medium-scale establishments, employing no fewer than ten persons, to large-scale establishments with more employees. These include private business establishments and federal and state government departments. The informal sector refers to smaller organizational units with no more than ten persons. This sector includes units of subsistence farmers, local artisans, and petty traders. It is seldom subject to government regulations, often relies on household labor, and rarely operates on a wage arrangement. See references in Alo and Adjebeng-Asem (1988:218–219).

7. See the "Anambra State Civil Service Handbook" (1989), and the "Collective Agreement between Nigerian Employers' Association of Banks, Insurance and Allied Institutions and the Association of Senior Staff of Banks, Insurance and Financial Institutions" (1990).

8. *The Economic Report on Africa* (UNECA 1990:21–22) also draws attention to the rapidly growing unemployment in most African countries, including Nigeria, which is "creeping up the educational ladder to include university graduates." Women, the report concludes, are "twice as vulnerable as men."

REFERENCES

Achebe, Christie. 1981. "Continuities, Changes and Challenges: Women's Role in Nigerian Society." In *Présence Africaine, Cultural Review of the Negro World*, 4th Quarterly, (120):7–16.

Afonja, Simi. 1990. "Changing Patterns of Gender Stratification in West Africa." In Irene Tinker, ed., *Persistent Inequalities: Women and World Development*, 189–209. Oxford: Oxford University Press.

Agbese, Dan. 1992. "Corruption: The Palm Oil That Stains the Palm of the Giver and the Receiver." *Newswatch*. March 9, 9–15.

Alarape, N. 1992. *The Nigerian Woman: Dawn of a New Era–The Better Life of Maryam Babangida*. Ibadan: Jenson International Limited.

Alo, Oladimejo and Selina Adjebeng-Asem. 1988. "Women and National Development: A Socio-Cultural Analysis of the Nigerian Experience." In M. Abraham Francis and Subhadra P. Abraham, eds., *Women, Development and Change: The Third World Experience*, 217–244. Bristol, England: Wyndham Hall Press.

"Anambra State Civil Service Handbook." 1989. *Annual Report*. Enegu, Nigeria: Anambra State Civil Service Commission.

Annual Abstract of Statistics. 1998. Abuja, Nigeria: Federal Office of Statistics.

Bujra, Janet. 1983. "Class, Gender and Capitalist Transformation in Africa." *African Development*, 8(3):17–42.

"Collective Agreement between Nigerian Employers' Association of Banks, Insurance and Allied Institutions and the Association of Senior Staff of Banks, Insurance and Financial Institutions." 1990. *Annual Report*. Lagos, Nigeria.

Ekiyor, M. O. 1989. "Formal Colonial Education: An Assessment of Its Impact on the Marriageability of *Acada* Women in Southern Nigeria." In *(I.A.S) Symposium*. Ibadan: University of Ibadan, Institute of African Studies.

Ekong, Sheila. 1986. "Continuity and Change in Nigerian Family Patterns." In Simi Afonja and Tola Pearce, eds., *Social Change in Nigeria*, 50–70. Essex: Longman.

Elias, T. O. 1958. "The Impact of English Law on Nigerian Customary Law." *Lugard Lectures*. Lagos: Ministry of Information.

Fafunwa, Babs. 1974. *History of Education in Nigeria*. London: George Allen and Unwin.

Fapohunda, Eleanor. 1983. "Male and Female Career Ladders in Nigerian Academia." Lansing, MI: Michigan State University, Women in International Development, Working Paper #17.

———. 1988. "Urban Women's Roles and Nigerian Government Development Strategies." In Christine Oppong, ed., *Sex Roles, Population and Development in West Africa*, 203–212. London: James Currey.

Fatton, Robert. 1989. "Gender, Class and the State in Africa," In Jane L. Parpart and Kathleen A. Staudt, eds., *Women and the State in Africa,* 47–66. London: Lynne Rienner.

Federal Office of Statistics, 1998. *Annual Abstract of Statistics.* Abuja, Nigeria. Federal Office of Statistics.

Karanja, Wa Wambui. 1983. "Conjugal Decision Making: Some Data from Lagos." In Christine Oppong, ed., *Male and Female in West Africa,* 236–241. London: George Allen and Unwin.

———. 1987. "Outside Wives and Inside Wives in Nigeria: A Study of Changing Perceptions in Marriage." In D. Parkus and D. Nyamwaya, eds., *Transformation in African Marriage,* 247–261. Manchester: Manchester University Press.

Kasumu, A. and J. Salacuse. 1960. *Nigerian Family Law.* London: Butterworths.

Mann, Kristin. 1985. *Marrying Well: Marriage and Social Change among the Educated Elite in Colonial Lagos.* Cambridge: Cambridge University Press.

Muhammed, Safiya. 1985. "Women, the Family and the Wider Society." In Ayesha Imam, Renée Pittin, and H. Omole, eds., *Women and the Family in Nigeria,* 29–36. Dakar, Senegal: Council for the Development of Economic and Social Research in Africa (CODESRIA) Series: National Universities Commission.

National Universities Commission. 1997. *Statistical Information on Nigerian Universities.* Abuja, Nigeria: National Universities Commission.

Obikeze, D. S. 1988. "Son Preference among Nigerian Mothers: Its Demographic and Psychological Implications." *International Journal of Contemporary Sociology,* 25(1/2):55–63.

Odu, Ike-Mark E. 1994. *Woman on the Move: A Course to Remember.* Lagos: Princess Communications.

Okeke, Eunice. 1989. "Nigeria." In Grace P. Kelly and Carolyne Elliot, eds., *Women's Education in the Third World: Comparative Perspectives,* 51–52. Albany: State University of New York Press.

Okeke, Philomena E. 1994. "Patriarchal Continuities and Contradictions in African Women's Education and Socio-Economic Status: An Ethnographic Study of Currently Employed University Educated Igbo Women in Nigeria." Ph.D. thesis, Dalhousie University Halifax, Nova Scotia, Canada.

———. 1999. "The First Lady Syndrome: The [En]Gendering of Bureaucratic Corruption in Nigeria." *CODESRIA Bulletin,* (3/4):16–19.

Okoronkwo, A. O. 1985. "Women's Participation in Trade Unions." In Tayo Fashoyin, Felicia Oyekanmi, and Eleanor Fapohunda, eds., *Women in the Modern Sector Labour Force in Nigeria: Issues and Prospects,* 79–89. Lagos: Leamson Printers.

Pittin, Renée. 1986. "The Control of Reproduction: Principle and Practice in Nigeria." *Review of African Political Economy,* 35:40–53.

———. 1990. "Selective Education: Issues of Gender, Class and Ideology in Northern Nigeria." *Review of African Political Economy,* 48:7–25.

Robertson, Claire. 1986. "Women's Education and Class Formation in Africa, 1950–1980." In Claire Robertson and Iris Berger, eds., *Women and Class in Africa,* 92–113. New York: Africana Publishing Company.

Shettima, Kole Ahmed. 1989. "Women's Movement and Visions: The Nigeria Labour Congress, Women's Wing." *African Development*, 14(3):81–98.

————. 1995. "Engendering Nigeria's Third Republic." *African Studies Review*, 38(3):61–98.

Smythe, H. and M. Smythe. 1960. *The New Nigerian Elite.* Cambridge: Cambridge University Press.

Taiwo, C. O. 1980. *The Nigerian Educational System: Past, Present and Future.* Ibadan, Nigeria: Nelson.

UNECA. 1990. *Economic Report on Africa.* Addis Ababa: United Nations Economic Commission for Africa, E/ECA/CM.16/3.

PART IV:

NEGOTIATING DIFFERENCE

13

THE POLITICS OF DIFFERENCE AND WOMEN'S ASSOCIATIONS IN NIGER: OF "PROSTITUTES," THE PUBLIC, AND POLITICS

Barbara M. Cooper

When I first arrived in the city of Maradi to do research for my book, *Marriage in Maradi, Gender and Culture in a Hausa Society in Niger, 1900–1989*, local authorities determined that I should make my contacts with women through the Association des Femmes du Niger (AFN), the women's wing of the military-dominated political party in power at the time. These male bureaucrats reasoned that Muslim Hausa men would be less likely to object to my interactions with their wives (some of whom were secluded) if it were clear that my research had been vetted through the appropriate state-controlled channels. The majority of the women I eventually managed to work with were not members of the AFN, and many indeed knew little or nothing about it. Nevertheless because I had made my earliest contacts through the women's association, AFN members took me under their collective wing, and I became something of a mascot for them whenever the AFN took part in highly visible public events. In a sense, if they were "my" informants, I was "their" researcher, and my public association with the AFN must have served them in some important way, given their insistence on my presence at these events. What was at stake here, I wondered? Why was it so important that I stand together with these women at parades and spectacles?

My puzzlement deepened the better I got to know some of the most active members of the women's association, especially as I became more alert to their ambivalence about the time-consuming activities of the AFN, and to their hostility toward the young unmarried women who were members of the Samariya youth organization. This antagonism became most pronounced when I had to choose my loyalties in a highly public and visible arena: would I use my car to transport key members of the AFN to and from a political rally, or would I carry some of the young women I worked with, who were prominent members of the Samariya? At one such moment a "big woman" in the AFN remarked to me with contempt that I would get no good "history" from the women in the Samariya. Such moments made it quite clear to me that any cultural feminist vision of a unified female sphere along the lines of Renée Pittin's early work in Katsina (1979) would not come close to describing the complex relations among women of differing age, marital status, and occupation in Maradi, and would in fact obscure some of the most important ways in which these women constituted themselves in formal political arenas.

I argue instead that women's associations in Maradi have not served to crystallize a Hausa female subculture. Maradi women have used the different women's associations to emphasize age, marital, and status distinctions among themselves as part of a larger move to create a legitimate public persona for both married and unmarried women. Women have thus participated in social transformation not by appealing to female solidarity or to a shared female culture but by drawing upon existing social forms to generate new possibilities for women in a changing political economy.

I refer to this contradictory tactic as a politics of difference, for by underscoring differences among them, women redefined marriage, respectable behavior, and access to external political spaces. The danger of such a maneuver was, of course, that in emphasizing difference by drawing upon existing categories to generate new political possibilities, there was a risk of heightening tensions among women and reinforcing accepted gender ideologies. I am not arguing that Maradi women as a whole consciously and deliberately engineered this tactic. To the contrary, I am suggesting that women's associations in Maradi in the late 1980s reflected fissures within the female body politic; in the pragmatics of bringing themselves into visibility at a time when Islamism had been on the rise in the region, women drew upon and emphasized those fissures. I characterize this politics of difference as tactical because the alliances and identities entertained by women engaged in struggles to improve their personal and collective circumstances are frequently provisional and preliminary. These approaches may succeed in moving them, in uneven and contradictory fashion, toward ends that may not be fully articulated and that cannot always be achieved through direct and confrontational means.

UNMARRIED WOMEN AND THE POLITICS OF NAMING

The word used for an adult woman, *mata*, is also used to designate a wife. Prior to her first marriage (generally at puberty in the Maradi region), a marriageable girl is known as a *budurwa*, a term that implies virginity. A married woman who loses her husband either through divorce or widowhood may be known as a *bajawara*, which implies that she and the male kin who serve as her guardians (with whom she may live and who support her) are interested in finding her a new husband. Finally, a previously married woman who earns her keep through sexual favors is known as a *karuwa*. Such a woman is likely to live in a house together with other *karuwai*, and her means of income is known as *karuwanci*. Renée Pittin's (1979) research in Katsina (Nigeria) on the female-centered "houses of women" in which *karuwai* live revealed that women may enter into *karuwanci* temporarily, that they may marry a "client," and that in general women treat movement into and out of marriages as career moves, with *karuwanci* serving simply as one "career" option among several.

Although the long-standing institution of *karuwanci* bears some resemblance to prostitution, the relative permanence of the sexual relationships involved, the courtship those relationships entail, and the lack of any enduring stigma for practitioners have prompted most English-speaking researchers to translate the word as "courtesanship" rather than "prostitution." In Maradi, streetwalkers who come from other ethnic groups and who do not practice the domestic courtesanship that women assimilated to Hausa culture prefer are openly derided and are not called *karuwai*; Hausa-speakers sometimes use the French loanword *passe-partout* to denote such women. In this work I shall use the word "courtesanship" to refer to *karuwanci*, retaining quotation marks to remind the reader that we, too, are contributing to a debate about the moral character of *karuwanci*, sex work, "prostitution," and female sexuality, even in this act of translation.

There is little ambiguity about how to name a young girl who has never been married—she is a *budurwa* (virgin). Increasingly when a girl manages to continue her schooling beyond primary school, she may not marry until she is in her late teens or early twenties. In this case her status is ambiguous: the possibility that such a young woman has been sexually active prior to her first marriage complicates the question of whether she can reasonably be considered a *budurwa*. In general, however, a girl is unlikely to enter into "courtesanship" without first having been married at least once. It is the large number of women who have been married at least once but are no longer married who are most difficult to categorize. The Hausa language does not distinguish a divorcée from a widow or provide a broad term such as "single woman." For convenience I shall refer to all such ambiguous women as "nonmarried" in order to distinguish them clearly from "unmarried" pubescent girls, who have never been married. In 1979 Pittin asserted from her work in Katsina that while men may refer to any nonmarried woman who is not kin as a *karuwa*, women "have little emotional, moral, or political investment in the concept of women outside their husband's houses occupying a negative or stigmatized position" (1979:98). Women are more likely to use the word *bajawara* to describe another adult woman who is living outside marriage; men can imagine no option for women outside marriage other than "courtesanship."

In Maradi in the late 1980s the situation was more complex. Certainly, men in Maradi characterized some nonmarried women as "courtesans," while women were more likely than men to characterize some nonmarried women as *bajawara*. In contemporary Maradi when women refer to another woman as a *bajawara* they mean two things: first, that she is living with relatives and is under the authority of a senior male, and, second, that she and her guardian are pursuing or anticipating her remarriage. The word *bajawara* is no more appropriate than is the word *karuwa* to describe an unmarried woman who lives on her own, earns her own keep without recourse to sexual favors, and has no immediate interest in remarrying. *Bajawara* is a more positive term, but it is not a more accurate term. The problem with conflating the categories of nonmarried women by promoting the notion that all nonmarried women ought to be considered *bajawara* is that it categorizes women who are pursuing remarriage with women who have no immediate interest in doing so. In Maradi, women emphatically consider certain women to be *karuwai*, with something close to the moral opprobrium attached to the English word "prostitute," although the stigma is of a less lasting character. They also recognize that there are some women who are not married, have no intention of (re)marrying in the near future, and whose primary source of income is not connected to sexual favors. These women are the subject of considerable debate among Maradi women themselves, for if they are not *karuwai* and they are not *bajawara*, what are they?

THE EVOLUTION OF WOMEN'S ASSOCIATIONS

Women's and youth associations have served as a means of mobilizing and making visible the power bases of the various political parties in Niger's postwar history. The major associations I will be discussing, the

Union des Femmes du Negre (UFN), the Samariya, and the AFN, were all created at various junctures by the party in power to shore up the regime and lend legitimacy to the single party state. The problem parties have faced in mobilizing women as a party base has been that the women who have the greatest mobility and visibility within the external public sphere are precisely those nonmarried women whose character and status are most ambiguous.

Thus in 1958, the Parti Progressiste Nigérien (PPN) founded its women's association, the UFN, which was promoted by the president's wife, Aissa Diori. Shortly thereafter, the UFN attempted to co-opt the "courtesans" of Maradi to form the nucleus of its women's wing. These *femmes libres* represented qualities that the party regarded as signs of modern, worldly women. As Jacqueline Nicolas observed at the time, the "courtesan" "embodies the woman who has succeeded in freeing herself of the family yoke and has overcome certain taboos, a woman who lives on her own and who therefore is more likely to choose for herself the husband who suits her. The 'independent woman' is used by the PPN as their Egeria [companion and advisor to kings]! It is the party which had the word 'karuwa' changed to 'zawara.'"[1]

However short-lived, this renaming—certainly it no longer held true in the late 1980s—underscores the importance of nonmarried women to politics in a Muslim society where very few married women are in a position to join a political organization publicly. Whether they were in strict seclusion or not, few respectable married women could have been called upon to parade on national holidays or to promote party propaganda. By choosing the word *bajawara* to replace *karuwa*, the PPN was automatically implying that these single women were temporarily between marriages. These women were to be held up as progressive women and potential wives, not as women who had chosen a lifestyle that rejected or threatened the traditional ideal of marriage. It would have been difficult then, as it is today, for a young woman to state in any public manner that she had no interest in remarriage.

Local Maradi practices included women in the political process through titled positions for a few women in the aristocratic class, while commoner women could become prominent through the *bori* spirit possession cult, still practiced openly here and overseen by its head, the Iya. Independent women could find some protection from the dangers of marginality through *bori* cult membership, so that many "courtesans" were also part of the broad *bori* network. The head of the *bori*, or Iya, is chosen from among senior women in the family of the ruler, and both the traditional ruler, the Sarki, and the Iya can lay claim to their right to office in part because their family is seen as being closely allied with the

bori spirits through inheritance: *su duk suna da bori* ("they all have spirits"). Such a traditional sanction does not exist in northern Nigeria, where
the cult is practiced very much in opposition to the desires of the Muslim rulers. The public acceptance of the *bori* cult, then, and the female
title of Iya altered the nature of women's participation in politics in
Maradi, making it possible for at least one variegated segment of the
female population (including some aristocratic women, *bori* members,
and "courtesans") to participate in political events.

Maradi's first formal women's association, then, capitalized on the potential represented in the *bori* cult and the office of the Iya. Although it
was directed by Umma Aguiyar, a well-educated midwife from the politically dominant Zerma-speaking region near the capital, the woman
who was chosen as her vice-president was Aisha Wandara, the sister of
the traditional Hausa ruler of Maradi. When her brother was first en-
throned, Wandara had briefly held the title of Iya, giving her authority
over the members of the *bori* spirit possession cult. Her relative youth
and independence, however, got her into trouble, and she was replaced
by another woman of the aristocratic class after four years in office.
Nevertheless, her spiritual and social ties to the spirit possession cult as
well as her genealogical ties to members of the aristocracy made her an
important asset to the UFN. Members of the cult, with which she remained closely associated, were often "courtesans," who as we have seen
made up the nucleus of the women available to join the UFN. Wandara
was the UFN's link to Hausa women, who for the most part were not as
well-educated as Zerma women in western Niger, and to the "courtesans"
who could most visibly represent the PPN's women's wing in Maradi.
Having lost her politically significant position as head of the *bori* cult,
Aisha Wandara could nevertheless wield some power by acting as the
state's link between a modern structure for women and the network of
women most available to participate in that structure. By integrating a
figure from the local female aristocratic hierarchy into the UFN, the PPN
could make a political analogy between traditional forms of representation for women and modern forms. The UFN could attempt to temper
the possible negative associations attached to members engaged in
"courtesanship" by drawing on the traditional sanction for *bori*, which,
as former head of the *bori* cult, Aisha Wandara represented.

In consolidating his control over the country, effectively creating a
one-party state, President Diori gradually alienated the Hausa traditional
rulers, who had continued to serve as the administrative apparatus under
French rule and whose networks and power bases Diori attempted to co-
opt through the creation of party committees in each village. With Diori's
fall in 1974,[2] the UFN slipped quietly into the background. When his

successor, Seyni Kountché, first took power, the new government had a reputation for integrity and concern for the rural population devastated by the Sahel drought. As his regime began building the structures of the "Development Society," local cooperatives and branches of the youth and women's associations were founded in areas outside of the capital. The traditional Samariya youth organizations were revived by the government in 1976 in part to carry out major development infrastructure projects and in particular to construct wells and classrooms (Decalo 1990:190). Samariya comes from the word *samari*, which means "youth" and, in particular, "young man." Traditionally in rural areas, when an invitation was sent out for men to work collectively on one another's farms, the *Sarkin Samari*, the head of the junior men, called them to work. Unmarried girls would be called by the corresponding leader of the young women, and while the young men labored the girls would sing and dance to make the farmwork more pleasurable. Such collective gatherings or *gaya* have become rare in rural areas today; hired labor has replaced the collective workforce.[3] Nevertheless the Nigérien government invoked this kind of collective work and festivity when it revived the Samariya in 1976.

The Association des Femmes du Niger (AFN) had a rather different genesis. In 1975, Kountché used the occasion of the International Year of the Woman to create a commission to study women's problems and to hold a series of public debates at the Institute for Research in the Humanities. These debates surveyed important issues ranging from women's status in the labor force to laws touching on women's rights in the family and to female education. While the efforts of the UFN to promote women's issues, particularly those of educated urban women in Niamey, were recognized in passing, the Kountché regime quickly succeeded in redefining the terms of the debate: the interests of rural women were emphasized, and, therefore, women's issues were seen as part of a broader national development agenda. The women's association that emerged, the Association des Femmes du Niger (AFN), was consequently firmly in the hands of the Kountché regime. While the AFN had some success in advancing issues relevant to women, notably the legality and availability of contraception (Dunbar 1991; Dunbar and Djibo 1992), other important efforts met with little success, most significantly the AFN's persistent attempts to promote a family code more favorable to women.[4] Despite Kountché's redirection of the women's association toward rural women's issues, the leadership and membership of the AFN remained concentrated in the major urban centers of Niamey and Zinder.[5] For women in Maradi, far from the capital, the significance of the AFN lay not in its specific social or economic programs, which in the end touched most of their lives only very marginally, but, rather, in the possibilities the AFN presented for redefining women's roles and their access to public activity.

STRUGGLING FOR LEGITIMATE INDEPENDENCE: THE AFN AND THE SAMARIYA

Women in Maradi often see the UFN and the AFN as one seamless whole and use the same Hausa term, 'kunjiyar mata (women's association), to refer to both. Nevertheless, when the AFN was set up in Maradi, Madame Aguiyar kept quietly in the background; any clear association of the AFN with the UFN in the wake of the military coup would have been dangerous for the survival of the women's association and possibly for Madame Aguiyar as well. In 1975 Aisha Wandara regained the titled position of Iya, making her the highest-ranking woman in the aristocratic class. Wandara's acquisition of full authority over the *bori* cult and its members, many of them "courtesans," made her the most logical choice to head the new women's association.

Despite the apparently seamless transition from UFN to AFN, the character of the new women's association was radically altered by the establishment of the Samariya youth movement. The Samariya evoked not gender but age and seniority as primary elements of social order. By calling upon the image of the collective work group under the authority of seniors, the Samariya heightened the differences between young women and senior women. In rural areas around Maradi, the Samariya of the late 1980s in some ways resembled the traditional model in which unmarried boys and girls worked cooperatively for the community. In the town of Maradi proper, however, the Samariya membership was notably older; many of the young men were certainly old enough to marry (25 to 35 years old) but perhaps could not afford to, and in some neighborhoods the girls were, in fact, young women, most of whom had been married at least once but were no longer married. Although the urban Samariya groups made an effort at dry season gardening, their agricultural duties were relatively insignificant compared with the entertainments they presented at the Maison des Jeunes and at the numerous political events that mark the year.

The character of the Samariya groups also varied from neighborhood to neighborhood. In the most conservative neighborhoods, only prepubescent girls were permitted to be members. In newer neighborhoods, where the availability of rental housing increased the population of women who were neither living with kin nor married, the women in the Samariya were frequently "courtesans." In the newer neighborhood of

Sabon Gari, for example, all of the young women in the Samariya lived in "houses of women" (*gidan mata*).[6] I asked a Samariya woman whether many of the members were *karuwai*, and she responded, "Not all of the women in the Samariya are *karuwai*, but lots of them are. Some of them are *budurwa* [unmarried virgins]" (Binta, November 13, 1989). It is striking that she and the other women in Maradi I spoke to never contended that these nonmarried women were *bajawara*. Either Samariya members were "virgins" who had never been married (girls of 10 to 13 or so), or they were "courtesans." There was no room for anything in between.

One consequence of this division was that by the late 1970s and early 1980s women in the public realm no longer had a single arena in which to act together in the interests of women. Nonmarried women who were "courtesans" tended to join the Samariya, while married women and more "respectable" nonmarried women took part in the AFN. Furthermore the number of "courtesans" who participated in the *bori* cult may have dropped; the newer medium for public display and the closer association with more modern structures made possible in the Samariya were more appealing, particularly to young women with some education. As the "courtesans" shifted to the Samariya, the utility of the *bori* cult as a source of female political support dropped significantly. Furthermore, as Maradi has adopted stricter Islamist practices as trade ties with conservative northern Nigeria have increased, the cult has become a political liability to politicians attempting to unite around a common Islamic cultural heritage. Once the Iya resigned from the presidency of the AFN in 1987, the few remaining *bori* members stepped into the background, leaving the AFN mostly to educated women, successful traders, and their clients.

The division of women into the Samariya, the AFN, and the *bori* cult undermined any solidarity the women might have been developing as a unified political group in the UFN. This fragmentation of women could serve the interests of the ruling regime, for it would work against opposition voiced by women at a time when the government was preoccupied with the demands of unruly students. Nevertheless, this division had the unexpected consequence of creating a more expansive political space for married and unmarried women who were not in fact engaged in "courtesanship."

DEBATING WOMEN

In the late 1980s, women who were not members of either the AFN or the Samariya often confused the two and saw no real difference between them, characterizing their membership as *matan zamani*, a euphemism for prostitute that means, literally, "modern woman." Members of the

AFN, however, insisted on a difference between themselves and members of the Samariya. AFN members were "married women" who engaged in respectable behavior. By separating the AFN from the Samariya, the government made it possible for married women to take part in public political manifestations without being grouped with unmarried "courtesans."

This separation enabled the Kountché regime and later the Ali Saibou regime to promote a nationalism founded on the image of women as mothers and wives, even as it drew upon young women as a powerful source of entertainment and propaganda, harnessing the image of the "free woman" as an icon of modernization. For women this also meant that those who were not "courtesans" could participate in political events, at least in principle, without damaging their reputations. Married women found a forum suitable for women of their status. However, the designation of AFN women as "married women" also made it possible for women who were not immediately interested in marriage to claim a terrain of public action without having to pretend to be potential wives (*bajawara*) under the tutelage of a senior male. This was new ground that the government, perhaps inadvertently, made available. Women themselves laid claim to and reinforced that territory through dialogue among themselves and through public performative statements about what it meant to be a "married woman."

Where women in the Samariya danced and sang, AFN women at public gatherings made an attempt to behave in a dignified manner, clapping and chanting slogans. AFN women chose behavior suitable to their purported age and marital status. AFN gatherings could be very jolly affairs, but the form of the festivity needed to be distinguishable from that of the Samariya. Where Samariya women were openly flirtatious, AFN women deferred to men without being subservient. This image of AFN women had become current nationally, as Janet Beik's observation of the stereotyping of AFN members for a play in Zinder illustrates: the director instructed the actresses "to shake hands with the préfet but not to bow over in respect (as traditionally women would do when meeting an important man)" (1987:109).

Samariya women had equally clear notions of suitable behavior for themselves. I asked one *karuwa* if the "courtesans" could join the AFN if they wanted to; she responded that they could but that it would be hard to get along with married women whose husbands might be clients and that, in any case, "there's no dancing in the women's association, so it wouldn't be appropriate" (Hajjiya Gobarci, November 13, 1989). The young Samariya members clearly enjoyed their dances and plays immensely, and no one seemed to feel that their behavior was inappropriate for their age or status as young girls and *karuwai*. One way a "courtesan" could demonstrate that she was a responsible citizen promoting the interests of society was to participate in the Samariya. Whereas in the past such women might have sought safety and refuge in the *bori* spirit possession cult, now they could turn to the government-sanctioned Samariya for legitimation, community, and protection.

While there were many AFN members who were not in fact married, their approach to legitimating their independence was to behave in a manner that resembled the married women's behavior as much as possible. They always wore headcloths and veils; they appeared restrained in public; they sat or stood with the married women in a crowd; they deferred to the older leaders of the association. They behaved as if they were married women. Nonmarried AFN members were generally very hardworking women, who made do with meager incomes and relied in part upon the generosity of their AFN patrons to help them stay out of "courtesanship." Some originally came from rural areas and had few connections in Maradi. A few were very successful traders or producers, but the more successful nonmarried women were invariably older—often old enough to claim that they were too old to bear children and thus not planning to remarry. A few were government functionaries whose careers made remarriage difficult.

Some nonmarried women in the AFN may have been *bajawara*, but not all were necessarily looking for a marriage partner. Their approach, rather, seemed to be to associate themselves with women who were responsible, respectable, and married in order to maintain a similar reputation for themselves. Since a Maradi woman's status as an adult is so closely associated with her status as a married woman, by mimicking the behavior of married women, nonmarried women could establish themselves as fully adult women. Ironically, the most subversive implication of this performance was perhaps that these women were beginning to disassociate female adulthood from marriage (the equation of "woman" and "wife"); in appearing publicly as *mata* (adult women) and not *samari* (youth) they forced the public recognition that some fully adult women were not, in fact, married.

Participation in the AFN was thus one way a woman could establish a reputation as an upright adult who behaved respectably, even if she was not married. This pushing at the edges of an accepted social category— *matan aure* (married woman)—is analogous to the strategy Catherine Coles observed among Hausa women in Kaduna: younger women manipulated the category of "old women" (*tsofuwa*) in order to enjoy the greater mobility of women beyond childbearing age (Coles 1990). However, such strategies are not guaranteed success. Popular perception of

AFN women in Maradi was not always generous; some women in search of a marriage partner might temporarily bow out of AFN activities to avoid any possible association with "free women" and to make their availability for remarriage clear.[7]

Women argued among themselves about what constituted appropriate behavior, and their appearance in external public spaces following various behavioral norms was a way to create new public norms and perceptions of women. An interchange in 1989 between the Iya and her niece, Rabi, illustrates the kinds of debates current in Maradi at that time. It is typical of many conversations I heard in which the respectability and status of various women was negotiated and established through gossip. The debate is unusual in that I happened to tape it while conducting a formal interview with the Iya, into which Rabi intruded. I asked the Iya whether there had been many *karuwai* in the women's association when it was started. I used the general Hausa expression, *'kunjiyar mata*, for "women's association" rather than either of the French acronyms, AFN or UFN.

Interviewer: When they first started the women's association, didn't they call upon lots of *karuwai* to join?

Iya: *Karuwai*? Yes, at that time the *karuwai* were put into the association.

Rabi: No, that's not right. They did not put *karuwai* in!

Iya: Well, they were the ones who weren't in seclusion; there were lots of them. All the married women were in seclusion.

Rabi: No, it's only recently that they've put the *karuwai* in!

Iya: No, today the married women are the majority.

Rabi [challenging]: Where are they?

Iya [amazed at the question]: The married women in the women's association? There are lots of them! The *karuwai* were all left to the Samariya.

Rabi: They separated them?

Iya: Yes. Each of the women you see is a married woman who has a husband. She is powerful in her home [*ta fi 'karfin 'dakinta*]. She may be an old woman whose husband has died; now she isn't a *karuwa*. You see, she has her own home, her daughters and children. She's not a *karuwa*. There aren't *karuwai* in the women's association. (Iya 'Yar Wandara, November 16, 1989.)

Rabi, who was not a member of either the Samariya or the AFN, did not initially see any difference between the two; because the Samariya was so highly visible, she thought of the Samariya when she heard me ask about *karuwai* and the women's association. Her remark that the *karuwai* had only entered the association recently may reflect her memory that when she was much younger the traditional rural Samariya work groups did not include "courtesans," who were more common in urban settings. Although the Iya knew very well that many of the women in the AFN were not married, when she generalized about AFN membership she described the typical AFN member as a married woman, a woman with *'karfin 'dakinta* ("the strength of her own room or home"). The expression is evocative, for it suggests both married women who have enough influence with their husbands to be able to go out to AFN gatherings, as well as any woman, married or not, who has the ability to maintain herself and her children or dependents in a home or room of her own. A woman who has the "the strength of her own room" does not rely upon a man to pay her rent, although she may rely upon her children for help. A woman who has been successful in trade might even own or rent a house herself. The phrase thus calls to mind a woman with either some economic self-sufficiency or enough intra-household stature to be able to negotiate with her husband for a degree of independence and mobility.

In the same exchange, Rabi, unconvinced, went on to enumerate women whom she considered to be *karuwai*, in order to prove that the women's association included them as members; the Iya explained to her that each of them was actually in the Samariya. Shifting tactics, Rabi then got Iya to name women in their neighborhood who were members of the AFN. Rabi pointed out that several of the women mentioned were not married. Iya then argued that they were older women who were beyond marriage age. Finally, Iya mentioned one woman who, she conceded, engaged in "courtesanship." Where Rabi found this woman's behavior indefensible, Iya was willing to make an exception for a woman who is temporarily having trouble making a living, but in her own mind she made very clear distinctions between women who engage in *karuwanci* and women who for the most part avoid it.[8] Rabi was less willing to see these distinctions, and as a married woman who rarely went out and saw little of how the two associations functioned, she had little understanding of why Iya would argue that some independent women are not *karuwai*. Note that neither woman made use of the word *bajawara*, which did not seem to be relevant to the discussion they were having.

This is not just verbal sparring, for much hangs on the issue of whether a woman, married or not, can take part in public activities—from politics to trading to education—without the perception of sexual impropriety. Despite Hausa ideology proclaiming the importance of men as providers for women, and despite the marginality of female enterprises, it is women who increasingly take on the burden of feeding themselves and their children (Coles 1991; Frishman 1991; Pittin 1991). Hausa women's contributions to the household and national economies are rarely recognized, and national and regional policies can actively thwart women's income-earning efforts (Pittin 1990, 1991). To secure their rights to trade in the home and to gain greater access to public sector employment, larger-scale trade, and significant education, women in this region must first fight for their right and their daughters' right to conduct their lives openly beyond the confines of their homes. One of the factors limiting girls' education in Maradi, for instance, is the perception that it is inappropriate for a young married woman to go out to school. In a region where girls marry shortly after the onset of puberty, this perception is a powerful constraint to female education. The use of young girls as hawkers for married women who cannot leave the home to carry out their trade also serves to discourage women from sending girls to school. Of the many battles that the women's associations could be waging, one of the most important is to earn for women the right to be seen publicly without being stigmatized morally. As in the conversation quoted above, this is a battle that is waged not simply with men but in debates among women themselves.

CONCLUSION

It is, I think, an impressive measure of the success women have had in contesting for access to external political space that on May 13, 1991, women in Niamey staged a well-publicized and highly visible protest against the virtual exclusion of female representation from the National Conference Planning Committee that was set up after the civilian coup d'etat. While the powerful national trade union had managed to eliminate all other "democratic" institutions created or co-opted by the Saibou regime from the planning committee (including the Samariya and the Islamic Association), women staged a massive demonstration in the capital when the AFN was denied any representation. If the Saibou regime attempted to co-opt women for its purposes, one might argue that women themselves managed to co-opt the AFN to gain representation for women even when the party with which it was originally allied had lost credibility.

The dangers as well as the promise of the politics of difference have been in evidence throughout the faltering transition to civilian rule Niger has undergone since 1990. While women demonstrating for representation in the early 1990s consistently held their ground in the face of "open hostility, public humiliation and even violence at the hands of Islamic leaders and supporters of the old regime" (Charlick and Ousseini,

1996:3), the visibility and audibility of women in this process generated a backlash against young women of precisely the ambiguous status discussed above—secondary school students of marriageable age. In the market at Zinder, several such women were beaten and stripped because of their "immodest" dress, and one was hospitalized (*West Africa* 1993). A powerful measure of the positive potential in the ongoing process of negotiating women's entry into public space is the fact that at such a moment large numbers of women rallied behind the young women rather than criticizing them for not dressing and behaving as if they were married women: once again women in the capital marched to protest the attacks and succeeded in forcing the government to intervene with police force (McCarus 1993a). While the attacks show how vulnerable single women are in times of national stress and suggest that repression in the name of Islam is growing not only in Maradi but throughout the country, these incidents show how important the work of establishing women's access to external public space is and how tenaciously women in Niger have fought for that access. Where the assertion of the right to public visibility is also, more concretely, a claim to women's moral right to go to the polling stations themselves to vote, democracy itself is in the balance.

In reworking what it means to be a "married woman," Maradi women were disrupting the most taken-for-granted of gender categories and enabling alliances between married women and nonmarried women. Making a beginning toward staking a claim to the right to enter into the external public spaces of formal politics and large-scale trade was an extremely important first step toward achieving economic independence and political autonomy. By 1990 Nigérienne women's visible participation in events marking national political life had become a cultural commonplace—it had become, as it were, a tradition. Thus when women protested their exclusion from the National Conference, the transitional government was compelled to intervene to protect the now "traditional" representation of women in public affairs, despite hostility from many quarters.[9]

The received image of Africa's rural and provincial women as ignorant, passive, and conservative mars Anne-Laure Folly's otherwise useful film *Femmes du Niger: Entre intégrism et démocratie* ("Women of Niger: Between Fundamentalism and Democracy") (1993), in which the historic women's marches of 1991 and 1992 are depicted as having emerged *ex nihilo* in the capital out of the crucible of economic crisis. In reality the mobilization of women for those protests was made possible, at least in part, by years of unglamorous and unrecognized performative labor on the part of AFN and Samariya women throughout the country. Their sustained and carefully staged engagement bespeaks a political acumen out of keeping with the film's predictable portrayal of mute and uncomprehending rural women in need of consciousness raising by their educated urban sisters. While it has been urban women, by and large, who have been the beneficiaries of what I see as a kind of popular female co-optation of the state's women's association, the possibility exists for rural Hausa women to carry through on what they helped to begin by supporting women's groups that protect the interests of women farmers. An attention to the concerns of such groups would have policy implications strikingly different from those emerging from the recognition of the needs of, for example, female bureaucrats.[10] For this reason I see some positive elements in the recent fragmentation and proliferation of women's groups in Niger.

Nevertheless, the gradual deterioration of women's representation in parliament since a high point in 1993 suggests that those initial gains have not, in themselves, guaranteed women's access to public office or the continued interest of rural women in the chaotic politics of the capital (Charlick and Ousseini 1996:2). Electoral politics, having failed to deliver any substantial reforms to benefit women economically, and having devolved yet again into military rule, may have little credibility for the very provincial and rural women that I argue here contributed to making electoral politics possible. Furthermore this politics of difference virtually guarantees that, whatever the initial advantages of the proliferation of women's groups, the intellectual, institutional, and material resources necessary for continuing mobilization and effective leverage are diluted. As Charlick and Ousseini remark, enhancing the participation of women in politics will mean "addressing them via their interests in . . . economic and productive activities" (1996:3), rather than through claims for female representation in government *tout court*. It remains to be seen how the ongoing struggles for accountable government will play themselves out and how women's groups will contribute now that the initial tactics of the politics of difference have failed to secure concrete material advances for women. To my Nigérien friends embarked upon this journey: *Allah ya kiyaye ku.*

NOTES

1. J. Nicolas (1967:59). Egeria was the companion and adviser to Numa, the mythical second king of Rome. Similar use of the *karuwai* by the PPN occurred in Arewa (Latour 1992:127–8). For parallel processes in Nigeria see Callaway and Creevey (1994:145).

2. Discontentment over the Diori regime's poor handling of negotiations for partial profits from the newly developing uranium mines, Diori's alienation of traditional rulers, and, most important, his administration's cynical and inhumane manner of distrib-

uting relief grain from international donors during the Sahel drought of 1968–74 eventually provoked a successful military coup in 1974. See Fuglestad (1983: 147–88); Charlick (1991: 40–52); Decalo (1990: 241–84).

3. The *gaya* were disappearing in the Maradi region when Guy Nicolas conducted his research there in the late 1960s. See G. Nicolas (1975:188). For the same institution in northern Nigeria, see M. G. Smith (1981:59–60).

4. A law facilitating women's access to contraceptives was passed only in 1988. Prior to that time a woman was required to present her husband's written authorization (République du Niger 1992:43). For a discussion of the pitfalls of promoting a family code in another Muslim context (Senegal), see Callaway and Creevey (1994:176–83). For a discussion of policies and practices surrounding contraception in Nigeria see Pittin (1986).

5. One of Miles' informant's remarks convey rural women's distant and subordinate relationship to the AFN in Zinder: "what they tell us to do, we do" (1994:282–83).

6. For a discussion of such houses in Katsina, see Pittin (1983).

7. One of my nonmarried acquaintances who had participated in street sweeping with married women in the AFN was severely chastised by her family for "going out with the Samariya." She stopped going to AFN events altogether in order to maintain a respectable image for potential suitors.

8. One reason it can be difficult to distinguish a *karuwa* from a nonmarried woman who lives on her own is that sexual access, even for married women, is closely associated among the Hausa with gifts, and any courtship, whether sexual relations are involved or not, also necessitates many gifts from the man.

9. My attention to the reformulation of tradition and the deployment of competing discourses resonates with Ayesha Imam's caution that real democracy requires autonomy for individual actors, not just the proliferation of parties, calling for "a focus on how to strengthen democratic processes at the level of daily life" (1992:105).

10. The focus upon women's interests in debates surrounding the Code Rurale (Rural Code) during the National Conference is perhaps a sign of a new and interesting elaboration in Nigérienne women's activism in the capital (Dunbar and Djibo 1992:27–30).

REFERENCES

Beik, Janet. 1987. *Hausa Theatre in Niger: A Contemporary Oral Art.* New York: Garland Publishing.

Binta [pseud.]. November 13, 1989. Interview by Barbara M. Cooper.

Callaway, Barbara and Lucy Creevey. 1994. *The Heritage of Islam: Women, Religion, and Politics in West Africa.* Boulder, Colo.: Lynne Rienner Publishers.

Charlick, Robert B. 1991. *Niger: Personal Rule and Survival in the Sahel.* Boulder, Colo.: Westview Press.

Charlick, Robert B. and Hadiza Ousseini. 1996. "Advancing the Participation of Women in Nigérien Political Life." http://www.csuohio.edu/polisci/nigerwom.htm (accessed November 26, 1997).

Clair, Andrée, ed. 1965. *Le Niger, pays à découvrir.* Paris: Hachette.

Coles, Catherine. 1990. "The Older Woman in Hausa Society: Power and Authority in Urban Nigeria." In *The Cultural Context of Aging: World-Wide Perspectives*, ed. Jay Sokolovsky, 57–81. New York: Bergin and Garvey.

———. 1991. "Hausa Women's Work in a Declining Urban Economy: Kaduna, Nigeria, 1980–1985." In *Hausa Women in the Twentieth Century*, ed. Catherine Coles and Beverly Mack, 163–91. Madison: University of Wisconsin Press.

Cooper, Barbara M. 1997. *Marriage in Maradi: Gender and Culture in a Hausa Society in Niger, 1900–1989*. Portsmouth, N.H.: Heinemann.

Decalo, Samuel. 1989. *Historical Dictionary of NIGER*. Metuchen, N.J.: Scarecrow Press.

———. 1990. *Coups and Army Rule in Africa*. New Haven, Conn.: Yale University Press.

Dunbar, Roberta Ann. 1991. "Islamic Values, the State, and 'the Development of Women': The Case of Niger." In *Hausa Women in the Twentieth Century*, ed. Catherine Coles and Beverly Mack, 69–89. Madison: University of Wisconsin Press.

Dunbar, Roberta Ann and Hadiza Djibo. 1992. "Islam, Public Policy and the Legal Status of Women in Niger." Study prepared for the GENESYS Project, The Futures Group, and USAID/Niamey.

Folly, Anne-Laure. 1993. *Femmes du Niger: Entre intégrisme et démocratie*. [Video.] New York: Women Make Movies.

Frishman, Alan. 1991. "Hausa Women in the Urban Economy of Kano." In *Hausa Women in the Twentieth Century*, ed. Catherine Coles and Beverly Mack, 192–206. Madison: University of Wisconsin Press.

Fuglestad, Finn. 1983. *A History of Niger 1850–1960*. Cambridge: Cambridge University Press.

Hajjiya Gobarci [pseud.]. 1989. Interview by Barbara M. Cooper, November 13.

Imam, Ayesha. 1992. "Democratization Processes in Africa: Problems and Prospects." *Review of African Political Economy* 54:102–5.

Iya 'Yar Wandara. 1989. Interview by Barbara M. Cooper, November 16.

Latour, Éliane de. 1992. *Les temps du pouvoir*. Paris: Éditions de l'École des Hautes Études en Sciences Sociales.

McCarus, Chris. 1993. "Election showdown." *West Africa*, February 22–28, 289–90.

Miles, William F. S. 1994. *Hausaland Divided: Colonialism and Independence in Nigeria and Niger*. Ithaca, N.Y.: Cornell University Press.

Nicolas, Guy. 1975. *Dynamique sociale et appréhension du monde au sein d'une société hausa*. Paris: Musée Nationale d'Histoire Naturelle.

Nicolas, Jacqueline. 1967. *Les "Juments des Dieu": Rites de possession et condition féminine en pays hausa (vallée de Maradi, Niger)*. Paris: Études Nigériennes.

Pittin, Renée. 1979. "Marriage and Alternative Strategies: Career Patterns of Hausa Women in Katsina City." Ph.D. dissertation, University of London (School of Oriental and African Studies).

———. 1983. "Houses of Women: A Focus on Alternative Lifestyles in Katsina City." In *Female and Male in West Africa*, ed. C. Oppong, 291–302. London: George Allen and Unwin.

———. 1986 "The Control of Reproduction: Principle and Practice in Nigeria." *Review of African Political Economy* 35:40–53.

————. 1990. "Selective Education: Issues of Gender, Class and Ideology in Northern Nigeria." *Review of African Political Economy* 48:7–25.

————. 1991. "Women, Work and Ideology in Nigeria." *Review of African Political Economy* 52:38–52.

République du Niger. 1992. *Enquête Démographique et de Santé 1992*. Niamey: Ministère des Finances et du Plan.

Smith, M. G. 1981 [1954]. "Introduction." In *Baba of Karo: A Woman of the Muslim Hausa*. Ed. and trans. Mary F. Smith, 11–34. New Haven: Yale University Press.

West Africa. 1993. "Constitution adopted." January 18–24, 72–73.

14

"WICKED WOMEN" AND "RESPECTABLE LADIES": RECONFIGURING GENDER ON THE ZAMBIAN COPPERBELT, 1936–1964

Jane L. Parpart

When work is over you see them sauntering about—many of them clad correctly in European clothes—hat at an absurd angle, sticks—and cigarettes—walking with an exaggerated swagger. I saw girls and women . . . some of them in the most modern clothing—one was in loose wide-legged pyjamas, gay and flaunting garments, she carried a sunshade and walked with her head thrown back—a cigarette held lightly between her teeth . . . a group of young men followed her admiringly. They were seen everywhere—girls and women in high-heeled shoes smoking cigarettes.[1]

INTRODUCTION

Mabel Shaw had no difficulty identifying the "wicked women" of Zambia. They were the young women who had fled the harmony and patriarchal order of rural Africa, and taken up the worst of Western life in the urban colonial centers. She described them with horror on her 1931 Copperbelt visit. She reflects the feelings of most Europeans in colonial Zambia in the 1930s,[2] who had accepted the dictum of indirect rule, namely that African salvation lay in rural social structures, not in the adoption of European ways. The urban centers springing up in Zambia were seen as "centres of mischief . . . [that] radiate evil through the territory" (Roebuck 1927), encouraging the worst aspects of Western life and destroying the harmony of rural life. African women, in particular, were expected to stay in the rural areas to maintain the rural social and moral order for returning male migrants (and the colonial system). Yet many African women went to towns, especially after the emergence of the copper mining cities in the late 1920s.[3] Some of them came and went as spouses, offering few challenges to gendered notions of social order. However, others discovered how to survive in town. They reveled in their independence, changed the terms of marriage and other institutions, and often chose to remain in town rather than return to the rural areas. These women became the "bad girls" of the Copperbelt—vilified by Africans and Europeans alike.

These women were held up as the opposite of everything moral, "civilized," and socially acceptable, providing a standard against which "respectable ladies" could be measured. Missionaries, colonial officials, and rural African leaders railed against them. The emerging African urban elite worried that "bad girls" would threaten their efforts to gain respectable status in colonial urban life. The discourse of opposition, this othering of "improper" African urbanites, especially women, surfaced intermittently during the pre-1945 period, and intensified after 1945, when colonial policy began to favor the establishment of a stable urban working class and emerging elite. The chapter will explore the way these Copperbelt women were represented by various groups of Europeans and Africans. It will examine the impact of these representations, their shifts over time and contexts, and the possibility that these women may have provided alternative models for thinking about and being women and men.

Zambia is a particularly appropriate site for this investigation because it experienced a high degree of urbanization after copper's development in the 1920s. Because neighboring mining centers in the Congo and Broken Hill[4] had permitted settled, married labor, the Zambian copper mines were forced to follow suit. Women took up this opportunity in droves. The Copperbelt towns thus provide an excellent site for exploring the lives of urban women during the colonial period, including the possibility that the "wicked women" of the Copperbelt may have contributed to the reconfiguration of gender in colonial Zambia.

THE COPPERBELT "BAD GIRLS": THE EARLY YEARS

After World War I, the policy of indirect rule emerged as a solution to governing African colonies on the cheap. It sought order and stability in the social structures and practices of rural African societies. Women played a central role in this vision. They were portrayed as docile, obedient wives and daughters, committed to ensuring the well-being of their families and rural communities—a discourse propagated by rural patriarchs and accepted as the norm by colonial officials and missionaries enthralled with the notion of indirect rule. "Good" women did not go to town, except when accompanying their husbands during periods of migrant labor. But all women were regarded as particularly susceptible to the corrupting influences of town life. The possibility that urban life would inspire women to throw off the constraints of rural life and enter a life of unbridled "wickedness" haunted the thinking of African and European leaders, particularly men (Parpart 1994; Ferguson 1992).

To counter this possibility, colonial officials and rural patriarchs tried to limit women's access to town. African women had to get permission to travel from rural leaders, and they were often denied. Road blocks turned back those without the necessary papers. Once in town, women were threatened with repatriation if they "misbehaved." The number of women on the Copperbelt rose anyway. By 1931 about 30 percent (or 5,292) of the 15,876 mine employees on the Copperbelt lived with women (Davis 1933:75–76). This figure had risen to about 40 percent in 1946 and 70 percent in 1956 (Wincott 1966:377). In 1943, the government townships had between 40 and 77 percent married inhabitants (Saffery 1943:52–53). In 1956, officials recorded 32,443 men, 15,575 women, and 24,111 children living in the municipal townships. Many more women and children lived informally in the townships and squatter compounds around the Copperbelt.[5] Officials tried to repatriate these squatters, but they often returned on the next available transport.

Women came to town for various reasons. For many, urban life was a holding pattern, to be endured until the family's return to the rural areas. Others came as obedient wives, but soon discovered the pleasures of town life. As a Roan compound manager reported, "women come to compounds very meekly. Next time you see them, they have donned a dress of stylish cut, and wearing shoes and stockings, they swagger along carrying the baby on their backs" (Spearpoint 1937:39). Some young women came to have a good time, intending eventually to marry or return home. Others fled unhappy marriages, heavy workloads, and patriarchal authority in the rural areas. Once in town, many came to prefer town life. As Audrey Richards reported, "women on the Copperbelt do not seem to want to go back to the villages and settle down as men may do."[6] "They have a much better time at the mines."[7]

Women soon discovered how to survive in town. They brewed beer, sold their sexual and domestic services, cooked and sold food, and engaged in other largely informal economic activities (Chauncey 1981). However, access to housing continued to be a problem, even for economically independent women.[8] Since most Copperbelt housing was tied to employment, which was predominately for African men, the easiest way to acquire housing was to live with a man. For settled married women, this was no problem, but women without partners had more difficulty. The temporary mine marriage emerged as a solution. These relationships endured any period from a few days to many years. Since location managers did not require proof of marriage, any self-proclaimed couple could acquire housing. One woman had been able to remain in one house by being the "wife" of three different contract miners.[9] Other women "changed hands four and five times respectively" (Davis 1933:77).

The marriage market thus became a key survival strategy for women wanting to remain in town. This "market" was fueled by lopsided demographics, with men dramatically outnumbering women.[10] Negotiations over sexual liaisons and partnerships often took place in the beer halls and shebeens. Audrey Richards visited the Roan beer hall in 1931—a large square building where beer was served to a large mixed gathering. "Expensive women congregated there." She found the verandahs

> filled with parties and little knots outside. Some women in pairs, obviously seeking adventure, and others single, definitely "soliciting." Marigold, the nightclub queen in coffee coloured silk dress and cap, earrings, and high heeled shoes, flirting in European fashion with two men. Many people just standing about drinking, and not a terrible disorder or amount of drunkenness.[11]

These activities offered venues where women could "upgrade" their marital partners, negotiate the terms of relationships, and establish an urban base. For some, these possibilities contrasted starkly with the hard work and constrictions of rural life. For others, town life at least offered increased autonomy, if rarely in conditions of their own choosing.

Attitudes toward urban "bad girls," and proposals for dealing with them, varied. Mine management and other colonial employers adopted a rather instrumental attitude. While acknowledging that African women "give a fair amount of trouble," mine management soon realized that "this is offset by the care they take of their husbands" and began to encourage married labor on the mines.[12] Management cared little about marital legality. They were "not primarily interested in Native morals, but in a contented and efficient labour force" (Davis 1933:76–77).[13] Thus for employers, "wicked women" were not bad mothers, but troublesome members of the community who should be sent back home. To that end, the mines hired police to patrol their townships, set up tribal representatives to enforce "traditional" mores, and supported the repatriation of "undesirable" characters, especially unattached women and adolescents.

Colonial officials and missionaries were more concerned with sexuality and "morality," although many colonial authorities accepted the inevitability (and benefits) of some urban prostitution.[14] The Copperbelt missionaries condemned African women who succumbed "to the glamour and the fascination of the things money can buy, to the social life of beer hall and dance hall, and to the merely physical side of their sexual life with men."[15] Both missionaries and colonial officials blamed this behavior on the evils of city life and the "callous brutality and lack of moral sense" . . . [due to] "lack of tribal restraint, over crowding, and an excess of material over spiritual well-being."[16] Like mine management, both missionaries and colonial officials believed the solution to urban decay, and to "wicked women" in particular, lay in repatriation.[17] The urban native courts, established in the mid-1930s, supported this initiative.[18] To encourage this policy, colonial officials restricted urban educational facilities and built up rural schools.[19]

By the late 1930s, however, the limits of this approach were becoming increasingly clear—African women (and men) could not be kept out of the urban areas, and urban "bad girls" were not going to go away. In order to deal with this "problem," stop-gap measures were introduced. The United Missions in the Copperbelt (UMCB) missionaries organized clubs and activities to counter the attractions of dances and beer halls.[20] Authorities set up a girls' boarding school on the Copperbelt, with the express aim of producing "town-bred girls who can become good wives and mothers in an urban environment."[21] The school accepted women who "were already adversely influenced by their industrial environment" in hopes of "wean[ing] them to a life of useful service as home demonstrators, teachers and housewives."[22] However, this discourse did little to undermine the belief that African well-being was irretrievably linked to the rural areas. The aspirations of the emerging African urban elite could do little to counter this bias (Moore 1940).[23]

The African community on the Copperbelt demonstrated a more nuanced and differentiated understanding of "wickedness" and "respectability" during this period. While no doubt most African men (and many women) condemned women who flaunted male authority and "traditional" mores, the more transient and often less skilled urban males also enjoyed the company of the women who frequented the beer halls and shebeens. They slept with them, "married" them, and spent much of their leisure time with them. Hence, they could not afford to be too critical, at least while in town. Many women also enjoyed the freewheeling atmosphere of the beer halls. In the early 1930s, some women in the Roan township told Richards, "Yes they got drunk. They had beer. They liked it."[24] Richards also discovered that young women used neighboring compounds, often of contractors, as staging grounds for finding new partners and sexual liaisons in the mines. There was much informal mingling at night, despite management's protestations to the contrary. Weekend parties outside the compounds attracted large crowds. Many of the unattached men and women saw these parties as a diversion from the daily grind rather than as a sign of decadence and moral decay.[25]

In contrast, most urban court assessors, tribal elders, and many "respectable" African urbanites regarded unattached women in town as potential renegades. Unlike many colonial officials and mine managers, they worried more about inter-ethnic sexual alliances, prostitution, and challenges to rural authorities, rather than issues of law and order or productivity. While opinion varied about the inherent promiscuity of various ethnic groups,[26] these more "respectable" Africans identified "wicked women" by their challenges to established beliefs and practices, particularly in regard to sexuality and drinking.[27] They blamed much of this behavior on the evils of urban life, and supported repatriation, "not only of out and out harlots, but also of divorced and unattached women in general."[28] The court assessors tried to send divorce cases to the rural courts, and urged the mining authorities to require marriage certificates before assigning housing. They also refused compensation for women engaged in serial adultery or prostitution.[29] Thus the issue of marital status and harmony increasingly entered African urban discourse.

In contrast, some more settled Africans on the Copperbelt had begun to develop very different notions of propriety and impropriety. Some survived on the margins, living off gambling and prostitution, with little desire to return to the rural areas or to identify urban life with "wickedness." Most aspiring urbanites, however, wanted to establish their position as "respectable" members of the urban community.[30] Generally more educated and skilled, although not always, many were committed Christians. These men and women sought to distance themselves from the sexual (mis)behavior of urban "bad girls," blaming their behavior on the beer halls and other temptations of urban life (Spearpoint 1937:32). Many avoided the beer halls, citing religious and cultural reasons.[31] They supported schooling and programs that would train young women for lives as "respectable" married urban women (Davis 1933:326). While some men despaired of finding "decent" wives in town and sought rural partners, they did so with the aim of establishing a respectable urban married life (Kaavu 1949).[32] Marital legitimacy, whether customary or church-based, became a potent symbol of respectability, and the emerging elite argued vehemently against offering married housing to unmarried Africans in town. Thus, notions of "propriety" became linked to marriage and sexuality in the minds of aspiring African urbanites before they became a concern for Europeans on the Copperbelt.[33]

"WICKED WOMEN" AND
"RESPECTABLE LADIES": 1945–1958

Efforts to constrain the freewheeling "bad girls/women" (and men) of the Copperbelt coincided with a shift in colonial policy after World War II, which recognized the need to encourage a more stabilized urban working and middle class in order to foster colonial development (Cooper 1989). This shift legitimated the struggles of Africans who had been trying to gain acceptance as respectable members of the urban community. Curbing "disreputable" behavior thus became a concern for many Europeans as well as African urbanites. The discourse against impropriety and "wickedness" intensified, as did the efforts to contain and eliminate this behavior. However, no single definition of respectability emerged—ideas varied with time and circumstances. Moreover, the initial authority of European notions of respectability came under fire in many quarters as political and class conflicts intensified after the mid-1950s.

The emphasis on a stabilized urban population fostered a growing concern with the nature of African urban family life. Among Europeans, Western notions of Christian family life shaped the concept of urban respectability. They condemned the "bad girls" of the Copperbelt, who upset this scenario with their promiscuous, quarrelsome, and irreverent behavior, their penchant for chasing other people's husbands, challenging social conventions, and refusing to accept their role as "proper" wives and mothers (Coppens 1952). Colonial officials joined the chorus.[34] Mine management reluctantly supported this position, although still inclined to define disruptive, antisocial behavior more by its impact on productivity and orderly compounds than on family values.

African urbanites interpreted "respectability" and "wickedness" in various ways. Many remained wedded to the notion of rural purity and traditional mores. Urban court assessors retained a general scepticism about urban life. Even Christian marriages were seen as prone to instability. "Girls living on the line of rail cannot be trusted. . . . It does not take long before a woman or girl comes to the court seeking a divorce."[35] They blamed urban social problems on easy marriages, especially inter-ethnic marriage, and lack of family guidance, but above all, on the bad influence of impudent, "uncontrollable" urban women.[36]

The emerging urban elite also vilified the "bad girls" of the Copperbelt. While the yardstick being applied had its roots in rural mores—the label stuck to women who insulted people, quarreled incessantly, and ignored the advice of their elders—strictly urban measures emerged as well. Movie-going, for example, was generally regarded as improper and dangerous. A clerk at Roan denounced the cinema. "If the bioscope was good, then I should attend with my family. . . . In fact, I am a church leader and it would be queer for me to attend such wicked shows" (Powdermaker 1953). Drinking in public places, especially in large beer halls and shebeens with local beer (*chibuku*) was frowned on, and women who frequented beer halls, caroused, and caused fights were condemned. The emerging elite valued "proper," generally Western-style housekeeping. A mine employee complained about his wife—"the house was untidy, chairs unpolished and many plates unwashed. . . . The house was . . . even stinking."[37] A former elementary school teacher criticized his wife for not knowing "how to clean his clothes or even press them well."[38] Thus "respectability" increasingly necessitated an ability to organize and maintain a modern/Western-style home.

What about the urban poor and working class, the group the elite called *bapanshi* ("the low ones")? How did they define "wicked women"? Clearly, long held assumptions of propriety influenced their thinking. Women who quarreled incessantly, insulted people, failed to respect their elders, and neglected their husbands, children, and homes, were regarded with disapproval, much as in the rural areas.

However, many members of the urban poor and working class aspired to respectable status and, like the elite, generally defined impropriety in relation to notions of "respectable" family life. But the definitions of proper family life varied a bit. Drinking in beer halls and shebeens was regarded as perfectly acceptable as long as one did not drink excessively, chase men, or neglect wifely duties. As one woman exclaimed, "I have no time for the radio, instead I go to the beer hall and drink. After drinking I go home and rest, and then cook for my children and husband" (Powdermaker 1953:27). However, most had no patience with women who became drunk and unruly at beer halls. A woman in Mikomfwa was criticized for "her bad manners, her fighting and losing her head after drinks."[39] Marital stability increasingly became seen as a sign of respectability, and women who lived on their own, changed partners frequently, or became involved in adultery and assault cases were regarded with suspicion.[40] Behavior that provided opportunities for sexual transgressions became increasingly suspect. The "champions" of the Copperbelt—women who lived openly as independent women or moved from short-term marriage to short-term marriage—were loudly condemned, although their independence of male control and social constraints had a certain glamour. People criticized promiscuous men as well. A Mikomfwa man was vilified for "changing wives like shirts."[41] Women sought respectability by choosing their friends carefully, avoiding the company of disreputable women, monitoring their children's movements, and accepting many of their husbands' dictates.[42]

Notions of respectability varied with age, sex, and religious affiliation as well. Young women and men had somewhat more latitude. Many saw no problem with going to beer halls and movies in search of excitement and potential partners. As one young woman confessed, "I went when I was young, but I was interested in no films, because then I was very interested in men. So cinema was my place where I could meet my darlings. I am married now and I do not go there" (Powdermaker 1953:60). When a woman reached a marriageable age, expectations often changed. As a young woman discovered, "My mother . . . says I have reached a stage where men are very serious to study women. So I have to abandon some of the things I liked while young, otherwise they lead me to some mischievious way, and men will have no desire to marry me" (Powdermaker 1953:60). Once married, most women were too busy for leisure. As one exasperated woman exclaimed, "Where can I find time now? No, I cannot go there [the movies]" (Powdermaker 1953:60). Many women sought respect by living harmoniously with their neighbors and being responsible wives and mothers. Some managed to become community leaders, sought out for advice by all.[43] More religious members of the urban poor often rejected drinking and movies altogether. A Seventh Day Adventist family in Mikomfwa refused to socialize with neighbors because they were all heavy drinkers.[44] Some women proudly declared that they never drank in beer halls or shebeens, because these places were full of wicked people.[45] Others hoped to better themselves and refused to socialize with disreputable neighbors.

A number of institutions, regulations, and practices were established in order to encourage "respectable" urban family life for Africans. The mining companies and government officials agreed to deny housing to couples without a marriage certificate, hoping this would restrict women's ability to change partners, and thus to survive in town outside marriage (Parpart 1988). In 1953, the mining companies expanded their social welfare activities, with an emphasis on producing good mothers, frugal wives, and modern homemakers—largely based on Western models. As one European social worker explained, "it is my job to break down the old prejudices so that African wives of the future will be enlightened partners of husbands in a middle-class community." She hoped her lessons to adolescent girls on scientific (Western) homemaking would make them more marriageable and prevent prostitution (Lloyd 1960). The mine newspapers glorified "respectable" women such as Mrs. M.—"a very fastidious woman. She keeps her house spotlessly clean. Everything is neatly arranged. . . . You would love seeing her smart, well-dressed children playing in the clean yard."[46] Government social welfare activities expanded as well. Model homes were set up to teach "proper"/Western housekeeping.[47] Although reduced in number and authority, the Copperbelt missionaries continued to foster responsible Christian family life in church and special classes. In 1958 they established a very popular Christian Home Making and Leadership Training Course to help wives of potential African leaders "take their place beside their husbands in home and community" (Johnson 1961).[48]

The mines set up formal advisory structures to deal with problems before they reached the urban courts. Roan established a Citizen's Advice Bureau (CAB) in the early 1960s to handle problems before they became too serious. While the CAB had no judicial authority, its advice was taken seriously. Moreover, it could embarrass miscreants, whose repeated appearances before the CAB made it "known that they [the clients] have failed to maintain peace in the home." Indeed, in the Bureau's first six months, 472 out of 525 marital cases ended in reconciliation.[49] The Bureau officials admonished women to keep a clean home, provide food for their family, and respect their husbands. They criticized insulting language, excessive drinking, especially in beer halls, infidelity, moving about the compounds at night, and lack of respect for husbands and their relatives. The CAB also condemned husbands who failed to provide for their wives and children, insulted their wife's relatives, drank excessively, used insulting language, beat their wives for "no reason," or indulged in sexual liaisons outside marriage. Polygyny was acknowledged, but regarded as unsuitable for the urban environment. Warring couples were offered advice, told to "discuss matters peacefully from time to time," and in insoluble cases, sent to the urban courts.[50]

The Urban Native Courts (UNC) played a central role in disciplining the emerging urban population on the Copperbelt. The courts maintained their rural bias for some time, sending divorce cases home and lecturing women on "proper" wifely behavior. They continued to believe repeat offenders and "troublemakers" should be sent home. In Ndola, for example, a man brought his granddaughter to court, claiming that "She is a most frightful cackler, and also causes me to lose all my money, for she loves only fornication and won't even consider marriage." Ignoring the woman's defense—her husband had deserted her and she wanted to stay in town—the court condemned her as "a prostitute beyond all doubt. You don't want your fellow women to have husbands, and those who are married you take theirs. What you want is that young men should kill themselves over you." They fined her, put her in prison, and ordered her repatriation upon release.[51]

However, the growing stabilization of the urban African community gradually forced alterations in the urban courts' policies. By 1953, the court assessors had reluctantly agreed to settle many urban marital cases, although they remained determined to reduce options for independent women (Parpart 1988; Mitchell 1961). At the same time, the courts did not simply condemn unmarried urban women. In 1948 an urban court awarded custody of a child to its mother as she "was a trained nurse, and had fed, clothed and cared for the child. Her home background was stable and satisfactory." She was accorded respectability, while her husband was vilified for his sexual misbehavior and unreliable character.[52] Thus the courts differentiated between those women who were regarded as a menace to the development of a settled, respectable urban population and those who were not.

The emerging urban elite supported efforts to constrain "disreputable" behavior in town. They used municipal associations, such as the Urban Advisory Board, as platforms to condemn loafers and other "undesirables," especially prostitutes and the unemployed. They also set up their own institutions, such as dance clubs, debating societies, and elite drinking establishments, where they could socialize with their own kind. The Roan Social Club, for example, provided a place where people living in the more elite area (section 2) of the mine township could socialize with each other and other elites. They "organized dances, debates etc., and had nice times."[53] The Chalimana Club in Luanshya was also popular. Some preferred to socialize and relax at home, away from "disreputable" people and behavior. A Form IV educated Luanshya man, for example, declared himself "a very private man," who only met his friends at home. After marriage, he abandoned his favorite club because his wife "doesn't allow me to take active part in organisations which entertain female membership and especially where things like dances can be practiced."[54] The emerging elite demonstrated a clear sense of class boundaries. A nurse at Roan rejected an invitation to go to the Mutamba Club for drinks because "she (and her kind) do not like going to these cheap clubs for drinks because they are always crowded with low class people who go there for chibuku. . . . The best club for us is Chilimana. No chibuku is sold there and the pub is decent. You find well behaved people there— *ba mama officer na ba bwana officer* (ladies and gentlemen) [who are] educated and or doing high grade jobs."[55] The emerging elite thus increasingly defined themselves in opposition to poorer urbanites, but most particularly "wayward" women.

Not surprisingly, the nationalist movement further complicated notions of "respectability," particularly in regard to the emerging elite.[56] Political leaders accused Africans who adopted Westernized practices such as wearing European clothes, wearing makeup, and straightening their hair of being European stooges. At the same time, they criticized women who drank excessively, engaged in prostitution (especially with Europeans), and neglected family duties. This discourse thus managed to pillory elite women and urban "bad girls" at the same time. The two political parties urged their women's groups and youth wings to discipline women engaging in such behavior. United National Independence Party (UNIP) officials unilaterally prohibited women from entering the Copperbelt beer halls, in order "to make them feed children and look after their homes properly. . . . If any man says this is unfair we take it he is only interested in having a nice time with women and is not helping the nation at all."[57] The Regional Youth Wing advised its members to rape the prostitutes, "not by touching their bodies but by laughing at them,"[58] while the Women's Brigade called on members to stamp out prostitution and hooliganism.[59] These criticisms undermined the emerging elite's moral authority over definitions of respectability, complicating notions of "wickedness" and "respectability," and providing openings for new interpretations and practices.

PUSHING THE ENVELOPE: RECONFIGURING GENDER

The language of "respectability" and "wickedness" implies a clear separation between these two "solitudes," but the evidence suggests a more complex process. Many supposedly "respectable" women adopted some of the strategies of their "wicked" sisters when seeking to challenge or at least redefine male (and even female) authority and control. Rejecting the norm that personal problems should be handled privately, some "respectable" women made full use of the urban institutions available to them, taking complaints about their husbands, partners, and sometimes their neighbors to various authorities. They convinced mine and government case workers to reprimand wayward and irresponsible partners, even threatening them with dismissal. The CAB at Roan handled the cases of many irate wives. In one instance, a wife insisted that she wanted a divorce because "her husband did not feed or clothe her . . . she had only three dresses. . . . She got only L1 per month from her husband to buy [her] own personal belongings; her husband also demanded the details of everything that she bought from the market or from shops." She would only drop the charges "if he could be persuaded to change his ways." The husband denied the accusations but agreed, under pressure, to be more generous.[60] Another woman took her husband to the CAB for beating her. The Bureau warned him, "if he hit his wife again, he might lose his job."[61] This "disreputable" behavior thus effected some change.

Some women took more direct action—the kind of action often associated with "wicked women." An Ndola woman, angered by her husband's preference for his second wife, tore up the wife's mattress, spoiled several articles in the house, and then took her husband to court. The court rejected her divorce application, but advised the husband to provide for both wives or face a divorce next time.[62] Even "respectable ladies" discovered that a public scene could achieve the desired results. Mrs. Yaka, the wife of a prominent urban court assessor, demanded a divorce on the grounds that her husband did not take proper care of her. When this was refused, "she returned to the court with the children all carrying the household goods so that they could be distributed. A large crowd of spectators gathered around the court to hear the proceedings." In despair, Yaka abandoned the case to his colleagues. "It did not matter. He was disgraced. Let the matter finish." The goods were divided between the husband and wife and the wife obtained her divorce.[63] Some women committed adultery to protest their husband's behavior and provoke a divorce.[64] Others took up with other men. A Mufulira woman told the urban court that she "married again because her husband was troubling her and did not clothe her."[65] Some simply left.

A discourse of confrontation between men and women underwrote and legitimated these challenges to male authority. A young woman in Luanshya, for example, admitted that she liked cowboy films because "I like to see how to throw good blows, so that I can kick anybody who interferes in my business, for example, if my husband interferes." Another was particularly interested in seeing women ride horses and "trying to shoot men" (Powdermaker 1953:45). Others adopted a less aggressive but still rather critical stance. Members of a Young Wives' Club in Mufulira agreed that "money spoils the relationship between husband and wife. The men never give us enough of their wages. Husbands take away money they earn and spend it on beer."[66] Indeed, it seems many women judged behavior in relation to larger issues. Anne Mwamba, for example, admitted that some women committed adultery because they were "too much fond of money," particularly if they had no children, but argued that "those who normally commit adultery are those who lack money to buy clothes and other things which are necessary to a woman."[67] Thus, while ideally women were expected to be good wives and mothers, in certain circumstances even "disreputable" behavior was acceptable to many.

Nationalist political struggles also inspired and legitimated the confrontational, aggressive behavior generally associated with "disreputable" women and men. In 1957, the Women's League of the African Nationalist Party (ANC) at Roan picketed the beer hall, and "when the lorry car-

rying supplies of beer arrived, the women lay across the road and refused to allow the lorry to proceed." A crowd of about two thousand,
mostly women and youths, participated. About thirty women and one man
were arrested.[68] The Ndola ANC Women's League sponsored a beer hall
protest that led to picketing and stoning the District Commissioner. Despite the use of tear gas against them, the protesters managed to set fire
to kiosks and the main beer hall.[69] As competition between the nationalist parties intensified, conflict increased as well. Women were at the center of many of these confrontations. Girls caught with petrol bombs
claimed they were "Junior Zambia Policewomen." Women burned their
marriage certificates, threatened those without political identity cards,
and took part in numerous protests and riots.[70] Leading women politicians, such as Foster Mubanga, spent long hours on the political campaign trail with male politicians, sometimes even overnight. She coun-
tered criticisms, especially of neglecting her family and home, with the
claim that she was working to end colonialism. Thus political needs legitimated behavior that otherwise would have been seen as disreputable
and improper—more characteristic of "wicked women" than of "respectable" urban ladies (Harries-Jones 1975:23–41).

CONCLUSION

"Wickedness," as defined on the Zambian Copperbelt, seems to have been
partly about resisting/challenging/escaping patriarchal control, but also about
the pursuit of pleasure, a site for negotiations around money and lifestyle.
Much of the literature on rebellious, "wicked women" has focused on their
challenges to patriarchal practices, whether rooted in "traditional" or Western notions of male authority and gender hierarchy (Parpart and Staudt 1989).
The pursuit of pleasure has received less attention, as has the possibility that
many women rebelled against male authority, not as a deliberate challenge
to gender hierarchies, but simply in order to remain in town—often in conditions not of their own choosing.

At the same time, "wicked women" (and men) were not simply a foil for
more respectable members of society, an "other" around which notions of
"respectability" could be crafted.[71] While the emerging Copperbelt elite often defined themselves in opposition to the "disreputable" classes, even seeking physical distance from them, the dichotomy between "respectability" and
"wickedness" was neither clear nor static. As we have seen, "respectable"
ladies adopted many of the strategies of their "disreputable" sisters when it
suited their purposes. Moreover, unacceptable behavior could garner sympathy if a woman was seen as a victim, especially of male abuse. While
notions of "respectability" and "wickedness" played a central role in emerg-

ing class distinctions, providing markers for distinguishing different groups, their very fluidity expanded the range of the possible/acceptable for women (and men) at various points in time.

The Copperbelt case also reminds us that "wickedness" is not a fixed set of assumptions and behaviors; it varies with time and circumstance. Moreover, assumptions about "wickedness" and "respectability" at once reflect and produce changes in state interventions, court sanctions, and marriage and gender roles. These debates opened possibilities for women and men to redefine gender roles and relations. Thus "wickedness" is not simply a concern for social workers and criminologists interested in studying deviant behavior, it is a key to understanding the reconfiguration of gender roles and relations in colonial and postcolonial Africa.

NOTES

1. Rhodes House Collection, Oxford (RHC), Mss. Afr. 1501, personal diaries of Mabel Shaw, 1931. A missionary with the London Missionary Society (LMS), Shaw worked at Mbereshi Girls School in Northern Rhodesia from the 1920s to the 1940s.

2. Zambia was known as Northern Rhodesia when under colonial rule (1898–1964).

3. From the 1920s, four towns grew up around the copper mines in the Northern Rhodesian Copperbelt. Two developed around Anglo-American mines: Kitwe around Nkana Mine and Chingola around Nchanga Mine. The Rhodesian Selection Trust Mining Company developed two centers: Luanshya, built around Roan Antelope Mine townships, and Mufulira, based at Mufulira Mine. Each town had municipal locations as well. A nearby commercial center, Ndola, although established in the early 1900s, expanded as the Copperbelt blossomed.

4. The Belgian Congo (later Zaire and now the Republic of the Congo) had developed copper mines earlier in the century. Broken Hill, a town just south of the Copperbelt, developed around a lead mine and railway.

5. University of Zambia, Institute for African Studies, Passmore, "Report on the Loafer Problem on the Copperbelt" (1956) (mimeo.).

6. School of Oriental and African Studies, University of London (SOAS), International Missionary Council/Conference of British Missionary Societies (ICM/CBMS) Box 1219, Ms. Wrong to Agnes Fraser, 15 March 1935. Ms. Wrong was citing Audrey Richards, an anthropologist who worked in Northern Rhodesia with the Bemba people.

7. SOAS, CBMS Box 1213, Audrey Richards, Talk to the Africa Circle, November 1934.

8. Even prostitutes often found it difficult to get housing on their own. Audrey Richards papers (AR) (at the London School of Economics), Large File W, Roan, 1934. See also White (1990).

9. AR, Large File W, Roan, 1934.

10. In Chingola in 1939, the sex ratio was about 2:1. National Archives of Zambia, Lukasa (NAZ) SEC/NAT/66G, Labour Department Annual Report, Chingola Station, 1939.

11. AR, Diary III, 1931.

12. This was to encourage stabilized labor, not permanent urbanization (Spearpoint 1937:38).

13. AR, Large File W, Nkana, 1931.

14. NAZ, ZA/7/4/8, V. R. Anley, District Tour of the Copperbelt, 8–23 May 1928.

15. SOAS, ICM Box 1214, Mary Shannon, Report on Women's Work in the Copperbelt, 1942.

16. NAZ, SEC/NAT/66G, Chingola Station Annual Report, 1939.

17. SOAS, CBMS Box 1213, Arthur Cross, Kitwe, to B. D. Gibson, London, 9 February 1937. Arthur Cross was the first head of the United Missions in the Copperbelt (UMCB), an ecumenical consortium established in the 1930s.

18. NAZ, SEC2/381, vol. 1, Meeting with the Representatives of the Native Courts of the Copperbelt, District Commissioner's Office, Mufulira, 12 May 1939. See also Epstein (1953).

19. Public Record Office, London (PRO), Colonial Office (CO) 799/17, Northern Rhodesian Administrative Reports (1938).

20. SOAS, ICM Box 1214, Mary Shannon, Report on Women's Work on the Copperbelt, 1942.

21. SOAS, ICM Box 1214, Memo on Girls' Boarding School, no date.

22. SOAS, LMS Box 32B, Director of Native Education, J. Tyndale Biscoe to B. D. Gibson, London Missionary Society (LMS), London, 5 November 1938.

23. Moore was one of the early UMCB/LMS missionaries.

24. AR, Large File W, Roan, 1931.

25. AR, Large File W, Nkana, 1931. Richards spoke Bemba with her informants.

26. Bill Epstein's private papers (EP). Bill Epstein was a researcher with the Rhodes-Livingstone Institute. I want to thank him for making these available to me. Conversations with urban court assessors and tribal elders in town revealed considerable variation in reputation. Bemba leaders told Epstein that Nsenga women were not as respectful toward their husbands as Bemba women were. Both Kasai (from the Congo) and Nsenga women were often branded as prostitutes.

27. AR, Large File X, Roan, 1931.

28. NAZ, SEC/NAT/66G, Chingola Station Annual Report, 1939.

29. NAZ, SEC2/381, vol.1, Meeting, Representatives of the Native Courts, District Commissioner's Office, Mufulira, 12 May 1939.

30. AR, Large File AA, Godfrey Wilson to Audrey Richards, 18 April 1940.

31. AR, Large File X, Luanshya and Roan compounds, 1931, and Roan, 1934, where a clerk's wife told Richards that "she never gets drunk like some other ethnic groups who get so drunk they give themselves to a man. She is a BaTonga, and they don't do that. Besides they have joined the African church."

32. Enoch Kaanu, *Namusiya at the Mines*, was written in 1943 by an African clerk who worked as a teacher at the mines.

33. NAZ, SEC2/406, vol. IV, Regional Council, Western Province, 17 July 1944.

34. Department of Labour, Northern Rhodesia, 1959. A colonial officer touring the Copperbelt reported that women on the Copperbelt should concentrate on "the breeding and rearing of the next generation." NAZ, SEC2/1124, I. Mackinson, District Commissioner, Fort Rosebery, Tour Report of Kitwe/Nkana, 30 August 1956.

35. EP, court records from 1950s.

36. Ibid.

37. Peter Harries-Jones papers (HJ), Citizens Advice Bureau (CAB), case no. 19, 11 June 1963. I am grateful to Peter for providing me full access to his research records on the Copperbelt.

38. HJ, CAB no. 30, June 1963.

39. HJ, Mikomfwa Ward 1B File, 20 January 1965.

40. EP, Life History of Anna Mwamba, Ndola, 1951; Powdermaker (1962).

41. HJ, Mikomfwa Ward 1B File, 20 January 1965.

42. Harries-Jones papers and Powdermaker (1952).

43. HJ, Mikomfwa Ward 1B File, 4 February 1965.

44. Ibid., 4 February 1965.

45. Ibid., 22 July 1964.

46. *Luntandanya* (August 1957), Kitwe.

47. SOAS, IMC Box 1219, D. Lehmann, Circular Letter, Mufulira, May 1955.

48. The course was based at the Mindolo Ecumenical Centre, which was established in 1958 to replace the UMCB. In 1960 there were four times as many applicants as places.

49. *Report of the Commission Appointed to Inquire into the Mining Industry in Northern Rhodesia* (The Morison Commission 1962); Harries-Jones (1964:63–65).

50. Harries-Jones (1964) and CAB case notes (early 1960s).

51. EP, Ndola court cases, 1951.

52. Epstein papers.

53. HJ, Roan Township, Section 2 File, 26 November 1964.

54. HJ, Roan, Clubs File, 1964.

55. HJ, Roan, Section 2 File, 1 December 1964.

56. The African Nationalist Party (ANC) spearheaded the nationalist movement in the 1950s in colonial Zambia, but a rival party, the United National Independence Party (UNIP) emerged in the late 1950s. UNIP won the election in 1964 and formed the government. Party rivalries divided the Copperbelt and other parts of Zambia during the final years of the colonial period and after independence (Harries-Jones 1975).

57. HJ, Political Meetings, UNIP meeting, Roan, 29 October 1964.

58. HJ, Political Meetings, UNIP Regional Youth Group, Roan, 18 September 1964.

59. HJ, Political Meetings, UNIP meeting, Roan, 9 August 1964.

60. HJ, CAB case 43, 1961.

61. HJ, CAB case 49, 1961.

62. EP, Case 72, Ndola court cases, 1951.

63. EP, Urban African Court (UAC), Luanshya, 21 May 1954.

64. EP, UAC, case 602, Ndola, 1951.

65. EP, UAC, case 729, Mufulira, 1951.

66. Dorothea Lehmann, Research Notes, Nchanga, 10 March 1958, in author's personal collection.

67. EP, Life History of Anna Mwamba, 1953.

68. Roan Consolidated Mines, Central Services Division (RCM/CSD), C202.7, files 9 and 10, Roan Antelope telex, Luanshya to Salisbury (Harare), Southern Rhodesia (Zimbabwe), 26 August 1957.

69. Hansard, Legislative Council, Northern Rhodesia, no. 94 (1958).

70. *Report of the Commission of Inquiry into the Unrest on the Copperbelt, July–August, 1963* (The Whelan Commission, Lusaka, 1963).
71. For more on respectability, see Ogden (1996).

REFERENCES

Chauncey, George. 1981. "The Locus of Reproduction: Women's Labour in the Zambian Copperbelt, 1927–1953." *Journal of Southern African Studies* 7:135–64.

Colson, Elizabeth and Max Gluckman, eds. 1951. *Seven Tribes of British Central Africa.* London: Oxford University.

Cooper, Frederick. 1989. "From Free Labor to Family Allowances." *American Ethnologist* 16:609–21.

Coppens, Betty. 1952. "Social Work in Urban Areas with Special Reference to Family Life." *International Review of Missions* 41:464–70.

Davis, Merle. 1933. *Modern Industry and the African.* London: Macmillan.

Epstein, A. L. (Bill). 1953. *The Administration of Justice and the Urban African.* Colonial Research Series No. 7. London: Her Majesty's Stationery Office.

———. 1992. *Scenes from African Urban Life.* Edinburgh: Edinburgh University Press.

Ferguson, James. 1992. "The Country and the City on the Copperbelt." *Cultural Anthropology* 7:8–92.

Harries-Jones, Peter. 1964. "Marital Disputes and the Process of Conciliation in a Copperbelt Town." *Rhodes Livingstone Journal* 35:29–72.

———. 1975. *Labour and Freedom.* Oxford: Oxford University Press.

Johnson, Essie. 1961. "Mindolo Women's Training Centre." *African Women.*

Kaavu, Enoch. 1949. *Namusiya at the Mines,* translated by R. Nabulyato and C. R. Hopgood. London: Longman.

Lloyd, Mavis. 1960. "Its My Job." *Horizon* (April) Johannesburg: Anglo American Corporation.

Mitchell, J. Clyde. 1961. "African Marriage in a Changing World." In *Report of the Annual Conference on Marriage and the Family.* Lusaka: Northern Rhodesia Council of Social Service, pp. 1–21.

Moore, R.J.B. 1940. *Man's Act and God's in Africa.* Livingstone, Northern Rhodesia: Livingstone Press.

Morison Commission. 1962. *Report of the Commission Appointed to Inquire into the Mining Industry in Northern Rhodesia.* Lusaka: Government of Northern Rhodesia.

Ogden, Jessica. 1996. "'Producing' Respect: the 'Proper Woman' in Postcolonial Kampala." In Richard Werbner and Terence Ranger, eds., *Postcolonial Identities in Africa.* London: Zed Books, pp. 165–92.

Parpart, Jane. 1986. "Class and Gender on the Copperbelt." In Claire Robertson and Iris Berger, eds., *Women and Class in Africa.* New York: Africana, pp. 141–60.

———. 1988. "Sexuality and Power on the Zambian Copperbelt: 1926–1964." In S. Stichter and J. Parpart, eds., *Patriarchy and Class: African Women in the Home and the Workforce.* Boulder, Colo.: Westview, pp. 115–38.

———. 1994. "'Where Is Your Mother?': Gender, Urban Marriage, and Colonial Discourse on the Zambian Copperbelt, 1924–1945." *International Journal of African Historical Studies* 27:241–71.

Parpart, Jane and Kathleen Staudt, eds. 1989. *Women and the State in Africa*. Boulder, Colo.: Lynne Rienner.

Passmore. 1956. "Report on the Loafer Problem on the Copperbelt." University of Zambia, Lusaka, Zambia: Institute of African Studies, mimeo.

Powdermaker, Hortense. 1953. "A Survey of Reading, Cinema and Radio-Audience Patterns, Preference and Attitudes in Luanshya." (mimeo.).

———. 1962. *Copper Town, Changing Africa*. New York: Harper and Row.

Richards, Audrey. 1940. *Bemba Marriage and Present Economic Conditions*. Manchester: Manchester University (Rhodes-Livingstone papers, no. 4).

Roebuck, Reverend Oliver. 1927. "Native Welfare Work in Industrial Centres." *Proceedings of the General Missionary Conference of Northern Rhodesia*. Lusaka.

Saffery, A. Lynne. 1943. *A Report on Some Aspects of African Living Conditions on the Copper Belt of Northern Rhodesia*. Lusaka, Northern Rhodesia: Government Publications.

Spearpoint, Frank. 1937. "The African Native and the Rhodesian Copper Mines." *Supplement to the Journal of the Royal Africa Society* 36:1–61.

Taylor, J. V. and D. Lehmann. 1961. *Christians of the Copperbelt*. London: SCM Press.

The Whelan Commission. 1963. *Report of the Commission of Inquiry into the Unrest on the Copperbelt, July-August, 1963*. Lusaka: Government of Northern Rhodesia.

White, Luise. 1990. *The Comforts of Home*. Chicago: University of Chicago Press.

Wincott, N. E. 1966. "Some Aspects of the Growth and Development of African Urban Society." B. Litt. thesis, Oxford University.

15

GENDER AND PROFITEERING: GHANA'S MARKET WOMEN AS DEVOTED MOTHERS AND "HUMAN VAMPIRE BATS"

Gracia Clark

When specific groups of women are held up as public examples of wickedness, they are often unusual in some way that transgresses accepted boundaries for wives and mothers in that society, and they are stigmatized for their deviance. According to this model, the virulent physical and verbal attacks on market women in Ghana during the decade 1975–1985 should never have happened. The remarkable autonomy and agency of these women are more deviant by Western standards than by local ones. Within southern Ghanaian cultural norms, their industry and separate incomes were wholly appropriate for mothers, and central to the local configuration of gender and kinship. Far from venturing into male-identified spaces or shirking their maternal duties, women traders follow the most common occupation for urban Ghanaian women, in markets considered stereotypically female spaces.

If traders were not pushing the boundaries of their gender roles, were their attackers pushing the accepted boundaries of misogyny? Apparently not. Measures aimed primarily at restricting traders, such as price controls and state distribution channels, were surprisingly popular among citizens. Most of these citizens must have numbered market women among their closest kin, and they included many traders themselves. Successive military and elected governments even initiated violent crackdowns to bolster their legitimacy, with considerable success. The bitter criticism of traders for abusing their economic power extended to condemning them as women and eventually challenged their right to continue trading at all.

The paradox of this widespread hostility to traders as women and women as traders arises from tensions more complex than obvious deviance. Unraveling its tangled causes involves unpacking several different historical trajectories that feed into it. The most sensitive transitions were precisely in the balance of power between sectors and between persons, rather than in absolute boundaries or definitions of right and wrong. Centuries of trade in the region had legitimated substantial market profits and state intervention in trade. Transformations in marriage and the gender division of labor, inside and outside of market trade, had affected the gendered moral framework in which women traded. Power shifts between trading and other economic sectors thus had implications for gender relations. Ideas of illegitimate profit also show historical continuities and changes when traced through concepts of witchcraft, theft, and corruption into the neoliberal moral vacuum of structural adjustment.

These transitions placed market women at the center of conflicts over control of the runaway economy and control of women. Even when their own work and income had not dramatically changed, the position of other significant groups had shifted around them. Market women exercised energetic, even desperate agency, but that did not trigger these conflicts or create their gendered content. Traders rather scrambled to preserve some viable combination of historical and contemporary values that promised community survival.

ATTACKS ON TRADERS

Scapegoating of women traders grew out of successive governments' efforts to deflect responsibility for soaring food prices and inadequate wages. During the First and Second World Wars, British colonial authorities tried to control the cost of provisioning barracks and prisons and the wages of miners and government workers by enforcing food price controls, with limited success (NAK 1, 2, 3). They blamed the high postwar prices of food and imports on parasitic market women, who burdened the consumer with useless layers of profit and hoarded scarce goods (NAK 4; Watson 1948). J. B. Danquah, a leading nationalist, strongly defended traders as "our hardworking mothers," while pressing for stricter controls on import prices at expatriate firms (Danquah 1947).

After independence, Nkrumah inherited both the wage bill and the enforcement power of the British authorities. He followed up both colonial and nationalist price control agendas, and echoed the colonial rhetoric against market women. He expanded price controls over imported and manufactured consumer items on the list of "essential commodities," and nationalized one large import firm into the Ghana National Trading Corporation (GNTC). He also challenged women's control of local food marketing by starting the Ghana Food Distribution Corporation (GFDC).

As Ghana passed through a succession of military and civilian governments in the 1960s and 1970s, this pattern of rhetoric and intervention in market trade continued. Strict enforcement episodes filled the official channels briefly with confiscated goods in addition to those the government could buy. The ensuing shortages raised pressures to smuggle goods across the porous borders and to divert the limited new legal imports into favored or generous hands. During these periods of toleration, well-connected traders in controlled commodities prospered, while still classified as illegal and wicked. New and old regimes alike could show their moral stature by launching another repressive episode.

When the Armed Forces Revolutionary Council (AFRC) brought in Flight Lieutenant Rawlings as head of state in June 1979, his "House Cleaning Exercise" centered on individual commercial morality. Once corrupt individuals had been removed and legal supplies distributed fairly, the system should work properly without fundamental structural reform. The AFRC targeted corrupt officials, and raised intervention in public markets to a new intensity. Government officials repeated publicly that they were targeting the wealthy wholesaler and middleman or woman, not the small-scale trader or producer. Nonetheless, their tactics of repeated confiscations and beatings damaged poorer traders most (Clark 1988).

The AFRC first followed the precedent of attacking sellers of essential commodities for violation of legal price controls. The renowned wholesale market in Accra, Makola #1, was looted immediately and demolished (Robertson 1983). In Kumasi and other regional capitals, soldiers confiscated and sold off the contents of stalls in the cloth and provisions sections of the main markets. They then moved down the main commercial streets, selling off controlled and uncontrolled goods from small and large stores, including the GNTC. Soldiers returned to the market day after day for weeks, acting with unprecedented brutality in beating and arresting traders, store owners, and government officials. A

Photo 15.1   Yam travelers rest and count money in a shed beside the wholesale yard. (From Gracia Clark, *Onions Are My Husband*. Chicago: University of Chicago Press, 1994. ©1994 by the University of Chicago. All rights reserved. Reprinted with permission.)

handful of women traders were flogged naked in the main lorry park before a crowd, finally triggering some public outcry against the disrespect to physical womanhood (*Daily Graphic* 1979).

The high level of street violence in these major cities, where soldiers faced turbulent crowds looking for goods to buy or loot, frightened away food traders and villagers. The resulting hunger may have actually pushed the AFRC to extend its price controls to local food crops. These began gingerly on a holiday (election day), with female police officers using little force. This caution vanished the next day; armed soldiers patrolled the wholesale yards and made forays into the retail stalls in the main market for food to sell or take away. Soldiers then chased food supplies back into village periodic markets, and finally lay in wait on the major highways to "hijack" produce in transit.

These new actions marked traders, as such, as legitimate targets, not only as price offenders. Even a single bag or basket of produce not yet offered for sale could be confiscated under threat of arrest, as evidence of intent to resell. Official national media echoed the colonial rhetoric about traders, condemning "those women" as greedy parasites, "bloodthirsty nation-wreckers," and "human vampire bats," who deliberately frustrated direct sales from farmers to consumers (*Daily Graphic* 1979). Opportunities for traders to counter these public attacks directly were severely constrained by government control of radio, television, and most newspapers.

The AFRC did manage to bring markets to a virtual halt, but this did not release a steady supply of cheap food as predicted or revive the moribund GFDC. Rawlings wanted to leave a lasting mark on the economy, before honoring his promise to hand over to elected civilians on schedule in October 1979. The AFRC initiated a further level of attack on the marketplace system and demolished sections of central markets in all the regional capitals.

Frustrated that Limann's civilian government soon returned to business as usual (including episodic price control enforcement), Rawlings returned to power on 31 December 1981, as head of the Provisional National Defense Council (PNDC) government. This government immediately launched a longer, more severe enforcement campaign, intensifying the familiar market confiscations and lootings, house-to-house searches, and blistering media attacks. Price controls had an even more drastic impact on urban food supplies this time, as the country entered the dry season. Poorer traders again suffered worst, because they lacked savings and had to continue working under the most violent and risky conditions. The PNDC also made a systematic effort to replace the marketplace system with consumer cooperatives, village brigades, and other official sources of consumer goods. When these legal channels proved ineffective, the remaining clandestine traders were accused of sabotaging PNDC efforts by offering farmers higher prices and better service.

The rapidly shifting and often extralegal rules and enforcement tactics of the PNDC and the informal civilian militias it sponsored meant that any commercial practice might be punished retroactively. Without respected price schedules, food traders could not even choose to cooperate with the military effectively. The moral taint once attached to diversion of official supplies and price control violations now enfolded all trading activities. Until late 1984, when the International Monetary Fund's Economic Recovery package stipulated deregulation of trade along with other neoliberal reforms, most private buying and selling was risky and furtive.

LEGITIMATE TRADE

Such stigmatization reversed a long history of enthusiastic support for trading, a highly respected occupation in Asante culture and throughout the larger Akan area for centuries. Since the foundation of the Asante confederacy in the 1700s, local and international trade and commercial production to supply them had been major organizing features of the local economy. The economy's boundaries straddled major international trade routes linking the coast to the savannah networks and included major producing areas for gold and kola. Both men and women participated actively in market-based trade, although more men than women enjoyed the advantages of chiefship or sponsorship by chiefs.

Money provides the building blocks of social solidarity, because most obligations between kin are conceived in terms of cash payments as well as presently fulfilled with cash. The concepts of money and varying individual wealth have been fully integrated into both male and female roles in lineage, marriage, and hometown. Without disposable cash income, an adult man or woman cannot easily discharge expected adult duties. Funeral donations, for example, are one of the most fundamental expressions of connections with relatives, affines, and neighbors. Men accomplish marriage by the payment of recognition fees to the wife's kin, and by the regular contribution of food money to the wife (Clark 1989). Community and lineage levies are customarily defined in cash terms for both men and women, although sometimes poorer members may contribute labor instead. Earning money through trading thus reinforced women's position as loyal and responsible pillars of lineage and community.

State intervention in trade, however, had equally strong traditional precedents. Asante principles of good governance not only allowed the chief to intervene in trade, but made promoting the profitable activities of citizens a central responsibility at any level of chiefship. Town chiefs took an active role in encouraging trade, establishing markets and improving the commercial position of their citizens. Leading male and female chiefs traded through court officials or by lending public funds to prominent traders. During public crises, they might control local food prices, requisition food for government needs, and embargo specific neighbors. The symbolism of the elephant tail gave the wealthiest Asante citizens ceremonial status, while also expressing a sense of complementarity or rivalry between the palace and trading hierarchies (Wilks 1975; McCaskie 1995).

After the conquest of Asante by the British in 1897, colonial officials also openly favored their fellow citizens, by providing building sites for British import firms in Kumasi, dismantling the controls favoring chiefly officials, and using regulations to defend the commercial position of British firms in times of war and depression. In response, Asante men moved out of market trading in favor of cocoa production for export and white-collar jobs retaining more upward mobility. After independence, the new Ghana government likewise protected the interests of its citizens by restricting the activities of British, Lebanese, Nigerian, and other foreign nationals. In the light of this history, Rawlings' expressed policy aim, to improve the terms of trade and redistribute profit margins, seems unexceptional and logical. Both socialist and liberal governments had already justified quite opposite interventions with the same ultimate goal.

Asante moral values do leave considerable room for debate over which state policies and commercial practices are fair and effective, and which goals are realistic and desirable. The distinction between good and bad profits comes not from how they are made (for example through trade or production), but from their results. Depending on the effect of a wealthy person's accumulation on others in the family or community, the process of accumulation is deduced to be good or bad. If others also end up better off, it is good. If others end up worse off than before, the wealthy person has profited at their expense. As with chiefs, increasing the prosperity of a broader group of associates secures personal power as well as moral approbation, by building a larger, stronger following willing to provide labor and loyalty as needed. In short, Asante believe that economic growth can in practice follow either a multiplier effect model or a zero sum game model, and that the first is virtuous and the second is wicked.

WITCHCRAFT AND THEFT

The concept of witchcraft is closely linked to theft, and can be considered as another form of wickedly selfish appropriation of resources. Witches steal the life substance from living persons by spiritually eating their organs at night, causing illness and death. Witches then use this life power to gain unfair advantage in a variety of pursuits, including business, court cases, and property disputes. Chiefs and wealthy people might not literally be witches, but they might well share the selfish ambition that steeled others to practice witchcraft. They were also natural targets of envy, and so needed protection from the witchcraft their powerful position would attract. Many Asante Christians retain beliefs in the reality and efficacy of witchcraft, even though they feel Christians should not resort even to protective magic but rely on prayer.

Tales of witchcraft included traders among other categories of persons, like envious relatives and politicians, liable to seek unfair economic advantages in their everyday pursuits. Thus, these tales connect indigenous spiritual beliefs to ideas of legitimate and illegitimate profit. Market charms fall into the more general category of *sika duru*, or money magic, used to protect or promote wealth in any economic enterprise. The main evidence for money magic was inexplicable success using economic strategies not noticeably different from those of one's peers. I never heard anyone admit to using money magic or claim that any specific individual used it, but most agreed that it existed.

The evil aspect of *sika duru* was not the profits it generated so much as what had to be done to "feed" or maintain it. Like most other powerful forms of magic, it was fed by human life in one way or another. Although it could be purchased with money, it would demand the sacrifice of the health or life of the owner's family members sooner or later. Women could sacrifice the lives of their own unborn children, recognizing some conflict between devoting time and resources to childrearing and accumulating wealth, but eventually this would not be enough. If not properly fed, *sika duru* would turn angrily on the owner.

In Kumasi, rumors and responses to questions about the use of magic charms in market trading centered around the famous Makola #1 market in Accra and Accra traders in general. The traders there exerted considerable control over trade in imports and manufactured commodities at the national level and included some of the wealthiest traders in Ghana. Their symbolic primacy was confirmed when this market was the only one completely demolished in 1979. Their disproportionate economic success while other traders suffered from scarcity of goods was particularly suspicious.

Makola women were reputed to have charms directly connected to money and business. Some charms were buried in front of their stalls, under their customers' feet. These acted to make these traders' goods seem irresistibly attractive, creating an overwhelming desire to buy them. Other charms confused the minds of customers during bargaining sessions, making them agree to unusually high prices. Another type of charm "doctored" a trader's money. When it was paid out, it wanted to return quickly to her hands. Some Accra traders reportedly wore magic wristwatches that turned into snakes at night, and vomited money. Snakes figure prominently in witchcraft and other spiritual beliefs in this part of Africa. When Makola was demolished, ostensibly to reveal buried hoards of illegal commodities and foreign exchange, rumors spread that soldiers had dug up buried boxes containing snakes. These proved their magic powers by disappearing on the way to the barracks.

Magic used against theft was judged wicked or not, depending on its effects. Ordinarily, protective charms against theft were considered justified because they harmed only the criminal and were effective only for the virtuous owner. The thief would fall ill and rapidly die, unless he realized the cause of his illness and returned the stolen goods. Property owners spent large sums of money for ominous bundles of herbs they displayed prominently in farms and other locations for their deterrent effect, and as fair warning of the consequences of theft.

Those who disapproved of protective magic did so because of potential conflicts with the higher value of mutual survival. Destitute passersby who harvested food crops to cook and eat on the spot should not be punished, although ideally they should then seek out the farmowner and volunteer to work for him. Only when they took the food home or sold it should this be regarded as criminal appropriation or theft. Young children were also considered innocent because they were incapable of controlling their hunger or understanding the warning. A charm could not make such distinctions, so it overemphasized personal rights without allowing for other legitimate claims.

Such drastic protective measures were also considered inappropriate for trading incidents. The swearing of ritual oaths that would have caused the death of a thief or liar were carefully prevented in several market disputes. Once in 1979, a trader selling from a table missed some money from under her basket and suspected a neighbor. It was impossible to prove, so instead of accusing the neighbor by name she dramatically threatened to swear an oath by eating earth, so that the thief, whoever she was, would die. The trader's other neighbors restrained her, making sure the earth never touched her lips, but also ridiculed her. One remarked that if everyone in the market did that whenever something was taken, you would see dead bodies lying everywhere. Others repeated the arguments made over farm protection, saying it could have been a child or someone else not fully responsible for his actions.

Ideas linking witchcraft to theft reinforce the distinction between legitimate prosperity and profit at others' expense. The witch gains economic and spiritual power by feeding on the life force of the very people who should be nurtured—unborn and young children and close relatives. The witch fattens while those around her (or him) wither through illness and misfortune. By analogy, profits generated by a zero sum game metamorphose into actual theft from others, a crime taken very seriously in Asante. Those whose good fortune is conspicuously not shared with fellow members of their lineage or community fall under suspicion of witchcraft.

IMMORAL CONDITIONS

The principles of relative benefit shaped Ghanaians' moral responses to broader economic conditions as well. According to those principles, something was clearly wrong and getting worse in the Ghanaian economy in the 1970s and 1980s. Real incomes dropped to half or even one-tenth their levels of twenty or thirty years previously, and the terms of trade continued to fall precipitously. The conceptual model of witchcraft, seeing a few get fatter while all those around them withered away, remained very salient to the shape of the economic polarization Ghanaians experienced. Not only had the standard of living deteriorated for most people old enough to remember former levels, but the economic crisis now obviously threatened the survival of their families. Many families were not only tangibly worse off than before, but visibly losing weight (through poor nutrition and medical care), just as witchcraft victims did. Traders and most other occupational groups found it increasingly difficult to provide basic foodstuffs and keep their children in school.

The abrupt reversal in public policy and rhetoric that came in 1985 under pressure from the World Bank and International Monetary Fund (IMF) did not disrupt these trends of increasing polarization and hardship, which continued for most Ghanaians, despite the promised miracle of the free market. Neither controlled nor free market prices were considered intrinsically fairer, but current relative price and wage levels were definitely immoral. Policy attacks against traders were only rejected by public opinion once they had caused enough damage to destroy traders' apparent advantage and once they had shown their inability to restore a more appropriate balance to economic life.

The apparent paradox of market women's lukewarm reaction to trade liberalization makes sense in terms of their relativistic, results-based framework of economic morality. They appreciated the reduction in physical harassment, although street clearance campaigns continued, but the falling terms of trade and rock bottom levels of real income made survival still seem impossible. The official rate of currency exchange rapidly rose up to and beyond rates featured on the black market, which had been traders' actual source of foreign exchange before. Rising official user fees approximated the cost of illegal exactions by public employees, which also continued. The PNDC government had not only stopped trying to change price levels, but was promoting existing conditions as ideal rather than condemning them as exploitative. Instead of contrasting the illegality and corruption of supply channels before 1985 with the freely available legal supplies of imported goods and foreign exchange afterwards, traders said that now even the government was price-gouging.

Positive comments on the new policies from traders in 1994 endorsed them on pragmatic rather than moral grounds. They accepted that the government needed to agree to World Bank policy demands in order to prevent bankruptcy. Technical and financial assistance from UN agencies and bilateral donors had virtually halted during the previous five years.

The new accords brought immediate access to foreign aid for road and rail rehabilitation that was much appreciated by traders among others. They also increased mining and other export production, although much of the increase was soaked up in debt service. The PNDC had misjudged its actual capacity to enforce internal price controls, or to defy the international donor consensus against them. Like starting a war the country could not win, this was worse than submission, since it victimized citizens caught in the middle and provoked retaliation from stronger powers. Still, the PNDC's previous goals and motivations were not necessarily wicked because they were unsuccessful or unrealistic.

WORKING MOTHERS

Market women could also point to culturally legitimated goals in support of their trading strategies, goals that had wide recognition as part of their appropriate gender role. They could invoke the powerful image of the maternal provider, one that still holds immense reverence and authority in matrilineal Akan culture. For Asante, the most central aspect of womanhood, being mothers, gives women as firm a commitment to the world of work as men have. A mother's responsibility for feeding her child is even more integral to motherhood than physical childcare or breastfeeding. Just as a U.S. father out of work feels emasculated by his inability to provide for his family, an Asante mother feels her children's hunger as a blow to her womanhood. Women traders constantly, in many contexts, referred to the need to work to provide for their children. This tireless work for the child's benefit distinguishes the child's relation to its mother from its relations to father, uncles, and siblings, whose support is more conditional and negotiable (Clark 1999). Traders could morally justify high levels of wealth by pointing to their goal of providing their children with such opportunities as higher education abroad.

Men may have ambivalent attitudes toward women's earnings because they have divergent relations with their mothers, sisters, and wives. Asante remark that a man is always glad for his mother to be wealthy, since that money will presumably be available to benefit him. His sister's wealth is almost as welcome, since it relieves some of his responsibility to contribute to his lineage, and to help her children as his heirs. His wife's wealth is suspect, however, because it gives her more personal independence from his control, and it will finally go to her lineage, not his.

This differentiated gender configuration sets up a contradiction between a woman's ideal behavior as a wife and as a mother. Women can take leadership roles within their own lineages as mothers and sisters, but should exhibit deference to their husbands. As in many West African societies, husband and wife do not establish a joint budget during marriage, but each contributes in cash and in kind to household expenses. A woman's children are her nearest kin and heirs, while a man divides his loyalties between his own and his sisters' children. Men and women are both expected to retain primary allegiance to their own matrikin after marriage, and to express this in continued financial support.

Class privilege and religious affiliation can shift this balance from kin to marriage, but the implied cost to women's personal agency inspires caution, if not outright hostility, among Asante women. Western ideals of marital respectability have more influence over the behavior of middle-class and devout Christian married women. The image of the "housewife," living with her husband and children alone in a "bungalow" or single-family house, is familiar from school and church. Ordinary women express some ambivalence toward the dependence, social isolation, and sexlessness required or created by this supposedly privileged position.

At the other end of the class spectrum, the village woman farmer appears equally virtuous, perhaps because her agency seems equally limited. Too poor to stay in the house, her poverty and hard work keep her relatively sexless and isolated in her remote location, with even fewer life options to tempt her. She may be more obedient to her husband; she certainly has all she can do to feed and school her children. Government attacks on traders lauded this rural ideal, urging women trading essential commodities to return to their home villages and farm. Kumasi traders more often mentioned returning to the home village and farming as their own last and worst personal option, even as their nightmare of a destitute old age.

VIRTUE AND BLAME

The principles of exercising wealth and leadership well extend directly into the ideology of virtue in market trading. The same positive values of mutual benefit, responsibility, and survival translate into specifically commercial contexts in traders' discussions of market relations. The proper way of treating "customers," the people who either bought from you regularly or supplied you exclusively, featured the criterion of mutual benefit. Ideally, you set price levels to allow them enough profit so that they could expand their operations as your own expanded. Again, it was a matter of self-interest as well as morality not to greedily keep all the profit for yourself. An expanding set of prosperous customers would increase your own economic strength and attract more customers, which a set of customers pushed to the edge of bankruptcy would not. Undue profit was defined relatively, by the apparent relative prosperity of your associates, rather than absolutely, in terms of any specific profit margin or price level.

Market leaders, the most conspicuous targets of government attacks, had to show the firmest commitment to shared benefits and prosperity. Candidates for commodity group offices needed to be competent, prosperous traders, but were unlikely to include the very wealthiest. The impartial judicial personality considered appropriate for prospective leaders ruled out the single-minded pursuit of self-interest needed to build up an extremely profitable business. The sparse material benefits of office and the unwanted government attention also discouraged those with the largest enterprises from seeking leadership positions.

Definitions of the good trader emerged from direct questioning. One mature trader who had served as leader of a commodity-based cooperative and took an active interest in civic issues was asked, "What does a good trader do?" "When she finds a source of some scarce goods, she does not keep the news to herself but tells her colleagues where she has found them, so they can also buy some." Spreading the benefit widely was her paramount positive virtue, not following rules or restraining her own price and profit levels. The emphasis, in attacks on traders, on hoarding goods in times of scarcity, thus preventing others from either consuming or selling them, appeals to the same value.

One bitter dispute revealed the positive commitment to mutual survival among competitors. A trader contesting the allegiance of a supplier-customer remarked sarcastically, "Perhaps you want to keep all the supplies for yourself? Perhaps you think you are the only one trading in this market?" The alleged intention of seeking to ruin competitors was anathema and had to be repeatedly disavowed. Again, unselfishness supported success in the longer term. Ideally, a trader wished to appear so firmly prosperous that she did not have to worry too much about her competitors. This attracted additional customers, since there was obviously more than enough profit to trickle down to them. Observers might construe unadulterated self-interest as desperation due to shaky personal finances.

The strongest concepts of economic wickedness that Asante culture recognize relate not to profit, but to theft, which is perceived as a constant danger in the market. It was historically a capital crime, and pickpockets are still stoned to death in Kumasi Central Market when caught in the act. Theft ranks among the most serious hereditary taints to a family's bloodline, along with alcoholism, tuberculosis, and asthma. The women elders in charge of approving marriages would veto suitors with tainted lineages, to protect the purity of their own lineage blood. During a period where large-scale corruption sometimes meant execution, reports circulated of grandmothers wondering whether to classify such corruption as theft, and therefore veto marriages into families well-known for corruption.

The values of mutual benefit and survival carried over to these discussions of public and private corruption. One common form of corruption affecting traders was the diversion of legal goods into the black market. Some considered it normal because employees should share in the wealth they had created. Others condemned it strongly on the grounds that it endangered the country's survival. Survival values could also be used to stigmatize legal distribution channels. Traders claimed, in order to justify using illegal currency exchange channels, that legal foreign exchange only went to buy Scotch for soldiers. Corruption made immediate survival possible, since desperately needed goods were not legally available, but the necessity for corruption made survival nearly impossible for less resourceful people.

RECRIMINATIONS

Although polarization of incomes between rich and poor was one primary sign of immoral profits, leveling trends also brought condemnation of women traders. The gap between their incomes and more prestigious white-collar occupational groups had narrowed significantly during the 1970s. Waged and salaried formal sector employees, in jobs that often required at least modest educational qualifications, saw their fixed incomes shrink to derisory levels with rapid inflation. Even after a respected high school teacher added a second job in order to get by, his total income hardly sufficed to reproduce his class status by educating his own children. Levels of wealth accepted for government officials or corporate executives seemed immoral for even a few illiterate women. Although most traders' incomes also declined absolutely during this period, no obvious technical innovation could legitimately account for the rapprochement between traders' and educated individuals' incomes. The most recent dramatic transformations in the marketplace network had happened during the 1950s, when opportunities in the civil service and formal sector were also expanding and keeping pay differentials high. Parents who had made immense sacrifices to educate their children also resented the fading of the security this once provided.

These class-based tensions were intensified by their gendered character, which added resentment of how the shrinking gap between male and female incomes undermined the authority of husbands. The ranks of salaried and waged workers, especially in Asante and farther north, were predominantly and historically male. Cocoa farming had drawn ambitious uneducated Asante men away from trading in the early 1900s, because it offered them better upward mobility. Now cocoa farmers grappled with low world prices and high indirect tax rates, which left hardly enough income to maintain their farms, let alone their families (Mikell 1989). Because economics played such a prominent and definitive role in gender relations, this fundamentally economic chaos generated a kind of gender chaos comparable to that of the 1920s (Allman 1991).

The sharpest conflicts arose within marriage, where husbands were supposed to provide financial support to their wives in return for their deference and services. Falling real incomes for both genders increased tensions between husband and wife, since both tended to blame shortfalls on the selfishness and irresponsibility of their individual partners, rather than simply on general conditions. Husbands fell short in their expected contribution to food money and school fees, and women could not easily make up the difference. Even men who appreciated their wives' increased financial contributions regretted the greater personal independence and reduced housework standards needed for wives to work full time. Since trading was often the first resort of hard-pressed women (rural and urban), much of the stigma of women's alleged insubordination and greed attached to that occupation.

Opportunities for traders to counter these negative images were limited. The government controlled most radio, television, and newspaper media directly or indirectly. Commodity group leaders did put forward alternative economic models energetically when possible. In the numerous meetings called by soldiers and government officials, these leaders blamed high food prices on the greed and selfishness of farmers, truck drivers, and managers of stores and government agencies. They described traders as hard-pressed mothers, only trying to feed their families under very difficult conditions. Traders selling local food crops underlined the old distinction between themselves and those selling cloth or other imported and manufactured commodities, subject to price controls and corrupt distribution. As eloquent as some speeches might be, they had little impact on official decisions, which were already made when the meetings were called. Public media gave them only limited coverage, for example, in the yam queen's brief annual televised interview on market conditions at Christmas.

Many traders themselves accepted that governments would and should try to manipulate prices. They wanted the government to make import firms or farmers sell to them at controlled prices, so they could resell more cheaply. They wanted price levels adjusted to meet the incomes of

Photo 15.2   A yam traveler bargains with farmers. (From Gracia Clark, *Onions Are My Husband.* Chicago: University of Chicago Press, 1994. © 1994 by The University of Chicago. All rights reserved. Reprinted with permission.)

ordinary citizens, including themselves. Women traders supported measures that victimized them as traders, because they felt their position as consumers and parents was more important, making them victims of these same conditions.

The eventual cooling off of public hostility owed less to traders' own resistance than to the damage hostile policies caused them. Partly due to the cumulative effect of repeated and prolonged repression, by 1985 urban traders were no longer the relatively prosperous group that had attracted envy and resentment. Their capital and buildings had been destroyed on a large scale, leading to a sharp decline in their average working conditions and living standards. Like other Ghanaians, they visibly lost weight during the terrible shortages of 1983–1984. Stringently enforced price controls and other hostile actions had obviously not solved the nation's problems, suggesting that traders were not the problem. This lent credibility after 1985 to their arguments that, like the vast majority of their neighbors, they were exhausting every possible effort merely to buy food and pay increased rents, school fees, and hospital bills.

WHO IS THE DEVIANT?

In this economic context, the nearly unbearable economic conditions certainly qualified as wicked, and posed a constant threat to family survival. Still, by 1994 they were accepted as normal, or at least unlikely to change in the foreseeable future. They persisted, yet they still felt outrageous. A similar paradox lies at the root of the gendered hostility to market women. A mother would and should work to support her children, and market trading was accepted as a respectable, even as a natural choice for women in Ghana. At the same time, the tense relations between men and women, especially as spouses but also as siblings, felt wrong on both sides, and in some sense unnatural. The wrongness of the relationship then reflected back on the actions that constituted or enacted it. Although historically unexceptional, they could nonetheless be wrong, or even wicked, because such moral judgments were usually based on the resulting relations between persons, not on the absolute characteristics of the actions themselves.

Without traders themselves committing acts or taking on personal characteristics that deviated from current or historical gender or economic norms, they could thus be condemned in terms usually reserved for deviants. Asante market women were not an ethnic minority in Kumasi or in Ghana generally, although ethnic minority traders were also repeatedly targets of government hostility in Ghana. Women's commercial presence and practices long predated colonial rule, and confirmed, not offended, primary cultural values. Trading in general and women's trading in particular had undergone historical transformations during the twentieth century, but these had been accomplished with little controversy, decades before hostility to market women peaked (Clark 1994).

This case suggests that wicked women need not always owe their stigma to their own transgression of gender or economic boundaries. The transgression of boundaries here was not by traders themselves, but by deviations located outside the marketplace system, within a broader economic configuration less vulnerable to direct public action. Market women in fact remained a relatively stable group through decades that saw dizzying transformations in the relative status of other, predominantly male, economic and social categories. Cocoa farmers and the entire range of waged and salaried workers were facing an economic disaster of prices that seemed to be no fault of their own. Since these painful historical shifts had affected traders less, though still to some extent, they changed the relationship between sectors of the population in ways that had serious gender implications.

Within a moral framework that judged by results and by the relative benefit to those affected, such changes were clearly wicked. Like witches' circles, the economy was defying accepted principles of mutual survival and shared benefit, and needed to be brought back under social control. Efforts by the state, unions, cocoa farmers, and other actors to influence wage and price levels directly had had little success. Market traders made an accessible and plausible target, because a group left relatively unscathed was most likely responsible. The marketplace system lay outside the existing discipline of the formal sector and government regulation, a highly visible symbol of its lack of control. Gender tensions about control of wives only sharpened a hostility rooted in economic frustrations that in turn sharpened marital tensions. Market women became de facto deviants, not because of their own increased agency, but because the whole economy had warped around them. This left them unable to unilaterally maintain an acceptable balance in their relations across gender and occupational divides, and vulnerable to attack on that basis. Their situation, though common, was still outrageous, and therefore someone wicked must be responsible for it.

REFERENCES

Allman, Jean. 1991. "Of 'Spinsters,' 'Concubines,' and 'Wicked Women': Reflections on Gender and Social Change in Colonial Asante." *Gender and History*, 3:2: 176–89.

Clark, Gracia. 1988. *Traders versus the State*. Boulder, CO: Westview.

———. 1989. "Money, Sex and Cooking: Manipulation of the Paid/Unpaid Boundary by Asante Market Women." In B. Orlove and H. Rutz, eds., *The Social Economy of Consumption*, pp. 232–348. Lanham, MD: University Press of America.

———. 1994. *Onions Are My Husband*. Chicago: University of Chicago Press.

———. 2000. "Mothering, Work and Gender in Urban Asante Ideology and Practice. *American Anthropologist*. 101(4): 717–729.

Daily Graphic. 1979. Letter to the Editor, 23 June 1979, p. 7.

Danquah, J. B. 1947. "Irregularities in Import Control." Motion in Legislative Council. 26 March 1947. Ghana National Archives, Accra, No. 0028 SF8.

McCaskie, Thomas C. 1995. *State and Society in Pre-Colonial Asante*. New York: Cambridge University Press.

Mikell, Gwendolyn. 1989. *Cocoa and Chaos in Ghana*. New York: Paragon.

NAK 1: Ghana National Archives, Kumasi, No. 1136, Foodstuffs and Meat Regulation, item 4, DC Juaso to Chief Commissioner of Ashanti, 1937; item 16, Officer-in-charge, Ashanti Division Department of Agriculture, Kumasi, to Chief Commissioner of Ashanti, 10 August 1937; item 63, Director of Agriculture to Chief Agricultural Officer, Kumasi, 2 September 1941.

NAK 2: Ghana National Archives, Kumasi, No. 1315, Kumasi Town Council, item 44, "Minutes of a Meeting of the Obuasi Sanitary Board Held on 18th July 1941."

NAK 3: Ghana National Archives, Kumasi, No. 124, item 18, "Report for the Period lst April 1935–31st March 1936." Ashanti Division, Department of Agriculture, 27 April 1936.

NAK 4: Ghana National Archives, Kumasi, No. 0734 SF1, "Cotton Piece Goods, distribution and sale of (ii) Price Control." "ACS Supply," 12 September 1946.

Republic of Ghana Statistical Service (RGSS). 1989. *1989 Ghana Living Standards Survey.* Accra: Republic of Ghana Statistical Service.

———. 1993. *1993 Ghana Living Standards Survey.* Accra: Republic of Ghana Statistical Service.

Robertson, Claire. 1983. "The Death of Makola and Other Tragedies: Male Strategies against a Female-Dominated System." *Canadian Journal of African Studies* 17(3): 674–695.

Shipton, Parker. 1989. *Bitter Money.* Washington, DC: American Anthropological Association.

Watson, Aiken, 1948. "Report of the Commission of Enquiry into Disturbances in the Gold Coast." June 1948.

Wilks, Ivor. 1975. *Asante in the Nineteenth Century.* New York: Cambridge University Press.

INDEX

Abacha, Maryam, 248 n.1

Aba Riots, 104

Abeokua, Nigeria, 27–40, 40 n.1. *See also* Egba state; Igbo society; Nigeria

Abiola, Iya, 70

Abortions, 220, 227, 240

Achebe, Christie, 238

Ada, 240, 248 n.5

Addae, Adwoa, 136–37, 141

Ado-Odo (S. W. Nigeria), 67–84; cocoa economy and, 82; concept of wayward women, 80–82; love and money, 76–80; marriage in the olden days, 70–72; modern times, 72–76; reference to the olden days, 68–69. *See also* Igbo society; Nigeria

Adultery: abolition of harsh deterrents, 178; acceptance of, 191–92; divorce for, 30–31, 42 n.19, 52; migrant labor and, 191; punishment by husbands for, 173–74; by royalty, 173

African Nationalist Party (ANC), 286–87, 290 n.56

Afua Fom, Eponuahemaa, 136–37, 141–42

Agency, women's, 14–16

Agriculture: cassava, 51, 116–17, 126 n.3; cocoa, 82, 139–43, 144 n.7, 145 nn.16, 19, 307; cotton, 177; by

women, 87, 177; yams, 126. *See also* Market gardening

Aguiyar, Umma, 260, 262

Ajisafe, A. K., 33, 42 n.16, 44 n.35

Ajose, Basiru, 73–74

Ajuwon, Chief, 73

Akinwonmi, Yele, 79

Ala/Ani, 110–11, 119

Alcohol: breweries, 195, 203; colonial campaigns against, 226–27; labor productivity and, 221; nightclubs, 195, 197–203, 277–79, 281; protests against, 286–87; respectability and, 281–82; urban elite, 284–85; venereal disease and, 221

Allman, Jean, 8, 130–48

Ambrose, Captain, 32

Anglo-Boer War, 193

Animal traction, 103 n.13

Animatu, 36

Asante culture, 130–48; autonomy of women, 136–37; capture of unmarried women, 143; cocoa farming, 139–43, 144 n.7; colonialist response to forced marriage, 132–33; concept of marriage, 134–35; control of trade, 297–99; demographics, 114 n.12, 135; Effiduasi order to marry, 130–31, 136–37, 145 n.13; husbands' obligations, 133–34, 136–37; registration of girls at puberty, 137–38; role of chiefs, 141, 143, 144 n.1; subversion of forced marriage, 142–43; working mothers, 303–4

Asare, Jean, 135

Asigyafo, 144 n.4

Association des Femmes du Niger (AFN): evolution of, 261–62; nonmarried women in, 265–67, 271 n.7; political representation protest, 268; politics of difference, 255–56; profile of membership, 263–64, 267; rural women, 271 n.5

Atta, Akosua, 135

Babangida, Maryam, 248 n.1

Bad women. *See* Wickedness

Bagandans. *See* Kampala-Kibuga

Bagenal, C. J., 227

Bajawara, 257–58, 263–65, 267

Banyanyagavu, 172

Bapanshi, 281

Basotho women, 188–209; defiance of police, 195–96; effect of migrant labor on, 189–96, 207–9; exodus of, 193–94; invasion by South Africa and, 207–9; russianism, 196–203; terminology, 209 n.1; traveling for independent work, 203–7

Bastian, Misty L., 8

Beatings, by husbands, 55–56

Beer. *See* Alcohol

Beik, Janet, 264

Betrothal, 44 n.32, 156. *See also* Bridewealth

Better Life for Rural Women program, 248 n.1

Bikazikazi, 172

Birth rates, declining, 213, 220, 222, 227–28

Bishop's Court, 31

Black market, morality of, 306

Blackwell, Captain, 36

Bloemfontein, 193. *See also* Orange Free State

Boama, Rosina, 135, 142

Bonyatsi, 191. *See also* Adultery

Bori spirit possession cult, 259–60, 262–63

Bottom power, 234–35, 243–47

Bridewealth: amount of, 37, 157, 179; in arrests of unmarried women, 131; as barrier to marriage, 176; behavior within marriage and, 47–48; betrothal, 44 n.32, 156; in British currency, 37–38, 44 n.36; legal identification of father, 157–59; legitimacy of marriage, 157; marriages arranged for, 54–55, 63 nn.37, 40, 41, 70; marriage without, 56–58, 64 n.57; in native currency, 117, 123; power and, 29, 165 n.6; repaid by wives, 76; restitution of, 56, 64 n.57; slavery of wives and, 56; women's independence and, 35–36

British Railway Commissioners: bridewealth disputes, 36–37; cases brought to, 35–38; encouragement of divorce, 38–40; judicial authority, 32–33; marital disputes, 28, 34–35, 39, 43 nn.25, 26, 27

Budurwa, 257, 263

Buha, Western Tanzania, 47–66. *See also* Tanzania

Bujra, Janet, 242

Buo, Afuah, 133–34

Byfield, Judith, 7, 27–46

Careers, professional, 238–40

Cassava production, 51, 116–17, 126 n.3

Celibacy, harmful effects of, 191

Chalimana Club, 284

Chanock, Martin, 53

Childbearing: British midwife training, 224; death during, 119; decline of, 219–22, 227, 229 n.4; as husband's decision, 240; *Nwaobiala* and, 116–17, 119–20; twins, 116, 126

Children: brought up by grandparents, 194; colonial infant welfare programs, 222–24; education of, 92, 306; girls and the marketplace, 122; inheritance, 165 n.9; lack of Manyema, 122; of migrant women, 205; naming, 165, 176; outside of marriage, 155; preference for sons, 241

Chineke, 119, 127 n.12

Chobeliso, 190

Cholera epidemics, 215

Christian community: arranged marriages, 73; Bishop's Court, 31; campaign against prostitution, 180–81; clothing, 122–23, 127 n.16; concern over marginalized women, 176; in the Egba state, 29, 41 n.10; mixed marriages, 30; monetization by, 128 n.17; *Nwaobiala* and, 122–23, 125; patriarchy and, 236; protest of husbands' power, 176; urban women, 278; Western-style homemaking, 282–83; witchcraft and, 299

Church Missionary Society (CMS), 176–78, 180

Cinema, 281–82

Cities, migration of women to, 12–13, 189–90, 194, 203–4, 276–78

Citizen's Advice Bureau (CAB), 283, 285

Clark, Gracia, 10, 140, 293–311

Clothing: Christianity and, 122–23, 127 n.16; on girls and young women, 116–17, 120–23, 269; stripping by *Nwaobiala,* 120–23

Cochrane, Kenneth, 104, 114, 120

Cocoa farming, 82, 139–43, 144 n.7, 145 n.16, 19, 307

Coker, Mary, 41 n.9

Cole, Thomas, 42 n.19

Coles, Catherine, 265

Collective work groups, 261–62

Colonial authorities: benefits of temporary mining marriages, 277; divorce, 38; efforts to raise birth rates, 220, 222, 227–28; enforced marriage, 132–33; German, 219–21; indirect rule, 141–42, 145 n.24, 274–76; *Mambo Leo,* 226–27, 230 n.13; Manyema women and, 212–13, 219–21; marital disputes brought before, 28, 35–38; morality campaigns, 12, 225–27; movement of people, 11–12, 193;

need for stabilized urban workforce, 280; *Nwaobiala* and, 114, 118; political status of women, 29, 40; prostitution, 180; role in internal trade, 298–99; rumors of Manyema women's sexuality, 212–13, 221–22; venereal disease eradication, 222–23; Western-style homemaking, 282–83

Contraceptives, 227, 240, 261, 271 n.4

Cook, A. R., 178

Cooper, Barbara M., 9, 255–73

Coplan, David B., 9

Copperbelt. *See* Zambian Copperbelt

Cornwall, Andrea, 7, 67–84

Cotton production, 177

Court system, women and, 14–15, 285–86

Cowries, 37, 44 n.35

Currency, British, 37–38, 44 n.36, 128 n.17

Currency, native, 103 n.5, 117, 123

Curses, 153–54, 162–63

Custody of children, 77, 79, 284

Dalasi, exchange rate, 103 n.5

Dance: as communication, 15; *famo,* 197–99; riots from, 225; in the Samariya, 264–65; sweeping, 112–16; as threat to system, 221, 225–28. *See also* Music; Shebeens

Danquah, J. B., 294

Davey, J. B., 222

Debt recovery, 32, 43 n.23

Decle, 216–17

Delano, I. O., 42

Desertion by wives, 71

Desola, Betsy, 29, 41 n.9

Diamond mines, 189–90

Diets, gender differences, 174–75

Diori, Aissa, 259

Diori, President, 260, 270 n.2

Dipomu (refuge in the palace), 31, 42 n.17

Disease, 215, 218. *See also* Venereal disease

Divorce: bridewealth as deterrent, 64 n.56, 123; for childlessness, 240–41;

custody of children, 77, 79, 284; disparities in income, 79; for husbands not fulfilling obligations, 133–34, 136–37; legal reasons for, 165 n.6; in marriages without bridewealth, 57–58; during migrant labor, 52, 62 nn.21, 24, 25; nineteenth century, 30, 42 nn.16, 17; prevalence of, 83 n.13; Railway Commissioners and, 28, 34–36, 38–40; refuge in the palace, 31, 42 n.17; remarriage after, 38; testimony of wayward women, 71–72; urban, 280

Dodds, Fred William, 128 n.17

Domestic violence, 103 n.11, 155, 157

Dowries, 82 n.2. *See also* Bridewealth

Dufie, Yaa, 135

Economic declines: bottom power during, 246–47; hostility towards market women, 306–10; Manyema women, 225–28; marriage and, 79, 135, 139, 183, 307; mobility of women, 193; unemployment in Nigeria, 243–44, 246–47; witchcraft and, 301–3

The Economic Report on Africa (UNECA), 249 n.8

Education of females: children, 92, 306; complaints about, 193; gender inequality, 237; as lure from wicked-ness, 278; rise of elite class in Nigeria, 237–38; struggle for, 268–69; use of legal system, 154; women's choices and, 75

Effiduasi, order to marry, 130–31, 136–37, 145 n.13

Egba state: colonial railway zones, 12, 15, 35–38; marriage during 1830-1899, 28–31; military, 41 n.7; political structure, 29, 33; treaty with the British, 31–32. *See also* Igbo society; Nigeria

Egba United Government (EUG), 31, 33, 40

Egwu, 15, 111–14, 119–20, 125, 127 n.6

Empala kitale, 172

Employment of women: bottom power, 243–47; outside wives, 241–42, 247; professional careers, 238–40; sexual harassment, 245. *See also* Income by women; Market gardening; Market women, Ghanaian

Epstein, Bill, 289

Eugenics movement, 222

Extramarital sexual relations. *See* Adultery

Fadipe, N. A., 30, 34, 42 n.11

Family Support program, 248 n.1

Famo, 197–99

Famong, Mamapetle Makara koa, 200

Famo Ngoanana, 200

Farganis, Sondra, 60 n.4

Fathers, legal definition, 157–60, 162

Fayawo boys, 78–79, 81

Female husbands, 39, 44 n.40

Femmes du Niger (Folly), 269–70

Fertility, colonial interests in, 213, 220, 222, 227–28

Fisher, Fanny, 41 n.9

Fish money, 95

Folly, Anne-Laure, 269–70

Funlayo, 43 n.27

Gambia, The, 15–16, 85–105. *See also* Market gardening

Gardens, women's, 15–16. *See also* Market gardening

Gaya, 261, 271 n.3

Gender identity: constructing subordi-nation, 53–59, 63 n.45; effect of migrant labor on, 52; ownership by men, 181–83; ranges of possible behavior, 48

Gender relations of power: disobedient Maasai daughter, 162–63; in Igbo elite circles, 237–42; relative income levels, 306–7

Gender roles: diets, 174–75; Ghanaian market women, 303–4; legacy of research on, 2–5; married women in public spaces, 268–69; nineteenth century Bagandan, 173–75; norms

during social chaos, 53; *Nwaobiala* on, 116–17; sitting postures, 174
German colonial administrators, 219–21
Ghana. *See* Asante culture; Market women, Ghanaian
Girls: kept out of the marketplace, 122; registration at menarche, 137–38; stripping by *Nwaobiala,* 120–23. *See also* Children
Gold Coast, ordering women to marry, 130
Gold mines, 194
Gramsci, Antonio, 164 n.2
Gutkind, Peter, 171–72, 181

Harcourt, Lewis, 40 n.2
Hattersley, C. W., 177
Hausa language, women in, 257–58
Healers, native, 224, 230 n.19
Hearth-holds, 82 n.10
Hegemony, 164 n.2
History of Abeokuta (Ajisafe), 42 n.16
History of the Yorubas (Johnson), 30
Hoa ikula, 195
Hodgson, Dorothy L., 1–24, 149–67
Housekeeping, Western-style, 281–83
Hunt, Nancy, 138
Hut taxes, 176–77, 225, 231 n.27
Hybrid spaces, 8

Igba atijo, 68–69, 71, 73, 81–82
Igbo society: bottom power, 234–35, 243–47; cocoa economy and, 82; deities, 110–11, 119; education of women, 238; gender relations, 237–42; marriage in, 70–76; pressures to marry, 238–42, 247; pressure to have children, 240–42; sweeping, 112. *See also* Nigeria; *Nwaobiala*
Ilari, 41n
Ilemoṣu, 75, 77, 80–81, 82 n.9
Imam, Ayesha, 271 n.9
Imprisonment of wives, 71
Income, importance of, 298
Income by men: child allowance payments, 243; marriage proposal and, 135; opportunities for, 72;

polygamy and, 78; relative to that of women, 306–7; support for sisters' children, 304
Income by women: bargaining power in marriages, 79, 307; bottom power and, 234–35, 243–47; cocoa farming, 139–43, 144 n.7, 145 n.19; control of, by men, 75, 93–97, 199; on the Copperbelt, 276–77; domestic service, 204–5; foodstuffs marketing, 72, 140–41; freedom to criticize men, 97; gender discrimination, 242–43, 245; Ghanaian market women, 303–4; by going from one man to another, 183, 203; hiding of, from men, 98; independence by, 75, 77–78, 80, 138; loans to husbands, 94, 98, 100, 103 n.9; lowered divorce rates and, 79–80. *See also* Employment of women; Market gardening
Infant welfare programs, 222–24
International aid, 87
International Decade of Women, 87
International Year of the Woman, 261
Irrigation rates, 87
Islamic society, unmarried women in, 259, 263
Itsebeletsa, 203
Iwofa system, 28–29, 39, 41 n.3
Iya, 259–60, 262, 266–67
Iyalodes of the Parakoyi, 29, 41 n.9

Jahally-Pacharr rice project, 102 n.2
Johnson, Samuel, 30, 37
Johnston, Sir Harry, 175
Jojolola, Madam, 30, 42 n.13

Kalindile, Rebeka, 60 n.5
Kampala-Kibuga, 171–84; effect of urban growth, 178–81; formation of, 184 n.1; historical construction of good women, 173–75; migration of women, 12–13; nomenclature of women, 185 n.24; restrictions on mobility, 178–79; as subjects of power, 181–83
Karanja, Wambui, 240

Karuwai (courtesans), 257–60, 262–67, 270 n.1, 271 n.8
Kepi, 197, 209 n.9
Kountché, Seyni, 261, 264
Kumasi market women, 140
Kuyebi, Chief, 79
Kwaku Afram v. Afuah Buo, 133

Labia minora, elongated, 195, 218
Language, graphic, 127 n.13
Language of avoidance, 189
Lawolu, Susannah, 41 n.9
Lead mines, 288 n.4
Lesotho, invasion of, 207–9. *See also* Basotho women
Liakhela (Majara), 194
Likoata, 199
Livingstone, David, 217
Loan repayment, by husbands, 94–96, 98
Lovett, Margot, 7, 47–66

Maasai culture: authority of elder men, 151; bridewealth, 157, 161; conflict with state laws, 161–63; disobedient daughters, 150–62; forced marriages, 152–57, 160–61; obligations of fathers, 157–60, 162. *See also* Tanzania
Macaulay, T. B., 30
MacGregor, Governor, 33, 121
Majara, Simon, 194
Makara, Azael, 190–91
Makola. *See* Market women, Ghanaian
Malan Pass, 196
Malitaba, 200, 203
Mambo Leo, 226–27, 230 n.13
Mandinka-speaking communities. *See* Market gardening
Manyema women: beauty of, 216–18; colonial rumors of hypersexuality of, 212–13, 221–22; as dangerous, 218–19; environmental threats, 214–15; fertility lowering, 215–16; population surveys, 219–21. *See also* Tanzania
Maradi women, 256
Market gardening, 85–105; animals for, 103 n.13; average income, 103 n.6;

control of income by men, 93–97; deployment of incomes, 91–93, 96, 100, 103 n.8; funding for, 102 n.2; gardens as second husbands, 86, 88–90, 101; loans to husbands, 94, 98, 100, 103 n.9; marital obligations and, 87–88, 101, 103 n.4; relationship among women, 91; resentment by men, 79, 91–92, 103 n.3
Marketplaces: cleanliness of, 113, 115–16; girls kept from, 122; Igbo, 121; protection within, 113
Market women, Ghanaian, 293–311; government attacks on traders, 294–97; legitimacy of trade, 297–99; legitimate gender roles, 303–4, 307, 309; morality of profits, 304–6; paradox of hostility, 293–94; pressure from World Bank for acceptance of, 301–3; price controls, 307–8; resentment of incomes of, 306–9; as scapegoats, 294, 309–10; witchcraft and theft, 299–302, 305–6
Marriage: in Abeokuta, Nigeria, 27–46; after children are grown, 77, 79–80; arranged, 54–55, 63 nn.37, 40, 41, 70, 151–56; beatings by husbands, 55–56; capture of unmarried women, 130–48; changes from the olden days, 74, 77, 81; by choice, 36, 74, 155–56; contingent on income by men, 194, 204–5; disobedient daughters, 150–62; economy and, 79, 135, 139, 183; efforts by colonialists to stabilize, 12; encouragement by churches, 176; female husbands, 39, 44 n.40; husbands' obligations, 134, 136–37, 162; incomes by women and, 6–7, 79, 94, 98, 100, 307; inheritance by wives, 146 n.25; legal definitions, 134; for love, 76–80; Marriage Law of 1971, 152, 154, 160; migrant labor in Buha and, 49–53; mixed religions, 30; by mutual consent, 38, 152, 154, 156, 160, 162; in the olden days, 70–72; patrilocal, 189; political power, 29; power of husbands, 176; by

registration, 131; reworking behavioral roles, 269; separation, 30; as social control, 53–59; as source of unpaid labor, 139–43; suicide to prevent, 153, 160; Tanzanian, 47–66; temporary mine, 277–79; without bridewealth, 56–58, 64 n.57, 82 n.11; wives as pawns, 145 n.18, 145 n.20. *See also* Polygyny; Unmarried women
Marriage in Maradi . . . (Cooper), 255
Marriage Law of 1971, 152, 154, 160
Masupha, Chief, 190
Mata, 257, 265
Matan zamani, 263
Matekatse, 193, 196, 203
Maternal altruism, 102 n.1
McCallum, Governor H., 31
McCurdy, Sheryl A., 1–24, 212–33
Men: changing domestic roles, 88; choice of wives, 54; control of daughters, 151–53; control of wife's income, 75, 93–97, 199; fears about women's income, 204, 303–4; left at home, 204–6, 208; obligations to wives, 70, 73; reinforcement of customary law, 3, 152, 164 n.5; resentment of wife's income, 79, 91–92, 103 n.3; seeking loans from wives, 94, 98, 100, 103 n.9; slave, 214; smuggling by, 79–80; useless, 75, 81, 82 n.1
Menarche, registration at, 137–38
Mental illness, 248
Midwives, British training for, 224
Migrant labor: control of wives, 50–51, 53; economic opportunities for women at camps, 192–95; effects on marriages, 52–54; freedom to choose one's wife, 73–74; gender identity of women and, 52; increase in women's labor at home, 51, 190–91; magnitude of, 207–8; *ma-weekend,* 203; prostitution, 34, 192–95; reasons to leave wives at home, 49–50, 61 nn.12, 13, 14; women following men, 189–90, 194, 203–4; women's networks, 206; by women with men

at home, 204–6, 208. *See also* Mobility of women; Zambian Copperbelt
Mining, 189–90, 194, 204. *See also* Zambian Copperbelt
Mobility of women: attraction to urban areas, 276–78; male control of, 174, 176; old women, 265; during poor economic times, 193; russian gangs, 202; state control of, 177, 192–93, 196, 276; working for oneself, 203–7. *See also* Migrant labor
Mobutu, concept of "authenticité," 13
Moir, Jane, 216
Money belts, 98
Moriamo, 43 n.26
Motekun, 43 n.25
Movies, 281–82
Muhammed, Safiya, 239
Music: russian gangs, 197, 199, 200–202; songs of the *Nwaobiala,* 116–18; as threat to system, 221. *See also* Dance; Shebeens
Musisi, Nakanyike B., 8–9, 171–87
Mutamba Club, 284
Mwamba, Anne, 286
Myarko, Beatrice, 135

Nationalism, demand for traditional ways, 13
Ngoma, 225–27. *See also* Dance
Nicolas, Guy, 271
Nicolas, Jacqueline, 259
Niger, 255–73; *bori* spirit possession cult, 259–60, 262–63; debates, 263–68; evolution of women's associations, 258–63; nomenclature of nonmarried women, 257–58; politics of difference, 256, 263, 268; rural women, 269–70, 271 n.5, 271 n.10
Nigeria: bottom power, 234–35, 243–47; change in gender relations in, 67–84; ethnic divisions, 236; First Ladies efforts, 235; formal *vs.* informal sector, 248 n.6; gender relations in elite circles, 237–42; rise of female elite class, 235–38. *See also* Ado-

Odo; Egba state; Igbo society;
    Nwaobiala
Nightclubs, 195, 197–203, 277–79, 281,
    285
Niven, A., 114, 116–17, 120–21
Nkanda, Chaisaba, 47, 57
Nkoebe, Chief Sempe, 192
Nkrumah, Kwame, 295
Northern Rhodesia, 13, 288 n.2. *See also*
    Zambian Copperbelt
Nso ani, 113
Nthako, Nthabiseng, 206–7
Nthunya Mpho, 202
Nwaobiala, 104–26; colonial response to,
    114, 118, 121, 127 n.14; demands of,
    12, 116–18, 120, 125–26; origin, 110–
    12; participation by local women,
    113; on roads, 124; stripping girls,
    120–23; sweeping activities, 15, 112–
    16
Nwa obolia, 126 n.4
Nyarko, Beatrice, 142

Obanjili, 110, 126 n.3. *See also*
    Nwaobiala
Ogboni political structure (Nigeria), 29,
    41 n.8, 43 n.21
Ogu Umunwaanyi, 120, 125
Okeke, Philomena E., 9, 234–51
Oloruntosin, Alhaja, 79
Orange Free State, 189–90, 193–96
Osigyani, 144 n.4
Osu stigma, 248
Owo onje (feeding allowance), 73

Parpart, Jane L., 9, 274–92
Passe-partout, 257
Pawns, wives as, 145 n.18, 145 n.20
Phelisa bana ba ka, 203
Pittin, Renée, 256–58
Planned Parenthood Federation of
    Nigeria (PPFN), 240
Police, antagonism towards, 196
Politics of difference, 256, 263, 268
Polygyny: female opposition to, 242;
    hut taxes, 176–77, 225, 231 n.27;
    income of wives and, 75, 78, 97;

inside and outside wives, 241–42,
    247; jealousy, 90; junior wives
    driven off by senior wives, 190;
    sleeping rotations, 103 n.7; in urban
    environments, 283
Population continuance: among
    Manyema, 215–16, 220–21; control of
    women for, 175, 177, 180; efforts to
    raise birth rates, 220, 222, 227–28
Pottery, Basotho, 194
Prostitutes: at centers of migrant labor,
    195; charges by, 117; confiscation of
    property, 192; forced marriage of,
    132, 134–36; free women as, 71, 73,
    77, 82, 182; *karuwai vs.,* 257–58, 271
    n.8; migrant laborers as, 206;
    Nwaobiala and, 114, 123; regulating
    mobility of women as deterrent, 177–
    79; russianism, 202; venereal disease
    and, 180, 222, 226, 228
Protests: Basotho women, 196; against
    beerhalls, 287; to end colonialism,
    287; for female political representa-
    tion, 268; russian gangs, 197–203. *See
    also Nwaobiala*
Puberty, registration at, 137–38
Punch, Cyril, 33, 37, 43 n.26

Railway, effects of, 34, 219
Railway commissioners. *See* British
    Railway Commissioners
Ransome-Kuti, Funmilayo, 42 n.12
Ransome-Kuti, I. O., 42 n.12
Ransome-Kuti, J. J., 30, 42 n.12
Rattray, R. S., 134, 137
Rawlings, Flight Lieutenant, 295, 297,
    299
Religion. *See* Christian community
Remarriage, 38, 42 n.16, 71–72
Respectability, 6, 8, 281–85
Richards, Audrey, 277
Rinderpest epizootic, 218
Roads, 124
Roan Social Club, 284
Roberts, P. A., 131–32
Roscoe, John, 173–77
Royalty, exemption from rules, 173

Rumaliza (Mohammed bin Halfan al
Barwani), 216
Rural women, 13, 269–70, 271 n.5, 304
Russian gangs, 197–203

Sacks, Karen, 173
Safuratu, Iya, 76
Saibou, Ali, 264
Samariya, 256, 259, 261–65, 267
Satan, russianism and, 200
Scarification, 127 n.15
Schroeder, Richard A., 7, 85–105
Sefwi Wiawso, 132, 145 n.16, 145 n.24.
See also Asante culture
Sesotho, 209 n.2. *See also* Basotho
women
Sexual harassment, 245
Sexual relations, 174–75, 234–35. *See
also* Adultery; Bottom power
Shaw, Mabel, 274
Shebeens (nightclubs), 195, 197–203,
277–79, 281, 285
Sheddick, Vernon, 194–95
Shina, Iya, 75
Sika duru (money magic), 299–300
Sitting on a man, 114
Slavery, African, 32, 39, 43 n.20, 56
Slave trade, 214–16, 219
Smallpox epidemics, 215
Snakes, in witchcraft, 300
So, Akosua, 136
Social clubs, 284. *See also* Nightclubs;
Women's associations
Socialization, 53–55, 59, 63 n.45
The Sociology of the Yoruba (Fadipe), 34
The Soul of Nigeria (Delano), 42 n.17
South Africa, 13
Southall, Aidan, 171–72, 181
Stealing, divorce for, 30
Structural Adjustment Program (SAP),
78–79, 243
Sweeping, by women, 15, 112–16. *See
also* Nwaobiala
Syphilis, 223. *See also* Venereal disease

Tanzania (Tanganyika): colonial interests
in women's fertility, 213, 219–21;

constructing female subordination,
53–58, 63 n.45; customary law, 152–
53, 164 n.5; marriage and migrant
labor, 49–53; marriage during 1943-
1960, 47–66; patriarchal legal system,
151–53, 162–63, 164 n.2. *See also*
Maasai culture; Manyema women
Theft, 299–301, 305–6
Thibella, 203
Throwing up one's skirt, 197
Tinubu, Madame, 29
Townsmen in the Making (Southall and
Gutkind), 171
Trade, chiefs role in, 298
Trade unionism, 243, 268
Tsekoa, Alinah, 197
Twins, 116, 126
Tyamzashe, Gwayi, 190

Uganda. *See* Kampala-Kibuga
Ujiji, 15, 214, 225. *See also* Manyema
women
Uli, 127 n.15
Union des Femmes du Negre (UFN),
259–60, 262
United Missions in the Copperbelt
(UMCB), 278
United National Independence Party
(UNIP), 285, 290 n.56
United Nations International Decade of
Women, 87
Unmarried women: *bajawara,* 257–58,
263–65, 267; by choice, 135–37;
detention and marriage of, 130–33;
economic reasons for, 135, 139;
importance to politics, 259; nomen-
clature difficulties, 257–58, 263–64,
267; registration of, 137–38; social
stigma, 80–82, 239–42; in women's
associations, 265, 271 n.7
Unyago puberty associations, 218
Urban Advisory Board, 284
Urban Native Courts (UNC), 283
Uwezo, 218

van der Merwe, G. C., 196
Vaughan, Megan, 139

322

Index

Vellenga, D. D., 131, 134
Venereal disease: colonial interest in
fertility and, 213, 220–21; eradication
efforts, 222–23, 226–28; justification
for enforced marriage, 130, 132–33,
135, 144 n.8; labor productivity and,
221; prevalence of, 223; prostitutes
and, 180, 222, 226, 228; restrictions
on mobility, 179–80

Wandara, Aisha, 260, 262
Waungwana, 214
Waywardness, in divorce narratives, 71
"Who Is a Wife?" (Vellenga), 131
Wickedness: appellation, 188; early
colonial period, 11–12; as feminine
power, 6; historical construction of,
172–75; maintenance of patriarchies,
149; precolonial period, 11; respectability and, 6, 8; as stigma, 5–6, 172–
73; timing of, 10–14; wayward
women, 71
Widows, 190, 192
Williams, Raymond, 164 n.2
Witchcraft, 299–302
Women: access to state power, 29, 40, 41
n.5; disdain for unmarried, 80–82;
entry into public space, 267–69;
freedom of old women, 265; intoler-
ance of bad behavior, 78;
marginalized, 176; married names,
176; networks, 206; ownership by
men, 181–83; political representation,
268–70; rural, 13, 269–70, 271 n.5,
304; sexual rights of, 134; slave, 214;
as source of moral decay, 13; urban,
276–82. See also Gender identity;
Unmarried women
Women in Development (WID) programs, 87, 102 n.2

Women's associations: bori spirit
possession cult, 259–60, 262–63;
debates over roles within, 263–68;
entry into public space, 267–69;
evolution of, 258–63; karuwai
(courtesans), 257–60, 262–67, 270
n.1, 271 n.8; politics of difference,
256, 263, 268; rural women, 269–70,
271 n.5; Samariya, 256, 259, 261–65,
267; Union des Femmes du Negre,
259–60, 262. See also Association des
Femmes du Niger
Women's League of the African Nationalist Party, 286–87
Women's Purity Campaign, 104. See also
Nwaobiala
Women's War, 104, 126 n.4
Wood, J. B., 31, 42

Yam production, 126
Yaws, 223
Yemowi, Lydia, 41 n.9
Yorubaland: change in gender relations,
67–84; marriage at the turn of the
century, 34–35; marriage during 1830-
1899, 28–31. See also Egba state

Zambian Copperbelt, 274–92; in the
early years, 275–80; economic
activities of women, 276–77;
enforcement of respectability, 282–85;
housing, 277, 282, 288 n.8; portrayal
of good and bad women, 276, 287;
temporary marriages, 277–79, 282;
towns in, 288 n.3; urban elite
respectability, 279–81, 284–85, 287;
urban poor respectability, 281–82,
287; wicked women in, 278–79;
women's use of courts, 285–86
Zawara, 259. See also Karuwai

ABOUT THE CONTRIBUTORS

JEAN ALLMAN teaches African history at the University of Illinois, Urbana-Champaign. She is the author of *The Quills of the Porcupine: Asante Nationalism in an Emergent Ghana* (1993) and (with Victoria Tashjian) *"I Will Not Eat Stone": A Women's History of Colonial Asante* (2000). Her studies of gender and social change in Asante have appeared in the *Journal of African History, Africa, Gender and History*, and *History Workshop Journal*. She is currently working on a social history of labor migration and religious belief in Ghana's Upper East region.

MISTY L. BASTIAN is an assistant professor of anthropology at Franklin and Marshall College in Lancaster, Pennsylvania. She has published several articles on topics ranging from popular media, gender, and fashion to witchcraft, the West African spirit Mami Wata, and Igbo religious practices. She is also the co-editor, along with Jane L. Parpart, of *Great Ideas for Teaching about Africa* (1999).

JUDITH BYFIELD is an associate professor in the Department of History at Dartmouth College in Hanover, New Hampshire. Her book, *The Bluest Hands: A Social and Economic History of Indigo Dyers in Abeokuta (Nigeria), 1850–1940*, is forthcoming. She has published on textile manufacturing and marketing, and gender and social change in the *Journal of African History* and the *Canadian Journal of African Studies*.

GRACIA CLARK teaches anthropology at Indiana University, Bloomington. Her work with women traders in Kumasi Central Market, Ghana, since 1978 is presented in her 1994 book, *Onions Are My Husband*, and in recent articles in *Africa* and the *American Anthropologist*. She has also consulted on gender and development with ILO, UNIFEM, and USAID. Currently she is editing life history narratives of Kumasi market women to present their ideas about economic process.

BARBARA M. COOPER teaches in the African Studies, Women's Studies, and History Departments at Rutgers University in New Brunswick, New Jersey. She is the author of *Marriage in Maradi: Gender and Culture in a Hausa Society in Niger, 1900–1989* (1997) and has published in *Signs*, the *Journal of African History*, and *African Economic History*. She is currently working on the implications of the Hajj for women and on the history of a minority Protestant community in Niger.

DAVID B. COPLAN is professor, chair, and head of the Department of Social Anthropology at the University of Witswatersrand in South Africa. He is the author of *Lyrics of the Basotho Migrants* (1995), *In the Time of Cannibals: Word Music of South Africa's Basotho Migrants* (1994), and *In Township Tonight! South Africa's Black City Music and Theatre* (1985). His numerous articles have appeared in such journals as *Cultural Anthropology*, *Ethnomusicology*, *Africa*, *Research in African Literatures*, and the *African Studies Review*.

ANDREA CORNWALL is a fellow at the Institute of Development Studies, University of Sussex. Her publications include the co-edited volume, *Dislocating Masculinity: Comparative Ethnographies* (with Nancy Lindisfarne, 1994). She is currently completing a book entitled *For Money, Children and Peace: Everyday Struggles in Changing Times in Ado-Odo, S.W. Nigeria.*

DOROTHY L. HODGSON teaches in the Department of Anthropology at Rutgers University in New Brunswick, New Jersey. She is author of *"Once Intrepid Warriors": Gender, Ethnicity and the Cultural Politics of Maasai Development* (2001) and editor of *Rethinking Pastoralism in Africa: Gender, Culture and the Myth of the Patriarchal Pastoralist*. She has several book chapters and articles both published and forthcoming on the interconstruction of gender and ethnicity, spirit possession and modernity, the production of masculinity, the politics of transnational ethnographic research, and ethnohistorical studies of development.

MARGOT LOVETT is an assistant professor at Saddleback College, Mission Viejo, California. She has published articles on gender and power, labor and matrilineality in the *International Journal of African Historical Studies*, *Critique of Anthropology*, and the *Canadian Journal of African Studies*.

SHERYL A. McCURDY is a postdoctoral fellow at the University of Texas-Houston in the School of Public Health. She has book chapters and articles published and forthcoming on the politics of secrecy in fieldwork, gender and colonial medicine, gender and identity politics, the creation of the Manyema diaspora in Tanganyika, spirit possession and associational life, and health, disease, and mortality. Her current projects focus on breast, cervical, and ovarian cancer in Houston and in Tanzania.

NAKANYIKE B. MUSISI is the Director of the Makerere Institute of Social Research at Makerere University in Uganda, and an associate professor at the University of Toronto in the Departments of History and Women's Studies. She is the author of articles on gender and state formation, gender and the environment, and the production of inequality in *Signs* and *Canadian Woman Studies*. Her current research interests are in the gendered development of Kampala as an urban colonial space.

PHILOMENA E. OKEKE is an assistant professor in the Women's Studies Program of the University of Alberta, Edmonton, Canada. Her research and teaching focus on women in the modern sector of developing countries as well as on issues of gender, race, and class in North America. Her research publications include "Female Wage Earners and Separate Resource Structures in Post-Oil-Boom Nigeria," "Post Modern Feminism and Knowledge Production: The African Context," and "The Politics of Cross-Cultural Feminist Research: Locating Scholars and Subjects." She recently served as guest editor of *Issue: Journal of Opinion*. She is in the final stages of completing her ethnography of working Igbo women in southeastern Nigeria.

JANE L. PARPART is a professor in the Departments of History, Women's Studies and International Development Studies at Dalhousie University in Halifax, Nova Scotia, Canada. She has written extensively on women and gender in Africa. Recently, she co-edited *The "Man" Question in International Relations* with Marysia Zalewski (1998) and *Great Ideas for Teaching about Africa* with Misty L. Bastian (1999). She has published books on gender and development theory and practice, most notably *Feminism/Postmodernism/Development* (1995), co-edited with Marianne Marchand.

RICHARD A. SCHROEDER is director of African studies and associate professor of geography at Rutgers University. He is the author of *Shady Practices: Agroforestry and Gender Politics in The Gambia* (1999) and co-editor with V. Broch-Due of *Producing Nature and Poverty in Africa* (2000). Other recent research has appeared in *Annals of the Association of American Geographers*, *Progress in Human Geography*, and *Africa*.

8570

Nyack College Library